Finance of International Trade

2nd edition

by
Alasdair Watson

THE INSTITUTE OF BANKERS
10 Lombard Street, London EC3

First published: June 1976
Second edition: September 1981

ISBN: 0 85297 059 5

Prepared by Hobsons Press (Cambridge) Limited, Bateman Street, Cambridge CB2 1LZ.

Printed in Great Britain.

FINANCE OF INTERNATIONAL TRADE

Preface

The second edition of *Finance of International Trade* not only incorporates all relevant developments since mid-1976 but also includes important new material. Foreign currency financing has been expanded to accord with the importance placed upon it by the relaxation of controls. Tender bonds and performance and similar types of guarantee, together with sections on merchanting, forfaiting and composite currency units, are included for the first time. There is a wider treatment of the foreign currency capital markets than was contained in the first edition, and, of course, account has been taken of the changes to all transactions brought about by the abolition of UK exchange control in October 1979.

The text and the up to date documents which illustrate it are intended to assist all students who seek to acquire the background information necessary to an understanding of the finance of foreign trade, foreign exchange and support services provided by London's financial institutions for importers, exporters and merchants.

The book is also designed for exporters and businessmen who need a basic understanding of financing the movement of goods, or an introduction to funding techniques in foreign currencies. The essential information contained in Chapter 1, sections 1-8, is intended specifically for the exporter and for those engaged in providing services for exporters.

I have concentrated in particular on the needs of students studying for the following examinations:

i   Finance of International Trade – Banking Diploma – *The Institute of Bankers*
ii   Financial Institutions and the Monetary System – direct entry to the Financial Studies Diploma – *The Institute of Bankers*
iii   International Trade and Finance of Overseas Trade – *Institute of Export*
iv   Finance of International Trade – *The Institute of Freight Forwarders*
v   International Trade and Payments – A foundation course in Overseas Trade – *British Overseas Trade Board.*

Past examination questions from some of the above syllabuses are given at the end of each chapter, and relate to the subject matter covered.

I have placed considerable emphasis on the integration of theory with practice, and have thus sought to stimulate independent thought on the part of the reader. The text includes numerous lists of facts and references to specimen documents and examples which are designed to illustrate the interrelationship of the subject matter.

All technical subjects seem to have attracted their own jargon, language or terminology over the years which, though common knowledge to the practitioner, may be confusing to the learner. To help the reader understand specialised jargon, buzz words, etc, and to pick up principles easily, I have included several new glossaries for ready reference. These appear in Chapters 2,3,4,5,7,8 and 10; they explain and describe terms used in the context of each chapter's particular subject matter. It is quite possible that the reader may find the same technical word, such as 'negotiation', appearing in different contexts in different chapters. It may also come as a surprise to the reader to note the number of different technical meanings the word 'credit' has in the vocabulary of the fully fledged professional international banker. No wonder we often suffer common misunderstandings about simple concepts.

There are certain areas of international business which are subject to frequent change, usually as a direct result of changes in the economic climate. Exchange control (there is still a need for a chapter on this subject, albeit a short one), the state of the foreign exchange market, developments in credit insurance and allied finance, and shipping documentation are particularly affected. As a result I have not dwelt on some of the more detailed technical aspects, but have endeavoured to state the general principles involved. I strongly recommend readers to study the following current publications:

The Financial Times
Journal of The Institute of Bankers
Export and *ECGD Services.*

The last is published free of charge and is available from the ECGD.

For the examination candidate there are four main subject themes in the various professional bodies' syllabuses that regularly feature in their examinations:

a *The methods of settlement of trade*
Why does open account trade favour the buyer, and to what extent? Why do advance payments provide the seller with the most secure position? What compromises are provided by means of clean or documentary collections, and by documentary credits? How do these work and what protection do they afford each of the trading parties?

b *Finance*
The meaning of the word 'finance' herein is the granting of credit to a buyer and/or provision of cash to a seller. Overdrafts, loans, negotiations, specialised advances, trade credit, factoring, leasing, hire purchase, forfaiting, discounting – are all associated with resolving the problem of *the timing* of settlement. A buyer normally wants to defer payment to assist his cash flow, whereas a seller wants his money as soon as possible. Finance usually relates to a lending technique often provided by banks to bridge the settlement timing problem of trading parties. One of the important techniques is the use of the documentary credit.

Examiners expect a thorough knowledge of how documentary credits function and a working knowledge of *Uniform Customs*. It is essential to know the advantages and protection that documentary credits afford to different parties; the procedures for establishing a credit; and the distinction between irrevocable and confirmed credits. Because of their practical importance these are questions that constantly recur; without a question on documentary credits no examination paper on finance of international trade would be complete. It is necessary to give a precise answer, for each examination question on the subject usually has a different 'slant', and no marks are gained if the answer is not directly relevant to the question set. Examiners look for evidence that the candidate knows:

i The basis of a documentary credit and its various types.
ii The benefits and disadvantages to both buyer and seller.
iii The means of settlement.
iv The nature of finance available.

c *Export Credits Guarantee Department (ECGD)*
The ECGD is assuming increasing importance in the finance of foreign trade, and this has been recognised by examiners. Recent papers have all included at least one

question on ECGD. Examiners look for up to date knowledge on this subject: they rarely get it.

It is essential to master the meaning of 'short-, medium- and long-term export finance', the risks involved and how the requisite finance is found. The parts played by the commercial banks, consortia and ECGD must be learnt. It is important for the candidate to keep abreast of all current developments, for conditions in this field change frequently.

Examiners may ask for detailed and accurate information regarding the different types of policies available to exporters. The candidate must know the different ways ECGD cover can be used to protect the exporter and the bank which may have provided finance for overseas sales.

d   *Foreign exchange*

Examiners are fond of setting questions that require some knowledge of the theory and practice of foreign exchange. The theory requires good knowledge of 'options', 'premiums' and 'discounts' – both the definitions of these terms and how to apply the principles. These are attractive questions for candidates who have really studied the subject, and marks are gained for correct definitions and the ability to choose correct rates, thereby displaying a full understanding of the problems posed.

Alasdair Watson, FIB, FIEx, MBIM
June 1981

Acknowledgements

In the first edition of this book, published in 1976, the author recorded his thanks to several experienced bankers and teachers who had kindly read and commented on his original manuscript. Their assistance was invaluable in the preparation of a new book that has since become one of the most popular of the textbooks published by The Institute of Bankers.

Since 1976, considerable changes have taken place in the financing of international trade and its documentation. This second edition, updated to June 1981, therefore contains much new material including most of the documents that now illustrate the text. The author and The Institute of Bankers would like to express their appreciation and gratitude to the following who have freely given their advice and/or assisted in obtaining suitable specimen documents for reproduction in this second edition of the book:

L.A. Barlow	(Williams & Glyn's Bank)
C.A. Brooks	(Midland Bank)
C.P. Dunham	(SITPRO)
C.A. Freebury	(SITPRO)
R.H. French	(British Insurance Association)
J.N. Gordon-Graham	(Lloyds Bank)
H.G. Sinclair	(Beecham Research International)
B.S. Wheble, CBE, Hon. FIB	(ex-Brown Shipley & Co.)
V.H. Wilding	(ex-Midland Bank)
C.W.G. Wilson	(Institute of Freight Forwarders)
M.H. Wright	(Glaxo Holdings)

and to The International Chamber of Commerce for granting permission to reproduce the texts of three of their publications – No. 290 *Uniform Customs and Practice for Documentary Credits* (1974), No. 322 *Uniform Rules for Collections* (1978), and No. 325 *Uniform Rules for Contract Guarantees* (1978); to the Export Credits Guarantee Department for permission to reproduce their flow chart of ECGD Services; to FIATA for permission to reproduce a set of their specimen documents; to Blue Star Line Ltd. for permission to reproduce a specimen of their bills of lading; and to the Simplification of International Trade Procedures Board (SITPRO) for their permission to reproduce the documents illustrated on pages 62, 66, 67, 75, 76, 77, 119, 137, 138, 139, 140 and 141.

[SITPRO, 26 King Street, London SW1Y 6OW, will be pleased to provide details of its export documentation systems, services, and publications for those requiring further information.]

In preparing this edition of the book, the author has very much appreciated the helpful advice and assistance given to him by the individuals and organisations to whom he has expressed his thanks; but he wishes to emphasise that the responsibility for the views expressed in this book rests with him and not with The Institute of Bankers or those who have been kind enough to offer their advice.

Finally, the author would like to thank the National Westminster Bank, The Institute of Bankers and members of his family, without whose assistance this publication would not have been possible.

Contents

CHAPTER ONE

Principles of International Trade and the Role of London's Financial Institutions

1.   INTRODUCTION TO INTERNATIONAL TRADE

A company with a healthy home market for its goods may consider exporting to be a waste of time and effort. This is usually an ill-advised policy, for the following reasons. If the home market is the only market, a company is more exposed to falling demand than if its products are being sold in several. For the same reason fund managers spread their investment portfolios over several stock exchanges to obtain a spread of risk over several markets. This spread of risk acts as a buffer and will enable a manufacturer to ride out recession periods more easily, particularly if the export markets were established when the home market was booming. A wider market should lead to lower unit costs; and the expansion of sales might prompt improved automation and production techniques, which in turn will lead to goods being priced more competitively, or to greater profits being made. A well-developed export market will often lead to economic growth, improved productivity, higher levels of employment, greater profits from which to pay higher wages, and yield an improved return to stockholders, as well as a safer margin against redundancy and failure during periods of recession.

The importance to the United Kingdom of exporting is well known since we often have a trade deficit which needs to be funded, sometimes by the falling value of our currency (sterling devaluation) and sometimes by foreign ownership of UK assets (the purchase of UK investments by non-residents of the UK). The falling value of sterling puts up the price of imports which of course include a large proportion of our raw materials and food, often being paid for immediately. On the other hand, exports are said to become more competitive as the value of sterling falls, but the exporter must pay for raw materials which then cost him more to import. Moreover, the exporter does not necessarily receive the proceeds from his manufactured goods straight away, and there will be a time lag between the effect of the inflationary costs of imports and the receipt of payments for goods which are often sold on credit terms abroad. It may be argued that apart from the obvious benefits to the balance of payments, an increase in UK exports will tend to lower inflation and increase the value of sterling. Over the last 30 years or so successive British governments have recognised the prime importance of exports in the UK economy. This is manifested in the proliferation of services offered by government departments (see section 3 of this chapter, and Chapter 6). Further stimulus has been developed by the Queen's Award for Export Achievement and the training of staff involved in exporting led by the Institute of Export and the British Overseas Trade Board.

2.   EXPORT MARKETS – WHERE TO START

'There are those who make things happen': fortunately these are usually the right things; but, to achieve results, *drive* is essential.

'There are those to whom things happen': very often the wrong things; this is frequently called bad luck but is often just bad management arising from lack of imagination and drive.

'There are those who are even unaware of what is happening': a successful businessman knows that continuous, accurate and up to date information plays a vital part in the success of a venture.

Most exporters have the drive required to achieve results by the well-tested formula of 'research', 'assess', 'decide', 'act', applied on a *continual* basis.

The sheer volume of information which can be obtained by an exporter is often daunting and can easily prove unmanageable. Unless one is selective it tends to be of little practical use. To someone new to exporting an answer to these basic questions is essential:

i   What information do I need?

ii   Where do I get it?

iii   What is relevant to my particular needs?

iv   What reliance can I place on the information?

v   How often should I review the information?

The first area for research is usually the product or service to be sold. A detailed study of this will help to establish the parameters for further research along more meaningful lines and probably at lower cost.

The kind of information which *could* be obtained before deciding whether to enter an export market will vary from company to company. It will depend primarily upon the nature of the goods manufactured or services provided, and also upon a company's *scale* of operations. Capital goods, consumer goods, and services each demand separate techniques. However, the information in general which exporters should consider is contained in this chapter. Consider the wide differences of approach between:

i   A manufacturer of capital goods designed to meet the specific requirements of each buyer.

ii   A manufacturer making a standard, unalterable product with sales linked to a well-developed home market.

iii   A manufacturer of consumer goods that may be varied without excessive cost or difficulty, given six to 12 months' notice of a need for design or production changes.

iv   A manufacturer of goods that can only be varied in a limited way and at considerable cost.

v   A service industry wishing to expand its network of finance operations/services internationally.

The emphasis in each of the above cases will be quite different, although the basic principles will be the same. Whether or not an outside professional research agency is employed, the steps which should be taken are as follows:

- obtain as much background information available in the UK as possible, particularly about the subject matter referred to in sections 4,5,6 and 7 of this chapter
- visit the market(s) for further on the spot research or to find or train an agent, or to plan sales campaigns, or to visit customers
- obtain a marketing survey in the market itself

3.   SOURCES OF INFORMATION

a   Technical Help for Exporters (THE)

THE was established in 1966 by the British Standards Institution (BSI) and the British Overseas Trade Board (BOTB) to assist manufacturers and distributors to overcome the problems of translating technical documents and complying with the many standards applicable to individual countries. Preliminary discussions between THE representatives, designers and production manager can save an exporter both time and money if he is entering a new export market.

b   The Department of Trade and Industry

Export Service and Promotions Division provides information and advice as follows:

i   Specific trade opportunities.
ii   Computerised export intelligence service.
iii   *British Business* (journal).
iv   Market assessments.
v   Invisible exports.
vi   Project information.
vii   Tariff and import regulations abroad.
viii Foreign samples.
ix   Help with overseas business missions.
x   Finding a buyer or representative.
xi   UK buying houses for overseas stores.
xii   Foreign importers.
xiii Commercial standing of overseas traders.
xiv   Resolving commercial disputes.
xv   Manufacture under licence: sale of know-how.
xvi   Group Export Representation Scheme.
xvii Export marketing research.

Overseas Projects Group (part of Export Development Division) co-ordinates official support for overseas projects.

Commercial Relations and Exports Divisions provide information and advice on:

i   Protection of commercial interests abroad.
ii   Exporting to communist countries.
iii   Tariff advantages overseas.
iv   Export prohibitions and restrictions.
v   Security export controls.
vi   Exchange control abroad.
vii   Documentation procedures.
viii Export documentation for statistics.
ix   Reducing work on export documents.

Statistics and Market Intelligence Library provides:

i   Statistics, trade directories, catalogues.
ii   Overseas market surveys and development plans, etc.

Fairs and Promotions Branch provides support for:

i   Trade fairs and exhibitions.
ii   Direct support for joint ventures.
iii   British pavilions.
iv   Information stands.
v   All-British trade fairs.
vi   British weeks.
vii   British shopping weeks.
viii Store promotions.
ix   Outward missions.
x   Trade drives.

Information and advice are given free of charge, and the Fairs and Promotions Branch is prepared to meet certain expenses arising from export promotions established under its auspices.

c   British Overseas Trade Board (BOTB) market entry guarantee scheme

Designed to help the smaller and medium-sized firms in manufacturing industry break into new overseas markets, the scheme aims to capture a significant increase in market share for the UK. The BOTB will fund 50 per cent of the following overhead costs which must be incurred specifically in relation to a proposed venture and its defined market and products:

i   *Overseas office accommodation* Rental; property and contents insurance; maintenance; services; local property taxes; office equipment; office consumable supplies; purchase and running costs, or rental, of cars.

ii   *Staff costs* Salaries, recruitment and relocation costs in respect of overseas-based administration, sales and warehouse staff.

iii *Training* Training in the selling and servicing of the venture product(s) of overseas-based staff only.

iv   *Travel and expenses* Travel and subsistence costs for overseas-based staff; and for home-based staff visiting the market directly in connection with a venture.

v   *Sales promotion* Advertising; publicity; sales literature specific to the venture market; product demonstration costs.

vi   *Overseas warehousing* Costs of storage facilities, including showrooms, under similar headings to those for overseas office accommodation.

vii *Commercial and legal costs* Legal costs in setting up the overseas operation; external audit costs; costs/fees for patents, trade marks, licences, testing and approval of venture product(s) to local standards.

The exporter is required to pay a 3 per cent flat charge for the funding, and also to pay a levy on sales receipts. This levy will be calculated to recover the funding costs plus interest at commercial bank lending rates. This means that, provided the venture is successful, the exporter will be expected to repay funds provided initially plus interest at 2½ per cent over the average of the UK clearing banks' base rate. The minimum funding is £20,000 and the maximum £125,000, and it will only be made available on production of independently certified evidence of eligible costs having been incurred.

d   Other sources of information

Association of British Chambers of
    Commerce
Association for Industrial Marketing
    Research
Banks
BBC External Services
British Export Houses Association
British Insurance Association
British Insurance Brokers' Association
British National Export Council
British Overseas Fairs Ltd
British Overseas Trade Board
British Standards Institution
Central Office of Information
Chambers of Commerce
Chartered Institute of Patent Agents
Confederation of British Industry
Council of Industrial Design
Department of Trade and Industry
Embassies
Export Credits Guarantee Department

Finance Houses Association
Finance for Industry
Foreign and Commonwealth Office
Foreign Press Association of London
HM Customs and Excise
HM Diplomatic Service overseas
HM Patent Office
HM Stationery Office
Industrial and Trade Fairs Holdings Ltd
Institute of Bankers
Institute of Credit Management
Institute of Export
Institute of Freight Forwarders Ltd
Institute of London Underwriters
Institute of Marketing
Institute of Trade Mark Agents
Market Research Society
Post Office
Trade Associations
Trade Indemnity Co Ltd
UK diplomatic representation abroad

4.   METHODS OF SELLING ABROAD

Developing an export market means participation. A company cannot expect to be in a market and enjoy its benefits without effective commitment by way of appropriate representation. It is therefore relatively unusual for a manufacturer to deal directly with a user abroad, except in the field of capital projects. One-off direct sales abroad to unload spare production capacity after home sales are satisfied is not serious exporting and can ruin an exporter's opportunity to develop a new market properly.

The sale of goods abroad may be carried out through sales outlets in the UK, or through sales outlets abroad. Dealing with each in turn . . .

a   The UK-based outlets include:

i   *General merchants:* some are specialists in certain types of commodity, others have their own retail outlets such as stores; there are a number who will try to sell anything anywhere so long as there is a profit.

ii   *Confirming houses:* some guarantee payment by the overseas buyer, others undertake to pay on behalf of the overseas buyer. There is normally no contact between manufacturer and buyer, which limits the flow of research information to the manufacturer. The exporter may derive benefits of reduced complexity in selling abroad by this method.

iii   *Export houses:* do not normally act as agents of the foreign buyer, but will be prepared to purchase the goods themselves. They frequently undertake the shipping, packing and insurance documentation and procedures, and often can arrange finance if required.

b   The overseas-based outlets may be:

i   *A branch:* the alternative activities are local manufacturing or local assembly and sales, or just sales and after-sales servicing. There are obvious advantages in having the prestige of one's name represented abroad through a branch. However, major points to consider before taking such a step will include the questions of local taxation, the remittance of quasi-capital (as a branch cannot be incorporated locally), repatriation of profits, and local laws in respect of ownership and the employment requirements of locally recruited labour.

ii   *A wholly owned subsidiary:* it sometimes pays to buy a going concern with the local expertise to go with it, rather than to establish a branch and train local staff from the beginning. The prestige value can still be obtained, but the purchase price to be paid might mean writing off a substantial figure to goodwill.

iii *A subsidiary with a controlling interest:* the prime role of such a subsidiary is normally the distribution and sales of the parent's products, not necessarily the subsidiary making a profit locally.

iv   *An affiliate or trade investment:* one of the most common direct outward investments by UK companies. There is no control over the policy of the affiliate, but an equity holding often helps to cement a closer working relationship with a well-established institution in the market.

v   *A representative or agency:* the type of agency will depend upon the agency agreement drawn up between the exporter and his overseas representative. The functions an agent may be asked to fulfil could include some or all of the following:
   * handling enquiries from potential buyers
   * giving or obtaining quotations and receiving orders
   * completing questionnaires on market conditions for the exporter
   * advising on sales policy, advertising and new products
   * dealing with complaints
   * assisting in obtaining payment (case of need; see Chapter 4)
   * keeping the exporter informed on local prices, competition, and technical information, and
   * generally protecting the exporter's interests

Sole agents are usually given exclusive rights in a specified area and do not deal with competitors' products; there is always the danger of a conflict of interests where general agents are concerned. Agents who hold stock are usually called distributors and they may also be required to provide after-sales servicing.

An exporter who is seeking assistance in establishing overseas representation as indicated in *i-v* above should consult his bank, the Department of Trade and Industry, and perhaps a law firm with experience of international commerce. Chambers of commerce and the Institute of Export may assist with agency agreements.

5.   PERMISSIONS EXPORTERS MAY REQUIRE

When examining the permissions which may be required (they are listed below), exporters should consider the following questions:
   * are these restrictions in force at present?
   * how important are they?
   * to what extent do they limit the marketing prospects?
   * can they be avoided or can approval be specifically obtained?
   * are there any impending regulations which will require permissions to be obtained?
   * is there a history or likelihood of retro-active legislation?

The permissions which are sometimes required may be in respect of goods or payments, as follows:

i   *Permissions and regulations affecting the goods:*
* export licensing
* import licensing
* anti-dumping legislation
* resale price restrictions
* trade embargoes
* registered trade marks and patents
* legal standards of marking, labelling and packaging
* legal standards of quality and specification of manufacture
* health requirements
* dangerous goods
* documentary requirements

ii   *Permissions and regulations related to payments:*
* import duty
* exchange control regulations in the buyer's country
* foreign exchange permits
* taxation

Sources of specific information on different markets relating to the above lists are given in section 3 of this chapter.

6.   MARKET CONDITIONS

Research into key facts relating to each potential market may be analysed under any of the following headings that may be likely to affect a product:

i   *Geographical and social conditions*
Political boundaries; physical features; location of ports and airports; transport systems; centres of population; climatic data; social and travelling habits; population trends and statistics (subdivided into income groups, age, sex, race and religion as appropriate); standards of living; health education and housing standards; types of employment and use of leisure time; eating and drinking preferences; local preferences for, and prejudices against, designs, symbols, packaging, colours, or brands and brand names.

ii   *Market conditions*
Local manufacturers' prices, production capacity, and output; importance and reputation of local producers; import trade statistics for similar goods; export statistics from UK competitors and other countries exporting to the market in question; level of duty, preferences, tax on goods made locally compared with imported goods from the UK and from elsewhere; the extent to which the product meets or is likely to meet market requirements, and details of all changes to the product that would be needed.

iii   *Methods of research in the market itself*
Market research agencies may arrange wholesale or retail trade surveys on distribution and marketing problems; consumer and user surveys on the basis of

quota or a random-sample area of the market, usually by means of mailed questionnaires and sometimes by personal interviews; test marketing by introducing the new product in a limited and selected area representative of the whole market, sometimes involving the distribution of free samples.

iv   *Advertising and promotion*

Exhibitions, cinema, radio, television, newspapers, magazines, trade journals, and posters; the coverage of the media; reading habits; languages used; methods used by competitors; promotional materials: samples, gifts, literature, films and display materials; organisation, presentation and cost of publicity.

v   *Payment terms and finance*

Costs of insurance, freight and transport expenses; details of the local currency, its convertibility, and stability of foreign exchange and interest rates; level of interest rates and availability of local finance; deferred terms of credit normally given, as well as details of any rebates, discounts, bonus or special incentive schemes; estimates of total expenditure needed to penetrate the market, and the period over which this is likely to be recovered, as well as financing arrangements to fund this cost; details of appropriate shipping terms (see Chapter 3). Subject to its availability as to the length of time involved and the amount required, finance for the UK exporter is normally available in London in sterling or foreign currencies, through the following facilities:

Overdrafts	Factoring
Floating rate loans	Invoice discounting
Fixed rate term loans	Hire purchase
Advances against collections	Leasing
Negotiation of outward collections	Special ECGD-backed bank finance
Discounts	for exports
Payments under documentary credits	Trade credit from the importer
Acceptance credit facilities	Funding from the exporter's own
Forfaiting	liquidity (working capital)

(Further details of these facilities are to be found in Chapters 4 to 7 inclusive.)

7.   RISK ASSESSMENT AND DECISION MAKING

i   *What are the risks?*

The risk to the goods includes: loss; damage; delay; loss on resale if not accepted; reshipment, warehouse, and insurance costs if not accepted.

    The risk of non-payment for the goods includes: exchange control and fiscal changes; buyer's default; agent's default; transfer of funds blocked for economic, war or political reasons; losses on foreign exchange.

    The risk on investments abroad in a branch or subsidiary company includes: nationalisation; sequestration; local recession; changes in taxation, local law, labour relations, ability to remit profits or dividends abroad.

ii   *How can potential risks be identified?*

By a regular flow of on the spot information on the following:

Market conditions: is there a boom, and when will it, or how likely is it, to break? Economic conditions: inflation and money supply barometers. Political conditions: war, strikes, riots, moratorium on payments, domestic politics. Customer data:

status reports and financial information.

A careful initial selection of agents and advisers, preferably from those with proven track records of success, should also be followed up by a continuing flow of information about their relative standing and activities and by regular visits to the market.

iii   *Reducing or eliminating the risks*

The decision to reduce or eliminate a risk must be based on a level of risk which is acceptable to the exporter, and on a cost of risk-reduction which is also acceptable. It is not unknown for large sums of money to be wasted by exporters whose company policy requires facilities or services to be provided which are never used to their full potential or are quite unnecessary for their particular needs.

It is essential for correct decisions to be made at the outset with regard to cargo insurance (Chapter 3), credit insurance (Chapter 6), invoicing policy and exchange rate protection (Chapter 8), as well as to the method of settlement to be negotiated with the buyer abroad (Chapters 2, 4 and 5).

The alternative methods of trade settlement (with their attendant risks to the exporter) are:

a   *Open account:* whereby the buyer obtains the documents and/or the goods prior to his sending his remittance on the agreed date. Risks: buyer's default; transfer of funds being blocked; absence of control by the exporter over the documents or the goods (see Chapter 2).

b   *Collections:* whereby bills of exchange and/or documents of trade are handled by the exporter's bank with instructions for the funds to be collected from the buyer (see Chapter 4). The risks may be similar to those listed under 'open account' above, except that control over the goods/documents may be possible through the banks involved.

c   *Documentary credits:* whereby payment may be received by the exporter for documents he presents to a bank in his own country which comply with stated terms and conditions given in the credit (see Chapter 5). Documentary credits contain the undertaking of the buyer's bank to make payment, and sometimes contain the undertaking of a bank in the exporter's country to pay. So, provided the exporter complies with the credit terms, the risk of the buyer's default is removed, and perhaps the transfer risks as well.

d   *Advance payments:* whereby the exporter is paid before he parts with his goods. While being the safest method of settlement for the exporter, it is the least satisfactory method for the buyer (see Chapter 2).

The buyer and the seller have the following basic points of concern to resolve:

	The buyer's problems are		The seller's problems are
i	Am I going to get the goods I have ordered, and will they arrive in good condition and in time for my purposes? The buyer will be concerned to obtain the security he needs from the settlement method to be agreed upon with the seller.	i	Am I going to be paid? A secure method of settlement for the exporter's needs must be considered.
ii	What deferred credit terms can I get? This is a question of finance rather than settlement, although open account settlement would provide a degree of satisfaction on this matter as well.	ii	When am I going to be paid? This is a finance problem, although advance payment settlement would also satisfy the exporter's cash flow considerations.

8.   LIST OF EXPORT SERVICES PROVIDED BY BANKS

i   Providing information and advice on:
* markets overseas (general economic reports and possibly undertaking or arranging market research)
* exchange control (overseas)
* tariffs and quotas
* methods and risks of selling overseas
* documentation and shipping
* appointing agents or establishing an overseas subsidiary
* names of overseas buyers and agents
* status reports
* ECGD matters
* foreign exchange and interest rate trends

ii   Arranging settlement: via branch network/correspondents abroad, banks will collect clean/documentary bills; pay, negotiate or accept under documentary credits; give indemnities covering discrepancies; exchange currency for sterling; maintain foreign currency accounts; provide international cash management.

iii   Eliminating exchange risk: through spot or forward cover or foreign currency loan.

iv   Providing finance:
* overdraft or loan
* negotiation, discount bill advance and forfaiting
* discount of acceptance under documentary credit
* acceptance credit – eg, 'accommodation bill' drawn on a bank (sometimes against security of collections) and discountable in the local discount market
* against appropriate ECGD cover

v   Obtaining marine insurance cover.

vi   Guarantees – eg, tender guarantees, performance bonds, guarantees for local overdraft facilities.

vii   Travel facilities and obtaining passports.

viii   Introductions to banks abroad, shipping and forwarding agents, ECGD, factoring and other relevant organisations.

9.   INTRODUCTION TO LONDON'S FINANCIAL INSTITUTIONS

a   There are geographical and historical reasons for the growth of London as a great financial centre. Britain was the first industrialised country, and London, as the capital and a major port, was most favourably placed on the trade routes of the world and was, indeed, a major trading city long before it developed into a financial centre.

The growth in merchanting and other commercial activity in London, together with the development of the British banking system (particularly through the early merchant banks), combined, with the expansion of the British Empire and the consequent growth in trade, to make London during the nineteenth century the world's major centre for finance and investment.

Today, despite the diminishing role of sterling, the importance of the gold and commodity markets, the stock exchange, insurance markets, banks, money markets and the Baltic Exchange, keeps London among the world's leading financial centres, with a range of services only paralleled in New York.

An expertise has grown up, and probably nowhere else in the world is there such an accumulation of skill in so many varied markets. The City of London plays a major part in maintaining stable markets and in financing trade (sterling is used to settle about 90 per cent of trade within the Commonwealth and about 20 per cent of total world trade). The Baltic Exchange accounts for two-thirds of the world's total shipping freight business and four-fifths of the world's air cargoes.

The City makes a most valuable contribution to the UK's income by its earnings on premiums, commissions and discounts in the various spheres of commercial activity.

b   In a recent survey of the UK insurance companies, members of the British Insurance Association were said to derive almost half their income from abroad. Lloyd's overseas business accounts for three-quarters of its total business. Some idea of the size of this unique industry may be obtained from the fact that in 1978 the estimated premium income was £14,275 million and approximately two-thirds of the premium income was paid in claims. There are some 168 branches, subsidiaries and agencies of foreign insurance companies based in London. It has been estimated that over half the insurance companies' general business, and about 10 per cent of their life business, originates abroad. One reason for the growth of London as an insurance centre is the comparative freedom from regulatory restraints which inhibit insurance companies overseas, and the fact that London is the leading re-insurance market in the world.

c   Since the ending of the gold pool in March 1968 the London gold market has changed in several ways. The arrangements whereby central bank operations held down the price to a maximum of $35.20 per troy ounce came to an end with the demise of the gold pool, and prices now fluctuate, at a higher level, in accordance with changes in supply and demand. Another development is that South African supplies of newly mined gold can no longer be counted on to arrive regularly, or to be placed on the London market. Since its monopoly of South African gold was one of the reasons for London's pre-eminence as a gold market, the current uncertainty leaves the way open for Zurich and Paris to compete for the status of the leading gold market. A third change was the creation of special drawing rights (SDRs) within the framework of the International Monetary Fund (IMF). These became operative on 1st January 1970 and added significantly to world liquidity (which was in danger of contracting following the loss of gold to hoarders before March 1968). SDRs were planned and created by the IMF to supplement international monetary reserves and were seen as offering a durable solution to the world liquidity problem. The scheme allowed members, subject to various conditions, to make temporary drawings of other foreign currencies to be repaid in due course. SDRs are an owned reserve and consequently constitute unconditional liquidity. They are denominated in units equivalent to the gold value of the US dollar and in most cases are counted as part of the individual country's reserves. By September 1975 fewer than 10,000 million SDRs had been issued, accounting for only 5 per cent of the total of international reserves. The value of the SDR is now based on a 'basket' of five leading currencies rather than on any objective standard of values. In October 1979, at the IMF annual meeting in Belgrade, the creation of a substitute account expressed in SDRs for US dollar reserve assets was discussed. In 1980 it was estimated that 16.5 billion SDRs were in member country revenues, and that these and the reserve positions in the IMF accounted for about 8 per cent of world reserves.

SDRs have been used in debt instruments such as Eurobonds and more recently in certificates of deposit (see Chapter 10), and certain major commercial banks have established SDR-denominated deposit accounts for some multinational customers. Lending in SDRs will follow during 1981.

d   The role of sterling as an international trading currency has diminished very considerably since the devaluation of 1976 and the subsequent change of government policy regarding its use in trading transactions. However, the exchange control relaxations of 1979 and subsequent weakness of other currencies in 1979–81 reversed this trend. The short-term sterling markets, however, are still extremely important and the removal of exchange control regulations in 1979 has encouraged a greater use of sterling. In the meantime attempts to control the money supply and high interest rates act as a brake on the growth of sterling borrowing. An outline of these markets follows.

Discount market
The 11 London discount companies provide a short-term money market for the purchase and/or sale of Treasury bills, short-dated British government bonds, certificates of deposit, and commercial bills.

The discount companies deal principally with the commercial and merchant banks in London, the Bank of England, and leading industrial and insurance companies.

i   *The Treasury,* through the Bank of England, floats a weekly issue of Treasury bills with a maturity of 91 days. The bidders at the tender include the discount houses, the Bank of England on behalf of its overseas central bank customers, and other banks.

ii   *Government bonds* that have a final maturity date of not more than five years may be bought and sold through the London discount houses. This is an extension of the facilities provided in the stock exchange by jobbers.

iii   *Certificates of deposit* are covered in greater detail in Chapter 10.

iv   *Commercial bills.* Trade and bank bills may be discounted directly by companies, or, more commonly, either held or re-discounted by a London bank with a London discount house. If the acceptor of a commercial bill is a first class London bank then payment at maturity is guaranteed and the bill will attract a lower discount rate when sold than, say, a trade bill accepted by an institution other than a bank. While the market in commercial bills is principally in sterling, foreign currency acceptances may be discounted in the London bill market.

The discount houses have diversified their activities still further to include foreign exchange broking, and dealing in the local authority, interbank, and finance house markets.

Interbank market
The prime market in London for short-term sterling is the discount market. However, the clearing and other banks in London have, since the mid-1960s, borrowed and lent each other money directly without going through the bill brokers on the discount market. The cost of interbank funds is about a quarter per cent more than for the equivalent period of borrowing on the discount markets. Transactions range from £100,000 upwards.

Local authority market
Local authorities (borough councils, etc) require long- and short-term capital to meet their financial commitments. Major projects such as building roads, etc, may not always be financed by way of stock issues because of statutory limitations. Income from rates does not provide an even flow of income for revenue expenditure, and at times gives rise

to considerable surpluses of short-term sterling. Local authorities are therefore large borrowers and lenders of sterling, and a further market for dealing in these funds has emerged. The clearing banks may directly or indirectly provide these funds. Negotiable bonds may be issued by local authorities for loans of between one ('yearling') and four years and the discount houses provide the secondary market for them.

Inter-company market

In the late 1960s, when lending restrictions were imposed on the clearing banks, a number of large companies started to use overdraft facilities which, in many cases, had never been used before but had been agreed as standby facilities in case of need. The rate of interest charged by the joint stock banks was invariably the finest borrowing rate available. Indeed, owing to the shortage of capital, other companies that had not previously arranged access to funds were only too happy to borrow from those companies that had, and at a higher rate of interest. Efforts have been made to curb this practice.

10. THE BANK OF ENGLAND

The banking structure of London is very complex and there is considerable overlapping.

At the centre is the Bank of England, the central bank, which holds the main accounts of the government and the leading commercial banks. It also maintains sterling accounts on behalf of many other central banks for their use in settling international transactions.

On behalf of the Treasury, the Bank of England handles the administration of the Exchange Control Act (still on the statute book, but see Chapter 9). It manages the Exchange Equalisation Account (which contains the gold and foreign currencies which are the international reserves of this country) and it operates, whenever necessary, in the foreign exchange markets, both in London and by dealing directly with other central banks abroad, to steady rates for sterling and keep them within the limits agreed from time to time with the International Monetary Fund (see Chapter 8). Ever since the international banking crisis of 1974, the authorities in various countries have imposed controls or insisted upon essential standards of practice in money market operations. The banking institutions have been subject to these measures. However, since an ordered market is of fundamental importance to the institutions themselves, the London banks exercise strict self-discipline. Within each bank are in-house regulations well inside those imposed by the central bank. The Bank of England's function in controlling the markets by means of returns submitted by the reporting institutions is all-important.

Until October 1979, when UK exchange control regulations were dismantled, the Bank of England required to be satisfied as to the competence of management, and exchange control and foreign exchange expertise, before granting 'authorised status' to any bank applying to carry out international banking business in London and thereby having access to the international money markets. The designation 'authorised bank' was an exchange control concept and now no longer applies. This does not mean that the Bank of England's role in bank supervision has diminished. In fact, its concern to ensure ordered markets has led to its requiring banks to maintain prudential accounting ratios.

11. CLEARING BANKS

The clearing banks have overseas branches in the City of London and in the provinces through which they transact their overseas business as outlined in the next section. Until the early 1960s they restricted their foreign business lending largely to the provision of short-term finance. Nevertheless, they handle a greater volume of foreign business than any other banking sector in the City. This reflects both the breadth of their foreign business services, extending from the provision of credit and payments facilities for foreign trade, to dealing in foreign exchange and offering information services to exporters. As primary deposit banks, and because of the extent of their branch networks, they hold the dominant position in British banking. This has enabled them to make their foreign business services available throughout the country, and has also brought them a large share of foreign business originating abroad. As a consequence, each of the clearing banks has built up a network of correspondent banks overseas, for which accounts are held and through which payments and other business are channelled. Since 1960 the clearing banks have extended their foreign business operations by entering the Euro-dollar markets, initially through subsidiaries, by forging closer links with overseas banks, particularly through the establishment of new international banks, acquisitions and investments in foreign banks and finance companies, establishing new branches abroad; and by broadening their export credit facilities and diversifying into leasing, hire purchase, factoring, confirming and other services to meet the needs of large multinational enterprises.

12. THE OVERSEAS BRANCH OF A JOINT STOCK BANK

While all foreign branches of the various banks deal with similar transactions, the internal structure of these organisations and the names given to the departments vary considerably. Consequently the nomenclature employed below is by way of illustration; a more detailed explanation of these services may be found in the chapters which follow. An overseas branch has two prime functions:
● it is a branch in its own right, often with its own customers, who include overseas banking correspondents, and
● it acts as a clearing house for the foreign business of its domestic branches

During the 1970s the joint stock banks experienced a period of considerable expansion, partially a result of mergers and diversification and partially as a result of exceptionally high inflation. The growth that followed led to a considerable amount of relocation of the larger-scale processing operations, which had hitherto been largely centralised on London. This gave the provincial overseas branches around the country enhanced importance, and at the same time gave economies on premises and staff. The money markets have remained in London.

a   Deposit services
The Accountancy Department will maintain:
i   The sterling accounts of the bank's foreign correspondents (*vostro* accounts).
ii   The sterling and currency accounts of private and corporate customers.
iii   Interest-bearing customers' currency deposit accounts, as well as sterling deposit accounts.
iv   Records of the bank's foreign currency (*nostro* accounts) maintained by banking correspondents abroad.

b   Transmission services
Payments Abroad Department:
i   Makes clean payments abroad in sterling or currency by means of The Society for Worldwide Interbank Financial Telecommunication (SWIFT) messages, mail transfers, telegraphic transfers, or drafts drawn on the correspondents abroad.

ii   Arrangements can be made for customers travelling abroad and staying in one place to cash their cheques at the counter of the bank's correspondents.

iii   Clean credits may be opened abroad for payments to third party beneficiaries.

Inland Payments Department:

i   Handles remittances for the credit of the accounts of overseas branch customers.

ii   Deals with remittances in sterling and foreign currency received from abroad for payment to firms, individuals and branches in the UK.

iii   Collects on behalf of branches the proceeds of cheques expressed in foreign currency, drawn on banks in the town clearing area.

iv   Operates the Insurance Companies' Currency Scheme (ICCS) for interbank London settlement of US dollar and Canadian dollar indebtedness, on behalf of insurance market customers.

v   Handles both the sterling and the US dollar clearing operations in London.

Mail Department:
May be divided into inward mail, outward mail, and translations sections.

Cable Department:
Handles inward and outward communications by cable, telegram, telex and SWIFT between branches abroad and correspondents abroad on behalf of domestic branches and departments of overseas branches.

Bills Department:

i   Outward bills for collection section; collects clean or documentary bills of exchange, cheques and documents, payable abroad in sterling or in foreign currencies.

ii   Inward bills section; obtains settlement of clean or documentary bills of exchange drawn on residents in the UK, or settlement against documents, on behalf of banks abroad.

Money Desk:
Deals with all types of foreign exchange transactions, quoting spot and forward rates (see Chapter 8). Quotes interest rates to be applied to all lendings and deposits in all currencies (see Chapter 10).

Foreign Exchange Settlement Department:

i   Handles the bookkeeping for the Money Desk.

ii   Ensures that the *nostro* accounts maintained with the overseas correspondents have sufficient funds to meet commitments, yet do not accumulate surplus funds which may be employed more profitably elsewhere.

Foreign Notes and Coin Department:
Buys and sells almost any foreign currency banknotes which are legal tender or exchangeable in their country of origin.

c   Lending services

Documentary Credits Department:

i   Supplies a full documentary credit service (see Chapter 5) covering the movement of goods all over the world. A documentary credit is one way of paying for imports, or receiving payment for exports, or undertaking merchanting transactions. For the importer it means the establishment of documentary credit in favour of his suppliers and in due course the receipt of shipping documents which give title to the goods. For the exporter it means the immediate notification of documentary credits established by foreign banks in his favour by order of his overseas buyers in order to facilitate payment for exports on presentation of shipping documents.

ii   Issues guarantees, indemnities and bid and performance bonds for fulfilment of contracts, etc, abroad (see Chapter 7).

Bills Department:
The sales section of this department negotiates or advances against clean or documentary bills of exchange, cheques and documents payable abroad in sterling or foreign currency. The inward bills section discounts bills payable in London and maintains the forfaiting portfolio.

Export and Shipbuilding Finance Department:
Arranges finance in support of exports from the UK where ECGD is prepared to guarantee the bank finance (see Chapter 6).

The management of the branch:
Managers arrange overdrafts, loans, negotiation and documentary credit lines of facilities for customers, and banks abroad, in sterling and foreign currencies.

d   Security and other services
The management of the branch
May deal with:

i   Status enquiries on UK and overseas buyers and sellers.
ii   Provision of economic reports on countries abroad.

Securities Department
Provides a full service for:

i   The purchase and sale of securities traded on stock exchanges abroad.
ii   The deposit of securities with correspondents abroad or with the bank's own depository in London.
iii   The receipt and delivery of securities abroad.
iv   The servicing of securities abroad, including the collection of income (dividends, etc).
v   Membership by invitation of the underwriting and/or selling group agencies of Eurobond issues.
vi   Purchase, sale and safe custody of gold, silver, coins and medallions.

Trade Enquiries:
i   Arranges introductions for customers who wish to engage in import or export trade.
ii   Maintains a comprehensive register of UK importers and exporters which specifies the goods manufactured and/or dealt in.
iii   Publishes a regular circular giving details of trade opportunities.
iv   Publishes a regular bulletin giving information on trading regulations, etc, in other countries.

Travel Department:

i   Issues and pays sterling travellers' cheques.

ii   Supplies domestic branches and banking correspondents with stocks of travellers' cheques to sell to their customers.

iii Issues worldwide letters of credit for travellers.

iv   Provides travellers' cheques expressed in other currencies.

v   Obtains passports and visas for customers.

The joint stock banks have developed international merchant banking services to a greater or lesser degree. These 'wholesale' services sometimes form part of their International Division and are usually separated to some extent from the 'retail' routine services outlined above which are carried out by a typical overseas branch.

13. MERCHANT AND INVESTMENT BANKS

The term 'merchant bank' is used rather loosely, for it is applied sometimes to merchants who are not banks, to banks which are not merchants, and to business houses which are neither banks nor merchants. There is a group of 17 houses in the City which are members of the Accepting Houses Committee and which are particularly active in the field of foreign trade. These and others make up the 56 members of the Issuing Houses Association. Each house has its own characteristics and its specialities on which it is regarded as an authority, but, in listing below the fields covered by the various houses in one way or another, it would be beyond the scope of this book to name the specialists for the individual fields.

In their various ways the merchant banks act as international banks, accepting houses, issuing houses and investment banks. The clearing banks, either directly, or through their many subsidiary companies, provide services as wide as any merchant bank. However, the merchant bank specialisations are as follows:

i   The acceptance credit line whereby the acceptance of a bill of exchange against documents taken on a collection basis provides the means of financing through the money market the movement of goods throughout the world. This is explained in detail in section 20 of Chapter 4.

ii   Foreign notes, gold and other precious metals, and commodities.

iii Maintenance of current and deposit accounts in sterling or foreign currencies for customers in the UK and abroad.

iv   Advances by loan and overdraft.

v   Foreign exchange and deposit dealing.

vi   Documentary collections, negotiations and advances against documentary collections, documentary credits, guarantees and performance bonds.

vii Confirming house business which under *del credere* arrangements also guarantees the solvency of approved buyers to whom their clients have sold goods.

viii Organising consortia to raise long-term finance, required for large overseas contracts, against ECGD guarantees, and the negotiation of financial agreements.

ix   Organising and participating in international consortia to raise foreign currency loans including Euro-credits, certificates of deposit, Eurobonds, floating rate notes, and domestic issues at home and abroad.

x   Assisting in raising new company capital by means of private placings, rights issues, public offers for sale, issues of loan capital, or equity participation loans ('nursery finance').

xi   Advising and assisting in public flotations.

xii Advising on mergers and acquisitions.

xiii Acting as company registrars.

xiv Promoting or managing investment trusts and unit trusts.

xv Providing an investment advisory service for clients.

xvi Acting as trustees and executors.

The accepting houses are active in all these fields, with particular emphasis placed on *i-vii*, whereas the issuing houses generally concentrate on *viii-xvi*. It should be noted that members of the Accepting Houses Committee are also members of the Issuing Houses Association and are active in corporate finance.

The term 'investment bank' is an American designation used to describe institutions which specialise in the transactions listed at *v, ix, x, xi, xii* and *xv* above. Certain indigenous merchant banks, a number of US-controlled investment banking subsidiaries, and the multinational consortia banks operate in the same international capital markets, sometimes in competition to obtain the business of, for example, lead-managing a new issue, sometimes in co-operation in an underwriting, selling or placing consortium with other banks and security dealers (see Chapter 10).

14. BANKING GROUPS

British overseas banks

The British overseas banks have developed banking services throughout the Commonwealth and in other overseas territories. In addition to providing domestic services in such areas as Australia, New Zealand, and South and Central Africa, they naturally handle a considerable proportion of the payments and finance for international trade between those areas and the UK.

They include the eastern exchange banks which are represented throughout the Far East, particularly India, Malaysia and Hong Kong, and which have tended to specialise in providing banking services for international trade, rather than in developing purely domestic banking within those countries.

Foreign banks and affiliates

The foreign banks and affiliates are the London offices and agencies of overseas banks (eg, the American, Japanese and Arab banks) and their British subsidiaries. By 1980 some 350 foreign bank operations were established in London. Naturally they compete actively for the inward and outward foreign business of their respective countries. Their business has expanded greatly in recent years, particularly in taking foreign currency deposits and making foreign currency advances from or to UK and overseas residents. US banks have been notably active in opening offices in London and competing for deposits on the London markets, especially by the issue of dollar certificates of deposit (negotiable receipts for deposits placed for a fixed period). Some foreign banks have London representatives only, who are active in trying to attract business to their respective organisations. In 1980 only a handful of the world's 100 largest banks were not represented directly or indirectly in London.

Multinational banks

Multinational banks are consortia whose shareholders usually include between 4 and 15 of the world's leading commercial banks. The majority, 27 in 1980, have London head offices as bases for their operations. Raising medium- and long-term finance in the wholesale banking sense, they provide capital for specific projects and for the expansion of some of the world's largest commercial enterprises. In addition to putting a 'package' together and negotiating large-scale financial facilities, they are able, through access to pooled resources, to raise funds on a very substantial scale. Many of the banks are engaged in securities-orientated business as investment banks.

A multinational enterprise may be described as one which owns or controls assets, such as factories, offices, plant, mines, etc, in more than one country. It has been estimated that by the end of the century more than half the world's total production will come from between 200 and 300 such concerns. The operations of these very large companies are massive and consequently benefit from the economies of scale.

Operating as a rule in many countries, the multinational company requires finance and allied services which may not be available locally where the funds are required. Funds are often raised internationally . . .

- to avoid the risk of national restrictions being imposed
- where the money required cannot be raised in the local money market in any one country

The financial and other services required by a multinational company may be considerable and varied, as the size and nature of its business is both large and diversified. Banks that wish to provide facilities for such organisations must operate internationally on a scale commensurate with the needs of such customers. This calls for a diversification of services, to embrace not only the traditional banking services, but also services such as factoring, invoice discounting, hire purchase, leasing, international money management, and medium- and long-term fund raising on a considerable scale. In order to raise funds for such customers, some 35 multinational banking groups have been established by the world's leading international banks.

15.   OTHER FINANCIAL INSTITUTIONS

a   Factoring

Export factoring is a service whereby the exporter passes copies of all his invoices on overseas buyers to a factoring company, the debts these represent being purchased by the factor, usually without recourse, who then undertakes all credit control, collection, and sales accounting work. The advantages of factoring for an exporter may be as follows, depending upon the extent of the factoring contract:

i   All bad debts, collection difficulties and the need for credit insurance are eliminated (the rights to the book debt being owned by the factor).

ii   The management of the exporting company may concentrate on production and sales and need not be concerned with non-profitable control and sales accounting procedures.

iii   Cost effective saving of staff, who would otherwise be engaged in sales accounting, and of premises such staff would have to occupy.

iv   Uneven cash flow arising from seasonal trade may be reduced by the facility to draw on invoices presented without having to wait until payment is made by the overseas buyer.

v   Elimination of foreign exchange risks.

vi   Subject to the factor's agreement, the exporter may trade on open account terms and thereby probably increase sales.

vii   Where the factor also provides shipping and forwarding facilities, the exporter may obtain most of the benefits he would derive from home sales.

London banks have acquired a controlling interest in the majority of large factoring companies. Bank lending by loan or overdraft may not necessarily be competitive with factoring finance. This depends upon the nature or size of the business and upon the balance sheet structure. There are occasions when bank and factoring finance together may enable a company to expand when selling consumer goods on short-term credit to a number of customers.

b   Leasing

There are occasions when foreign buyers of capital plant and machinery are unable to buy the equipment even on deferred credit terms, either because of insufficient funds or perhaps as a result of licensing regulations in the buyer's country, or because the plant carries a high obsolescence risk. Such buyers might consider leasing the plant or machinery they require. To do this, they approach a leasing company which will buy the goods from the manufacturer. The manufacturer gets paid in full by the leasing company, usually after shipment and installation at the hirer's premises. Many leasing companies are wholly owned subsidiaries of leading London banks. Additionally, the joint stock banks in consortium with other banks have formed a partnership, Airlease International, which specialises in ship and aircraft leasing. Taxation and depreciation play a large part in making leasing transactions attractive to the various parties, and financial packages for major projects sometimes include 'off balance sheet' schemes involving a leasing agreement.

c   Hire purchase

In the 1960s the joint stock banks took a large interest in the UK hire purchase business. Many of the leading hire purchase companies are now either partly or wholly owned by a joint stock bank. Export finance may be provided by a number of the large hire purchase finance houses in one of two ways:

● through a branch network of overseas offices
● through a correspondent relationship with other hire purchase houses abroad forming a credit union (or club)

It is possible through a branch network or a credit union to arrange for an overseas buyer of UK goods to receive a hire purchase agreement from a hire purchase company in his (the buyer's) country. The UK exporter receives immediate payment and the buyer obtains deferred credit terms. The system, however, may suffer from the following constraints:

● the limited extent of the branch or correspondent network
● local hire purchase restrictions or regulations
● exchange controls abroad
● relatively higher cost of finance than provided directly by banks

d   Confirming and export houses

i   *Confirming houses* confirm orders placed with them by overseas buyers by guaranteeing payment to the exporter on goods shipped and acting as agents of the overseas buyer. Should the buyer require credit, it will be arranged by the confirming house. The exporter will not run any overseas credit risk.

ii   *Export houses* often carry out the functions of a confirming house, above, but more often act either as an export merchant in buying and selling the goods on their own account or as agent of the exporter. The export house may arrange:
   * to promote the sale of the goods abroad
   * cover the credit risks involved
   * carry out the functions of an export sales department
   * carry stocks at home or abroad

Naturally, the wider the service provided the greater the cost to the manufacturer. Most houses engaged in this business are members of the British Export Houses Association (BEHA).

e   Invoice discounting

This is a method of finance provided by certain confirming and export houses whereby an advance is made to the manufacturer of a proportion of the value of his invoices. The invoice discounter retains a right of recourse on all transactions and looks to his client for repayment. The charge is usually a flat rate per month, and further charges are levied on extensions which are frequently required because not all debtors pay promptly. The invoice discounter does not keep his client's sales ledger, nor does he collect debts due as would a factoring company. In short, no service is provided, only finance.

PAST EXAMINATION QUESTIONS

1   Describe how a British bank can assist traders to settle their international indebtedness. What are the relative advantages and disadvantages of the methods you have outlined?

(Institute of Freight Forwarders)

2   How could a UK bank:

a   assist a British importer to pay his overseas supplier against documentary evidence of the shipment of goods?

b   provide the importer with three months' credit against the security of the goods?

(Institute of Bankers)

3   Your customer, Home Industries Limited, has found home demand for its products flat and the directors have decided to investigate the possibilities of selling overseas. The managing director comes to you for advice on how to start. What are the main factors to be considered?

(Institute of Bankers)

4   What other documents, apart from the usual set of shipping documents, would a merchant bank require for financing an exporter's clean accepted D/P or D/A bills of exchange? Comment upon the four means by which finance might be made available to you by your banker in respect of such bills.

(Institute of Export)

CHAPTER TWO

Clean Payments and Settlement

1. INTRODUCTION

a   A major function of any banking system is of course the transfer of money from one customer to another. Sometimes the transfer requested by a customer is in favour of a beneficiary who banks with the same bank, in which case the procedure is simple: one customer is debited and the other credited. Sometimes there has to be a transfer of money to another bank, as the beneficiary has his account elsewhere. Internally, within the UK, the methods of transfer usually used are cheque or credit transfer, with interbank settlement effected through the clearing houses. The vast majority of all international payments are also made through the banking system, although settlement as a rule is not made across a clearing house. Instead, if a UK bank, for example, wanted a bank abroad to pay money to a beneficiary on its customer's behalf, the UK bank would arrange to credit the account of the foreign bank in London or give instructions for the foreign bank to enable the foreign bank to obtain reimbursement to the debit of a foreign currency account of the UK bank maintained by a bank abroad. These instructions may be conveyed by mail or cabled payment orders between the banks, or by means of banker's drafts or international payment orders.

Apart from notes, and to a lesser extent coin, used to satisfy travel requirements, no large sums of money in the form of cash are normally moved physically across frontiers. Although there is nothing to prevent anyone carrying suitcases full of notes or coin in or out of the UK, certain other countries have exchange control regulations to prevent this. In any event, it is not a particularly safe or sensible thing to do. What *does* move from one country to another is an instruction from one bank to 'pass entries' (credit one account and debit another) sent to a correspondent bank abroad so as to effect the payment. What these instructions are, and what types of accounts banks keep with each other for this purpose, will be seen later in this chapter.

b   The London joint stock banks have centralised overseas or foreign branches with departments which specialise in different aspects of foreign business on behalf of their branch banking networks and of banks abroad for which they act as correspondents. Whilst the names of departments, and certain functions carried out in them, of different banks vary in their detail, the broad picture of the work processed in an overseas branch of a joint stock bank may be summarised as follows:

| Department | Functions | | Some other functions |
	Inward payments	Outward payments	
†*Accountancy* See sections 4 and 5 in this chapter	Pays drafts drawn by correspondents abroad upon presentation. Usually they have been pre-advised by the drawers	—	Records all transactions made over *vostro, nostro* ICCS (Insurance Companies' Currency Scheme), or customers' currency accounts
†*Inland Payments* See sections 2 and 3 in this chapter	*a* Pays UK beneficiaries in accordance with instructions from abroad in £ or foreign currency *b* Handles drafts, cheques, travellers' cheques, etc, payable in the UK and remitted for collection or payment, often from abroad *c* Handles ICCS transactions *d* Collects cheques drawn on other London banks	—	Maintains cashiering services Manages the sterling and US$ clearing functioning on behalf of the branch
†*Payments Abroad* See sections 7, 8 and 9 in this chapter	—	*a* Mail payment orders *b* Cable payment orders *c* Issue of drafts *d* Opens clean credit facilities	
Bills – Inwards See Chapter 4 (the bills come *in* from abroad)	—	Collects clean and documentary bills in sterling or currency drawn by overseas drawers on UK drawees	Discounts bills of exchange
Bills – Outwards (the bills go *out* abroad)	Remits clean and documentary bills and cheques in sterling or foreign currency for collection and payment abroad, including Eurocheques negotiated in the UK	—	Negotiates and advances against bills of exchange and cheques
Documentary Credits See Chapters 5 and 7 – Imports		*a* Authorises banks abroad to make settlement for imports, etc, against *documentary* evidence	Issues guarantees, indemnities, performance and tender bonds
– Exports	*b* Is authorised by banks abroad to make settlement for exports, etc, against *documentary* evidence		
– Transits	*c* Receives instructions from abroad to make settlements	*d* Payments made abroad on presentation of evidence required by overseas correspondent	
†*Travel* See sections 11 to 13 in this chapter	Issues sterling and foreign currency travellers' cheques for sale through the branch network and abroad	(For payment of travellers' cheques abroad, see *Inland Payments*)	Obtains passports and visas

Department	Functions		Some other functions
	Inward payments	Outward payments	
*Securities See Chapter 10	a Collects drawn bonds, dividend warrants payable overseas and foreign coupons c Purchase of sterling securities for banks and customers resident abroad	b Sale of sterling securities for other banks and customers resident abroad	Deals in stocks, shares, bonds, certificates of deposit, gold, platinum, silver and medallions
†Foreign Notes and Coin See section 14 in this chapter	a Repatriation of foreign currency to banks abroad b Foreign currency bought from UK residents returning from abroad and foreign visitors requiring sterling	c Foreign currency sold to UK residents and others going abroad d Foreign currency bought from banks abroad for sale in the UK	
Mail and Cables	Deals with the communications inwards and outwards, translating letters in foreign languages when required		

*The work of these departments is covered in the following chapters
†The work of these departments is dealt with elsewhere in this chapter

2. OPEN ACCOUNT TRADE

Open account business is an arrangement between buyer and seller for the buyer to settle his debts with the seller at a predetermined future date, perhaps at the end of the month or, say, one month after each shipment. In the meantime, the goods and shipping documents are sent directly to the buyer so that he can take delivery of the goods and dispose of them as he pleases. The essential features of open account business are that:

● the seller has absolute trust that the buyer can and will pay at the agreed time
● the seller is confident that the government of the buyer's country will not impose regulations deferring or blocking the transfer of payments
● the seller has sufficient liquidity to provide any necessary credit to the buyer, or has access to export finance

When the agreed date of payment arrives it is up to the buyer to make arrangements to transfer funds in settlement to the seller. The methods he might adopt are as follows:

i Sending his cheque to the seller.
ii Asking his bank for a banker's draft which he sends to the seller.
iii Asking his bank to remit funds by airmail via another bank in the seller's country.
iv Asking his bank to remit funds by telex or cable or SWIFT message via another bank in the seller's country (see section 8 of this chapter).

Settlement of open account trade is *un*likely to be arranged by:

● international money orders
● physical transfer of notes or coin through the post or by hand
● travellers' cheques

Perhaps it is significant that approximately 60 per cent of trade between the UK and her EEC partners is on open account terms. There is usually a long-standing or regular business relationship underlying open account trading. It requires that the seller lose complete control over the goods and place the onus of settlement on the buyer.

What comfort should the seller seek before selling on open account terms?
- knowledge that the buyer is of good standing and reliable
- knowledge that the buyer's country is economically and politically stable. An economic report may be obtained from a bank
- ECGD or other credit insurance (see Chapter 6) if appropriate

3.   ADVANCE PAYMENTS

Business conducted on the basis of payment in advance will mean that the seller has both goods and money, and the system implies that the following factors are present:
- absolute trust by the buyer that the seller will deliver the goods the buyer has ordered
- confidence by the buyer that the government of the seller's country will not prohibit the export of the goods, after payment
- knowledge by both buyer and seller that the exchange control authorities in the buyer's country will permit advance payments to be made; the majority of countries do not
- knowledge by the seller that the buyer has sufficient balance sheet liquidity or can obtain working capital by way of import finance

Advance payments are most usual in conditions favouring a 'seller's market'.

The buyer may make payment as follows:

i   By cheque (goods will be despatched after the cheque is cleared).
ii   By banker's draft.
iii By mail payment order.
iv   By cable or telex payment order.
v   By SWIFT message.
vi   By international money order.

What security may be obtained by the buyer to ensure he will receive the goods for which he has already paid? Only pre-knowledge of the integrity and standing of the seller, and the economic and political stability of the seller's country. A status report and economic report should be obtained. A further security may be obtained in some cases, namely a repayment guarantee from the seller, by which means payment can be obtained if the goods should not be shipped. Buyers may obtain significant cash discounts by making advance payments to sellers overseas. As a result of the exchange control changes of 1979 it is expected that this method of settlement will increase considerably during the 1980s.

4.   VOSTRO ACCOUNTS

Banks throughout the world play a major part in settling debts incurred in international trade. An importer wishing to pay a foreign exporter, for example, may ask his bank to make the payment in a variety of ways but, whichever method is adopted, the result will be reflected in the accounts which banks maintain with each other.

From the viewpoint of a UK bank, *vostro* accounts are the sterling accounts maintained with it in the names of other banks situated abroad. *Vostro* is a Latin word meaning *your*. Foreign banks wishing to make payments in sterling on behalf of their customers to UK beneficiaries will often instruct the UK bank to pay the beneficiary to the debit of such an account (*vostro*) held by the UK bank. It also follows that sterling funds due to customers of foreign banks abroad will be received by a UK bank in England for the credit of the same (*vostro*) accounts.

It will be understood, therefore, that a *vostro* account is the name given, so far as a UK bank is concerned, to the current account of one of its correspondent banks, maintained with it in sterling. As approximately 20 per cent of world trade is settled in sterling, it is necessary for foreign banks which engage in international business to be able to make and receive payments from time to time in sterling. These banks must, therefore, have accounts in sterling maintained in the UK. A foreign bank, say a Swiss bank in Switzerland, might refer to the Swiss franc accounts it keeps of British, American or French banks, as *vostro* accounts, since to the Swiss, the Swiss franc is the home currency, as sterling is to a UK bank.

5. NOSTRO ACCOUNTS

Nostro accounts from the viewpoint of a UK bank are its foreign currency accounts which it has with foreign banks abroad. *Nostro* is a Latin word meaning *our*. The real banking account is therefore maintained in the books of the bank abroad; however, in the books of the UK bank there is a record of the transactions passed abroad. This record account shows the bank abroad with whom the account is kept and provides a mirror image (in other words a reversed picture) of the affairs of the *nostro* acc__nt abroad. An importing customer, for example, may wish his UK bank to arrange for payment in US dollars to be made to the US supplier. The importer would be debited in sterling, if he needed to purchase the currency, whilst the record account in the UK bank's books of its account abroad would be credited with the US dollars bought. The bank abroad would be instructed to pay US dollars to the beneficiary in America to the debit of the UK bank's account with them. Thus when money is to be paid from an account abroad, which will be debited, the UK bank passes a credit entry over the record account it keeps. As a result, when the *nostro* account abroad is in credit, as is usual, the record account will show a debit amount and *vice versa*. It is important for a bank to know how much money it has at any particular time on its accounts abroad. Too much money held on *nostro* accounts will be uneconomic, since these balances are current accounts in the eyes of the account-holding banks (to them, of course, they are *vostro* accounts), and as a result, do not usually earn interest. It is also of great importance to keep a record of what liabilities are pending and when they are likely to be paid, so that there are sufficient funds on the *nostro* accounts to meet them. In the majority of cases, entries over the *nostro* account and record *nostro* account will be passed on different dates for the same transactions. This, because of time differences between countries, makes it difficult for a bank to assess its position accurately on the *nostro* account abroad. To ensure that the *nostro* accounts are being operated efficiently and accurately, the following procedures are adopted:

i   Value-dating the items passed to the *nostro* account. This will indicate when the funds on the account abroad are available for use or, conversely, when they are likely to be withdrawn. The same principles apply to your personal bank account: it may be credited with cheques you pay in, but, until those cheques are cleared, you do not get good value.

ii   Switching funds from one account to another in the same currency to ensure that each *nostro* account has a sufficient balance to meet current payment orders; a foreign exchange dealer will buy more currency if there is an overall shortage in that currency.

iii   Checking the record account with the foreign exchange dealer's overall position.

iv   Examining statements from the account-holding bank on a regular basis. These are reconciled when they are received, but are certain to be retrospective and rarely help to provide an up to date picture of the *nostro* account abroad. Checking the statements ensures that any transactions can be investigated which should appear on the statement but do not, as well as those transactions shown on the statement but not recorded in the record account.

British banks need foreign currency accounts (*nostro* accounts) with banks abroad, particularly in countries that have major trading currencies. This is to enable them to make and receive payments in such currencies. The major trading currencies are the US dollar, Canadian dollar, Japanese yen, and the majority of West European currencies.

A final word about *vostro* and *nostro* accounts. One bank's account with another bank abroad is at the same time both a *nostro* and *vostro* account: it depends on the viewpoint of each bank. For example, an American bank's sterling account in London with a UK bank is *vostro* from the UK bank's viewpoint, but *nostro* from the American bank's.

Examination candidates are advised to look at *vostro* and *nostro* accounts through the eyes of banks in their own country.

6.   OTHER FOREIGN CURRENCY ACCOUNTS

Apart from *nostro* accounts, banks in the UK may also hold foreign currency accounts for any of their customers. The funds represented on these accounts are usually part of the UK banks' *nostro* accounts abroad, although they are not separately identifiable there, except by entries in the UK banks' books. Entries passed over customers' currency accounts are therefore usually interlinked with *nostro* accounts.

After all, one expects to find US dollars in America, deutschemarks in Germany, and pounds in the UK.

The advantage of having such an account is that the customer will not lose money in exchange rates and commission on each transaction but may offset receipts and payments in a foreign currency. Many insurance companies have accounts in US and/or Canadian dollars to receive premium income in those currencies and to effect payment of claims. Banks as well as insurance companies in London regularly have occasion to settle indebtedness between themselves. Bankers' payments may be issued when the amount to be paid is in sterling; however, if the amount is in Canadian dollars settlement might be made in London through a scheme known as the Insurance Companies' Currency Scheme (ICCS). There are about 30 banks in London which subscribe to what is in effect a local London clearing of Canadian dollars for insurance transactions.

Receipts or payments of foreign currency destined for or originating in London may be settled as follows:

● over a *nostro* account maintained by a bank abroad
● through a customer's currency account maintained by a London bank
● through the ICCS (for Canadian dollars only) between one bank in London and another
● through the US dollar clearing in London (US dollars only)

US dollar clearing in London

The dollar clearing was first introduced as a pilot scheme in 1974. Before that the ICCS had provided an unofficial clearing for some dollar payments superimposed on the insurance company transactions. The new scheme was widened in February 1978 to include more member banks.

Cheques, travellers' cheques and bankers' drafts expressed in US dollars may be exchanged at the Bankers' Clearing House in London by the member banks. Items to be cleared in this manner must be taken from the customer or branch concerned before 2.00 pm. The exchange takes place at 3.00 pm, and at 3.45 pm the cables are sent to the foreign correspondent banks. Unpaids and wrong deliveries can be returned up to 10.00 am on the following day.

7. BANKERS' DRAFTS

A UK resident wishes to pay a beneficiary in the USA by means of a banker's draft. The procedure adopted is as follows:

i   Formal request to issue a draft is provided by the UK resident in writing.

ii   The customer authorises the purchase of US dollars spot or requests that it be applied against an existing forward exchange contract, or to the debit of a currency account if he has one.

iii   The customer authorises the issuing bank to debit his account with the sterling equivalent of the draft plus bank commission; alternatively, he authorises the debit to his currency account.

iv   The UK bank debits the customer's account, hands the draft to the customer and credits its *nostro* record account.

v   The UK bank advises by airmail the US bank on which the draft is drawn of the issue of the draft and asks them to pay it on presentation to the debit of the UK bank's *nostro* account with them.

vi   The UK resident forwards the draft to the US beneficiary.

vii   The US beneficiary presents it to the drawee bank for payment.

viii   The US bank pays the draft in accordance with the airmailed advice.

ix   The US bank debits the UK bank's dollar account.

Note: Points *i* to *iii* above are all dealt with at the same time and are completed on the draft order form.

Bankers' drafts, though widely used, are not so popular as payments made by mail or cable transfer. It should be noted that bankers' drafts are issued in sterling or in foreign currencies as required; the procedure indicated above relates to drafts issued in foreign currencies.

8. MAIL PAYMENT ORDERS AND CABLE PAYMENT ORDERS

Mail payment orders are often referred to as MTs, this being the abbreviation for *mail transfer*. A mail payment order may be described as follows:

- an authenticated order in writing
- addressed by one bank to another
- instructing the bank to which it is addressed to pay a sum certain in money
- to, or on application by, a specified person or beneficiary

Inward MT

Before a UK paying banker will carry out the instruction contained in a mail payment order he will have to be satisfied that the following points are in order:

i   That the instruction can be authenticated; that the order has indeed come from the bank it purports to have come from, which may be verified by checking the remitting bank's authorised signatures index showing the signatures of those officials authorised to sign on behalf of their bank.

ii That the remitting bank has sufficient funds on its account with the paying bank, or that other satisfactory reimbursement instructions are given to the paying bank (see section 9 of this chapter).

Outward MT

A UK resident wishes to pay, say, US dollars to a beneficiary in the USA by means of a mail payment order. The procedure adopted is as follows:

i   The customer gives his written and signed instruction to his bank to issue an MT stipulating the beneficiary's full name and address, and the name of his banker if known.

ii   The customer authorises the debit of the sterling equivalent of US dollars at the spot rate or against a forward exchange contract to his account, or to the debit of a currency account if he has one.

iii The UK bank debits the customer's sterling account with the sterling equivalent plus charges and exchange commission, or debits his foreign currency account and credits the *nostro* record account.

iv   The UK bank airmails the authenticated payment instructions to the US bank, giving reimbursement details, perhaps to the debit of the UK bank's account with them (see 'Inward MT' above).

v   The US bank pays or credits the account of the beneficiary and obtains reimbursement by debiting the remitting bank's account, or in accordance with instructions given in the MT order (see 'Inward MT' above).

Note: If the amount to be paid to the US beneficiary *is in sterling*, the *vostro* account of the US bank is credited.

Cable payment orders, known as TTs, the abbreviation for *telegraphic transfers,* differ from MTs as follows:

a   The means of transmitting the message is cable or telex instead of airmail. It is therefore faster, but slightly more expensive, to transmit. However, as money in transmission will not earn interest for the beneficiary until it is received by him, large amounts should be remitted by telex, cable or SWIFT (see below). If the remitter has the use of the funds until the last moment, and then arranges for a telex or cable remittance to be sent, he too will benefit from the extra time the funds remain on his account.

b   The means of authentication instead of by signature is by a test key: although it is possible it is not a normal procedure to transmit a signature by cable or telex. The test key is a coded system of numbers which enables correspondent banks to verify that the message has been sent from the bank from which it purports to have come and also to verify its content including the amount stated therein.

SWIFT

The Society for Worldwide Interbank Financial Telecommunication is a co-operative society created under Belgian law and registered in Brussels. It is wholly owned by some 240 of the largest European and North American banks.

The aims of SWIFT are to enable members to transmit between themselves:

- international payments
- statements, and
- other messages connected with international banking.

As 80 per cent of international money transfers are carried out by mail payment orders (20 per cent by telex or cable), the SWIFT system is designed to speed up international settlement. During 1977 the principal banks in the UK started to use the SWIFT system for settlement with other SWIFT members. Messages previously sent by cable or telex are to be transmitted by an 'urgent SWIFT message', and an MT becomes a 'SWIFT message'.

Type of payment	Comment	Cost	Speed
Banker's draft	Could be lost, stolen or destroyed. Banks are reluctant to place a stop on a draft they have issued themselves, since it could mean dishonouring their own paper which creates a poor impression on the public generally	Same as MT	Generally slower than MT or TT as draft is normally given to customer to send to the beneficiary, who on the other hand will receive notice of payment earlier as it is sent directly to him, which is important when he is waiting to execute an order
Mail payment order (MT)	Payments are made to named beneficiaries through banking channels; however, such payments might be delayed or lost in the post between banks	Same as banker's draft	Slower than TT remittance; instructions sent by *airmail*
Telex or cable payment order (TT)	Quite safe; payments are made to named beneficiaries through banking channels	Marginally more expensive compared with MTs but, if amount transferred is large, perhaps a cost saving in interest charges	Faster method of remittance than an MT. Instructions sent by cable or telex
Cheque	Could be lost, stolen or destroyed. Payments may be made in any currency	Cheap, but payee will incur collection charges and perhaps negotiation interest. Drawer gets the use of the money during the time taken for the cheque to be cleared	Slowest method of settlement in one respect, as payee has to wait for cheque to be returned to drawer's bank for clearance; faster method in another in that the cheque if sent direct to payee may be negotiated locally, usually with recourse (see Chapter 4, section 18)

9. METHODS OF REIMBURSEMENT

Method of reimbursement	Types of transactions
a Sterling payment to London office of paying agent	Sterling payments and currency payments where rates are stable against sterling
b Credit to *vostro* account of paying agent	Sterling payments, or where there is no market for the currency of payment (eg, for a payment in roubles, the Russian bank would be asked to advise the exact amount of sterling to be credited to its account in London)
c To the debit of UK bank's *nostro* account	Currency payments where the paying agent holds the UK bank's account

Method of reimbursement	Types of transactions
d To claim reimbursement from another branch of the same bank or another bank in the vicinity	Currency payments where the paying agent does not hold the UK bank's account. The branch of paying agent or other bank in the vicinity that does have the *nostro* account is instructed to honour claims of the paying agent to the debit of the UK bank's *nostro* account
e To instruct a reimbursing bank to pay the paying agent to the debit of the UK bank's *nostro* account	Currency payments where the paying agent does not hold the UK bank's *nostro* account
f Pay the London office of the shipping company by banker's draft and instruct the shipping company to contact the purser by radio to make the payment	Payments to beneficiaries on board a ship

10. CHEQUES

a Flow diagram of a cheque drawn and payable abroad in favour of a UK payee

b Flow diagram of a cheque drawn and payable in the UK in favour of a foreign payee

Cheque books are issued by UK banks to customers who open sterling current accounts. Banks in the UK will provide cheque books for certain foreign currency current accounts maintained in the UK. This will depend on the currency, the use for which the account is required, and a bank's own internal policy.

Eurocheques

The Eurocheque scheme, to which a number of leading European banks, including the UK joint stock banks, subscribe, is a system whereby travellers may encash their personal cheques abroad with the minimum of formality.

To a certain extent the development of this scheme must have reduced the sale of travellers' cheques which might otherwise have been bought. Full details of encashment arrangements may be found in the Eurocheque manual, but the procedure may be summed up as follows:

i   The traveller draws his cheque in the presence of the collecting banker; the cashier must see him sign it. Certain countries also require that a particular form of cheque be used.

ii   Most countries require that the cheque be drawn in the currency of the account holder for an amount not exceeding the guaranteed maximum. Others stipulate the currency of the country of encashment. For customers of UK banks, the maximum encashable abroad per cheque is the amount shown on the cheque guarantee card.

iii The traveller must present a valid cheque guarantee card issued by his bank.

iv   The account number on the cheque card must be indicated and agree with that on the cheque. Some banks' cheque cards have no account number, in which case the surname and first names or initials on the guarantee card must tally exactly with those printed on the cheque.

v The signatures on the card and cheque must agree.

vi The card number, if there is one, must be written on the reverse of the cheque by the paying cashier.

vii The traveller is paid the local currency equivalent of his cheque amount at the rate of exchange given by the encashing bank less commission.

viii The encashing bank forwards the cheque for payment and reimbursement to the drawer's bank, by which it must be received within 20 days of the issue date.

ix Should a traveller cash more than two cheques at the same time, his passport or identity card number and details should be checked and noted on the reverse of one of the cheques.

x When the traveller's bank receives the cheque it must be honoured, and will be provided the encashing bank has done everything expected of it (*i–ix* above), even if its customer, the drawer, has no funds to meet it.

11. TRAVELLERS' CHEQUES (sometimes referred to as travel cheques)

Sterling travellers' cheques are normally issued in denominations of £10, £20, £50, and sometimes £5 and £100. Currency travellers' cheques may also be sold in the UK for people intending to visit the country of the currency, or, in the case of US dollars, deutschemarks or Swiss francs, any country where they are readily acceptable. The benefits to a traveller of buying travellers' cheques are that:

● travellers' cheques are safer than notes and coin. If they are lost or stolen, the issuing bank, if notified immediately, may be able to (and probably will) refund the customer's money. Refund will depend upon the reasons surrounding the loss and whether the cheques are presented for payment in the meantime

● travellers' cheques are less bulky than an average wallet full of notes for the same total amount

● they are readily encashable at banks, hotels, railway stations and many commercial firms abroad. (*Note*: sterling travellers' cheques are not always readily acceptable in the USA even when issued by one of the British joint stock banks)

● travellers who buy foreign currency travellers' cheques fix the rate of exchange at the time of purchase, thereby determining the amount of sterling payable by the traveller for the foreign currency he wants. This is of great advantage in times of foreign exchange crises, particularly when sterling is under pressure in the foreign exchange market. (*Note*: unused cheques may have to be sold back at a rate less favourable than that at which they were bought unless they are credited to a customer's foreign currency account, if he has one)

● unused sterling travellers' cheques may be paid into the issuing bank at their face value without any loss in foreign exchange conversions when the traveller returns to the UK

The progress of a travellers' cheque from issue to payment is as follows:

i Customer or non-customer calls at the bank in person requesting travellers' cheques.

ii The travellers' cheques are prepared in sterling or foreign currency, as the traveller wishes, and in the available denominations of his choice; travel facilities expressed in foreign currency may be bought and held by the applicant at any time and for any purpose.

iii   If the cheques are in foreign currency the sterling equivalent is calculated by the bank at the rate of exchange for travellers' cheques in that currency ruling on the day of purchase, unless the cost is met by payment in foreign notes or by the debit of an account in the foreign currency held by the applicant.

iv   The customer's account is debited or cash taken for the value of the cheques plus commission.

v   The traveller signs each cheque in the presence of the issuing banker.

vi   In due course the traveller tenders a sterling cheque to, say, a hotel for encashment.

vii   The hotel pays the cheque in local currency (at a rate of exchange sufficient to cover possible short-term fluctuations in the rate) after the customer has signed the cheque in the presence of the payer who will check that the two signatures tally.

viii   The hotel will hand the cheque to its own bank for collection and credit to its account.

ix   The foreign bank will forward the cheque to the UK issuing bank for payment through its UK correspondent.

x   The foreign bank receives reimbursement from the UK issuing bank.

If sterling travellers' cheques are concerned, a *vostro* account in London of the foreign collecting bank will be credited. If foreign currency travellers' cheques are concerned, the foreign bank will be reimbursed by the debit to a *nostro* account of the UK issuing bank. There are some UK banks which issue their own *foreign currency* travellers' cheques, but the majority of those sold by UK banks expressed in foreign currency are issued by correspondent banks abroad. This pattern is likely to change with the developments planned for example by Visa and Master Card, etc.

12.   OPEN CREDIT FACILITIES

There are two ways in which funds may be drawn, by prior arrangement, from a specified branch of a bank abroad:

i   The 'encashment of cheques credit', as it is usually known, is an identical method to the 'credit opened' facility in the UK. The branch of the bank abroad is requested to honour cheques presented by the named customer. The advice will quote the total amount that can be drawn at any one time and the expiry date of the facility. The customer presents his own cheque, in sterling, at the bank and obtains local currency, less charges, in exchange. The cheque is presented to the drawee bank for reimbursement.

ii   A beneficiary, resident abroad, may wish to receive regular payments due to him, such as a salary or pension. Such payments may of course be remitted by mail, telex or SWIFT transfer through the remitter's bank every month when due. A facility may be established for a regular standing order to be made whereby the remitter's bank may authorise a bank local to the beneficiary to make regular payments at stated intervals and for stated sums. The paying bank will receive from the issuing bank a specimen of the beneficiary's signature which may be compared with the beneficiary's receipt for funds paid to him. After each payment is made in accordance with the issuing bank's instructions, the paying bank will claim reimbursement, in the manner described in the credit, from the issuing bank. Such credits may be used to make regular standing order payments to an overseas beneficiary.

13. TRAVELLERS' LETTERS OF CREDIT

Whilst the name may suggest it, there is no similarity between a traveller's letter of credit and a documentary credit (see Chapter 5), the purpose and details of the two facilities being entirely different.

A large number of travellers use travellers' cheques. There are still those, however, who prefer to carry a traveller's letter of credit, even though drawings can be made only from banks specified by the issuing bank. The issuing bank may require the traveller to pay for the credit in full at the time of issue, or may permit a 'drafts as presented' basis for settlement.

Two documents are issued, the letter of credit itself and a letter of indication. The traveller will also be given a list of the correspondents of the issuing bank throughout the world from whom drawings under the credit may be made. The traveller should be instructed that the letter of indication and the letter of credit should at all times be kept separate.

The credit will:
- be addressed to 'the correspondents of the bank'
- contain an authority to cash drafts drawn in the manner described
- state the bank on which the drafts are to be drawn
- state the total amount available and in what currency
- stipulate the expiry date
- bear the number and date of the credit

The encashing correspondent will check the signatures of the issuing bank of the credit to ensure the document is authentic. Each drawing is recorded on the back of the credit together with the encashing bank's stamp and date. This ensures that the limit is not exceeded. A draft is drawn on the issuing bank, signed by the traveller, and negotiated by the encashing bank after it has checked the traveller's signature against that shown in the letter of indication which was signed by the traveller on the day of issue. The draft is sent for collection by the encashing bank to the issuing bank for payment.

These documents have been frequently subject to forgery, and encashment agents are quite right to be extremely cautious when asked to make payment. Several leading UK banks no longer issue travellers' letters of credit as encashing correspondents abroad have been known on many occasions to refuse payment, despite the existence of an agency arrangement with the UK bank to provide the service. This can cause the traveller considerable difficulty, and alternative travel facilities are to be recommended.

14. FOREIGN NOTES AND COIN

Foreign notes and coin are required by travellers visiting countries abroad. Banks supply these needs by importing notes and coin, sometimes from banks in Switzerland and sometimes from banks in the countries of origin, or by buying them from other banks in London.

When visitors from abroad want sterling in exchange for their own notes and coin, or whenever UK residents return with surplus foreign currency, UK banks will buy the foreign currency and give sterling in exchange.

UK banks will not wish to hold large stocks of foreign money in the form of non-interest earning cash, and therefore will sell the surplus at the best rates possible.

Diagram of purchases of foreign notes and coin by travellers

Diagram of sales of foreign notes and coin by travellers

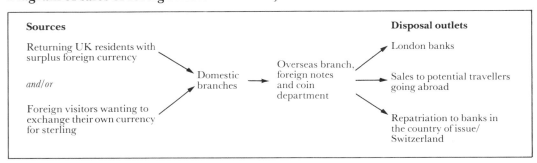

When notes or coin are imported or exported the banks involved must pay the cost of freight and also the insurance premium. In the case of coin freight costs are significant. As a result, better rates of exchange may be obtained on the London foreign notes and coin market where the London banks requiring a particular currency may find a seller who wishes to dispose of a surplus. The major European currency requirements follow a similar pattern to the tourist exodus. For example, the summertime migration to Spain by many UK tourists creates a need for most London banks to import pesetas during spring and summer months, perhaps selling surplus pesetas later in the season on the London market or repatriating them.

The exchange control regulations of certain countries abroad prohibit or limit the export of their notes, and consequently prohibit or limit their repatriation; hence the references to Switzerland, which like London has a large market in foreign currency notes.

15. MEANS OF SETTLING DEBTS INCURRED IN INTERNATIONAL TRADE

The systems of trade which have evolved over the years cater for the varying degrees of trust between buyer and seller. Trust often comes with knowledge of the other party, and the banks assist in this by obtaining status reports for the benefit of either or both of the parties concerned. Sections 2 and 3 of this chapter deal with open account trade and payments in advance; Chapter 4 deals with collections which tend to favour the importer, and Chapter 5 with documentary credits which tend to favour the exporter.

The position can be expressed as follows:

Can you trust him to pay for the goods you have sent?
Does he trust you completely to supply right content?
For you trust with your goods
Or you trust with your cash,
And traders go bankrupt
If traders are rash.

To resolve this stalemate, a status report
Establishes actions to which traders resort.
For you trust with your goods
Or you trust with your cash,
And traders go bankrupt
If traders are rash.

Now 'open account' is a system of trade
Where buyer has goods before seller is paid.
For you trust with your goods
Or you trust with your cash,
Note, sellers go bankrupt
If sellers are rash.

To pay in advance before goods are exported,
May result in non-shipment, goods wrong or distorted.
For you trust with your goods
Or you trust with your cash,
Note, buyers go bankrupt
If buyers are rash.

Where little trust from each side applies,
The banks can assist with a compromise.
For you trust with your goods
Or you trust with your cash,
And traders go bankrupt
If traders are rash.

A bank can collect clean bills on the buyers
But by then he has got the goods he requires.
For he pays for the goods
Or he's sued for the cash:
But, sellers go bankrupt
If sellers are rash.

Collections may be D/A or D/P;
It depends what sellers want them to be.
Should they part with their goods
Before payment in cash?
As sellers go bankrupt
If sellers are rash.

Both buyer and seller may consider with merit
A bank's documentary letters of credit.
Where the title to goods
And the transfer of cash
Is up to the banks
Not to be rash.

The methods of settling debts incurred in international trade are:
- open account trade (see this chapter, section 2)
- clean collection (see Chapter 4, section 3)
- documentary collection (D/A) (see Chapter 4, section 5)
- documentary collection (D/P) (see Chapter 4, section 5)
- revocable documentary credit (see Chapter 5, sections 3 and 4)
- irrevocable documentary credit (see Chapter 5, sections 3 and 4)
- confirmed documentary credit (see Chapter 5, sections 3 and 4)
- advance payment (see this chapter, section 3)

16. GLOSSARY OF TERMS USED IN THIS CHAPTER

Authentication
act of certifying the genuineness of a transaction; official bankers' signatures and cable codes are distributed between banking correspondents for this purpose.

Beneficiary
payee or recipient, usually of money.

Correspondent bank
agent bank to which the principal bank communicates instructions for action.

Currency
usually implies *foreign* money rather than money in general.

Draft (1)
a bill of exchange.

Draft (2)
a banker's payment or banker's cheque.

Drawer
one who draws, writes, or issues a cheque, a draft, or bill of exchange.

Economic reports
available for customers from all leading international banks; they may relate to specific countries, regions, industries or markets, and provide up to date local and statistical information.

Facilities
a word used to describe a range of banking services, but more particularly lending services such as loans, negotiations, overdrafts, etc; a facility letter is in fact a simple form of loan agreement.

Funds   money in any currency, unless specifically stated; see the glossary of terms in Chapter 10 for 'funding'.

Local currency   usually employed in the context of the indigenous money of the country of payment; the local currency of the UK is 'sterling', of Burma 'kyat', or Nigeria 'naira', etc.

Paying agent   bank which, on the express instructions of another bank or branch, makes payment to a named beneficiary or to the bearer of a banker's draft.

Reimbursement   act of repaying, settling or funding a paying agent which pays money to a beneficiary at the request of its principal, normally another bank or a customer.

Status report   credit information obtained regarding an individual, firm or company, by enquiry made through a bank or credit information bureau.

SWIFT   see section 8 of this chapter.

PAST EXAMINATION QUESTIONS

1   Define a *nostro* account.
    Starting with the customer's instructions, describe how a UK bank transfers a sum of money in US dollars on behalf of a UK resident customer to a beneficiary in New York by means of:
a   a banker's draft on New York
b   a mail order payment
c   a telegraphic transfer   *(Institute of Bankers)*

2   What are the various methods which travellers can use to obtain their cash requirements abroad? Discuss the advantages and disadvantages of each method.

                                                        (Institute of Bankers)

3   A manufacturer sells components to continental buyers on 'open account' terms. Explain the forms in which the buyers can effect payment and compare them from the exporter's viewpoint.

                                                        (Institute of Export)

4   How may a bank in London use an agent in another country to make a payment in the currency of that country, even though the London bank has no currency account with the agent?

                                                        (Institute of Bankers)

CHAPTER THREE

Shipping Terms and Documents of Foreign Trade

1. INTRODUCTION AND SHIPPING TERMS

International sales contracts have certain characteristics not present in sales on the domestic market. They also necessitate one or other, or both, of the commercial parties entering into other contracts, such as contracts of carriage and of insurance; and documentation relating to these other contracts is frequently required to evidence or to ensure the due performance of the sales contract. The payment aspect also may call for a separate contract with a bank, as an integral part of the performance of the sales contract with regard to the settlement for the goods (the difference between internal and international settlement is described in the introduction to Chapter 2).

The terms of trade which buyer and seller agree to adopt are often those defined in the International Chamber of Commerce publication No. 350 *Incoterms*. These are designed to avoid misunderstandings which could arise between contracting parties in respect of interpretation of responsibilities, liabilities, ownership, risk, and, to a certain extent, documents. There are, however, other sets of trade terms in use in the world, including those of the socialist bloc and a set known as *Combiterms*, as well as those of the International Chamber of Commerce. The USA formerly used its own set of trade terms, but has now agreed to adopt the ICC *Incoterms*. (These were updated in 1980, and students and others interested in more detailed knowledge should note the *Guide to Incoterms*, ICC publication No. 354.)

The production of many of the commercial documents referred to in *Incoterms*, and also in this and other chapters, is the responsibility of the exporter or that of his freight forwarding agent. During the past ten years there have been developments which have resulted in improving the production and efficiency of export documentation, with considerable cost savings to the exporter. The developments are, in part, changes in the nature of the documents themselves and the methods by which they are produced: in part also the documents have had to reflect the changing pattern of the handling of the movement of the goods. A comment on the second point first: the growth of palletisation and containerisation (unitisation of cargo) has required new documents and documentary procedures to be accepted internationally. As for the first point, the changes in the documents themselves result from:

a   Changes in UK trading relationships from links with EFTA and the Commonwealth to the forging of a close partnership within the European Economic Community.

b   The new transport techniques referred to above.

c   An improved international understanding of obligations, trade terms and procedures, due in part to the increasing acceptance of, and the new developments in, International Chamber of Commerce standardised uniform rules and documents. Some of the most important are covered by ICC publications:

> No. 290 *Uniform Customs and Practice for Documentary Credits*
> No. 305 *Guide to Documentary Credit Operations*
> No. 322 *Uniform Rules for Collections*
> No. 323 *Standard Forms for the Issuing of Documentary Credits*
> No. 325 *Uniform Rules for Contract Guarantees*
> No. 350 *Incoterms*
> No. 354 *Guide to Incoterms*

d   Standardised layout of individual documents to reduce the incidence of error and to speed up production thereof. Leading the international field in this respect is SITPRO, the Simplification of International Trade Procedures Board. Established in 1971, SITPRO took over from the Department of Trade the responsibility for developing and promoting an aligned series of documents for British exports. The SITPRO publication, *Systematic Export Documentation*, should be obtained by all potential exporters or by those already producing export documents who have not yet seen it.

Whenever a sale of goods takes place there may be, in addition to the cost of the goods themselves, a number of other costs which must be paid by the buyer or the seller, or shared between them.

In internal or inland trade the commercial parties to the sales contract will normally agree a price based on the buyer taking over the goods at the seller's or supplier's warehouse, or on delivery by the seller to the buyer's warehouse, or, perhaps, on the basis of delivery by the seller to a specified rail or road carrier. This is because it is simple for either buyer or seller, as appropriate, to arrange and pay for all formalities involving the movement, and insurance, of the goods from one place to another in the same country.

In international trade the position is more complicated. There are likely to be three separate contracts of carriage for the goods – ie, from the seller's or supplier's warehouse to a place within the seller's country, from which there will be an international movement of the goods to a place of arrival within the buyer's country, with a possible further internal carriage within the buyer's country to his warehouse. There may also be official formalities. For these reasons it was customary to trade on terms whereby the 'cut-off' point for responsibility for arranging and paying for transport was either a port of departure in the selling country, or a port of arrival in the buying country. Thus, with an FOB (free on board) sale the seller had to deliver the goods on board a vessel nominated by the buyer, with the buyer responsible for charges from that point on. Alternatively, the seller could be responsible for all charges (CIF – cost, insurance and freight) or part charges (C & F – cost and freight) to the port of arrival. The ICC *Incoterms* explained clearly the relative responsibilities, risks and duties of the two parties, but with the changes in transport technology which have led to unitisation of cargo, fresh trade terms have been developed. These appear in the 1980 revision of *Incoterms* (see above list of ICC publications). Below is a brief resumé of the 14 terms now current.

Shipping terms	ICC international abbreviations	The seller must:	The buyer must:
Ex-works	EXW	Deliver goods at his premises	Make all arrangements at his own cost and risk to take goods to their destination
Free carrier . . . at a named point	FRC	Provide export licence and pay any export taxes; provide evidence of delivery of goods to the carrier	Contract for the carriage, pay the freight and nominate the carrier; pay insurance premium
Free on rail, or free on truck	FOR	Deliver goods to railway; provide buyer with an invoice and transport document	Pay freight; notify seller of destination of the goods; obtain export licence and pay any export taxes
FOB airport	FOA	Deliver goods to airport of departure; contract for carriage or notify the buyer if he wants him to do so	Pay freight; notify seller if he does not wish him to contract for carriage; pay insurance premium
Free alongside ship	FAS	Deliver goods alongside ship; provide an 'alongside' receipt	Nominate the carrier; contract for carriage pay freight, obtain export licence and pay any export taxes; pay insurance premium
Free on board	FOB	Deliver goods on board and provide a clean on board receipt; provide export licence, pay export taxes and loading costs if not included in the freight charge	Nominate the carrier; contract for carriage and pay the freight; pay discharge costs and loading costs if included in the freight charges; pay insurance premium
Cost and freight	CFR (often seen as C & F)	Contract for carriage, pay freight to named destination; deliver goods on board and provide buyer with an invoice and clean on board bill of lading; obtain export licence and pay export taxes, loading costs and unloading costs if included in the freight charges	Accept delivery of goods on shipment after documents are tendered to him; pay unloading costs if not included in the freight charges; pay insurance premium
Cost, insurance and freight	CIF	As with 'cost and freight' above, *plus* contract for the insurance of goods, pay the premium and provide the buyer with the policy or certificate	Accept delivery of goods on shipment after documents are tendered to him; pay unloading costs if not included in the freight charges
Freight/carriage paid to . . .	DCP	Contract for carriage, pay freight to named destination; deliver goods to first carrier; obtain export licence and pay any export taxes; provide buyer with invoice and transport document	After tender of documents, accept delivery of goods when they are delivered to first carrier; arrange and pay insurance premium
Freight/carriage and insurance paid to . . .	CIP	As with 'freight/carriage paid to' above, *plus* contract for insurance of goods and pay the premium, providing the buyer with a policy or certificate	Accept delivery of goods after documents are tendered to him
Ex-ship	EXS	Deliver goods on board at destination; provide buyer with documents to enable delivery to be taken from the ship	Pay discharge costs, import duties, taxes and fees, if any; obtain import licence

Shipping terms	ICC international abbreviations	The seller must:	The buyer must:
Ex-quay	EXQ	Deliver goods on to quay at destination. Provide buyer with documents to enable him to take delivery; obtain import licence and pay import duties, taxes, fees, unloading costs and insurance	Take delivery of goods from the quay at destination
Delivered at frontier	DAF	Deliver goods cleared for export at a place named on the frontier; provide the buyer with documents to take delivery	Pay for on-carriage; obtain import licence and pay import duties, taxes and fees if any
Delivered duty paid	DDP	Obtain import licence and pay import duties, taxes and fees if any; arrange and pay insurance; provide documents to enable the buyer to take delivery	Take delivery of the goods at the named place of destination

2.   COMMERCIAL DOCUMENTS

The following commercial documents are briefly described below and are illustrated with examples shown at the end of this chapter.

a	Pro-forma invoice	*Exhibit 1*
b	Commercial invoice	*Exhibit 2*
c	Certified invoice	*Exhibit 3*
d	Weight note	*Exhibit 4*
e	Packing list	*Exhibit 5*
f	Specification	*Exhibit 6*
g	Manufacturer's or supplier's quality or inspection certificate	*Exhibit 7*
h	Third party certificate of inspection	*Exhibit 8*
i	Manufacturer's analysis certificate	*Exhibit 9*

a   Pro-forma invoice *(Exhibit 1, page 62)*

The pro-forma invoice is a form of quotation by the seller to a potential buyer. The only difference in appearance from a commercial invoice is that the words 'pro-forma' will appear on it. It may be an invitation to the buyer to place a firm order and is often required by him so that the authorities of the importer's country will grant him an import licence and/or foreign exchange permit. The pro-forma invoice normally shows the terms of trade and price so that once the buyer has accepted the order there is a firm contract to be settled as stipulated in the pro-forma. Details from the accepted pro-forma must be transposed identically to the commercial invoice which is issued in due course, and quite frequently the seller is required to certify on his commercial invoice 'that goods are in accordance with pro-forma invoice No . . . .'. Pro-forma invoices are also used where settlement is to be made:

i   In advance – ie, pending cash payment of goods stated or before shipment.

ii   On consignment, where goods are exported before a firm sale contract and placed in the hands of an agent to whom the pro-forma will act as a guide for prices he should obtain.

iii   Subject to tender, where the pro-forma is used to support a tender for a sale contract which if accepted by the buyer will win the contract from other suppliers also tendering in competition.

iv After an invitation to tender has been accepted by the seller. The pro-forma will not have any amounts shown against the goods, and potential buyers are invited to make an offer or tender which, if accepted by the sellers, will form a firm contract of sale (see also Chapter 7, section 5).

b Commercial invoice *(Exhibit 2, page 63)*

The following information should normally appear on a commercial invoice used for international trade:

i Names and addresses of buyer and seller, and date of invoice.

ii Complete description of goods. If payment is to be obtained by means of a documentary credit this description of the goods must *exactly* match that given in the documentary credit.

iii Unit prices where applicable and final price against shipping terms.

iv Terms of settlement – eg, under documentary credit, or 30 days' sight D/A (documents against acceptance) (see Chapter 4, section 5).

v Shipping marks and numbers.

vi Weight and/or quantity of goods.

vii Name of vessel, if known or applicable.

The following sometimes need to be shown, usually for the customs authorities in the buyer's country:

viii Seller's signature.

ix Origin of goods.

x Ports of loading and discharge, or places of taking in charge and delivery.

xi Details of freight and insurance charges specified separately, where applicable.

c Certified invoice *(Exhibit 3, page 64)*

A certified invoice may be an ordinary signed commercial invoice specifically certifying:

- that the goods are in accordance with a specific contract or pro-forma, or
- that the goods are, or are not, of a specific country of origin, or
- any statement required by the buyer from the seller

There are also formal certified invoices, which, when submitted to the importing authorities, will provide them with the necessary evidence to pass the goods through customs with a lower import duty or none at all. Combined certificates of value and origin (CVO) are used between members of the Commonwealth, and special invoices for the other major free trade areas such as the EEC and LAFTA. All certified invoices must be signed, and in the case of combined certificates of value and origin they should be signed by a witness as well.

Exhibit 2 bears the certification of the issuer that the information contained in it is true and correct.

Exhibit 3 is a CVO, signed and witnessed, which certifies that the value and origin of the goods are as stated.

d Weight note *(Exhibit 4, page 65)*

This document may be issued by the seller, or often by a third party; it merely indicates the weight of the goods, which should tally with that shown on all the other documents. Weighbridge tickets are sometimes produced for road or rail shipments. (See *Uniform Customs and Practice*, Article 25, wherein banks will accept a superimposed declaration of weight on the shipping document, unless the credit calls for a separate or independent document.)

e and f   Packing list and specification *(Exhibits 5 and 6, pages 66-7)*

These documents set out the details of the packing of the goods. They are often required by the customs authorities to enable them to make spot or more thorough checks on the contents of any particular package. The packing list does not necessarily give details of the cost or price of goods; the specification does.

g   Manufacturer's or supplier's quality or inspection certificate *(Exhibit 7, page 68)*

This is a signed declaration by the manufacturer or supplier that he has examined the goods and found them to be as required under the contract of sale. Despite trades description legislation the practical value of this document is clearly limited. (See *Uniform Customs and Practice*, Article 33, wherein banks will accept such documents as tendered, unless specifically defined in the credit, even if issued by the supplier himself.)

h   Third party certificate of inspection *(Exhibit 8, page 69)*

This is a certificate declaring the result of an examination of the goods by a recognised independent inspection body. In order to protect himself from paying when substandard or worthless goods have been shipped, an importer can call for an independent check or examination of goods before they are despatched. This is particularly important for the buyer, as banks, unless lending against the security of the goods represented by the documents, are often concerned with documents only and not the underlying goods. With regard to a bank's liabilities and responsibilities under a documentary credit, it is essential to read very carefully *Uniform Customs and Practice for Documentary Credits*. Case law has also underlined these principles many times.

i   Manufacturer's analysis certificate *(Exhibit 9, page 70)*

This certificate states the ingredients and proportions revealed by an analysis of chemicals, drugs, etc.

3.   OFFICIAL DOCUMENTS

The following official documents are briefly described below and are illustrated with examples shown at the end of the chapter.

a	EUR 1 form	*Exhibit 10*
b	T2L form	*Exhibit 11*
c	Consular invoice	*Exhibit 12*
d	Legalised invoice	*Exhibit 13*
e	Combined invoice and certificate of origin	*Exhibit 14*
f	Chamber of commerce certificate of origin	*Exhibit 15*
g	Blacklist certificate	*Exhibit 16*
h	Veterinary certificate	*Exhibit 17*

a and b   EEC documents, EUR 1 and T2L *(Exhibits 10 and 11, pages 71-3)*

These forms are European Economic Community documents. The EUR 1 form is used in respect of preferential exports from an EEC country to a non-EEC country.

The T2L form is used in respect of trade between EEC member states where the goods in question are being transported directly between member states and without passing through the territory of a non-member country.

c   Consular invoice *(Exhibit 12, page 74)*

The importing authorities of several countries require consular invoices to be produced before goods may be cleared by customs. Regulations differ from country to country, and countries that require consular invoices have designed their own forms. These are obtained from the embassy of the importer's country by the exporter, who completes the details and submits them to the embassy for stamping, for which a charge is made. Sometimes a chamber of commerce is required to certify on the consular invoice that the origin of the goods is as stated. This type of document is called for by some South American and a few other countries and it is designed for official use. In the first instance, the selling price is examined in the light of the current market price, to ensure that 'dumping' is not taking place or that importers are not syphoning money overseas; secondly, it forms the basis for determining the import duty levied by the customs authorities.

d   Legalised invoice *(Exhibit 13, page 75)*

A number of countries require the commercial invoice to be legalised by their own embassy or consulate in the seller's country. Instead of having a particular invoice form the seller presents his own signed commercial invoices to the embassy or consulate for stamping. These are sometimes called visaed invoices, and several Middle East countries require them.

e and f   Certificates of origin *(Exhibits 14 and 15, pages 76-8)*

These constitute signed statements evidencing the origin of the goods. They may be issued by the exporter on a document incorporating the invoice. The Commonwealth certificate of value and origin, or the exporter's own certified (as to origin) invoice, may be used as certificates of origin. On the other hand the certificates may be issued by a third party, normally a chamber of commerce. A chamber of commerce certificate of origin must contain details of the goods and the signature and seal of the chamber. It is often used by importing authorities to determine tariff rates where applicable.

g   Blacklist certificate *(Exhibit 16, page 79)*

Countries at war or with badly strained political relations with other countries may require evidence that:
- the origin of the goods is not that of a particular country, or
- the parties involved (manufacturer, bank, insurance company, shipping line, etc, which might be friendly or associated with such a particular country) are not blacklisted, or
- the ship or aircraft will not call at ports in such a country unless forced to do so

   Institutions in many countries, particularly chambers of commerce, try to resist giving such certificates.

h   Health, veterinary and sanitary certificates *(Exhibit 17, page 80)*

These are sometimes required for official purposes in the purchase of foodstuffs, hides and livestock and in the use of packing materials. The example is of a veterinary certificate.

4.   INSURANCE DOCUMENTS

The following insurance documents are described below and are illustrated with examples shown at the end of this chapter.

a	Letter of insurance	*Exhibit 18*
b	Insurance company's open cover certificate	*Exhibit 19*
c	Lloyd's open cover certificate	*Exhibit 20*
d	Insurance policy	*Exhibit 21*

a   Letter of insurance *(Exhibit 18, page 81)*

A letter of insurance is normally issued by a broker (often a bank acting in that capacity) to provide notice that an insurance has been placed pending the production of a policy or certificate. Sometimes this takes the form of a cover note. Such documents do not contain full details of the insurance said to be effected and therefore are not considered satisfactory by banks which normally require evidence of an insurance contract in documents called for under a documentary credit.

A broker's certificate is a document that is no better from the insured's point of view than a cover note. It has been issued by a third party, not the insurer, and therefore if appropriate cover has not been effected the course of action in the event of a claim could not be against the insurer but against the broker.

b and c   Insurance certificates *(Exhibits 19 and 20, pages 82-5)*

Insurance company and Lloyd's certificates are frequently drawn up by the insured on forms printed on behalf of and issued by insurance companies under either a floating policy (now comparatively little used) or open cover. The systems of open cover and floating policies are similar in the following particulars:

i   Once the system has been arranged the insured is covered for all his shipments on the terms and for the risks agreed. The insured will declare to the insurance company the value and details of each shipment made and will issue for the purposes of export documentation a pre-printed insurance certificate made valid, when completed with the details of the shipment, by the signature of the insured. This document will show the risks covered and be pre-signed by the insurer.

ii   No legal action may be taken in UK courts, and many foreign courts of law, on a contract of insurance evidenced solely by an insurance certificate. As a result, any action to be taken against the insurers must be preceded by the insurers making the action possible by providing the insured with a policy to be sued upon! Knowledge of the insurance company's procedures, policy, reliability, etc, are important to a lending banker accepting such a document instead of a policy. Certificates issued against cover from Lloyd's, reputable companies, or the Institute of London Underwriters, are considered entirely satisfactory by bankers, in place of insurance policies (see Exhibit 21).

d   Insurance policy *(Exhibit 21, page 86)*

Insurance policies provide actionable evidence of a contract of insurance. Full details of the risks covered are shown on the policy. The right to claim from the insurers may be assigned by the insured in the first instance to someone else, usually the overseas buyer or a bank, by endorsement and delivery.

Risks that may be covered

Insurance cover is often effected on the basis of what are known as 'Institute cargo clauses', and these may be FPA, WA or 'all risks'. War risks have to be covered specifically.

Perils of the sea covers accidental loss or damage such as that caused by sea water, storms, stranding, collisions, etc. *Fire* covers smoke damage as well but does not cover goods which by their nature are likely to self-ignite. *Jettison* covers an act of the master of throwing the goods overboard, usually to lighten the vessel in time of emergency. *Assailing thieves* covers the forcible taking of the goods rather than mere pilferage and is just described in the policy as 'thieves'.

Insurance cover is only effective against risks expressly stated in the policy. The above-mentioned risks are invariably covered to some extent at least. The following risks are sometimes covered in the standard form of cargo insurance policy, those normally subject to additional premiums being marked † or ‡:

Latent defects of the ship's hull or machinery.

Shore risks: collision, derailment, earthquake, flood, overturn, windstorm.

† Theft, pilferage and non-delivery (TPND).

† Strikes, riots and civil commotions (SRCC).

† War.

† Freshwater damage, oil damage, sweat damage, contact with other cargo.

† Breakage and leakage.

‡ Damage caused by hooks or breakdown of refrigerating machinery.

‡ Inherent vice.

‡ Delay.

‡ Damage to labels and packing.

(For the meaning of ‡ see *iv All risks*, in section below)

e The extent to which the risks are covered in the Institute of London Underwriters' 'Institute cargo clauses':

i   *FPA*: the letters stand for free from particular average; they mean that the insurers are free from paying claims for partial loss, accidentally caused unless the ship is stranded, sunk or burnt. The phrase 'particular average' originates from the medieval Italian *avaria particolare* which means a loss not to be shared, a private partial loss as opposed to a 'general average' loss as described below. This has now come to mean 'partial accidental loss or damage'.

ii   *WA* or *WPA*: the letters stand for with average or with particular average; they mean that the insurers will pay for partial losses accidentally caused by a risk covered. Each separate package is deemed to be separately insured for the purposes of FPA cover, and therefore if one package is lost then it constitutes a total loss and is covered.

iii *WA subject to a specified franchise*: the franchise is a stated percentage of loss up to which the insurers are not liable to pay. Any insured loss of the franchise percentage or more will be paid in full. (The standard WA cover also has a built-in franchise which will apply to most goods and under certain conditions of loss.)

iv   *All risks*: this cover is not what it first appears to be; not all risks are covered. It is an extension of the WA coverage and normally excludes the risks marked ‡ in section (d) above.

v   *General average*: loss resulting from an intentional sacrifice or expenditure, incurred by the vessel's master in time of danger for the mutual benefit of all parties including that of the vessel whose interests share the common danger. The parties may be considered in three groups: the owners of the goods, the owners of the ship, and those entitled to receive payment of freight. The last group is normally the shipowner, unless the vessel has been chartered. It is reasonable that all should share in the loss occasioned by an act of general average in proportion to the value of their own interest in the venture. A good example of an act of general average is when a vessel opens the sprinklers or uses steam to douse a fire on board. The ship's fittings and some cargo would probably be damaged by such action and the loss occasioned by the water from the sprinklers or the steam would be borne by all parties in proportion to their interest. All cargo insurance policies cover the risk the insured runs of having to contribute to a general average claim, whether or not his goods are damaged, provided that the peril leading to the general average expenditure is covered by the policy (see Chapter 7).

f   Points of significance to a banker in considering acceptability of insurance documents

A banker is required to examine insurance documents both under documentary credits and when making advances against the security of goods or documents relating thereto. In doing so he should consider the following:

i   The class of document (policy, certificate, cover note); is it acceptable for the purpose?

ii   Does it bear the signature of the insurer if necessary and is it countersigned where required?

iii Are the rights therein available to the party requiring them – eg, have they been assigned to the bank or buyer by endorsement, or has the document been issued in the bank's or buyer's name?

iv   Is the sum insured in the correct currency?

v   Is the insured value sufficient? (It should always be for at least the invoice amount.)

vi   Are the risks covered those required or stipulated? *Note*: under a documentary credit a document may be refused, because cover is in excess of that stipulated.

vii Where and by whom are claims payable?

viii What is the duration of the insurance? (Normally from seller's warehouse to buyer's warehouse.)

ix   Is the description of the goods insured sufficient for identification purposes?

x   Do the marks and numbers and other details on the document coincide with other shipping documents presented with the insurance?

xi   When shipment has been made on deck or in a container, has this been noted on the document?

xii Does the document evidence that cover was effective not later than the date on which it was required to be?

5. TRANSPORT DOCUMENTS

The following transport documents are described below and are illustrated with examples at the end of the chapter.

a Air waybill *(Exhibit 22, page 88)*

The IATA air waybill (sometimes called an air consignment note or air freight note) is issued in a set of 12, of which three are commercially important; the remainder are copies for airline purposes. 'Originals' are produced:

- for the issuing carrier
- the consignee, and
- for the shipper

The waybill is a receipt only and not a document of title, and the goods are delivered to the named consignee without further formality once customs clearance has been obtained. However, if the third 'original' above is still in the hands of the shipper and can be surrendered by him to the airline before delivery has been made to the consignee then the shipper can give amended instructions as to the person to whom delivery is to be made. In order that the exporter or his bank may retain control over the goods, the goods might be consigned to or to the order of a correspondent bank (assuming the correspondent is agreeable to this) for such bank to release the goods or documents as instructed. The document should bear the airline's stamp with the date of despatch. The flight number should be indicated and the document signed on behalf of the airline.

b Parcel post documents *(Exhibits 23 and 24, pages 89-90)*

When goods are to be despatched by post, the post office will issue a receipt for the parcels (see Exhibit 23), and the goods will be delivered directly to the addressee. Control over the goods may sometimes be exercised by having the parcels addressed to a bank in the buyer's country. Many banks however do not wish to deal with goods in this manner, as postal authorities abroad are not always prepared to hold parcels to a bank's order, and banks themselves often have no suitable storage space. Indeed Article 6 of *Uniform Rules for Collections* (see Chapter 4) states that 'goods should not be despatched direct to the address of a bank, or consigned to a bank, without the prior agreement of that bank'.

The receipt normally contains the following information:

- branch stamp of the post office indicating the date of despatch
- signature of the checking officer of the post office
- full name and address shown on the parcel(s)

- shipping marks and numbers for identification with other documents
- postage paid
- name of sender

Exhibit 24 is designed by SITPRO as part of a special pack of forms for parcel post transactions. This is a certificate of posting.

c d e FIATA documents *(Exhibits 25, 26 and 27, pages 91-4, and see also (e) below)*
FIATA is the International Federation of Forwarding Agents Associations. Its documents include important conditions and clauses on liabilities accepted by the issuing forwarder. The Institute of Freight Forwarders Limited, under licence from FIATA, has to authorise trading members of the Institute to issue these forms, which incidentally are not available to non-members of the Institute.

Exporters who use the services of a freight forwarder will often obtain the forwarder's own receipt in exchange for their goods (see Exhibits 25 and 26). Freight forwarders will, where possible, seek to obtain the cost benefits of grouping a number of different consignments into one container for delivery to the shipping company. A shipping company will sometimes issue individual bills of lading to shippers of part-cargoes stuffed by the carrier/forwarder into one container. It is therefore not only the freight forwarder who will sometimes give a receipt for a part container load but also the shipping company when required to do so. It is, however, quite normal practice for freight forwarders to conduct groupage shipments in the following manner:

The goods	The receipts
UK exporters deliver their goods to a *UK freight forwarder*, the shipper, who places them in, say, *one* container going to the same destination. The container is delivered to a *shipping company* which carries it to the port of destination for delivery to an *overseas freight forwarder* who opens the container and delivers the goods to the respective *overseas importers*	*UK exporters* obtain the forwarding agent's receipts for their goods and send them directly or through their bank to the *overseas importers* who, on arrival of the goods, present the UK freight forwarder's receipts to the *overseas freight forwarder* who has previously received the title documents to the container (bills of lading) from the shipper in the UK. The bills of lading are required before the container is released by the *shipping company* at the port of destination to the *overseas freight forwarder*

These documents are normally no more than receipts. They do not as a rule evidence a contract of carriage nor are they title to the goods whilst under the control of the shipping company. Nevertheless, they provide the means by which consignees can obtain the goods from the forwarding agents at destination. To that degree, unless the forwarding agent is *also* the carrier, the people who assume responsibility for the goods are the forwarding agents as opposed to the carrier.

e Combined transport bill of lading *(Exhibit 27, pages 93-4)*
As a natural sequel to unitisation of cargo it has become increasingly customary for the 'unit load', especially where the cargo has been stuffed in a container of 20 feet length, to be shipped on one contract of carriage from a 'place of taking in charge' to a 'place of delivery'. This is known as a 'combined' or 'multi-modal' transport, and in place of the traditional port-to-port bill of lading (Exhibit 32) a 'combined transport bill of lading' is used (see Exhibit 27). When such a document is required under a documentary credit it does not make sense for such credit to specify ports of loading and discharge, as the essentials are the places of taking in charge and delivery, or to prohibit transhipment.

The issuer is responsible for the whole combined transport being correctly completed and for loss or damage to the goods wherever occurring.

The freight paid includes all the costs of forwarding to final destination, and it is clearly stated on the combined transport bill of lading that delivery at destination will be given only on due presentation of an original example.

A traditional 'through' bill of lading also covers a multi-modal transport transaction. However a through bill must be issued by a shipping company or its agent. There must be a sea-leg and the issuing shipping company does not necessarily accept responsibility for performance of the non-sea-leg portion of the journey, nor liability for loss or damage other than that occasioned during the sea-leg.

There is an increasing tendency to use one document as either a traditional port-to-port bill (Exhibit 32) or a combined transport bill, according to the information inserted by the shipper.

f   House bill of lading (*Exhibit 28, pages 95-6*)
These documents are issued by freight forwarders for their own services. This exhibit is the form recommended by The Institute of Freight Forwarders Limited for trading members of the Institute and bears the IFF Standard Trading Conditions.

Under the Carriage of Goods by Sea Act 1971, any sea waybills, data freight receipts, house bills, forwarding agents' receipts or similar non-negotiable documents, not being bills of lading or title documents, are nevertheless subject to the *Hague Rules* relating to bills of lading where the non-negotiable documents provide evidence that they relate to contracts of carriage of goods by sea.

g   Rail consignment note (*Exhibit 29, page 97*)
With the growth of freightliner traffic the volume of goods being exported by rail through to final continental destination is increasing. Consequently the carrier's receipt, or duplicate copy, frequently accompanies the other documents. Goods will be released to the consignee, upon application and nominal proof of identity, by the rail authorities at destination or by delivery direct. Control over the goods would be arranged in the same way as for an air consignment. The rail consignment note should bear the stamp of the station of departure and the date of departure.

h   Road waybill (CMR) (*Exhibit 30, page 98*)
The CMR (Convention Merchandises Routiers) consignment note is an internationally approved and recognised non-negotiable transport document used when goods are travelling by road through or to countries which are parties to the CMR. The contracting countries are Austria, Belgium, Bulgaria, Czechoslovakia, Denmark, Finland, France (including overseas territories), Federal German Republic, German Democratic Republic, Gibraltar, Greece, Hungary, Italy, Luxembourg, Netherlands, Norway, Poland, Portugal, Rumania, Spain, Sweden, Switzerland, United Kingdom (including Northern Ireland), and Yugoslavia.

As well as its function as a receipt and delivery document, the note provides written evidence that goods are being carried under the terms of the CMR.

i and j   Bills of lading (*Exhibits 31 and 32, pages 99-101* and *see also (i) and (j)* below)
This document is the receipt given by the shipping company to the shipper for goods accepted for carriage by sea. If in negotiable form it also conveys title to the goods, and the goods will only be released by the shipping company at destination against surrender of a signed original of the bill of lading. Finally, the bill of lading evidences a contract of carriage.

Bills of lading are usually issued in sets of two, three or more original examples, any one of which may be presented to obtain delivery of goods from a vessel. Traditionally they are issued in a set of more than one, in case of loss in the mail. Currently, to cut the cost of documentation, the United Nations Facilitation's working party is recommending a 'set' of one original only, if commercially acceptable. The first original presented will be enough to obtain the goods and the shipping company will be discharged from liability even if the bill of lading was issued in a set of more than one and the true owner was subsequently to present another original. If complete control over the goods is required then possession of a full set of bills of lading is imperative. Bills of lading are prepared by the exporter or a freight forwarder and then presented to the shipping company for completion and signature. If the goods have been received in apparent good order a 'clean' bill of lading will be given; otherwise the shipping company will indicate on the bill of lading what it considers to be defective in respect of the goods and/or their packaging. Such bills are known as 'claused' or 'dirty bills of lading'. As the statement or clauses indicate a condition detrimental to the goods the buyer may have contractual reasons for not accepting the goods in such condition. Under Article 18 of the ICC *Uniform Customs and Practice for Documentary Credits,* banks will refuse tender of claused bills of lading under a documentary credit unless the credit specifies that a particular clause is acceptable.

The consignees are usually anxious to ensure that the goods they have ordered are actually on the way to them when documents are tendered for payment. This would be indicated in the bills of lading by the word 'shipped'. Sometimes there is no evidence, as for instance when bills of lading state 'received for shipment' (see Exhibit 31); then there is a risk that the goods are just lying at the port of loading waiting for the next vessel. 'Received for shipment' bills often have a clause 'Since shipped'; this clause is known as an 'on board notation' and should be dated, and signed or initialled by the carrier or his agent.

The rights of title to the goods may be transferred by:
● issuing bills of lading to order and endorsing them in blank, or
● issuing the bills of lading to the order of the buyer or bank abroad, or
● issuing the bills of lading consigned to the buyer only; and then arranging for the bills of lading to be delivered to the consignee directly through the banking system

When a vessel is chartered carriage of goods is subject to the terms of the contract of hire, or 'charter party', and any bill of lading issued will be claused 'subject to charter party'. If settlement is being made under a documentary credit, banks will not accept such bills unless specifically authorised to do so in the credit. The legal complexity of the usual charter party contract and the consequent difficulty of ascertaining whether any of the terms may be detrimental to the interests of the consignee make banks hesitant about accepting charter party bills of lading as security.

i Short form bill of lading *(Exhibit 31, page 99)*
One of the three functions of a bill of lading is to provide evidence of the underlying contract of carriage by sea which comes into being with the reservation of space on board a ship. The shipping company's terms are usually given in full on the reverse, but with the short form bill this is not the case. The essence of the 'short form' is the complete removal from the reverse of the bill of lading of the 'small print' which gives

details of the contract of carriage. Article 19(b)(ii) of *Uniform Customs and Practice for Documentary Credits* defines such short form bills of lading as 'bills of lading issued by shipping companies or their agents which indicate some or all of the conditions of carriage by reference to a source or document other than the bill of lading'. In a number of countries, including the UK, the use is being encouraged of a short form bill of lading common to a number of different shipping companies. This is not pre-printed with the name of the shipping company, so the 'name of the carrier' has to be typed in with the other data relating to the specific shipment. This type of document is known as the 'common short form bill of lading' (see Exhibit 31). Banks will accept such bills of lading when presented under documentary credits unless the credit specifies otherwise.

j   Bill of lading (liner) *(Exhibit 32, page 100-101)*
These are issued by shipping companies in respect of goods carried on regular line vessels with scheduled runs and reserved berths at destination. Such means of transport has possible advantages over tramp vessels which do not necessarily adhere to a very strict schedule and may make unscheduled calls at various ports on the way to the ultimate destination.

   Shipping lines serving the same routes or destinations may form a conference, within which agreements are made over such matters as the terms and conditions of bills of lading, freight rates, and sometimes times of sailing and use of berthing facilities.

k   Non-negotiable sea waybill *(Exhibit 33, page 102)*
The processing of bills of lading is slow since they may have to pass through several hands. Therefore these documents may not be received by the consignee on or before arrival of the vessel. The non-negotiable sea waybill was developed to avoid delay in the handling of goods at destination, and has been adopted by a number of shipping lines as an alternative to bills of lading. It resembles the air waybill, as the goods are delivered to the named consignee without any need to hand over the waybill.

l   Mate's receipt *(Exhibit 34, page 103)*
Rarely seen in banking circles, and rightly so, for this is merely a receipt for goods shipped aboard. Not being a document of title, it should be exchanged for the set of bills of lading by the shipper at the offices of the shipping company.

m Points of significance to a banker required to examine bills of lading
i   Each original example must be signed by or on behalf of the ship's master, or the shipping company, and a full set must be presented (unless stipulated otherwise in a documentary credit).
ii   The date of shipment must be indicated.
Article 41 of *Uniform Customs and Practice*, permits banks to accept shipping documents presented within a period after their date of issue stipulated in the credit. If no such period is given in the credit the period is 21 days, as stated in Article 41. There is therefore no such thing as a 'stale' bill of lading under a documentary credit. Nevertheless, a penalty is usually levied by the port authorities at destination when goods are not collected within a certain time after arrival. This charge is known as 'demurrage' and the cost, often considerable, will have to be met before the goods may be taken away. It follows that it is important to pass the bills of lading forward

quickly. Nevertheless, goods now tend to move more quickly than documents, which is why the negotiable bill of lading, which must be produced at destination to secure delivery of the goods, is being replaced by the non-negotiable waybill (see item (k), above).

iii Freight must be paid by the seller on C & F or CIF terms and the bill of lading must be marked 'freight paid'. When a bank is lending against the security of an importer's shipping documents where the contract is FOB, the bank should debit the importer's account with the amount of freight payable and pay the London office of the shipping company, obtaining a 'freight paid' statement on the bills of lading. Shipping companies retain a right of lien over the goods until payment of freight has been made.

iv A 'notify party and address', where required, must be shown on the bill of lading. The shipping company will advise the notify party when the vessel arrives.

v If the goods are shipped on deck the law requires that the bill of lading specifically states this fact. If the bill of lading does not so state, the goods will be considered to have been shipped under deck. 'On deck' bills of lading are generally unacceptable to banks owing to the dangers of jettison and washing overboard. They are unacceptable under documentary credits unless the credit specifically states that they are acceptable. Bills of lading will not be refused under a documentary credit merely because the bill of lading contains a provision that the goods 'may be carried on deck'. Most goods should be shipped 'under deck' but certain dangerous or very large cargoes, and some livestock, have to be shipped 'on deck'.

vi As an aid to remembering the points required for ensuring a bank's security with this document, look in Chapter 5 at the bank's application form to open a documentary credit. There you will see that the requirements for this document are: Full set/clean/on board/ocean bills of lading/to order (of shipper)/blank endorsed/(marked notify). If each of these points, as the phrase is divided up, is satisfied, and provided the names and goods tally (and you are dealing with honest traders and shipowners) then the security is practically complete. In respect of documentary credits or when documents are accepted as security for an advance it then remains to see that certain other points are correct – ie, signed, dated, and alterations authenticated, shipped by a certain date if that be stipulated in a credit and, of course, marked 'freight paid'; if applicable, from and to the named ports, etc.

6. FINANCIAL AND FINANCING DOCUMENTS

The financial documents, bills of exchange and promissory notes are described first below and then the documents encountered in connection with the financing of goods. Examples of the documents are given at the end of the chapter.

a	Bill of exchange drawn in foreign currency and payable at sight	*Exhibit 35*
b	Bill of exchange drawn in sterling and payable at 60 days' date	*Exhibit 36*
c	Bill of exchange accepted payable at 30 days' sight	*Exhibit 37*
d	Promissory note	*Exhibit 38*
e	Inspection and sampling order	*Exhibit 39*
f	Delivery order	*Exhibit 40*
g	Warehouse receipt	*Exhibit 41*
h	Trust receipt	*Exhibit 42*

a, b, c Bills of exchange *(Exhibits 35, 36 and 37, pages 104-6)*
The legal definition (Bills of Exchange Act 1882, section 3): a bill of exchange is an unconditional order in writing, addressed by one person (drawer) to another (drawee), signed by the person giving it (drawer), requiring the person to whom it is addressed (drawee) to pay on demand, or at a fixed or determinable future time, a sum certain in money to, or to the order of, a specified person (payee), or to bearer. The words in brackets do not appear in the Act, but have been inserted for clarity.

The function of bills of exchange: widely used in international trade, partly since they are convenient vehicles for collecting debts from traders abroad. Finance may be arranged in a number of ways using bills of exchange, both for the buyer (drawee) and for the seller (drawer). Bills of exchange which have been dishonoured may be used in their own right as the basis for legal action. After payment, the discharged bill of exchange is retained by the drawee as evidence of payment; in other words it becomes a receipt for the money. Further details of the use of bills of exchange under collection facilities and documentary credits may be found in Chapters 4 and 5.

It is the practice in some European countries for banks to 'aval' bills of exchange by adding the bank's name to the bill; this raises the status of the document, as the avalising bank has guaranteed payment at maturity (see Chapter 7).

d Promissory note *(Exhibit 38, page 107)*
Whilst not bills of exchange, they are largely subject to the same rules and are used for a somewhat similar purpose, the settlement of indebtedness. Instead of being drawn like a bill of exchange, by the person expecting to be paid, they are made by the person who owes the money (maker), in favour of the beneficiary (payee). A simple way of looking at a promissory note is to consider it an IOU. When due, it is presented for payment by the holder, who may be the payee or someone to whom the promissory note has been negotiated.

e Inspection and sampling order *(Exhibit 39, page 107)*
When banks are protecting consignment stocks for foreign exporters to the UK, or if they are lending to a UK importer against a pledge of goods, the goods are usually warehoused in the bank's name pending sale to buyers. Prospective buyers frequently need to inspect and sometimes sample the goods before buying them, and it is necessary to be able to authorise a warehouse to permit this to take place. Assuming that the overseas seller or UK importer authorises sampling and/or inspection, a bank may issue such an order on a warehouse and hand it to the prospective buyer.

f Delivery order *(Exhibit 40, page 108)*
This is an order on a warehouse instructing it to deliver goods to bearer or a party named in the order. Banks issue such orders when goods stored in their name are to be delivered to a buyer or are to be reshipped and have to leave a warehouse.

g Warehouse receipt *(Exhibit 41, page 109)*
This is a receipt for goods issued by a warehouse. The document is not negotiable and no rights in the goods can be transferred under it. Delivery orders may be issued against the receipt for the goods which relate to it.

h Trust receipt *(Exhibit 42, pages 110-11)*
When a bank wishes to release documents of title, or the goods themselves, to a customer of *undoubted integrity,* whilst still retaining its security rights in those goods

and/or the proceeds of their sale, it may obtain a completed trust receipt from its customer to whom a loan has been made. This is an acknowledgement of the pledge of the goods to the bank and an undertaking of the customer to take the documents as trustees for the bank and to:

- arrange for goods to be warehoused in the bank's name, or
- arrange for processing of the goods and their return to warehouse in the bank's name, or
- arrange for sale of the goods and to pay all sale proceeds without deduction to the bank immediately on receipt or within a short, stated, period of time

The reason why a bank sometimes gives this facility is that it retains the bank's security against the possibility of the customer's liquidation or bankruptcy. It denies the liquidator or trustee in bankruptcy the legal right to distribute the proceeds of the bank's security (goods or documents relating to goods) for the benefit of creditors in general. The defect is that if a customer fails to keep to the terms of a trust receipt undertaking and behaves in a dishonest way, then, as was shown in Lloyds Bank Ltd v Bank of America NT & SA 1938, the undertaking provides no security for the bank. Indeed it was held that the bank which released the documents (and took the trust receipt) thereby enabled the fraud to take place, and must therefore suffer the loss.

7. GLOSSARY OF TERMS USED IN THIS CHAPTER

Agent
one who agrees to act in accordance with the terms of a mandate on behalf of another, his principal; banks act as agents for other banks in a variety of ways; the services carried out largely depend upon the agency agreement existing between the banks in question.

Broker (insurance)
one who arranges a contract of insurance between an underwriter and an insured; a broker is not a party to the contract but merely acts as an agent for the insured; it follows that a good broker should obtain for his client the best cover and terms available by approaching a wide variety of insurers.

Carriage forward
implies that freight is payable at destination; the clause may be found on bills of lading or other shipping documents that are likely to cover a shipment of goods on FOB terms.

Carriage paid
implies that the carrier has received payment for freight, probably prior to shipment, as it is an essential ingredient of a CIF or C & F contract.

Chamber of commerce
a body organised to protect the interests of commerce in a town or district; in the UK chambers of commerce are independent voluntary bodies, although some foreign chambers of commerce are government controlled.

Clearance charges   the costs incurred in obtaining goods from a shipping company or carrier; the charges may include freight, customs duty, landing charges, warehouse charges if stored in the meantime, and freight forwarders' disbursements; it is as well to ascertain a customer's precise instructions before paying such charges on his behalf.

Consignment (1)   in general terms 'something which is despatched', or a sending of goods.

Consignment (2)   system of exporting goods which have not been sold, but which are entrusted to a bank in the importing country to warehouse pending receipt of payment from interested buyers.

Contract of carriage   usually an oral contract concluded over the telephone at the time freight space is booked; the evidence of the contract is conveyed in the document of movement.

Contract of sale   bargain concluded between buyer and seller; the contract may be arranged by word of mouth informally, or may be the subject of a detailed sales agreement in writing and signed formally.

Customs   official inspectors empowered to levy taxes according to tariff on goods entering or leaving a country; customs examination of TIR (below) consignments are usually located away from ports or frontier sites to reduce congestion and speed up the movement of goods.

Discharge   unloading from a ship or other vehicle.

Dumping   the exporting of large quantities of a particular product, often surplus production, at a very low price, thereby undercutting local and other manufacturers.

Duty   levy or tax imposed by the authorities on goods imported, normally payable on entry of the goods to the customs.

Foreign exchange permit   required in certain countries abroad, *not* in the UK; normally this permit must be obtained by a commercial bank on behalf of a customer prior to the bank's paying foreign currency.

Free trade area	one of the objectives of the EEC is to reduce and/or remove tariffs on goods moved between member states; the idea is to develop competition and reduce national subsidies, thereby stimulating a more widely based and healthier economy with a greatly enlarged 'domestic' market.
Freight (1)	goods or merchandise.
Freight (2)	payment due to a carrier for transporting goods; this is the meaning most commonly used in this book.
Inherent vice	propensity of a commodity to self-destruct; this gives rise to a high insurance risk, and therefore cover may be given only after payment of an additional premium.
Institute cargo clauses	clauses covering goods in international transit against marine risks produced by the T & CC (see Institute of London Underwriters, below); war risks are covered by the Institute war clauses and strikes risks by the Institute strikes, riots and civil commotions clauses.
Institute of London Underwriters	founded in 1884; it is the association of marine insurance companies working in the London market issuing policies known as 'companies' combined policies' and certificates on their behalf; it also issues standard Institute cargo clauses for both company and Lloyd's underwriters which are used in many parts of the world, through the Technical and Clauses Committee (T & CC).
Landing	discharging of cargo from a ship or aircraft on to land rather than into a lighter (below).
Lien	legal right to retain possession of a tangible asset; the right of a warehouse to retain goods pending payment of their charges.
Lighter	barge, often employed at ports with few or no quayside facilities; goods are discharged into lighters when the ocean-going vessel must anchor offshore.
Marine insurance	branch of the insurance industry which includes hull insurance and other aspects of insuring ships and which also embraces cargo insurance in respect of air, land and water-borne risks.

Marks and numbers	the identifying marks placed upon the cargo; the 'port mark' enables the shipping company to stow and discharge cargo in the correct order; marks and numbers are to be found on all shipping documents, and often help those handling documents to ascertain whether the documents constitute the same set or not.
Ship's hooks	apart from a port's own facilities for unloading general cargo, most vessels carry their own lifting equipment; 'under ship's hooks' implies the use of a vessel's own lifting gear, which of course will have hooks to lift goods.
Ship's rail	the rail follows the perimeter of the deck of a vessel, over which goods must pass on loading and discharge.
Tendering (1)	presenting, offering, giving.
Tendering (2)	submission of a formal offer to perform a contract.
TIR	Transit International Rapide carnets which comprise either 6 or 14 pages on which all details of the goods carried are listed (one page per journey); the carnet must be presented at the port of exit, all transit frontiers, and at the final customs shed in the country of destination; the vehicle will be sealed by the customs at the port of exit and will bear the international marking plate 'TIR'.

Specimen Documents

The 42 documents which are illustrated on pages 62 to 111 are described on pages 44 to 58.

Full sets of shipping documents presented for collection and also under a documentary credit appear in Chapters 4 and 5 respectively (see pages 137 to 145 and 189 to 212).

Exhibit 1 **Pro-forma invoice**

PROFORMA **INVOICE** FACTURE FACTURA	RECHNUNG FACTUUR		
Seller (Name, Address, VAT Reg. No.) Weybridge Office Equipment Ltd Ford Street House Weybridge Surrey			Brussels Tariff No.
	Invoice No. and Date (Tax Point) PFI- 6648	Seller's Reference	
	Buyer's Reference		
Consignee J.Panalogliou 1433 Elysi Athens 410 Greece	Buyer (if not Consignee)		

Country of Origin of Goods United Kingdom
Terms of Delivery and Payment FOB London

Vessel/Aircraft etc.	Port of Loading
Port of Discharge	

Marks and Numbers; Number and Kind of Packages; Description of Goods	Quantity	@	Amount (State Currency) £
Specification number:			
13575 Minichrome markers	each		0.65
13488 French oil sets	set		2.94
13679 Diffusing ink 500ml	each		1.08
12977 Easel mark 3A large	each		24.16
13698 Ball pens Blue	50		4.00
13444 A4 cartridge paper brand VW	ream		8.40
13986 Columbus stapler	each		3.95
12189 Artist's tape 3cm – red	roll		1.60
12337 Zeffra plastic overlays 6x4 cm	25		11.90
12446 24 Brush set 00 – 8	set		12.00

TOTAL £	
Gross Weight(Kg)	Cube (M3)

When ordering please quote specification number and quantity required, and indicate as per proforma PFI – 6648

Name of Signatory
Place and Date of Issue Weybridge   3.4.19..
Signature

It is hereby certified that this invoice shows the actual price of the goods described, that no other invoice has been or will be issued and that all particulars are true and correct.

Exhibit 2 **Commercial invoice**

GLAXO GROUP LTD.	INVOICE FACTURE RECHNUNG
166 High Holborn, London WC1V 6PD	FACTURA FACTUUR

Invoice No. 37218		Log No. SD4/5216	
Customer Order No. GW/429		Customer A/C No. 2761	

Telephone 01-240 1255
Telex 261657
Cables Glaxaply, WC1   VAT Reg No. 239 8208 39

Invoice Address
IMPORTER LTD
VIENNA
AUSTRIA

Bankers

Country of Origin of Goods	Country of Final Destination
E.E.C. (UK)	AUSTRIA

Terms of Delivery and Payment CIF VIENNA

DRAFT AT 30 DAYS SIGHT

Vessel / Aircraft etc.	Port of Loading
OVERLAND	LONDON

Port of Discharge	Insurance
VIENNA	EFFECTED

Marks and Numbers	Description of Goods	Quantity	@	Amount (State Currency)
GW 429	MOVEMENT CERTIFICATE NO. EUR.1 R874153		per pack	£ sterling
1–6	6 CASES PHARMACEUTICAL PRODUCTS EACH CONTAINING 100 PACKS	600 packs	1.26	756.00
CASES 1–6	GROSS 10.50 Kilos NETT 2.30 Kilos MEASUREMENTS 455 x 360 x 320 mms each		OVERLAND FREIGHT	40.00
			INSURANCE	1.20
			Selling Price	£797.20

We hereby certify this invoice true and correct.
for GLAXO GROUP LTD.

Place and Date of Issue
London 4.12.79
Signature

Exhibit 3 **Certified invoice**

GLAXO GROUP LTD.

166 High Holborn, London WC1 V 6PD
Telephone 01-240 1255
Telex 261657
Cables Glaxaply, WC1   VAT Reg No. 239 8208 39

INVOICE   FACTURE   RECHNUNG
FACTURA   FACTUUR   RH

Invoice No.	Log No.
72436	SD4/0274

Customer Order No.	Customer A/C No.
BC/728	4216

Invoice Address

IMPORTERS LTD
SYDNEY
AUSTRALIA

Bankers

National Westminster Bank Ltd
52 Threadneedle Street
London EC2R 8AL
Code 60-00-02
Account Number 00462136
Glaxo Group Ltd

Country of Origin of Goods	Country of Final Destination
E.E.C.(UK) CODE A	AUSTRALIA

Terms of Delivery and Payment   FOB LONDON

CASH AGAINST DOCUMENTS (C.A.D.)

Vessel / Aircraft etc.	Port of Loading
S.S. ARMADICE	LONDON

Port of Discharge	Insurance
SYDNEY	EFFECTED

Marks and Numbers	Description of Goods	Quantity	@ each	Amount (State Currency) £ sterling
BC.728 SYDNEY 1–60	60 CARTONS BABY FOOD EACH CONTAINING 12 PACKS OF 200gm	60 cartons	2.00	120.00
CASES 1–60	GROSS NETT MEASUREMENTS 8.00 Kilos 2.40 Kilos 380 x 275 x 275 mms each			

Selling Price   £120.00

COMBINED CERTIFICATE OF VALUE AND OF ORIGIN OF GOODS FOR EXPORTATION TO THE
COMMONWEALTH OF AUSTRALIA—4

CHARLIE BROWN
IMPORTERS LTD, LONDON.

1 Value of outside packages containers	£10	Included
2 Labour in packing goods into outside packages containers	£14	Included
3 Inland transport and insurance charges to dock airport area	£ 6	Included
4 Dock and port charges		
5 Overseas Freight		
6 Overseas Insurance		
7 Details of any other charges relating to delivery of goods		
8 Royalties (State full particulars)		
9 Commission and sundry charges (State full particulars)		

Witness

London   the   4th   day of December   '79

Exhibit 4   **Weight note**

THE MERSEY DOCKS AND HARBOUR COMPANY

WEIGHT NOTE

NO. __689__

DATE __2.4.19..__

VESSEL: __Jnausir__

BERTH: __Victoria 4__

A/C: __Flat Tyres Ltd__

PORT & B/LADING NO. __79__

COMMENCED WEIGHING __30.3.19..__

COMPLETED WEIGHING __30.3.19..__

MODE OF WEIGHING __Weighbridge__

Marks	Particulars of Goods	Kilograms
D F G LIVERPOOL 1 - 104	104 cases KD MOTORCYCLES	5428

THE ABOVE CERTIFIED TO BE THE CORRECT WEIGHT TAKEN ON LANDING/DELIVERY OF THE GOODS SHEWN ABOVE.

SIGNED _____

Cargo Handling Manager

01964

Exhibit 5 **Packing list**

CONTINUATION SHEET /PACKING LIST		

Exporter/Shipper (Name and Address)	UK Customs Assigned Number CAN 99999	Sheet No. 2 of 2
SITPRO Export Ltd High Street Burton On Trent DE15 1YZ England	Invoice No. and Date (Tax Point) (Various)	Exporter's Reference 12345/6/8/52/53
	Buyer's Reference (Various)	Other Reference(s)

Consignee	For Official Use
SITPRO Overseas (Demonstration for use with shipment Ref.Nos 12345, 12346,12348, 12352 or and based on 12345). 12353	Based on shipment No.12345

Marks and Numbers; No. & Kind of Packages; Description of Goods	Quantity	Gross Weight (kg)	Cube (M³)
CASE NO.			
1 Automatic Lathe Ref 347-1 25mm	1		
2 Automatic Lathe Ref 347-2 50mm	1		
3 Automatic Lathe Ref 348-1 55mm	1		
4 Automatic Lathe Ref 348-3 75mm	1		
5 Screws – Self tapping 1"xNo.8	1000		
Grommets composition – 10mm	300		
Electric Motors – 75w/240v	14		
Small brass collars	25		
Large brass collars	40		
Huge brass collars	20		
Chucks 25mm	50		
Chucks 50mm	20		
Chucks 55mm	40		
Chucks 75mm	10		
Castors – special 10" round	20		
Washers – mixed – in sets of 10	100		
6 Cable harness for 347-1	10		
Cable harness for 347-2	5		
Cable harness for 348-1	15		
Cable harness for 348-3	4		
Control wheels 47172	10		
" " 47171	10		
" " 47170	5		
Solenoid sets for 347-2	5		
" " 348-3	1		
Restrictors – mixed – in packs of 10	100		
Circuit Control Boards for 347-1	20		
Circuit Control Boards for 347-2	20		
" " " " 348-1	20		
" " " " 348-3	10		
7/9 Pipe joints 4" x 90°	3		
10/11 Pipe joints 6" x 45°	2		
12/17 Cutting oil 50kg net drums	6		
Total CIF			

See Principal Sheet for further details of this Consignment

Exhibit 6 **Specification**

CONTINUATION SHEET /SPECIFICATION

Exporter/Shipper (Name and Address)			
SITPRO Export Ltd High Street Burton On Trent DE15 1YZ England	**UK Customs Assigned Number** CAN 99999		**Sheet No.** 2 of 2
	Invoice No. and Date (Tax Point) (Various)		**Exporter's Reference** 12345/6/8/52/53
	Buyer's Reference (Various)		**Other Reference(s)**

Consignee	For Official Use
SITPRO Overseas (Demonstration for use with shipment Ref.Nos 12345, 12346,12348, 12352 or and based on 12345). 12353	Based on shipment No.12345

Marks and Numbers; No. & Kind of Packages; Description of Goods	Quantity	HMV * @	@	Amount (State Currency)
CASE NO.				Selling Price
1 Automatic Lathe Ref 347-1 25mm	1	2400		2571.00
2 Automatic Lathe Ref 347-2 50mm	1	3000		3017.00
3 Automatic Lathe Ref 348-1 55mm	1	3134		3642.00
4 Automatic Lathe Ref 348-3 75mm	1	5010		5341.55
5 Screws - Self tapping 1"xNo.8	1000	0.01	0.01	10.00
Grommets composition - 10mm	300	0.18	0.20	60.00
Electric Motors - 75w/240v	14	15.15	15.20	212.80
Small brass collars	25	0.10	0.10	2.50
Large brass collars	40	0.18	0.20	8.00
Huge brass collars	20	0.30	0.30	6.00
Chucks 25mm	50	4.00	4.30	215.00
Chucks 50mm	20	6.10	6.20	124.00
Chucks 55mm	40	6.00	6.50	260.00
Chucks 75mm	10	8.25	8.20	82.00
Castors - special 10" round	20	1.25	1.27	25.40
Washers - mixed - in sets of 10	100	1.00	1.00	100.00
6 Cable harness for 347-1	10	22.50	22.50	225.00
Cable harness for 347-2	5	22.50	23.00	115.00
Cable harness for 348-1	15	22.50	22.50	337.50
Cable harness for 348-3	4	23.10	24.00	96.00
Control wheels 47172	10	3.75	3.74	37.40
" " 47171	10	4.20	4.21	42.10
" " 47170	5	4.20	4.21	21.05
Solenoid sets for 347-2	5	21.25	24.70	123.50
" " " 348-3	1	21.25	24.70	24.70
Restrictors - mixed - in packs of 10	100	1.20	1.21	121.00
Circuit Control Boards for 347-1	20	73.00	75.00	1500.00
Circuit Control Boards for 347-2	20	76.00	79.00	1580.00
" " " " 348-1	20	72.00	74.00	1480.00
" " " " 348-3	10	78.00	81.00	810.00
7/9 Pipe joints 4" x 90°	3	12.75	12.50	37.50
10/11 Pipe joints 6" x 45°	2	25.00	24.00	48.00
12/17 Cutting oil 50kg net drums	6	28.50	28.50	171.00
Total CIF			GBP	£22447.00

* Home market value (HMV)
required for USA, Canada
New Zealand, Zambia.

See Principal Sheet for further details of this Consignment

Exhibit 7　**Manufacturer's or supplier's quality or inspection certificate**

```
                        J.A.K.T.  Co.  Ltd.

                                                  15 The Way,
Our reference B/44792                             Northwood
                                                  Middlesex.
                                                  4.5.19..

China National Machinery Import
                & Export Corporation,
Tientsin Branch,
Ho Ping District,
Tientsin.
The People's Republic of China.


Dear Sirs,
          Order 7739909-18E -14.7.19..
          Our ref.  B/44792
          6 cases marked 7739909-18E
                    Hsinkang China

          We hereby certify that the guides and spindles
supplied against the above order are made from the best quality
steel suitable for the purpose and they are guaranteed for
accuracy of shape, dimensions quantity and quality.

          We further certify that the goods are of our manufacture
and are brand new and are free from rust.   They have been
packed in lined cases.   The goods have been examined at the
time of manufacture and found to be up to standard.



                        Yours faithfully,
                        J.A.K.T.  Co.  Ltd.
```

Exhibit 8 **Third party certificate of inspection**

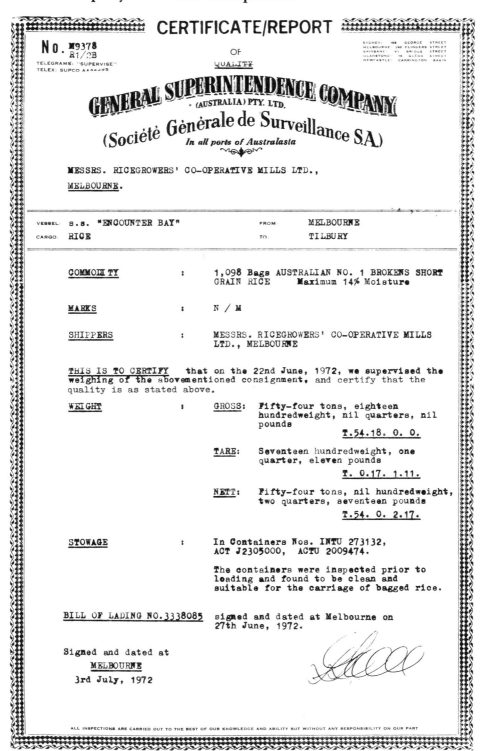

CERTIFICATE/REPORT

No. M9378
R1/2B

TELEGRAMS: "SUPERVISE"
TELEX: SUPCO AA94395

OF
QUALITY

SYDNEY: 188   GEORGE   STREET
MELBOURNE: 590 FLINDERS STREET
BRISBANE: 91   BRIDGE   STREET
GLADSTONE: 16   GLEGG   STREET
NEWCASTLE: CARRINGTON   BASIN

GENERAL SUPERINTENDENCE COMPANY
(AUSTRALIA) PTY. LTD.

(Société Générale de Surveillance S.A.)
In all ports of Australasia

MESSRS. RICEGROWERS' CO-OPERATIVE MILLS LTD.,
MELBOURNE.

VESSEL:	S.S. "ENCOUNTER BAY"	FROM	MELBOURNE
CARGO:	RICE	TO:	TILBURY

COMMODITY : 1,098 Bags AUSTRALIAN NO. 1 BROKENS SHORT
GRAIN RICE   Maximum 14% Moisture

MARKS : N / M

SHIPPERS : MESSRS. RICEGROWERS' CO-OPERATIVE MILLS
LTD., MELBOURNE

THIS IS TO CERTIFY that on the 22nd June, 1972, we supervised the
weighing of the abovementioned consignment, and certify that the
quality is as stated above.

WEIGHT : GROSS: Fifty-four tons, eighteen
hundredweight, nil quarters, nil
pounds
                      T.54.18. 0. 0.

TARE: Seventeen hundredweight, one
quarter, eleven pounds
                      T. 0.17. 1.11.

NETT: Fifty-four tons, nil hundredweight,
two quarters, seventeen pounds
                      T.54. 0. 2.17.

STOWAGE : In Containers Nos. INTU 273132,
ACT J2305000, ACTU 2009474.

The containers were inspected prior to
loading and found to be clean and
suitable for the carriage of bagged rice.

BILL OF LADING NO.3338085 signed and dated at Melbourne on
27th June, 1972.

Signed and dated at
    MELBOURNE
3rd July, 1972

ALL INSPECTIONS ARE CARRIED OUT TO THE BEST OF OUR KNOWLEDGE AND ABILITY BUT WITHOUT ANY RESPONSIBILITY ON OUR PART

Exhibit 9   **Manufacturer's analysis certificate**

Fabriek van Chemische Producten
VONDELINGENPLAAT N.V.
Rotterdam   Date 4.5.19....
Holland.

C E R T I F I C A T E   O F   A N A L Y S I S

Buyer: Antcrushers Ltd, 6 Mallett Way, Exeter.

Product: Formic Acid
Code number: 24.56.78.   Order number 088753

Molecular weight 46

Batch Number	Package Number	Kilos Net per package	Kilos Net	%	Kilos 100%
215	76	1429 x 35	50015	85	(min)

VONDELINGENPLAAT

P. Clogg
Laboratory Supervisor

Exhibit 10 **EUR 1 form** *(front)*

MOVEMENT CERTIFICATE	

1. Exporter (Name, full address, country)

SITPRO Export Ltd
High Street
Burton-on-Trent DE15 1YZ
England   VAT No. 241 8235 77

EUR.1 No.   J   492116

See notes overleaf before completing this form

752-12350 LD

2. Certificate used in preferential trade between

THE EUROPEAN ECONOMIC COMMUNITY

and

....

(Insert appropriate countries or groups of countries or territories)

3. Consignee (Name, full address, country) (Optional)

SITPRO Scandinavia AB
Fack,
S10260 Stockholm
SWEDEN

4. Country, group of countries or territory in which the products are considered as originating

EEC

5. Country, group of countries or territory of destination

Sweden

6. Transport details (Optional)

Triangle Vessel

7. Remarks

None

(1) If goods are not packed, indicate number of articles, or state "in bulk" as appropriate.

8. Item number: marks & numbers Number and kind of packages (1): description of goods

<u>1 x 12m TILT Trailer holding</u>

1) 6140
   1/200   200x25 kg net polythene
                lined steel drums
                ANTIMONY TRICHLORIDE
                Class 8 UN No 1733

2) 6140
   201/400   200x25kg net polythene
                lined steel drums
                HYDROFLUORIC ACID
                SOLUTION 50% W/W
                Class 8 UN No 1790

9. Gross weight (kg) or other measure (litres, m³, etc.)

10540
5600
kg

10. Invoices (Cpt.cr.al)

(2) Complete only where the regulations of the exporting country or territory require.

11. CUSTOMS ENDORSEMENT

Declaration certified   Stamp
Export document (2):

Form .... No ....

Customs office ....

Issuing country or territory:
UNITED KINGDOM ....

Date ....

....
            (Signature)

C 1299

12. DECLARATION BY THE EXPORTER

I, the undersigned, declare that the goods described above meet the conditions required for the issue of this certificate.

(Place and date)
Burton 3 Jul 1981 ....

(Signature),

1

TB/Bn 52/1199/2A 5/77   F.4265 (Jul. 1977)

Exhibit 10 **EUR 1 form** *(back)*

13. REQUEST FOR VERIFICATION	14. RESULT OF VERIFICATION
To: H M CUSTOMS AND EXCISE, INTERNATIONAL CUSTOMS DIVISION E BRANCH 4, ADELAIDE HOUSE, LONDON BRIDGE, LONDON EC4R 9DB, ENGLAND	Verification carried out shows that this certificate (1)
	☐ was issued by the Customs Office indicated and that the information contained therein is accurate.
	☐ does not meet the requirements as to authenticity and accuracy (see remarks appended).
Verification of the authenticity and accuracy of this certificate is requested.	
.... (Place and date)	.... (Place and date)
.... (Signature) Stamp	.... (Signature) Stamp
	(1) Insert X in the appropriate box

NOTES

1. Certificates must not contain erasures or words written over one another. Any alterations must be made by deleting the incorrect particulars and adding any necessary corrections. Any such alteration must be initialled by the person who completed the certificate and endorsed by the Customs authorities of the issuing country or territory.

2. No spaces must be left between the items entered on the certificate and each item must be preceded by an item number. A horizontal line must be drawn immediately below the last item. Any unused space must be struck through in such a manner as to make any later additions impossible.

3. Goods must be described in accordance with commercial practice and with sufficient detail to enable them to be identified.

Exhibit 11   **T2L form**

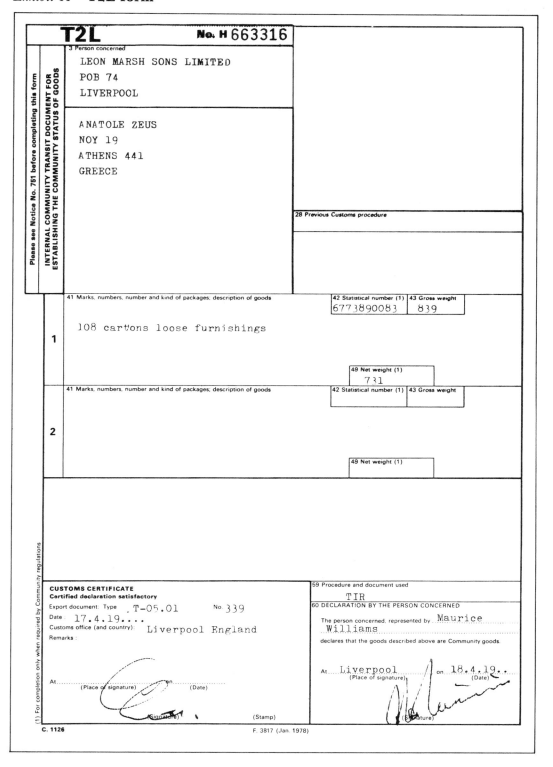

T2L   No: H 663316

Please see Notice No. 751 before completing this form

INTERNAL COMMUNITY TRANSIT DOCUMENT FOR ESTABLISHING THE COMMUNITY STATUS OF GOODS

3 Person concerned

LEON MARSH SONS LIMITED
POB 74
LIVERPOOL

ANATOLE ZEUS
NOY 19
ATHENS 441
GREECE

28 Previous Customs procedure

41 Marks, numbers, number and kind of packages; description of goods	42 Statistical number (1)	43 Gross weight
1 108 cartons loose furnishings	6773890083	839
	49 Net weight (1) 731	

41 Marks, numbers, number and kind of packages; description of goods	42 Statistical number (1)	43 Gross weight
2		
	49 Net weight (1)	

(1) For completion only when required by Community regulations

CUSTOMS CERTIFICATE
Certified declaration satisfactory
Export document: Type T-05.01   No. 339
Date: 17.4.19....
Customs office (and country): Liverpool England
Remarks :

At..on............................
(Place of signature)   (Date)

(Signature)   (Stamp)

59 Procedure and document used
TIR

60 DECLARATION BY THE PERSON CONCERNED

The person concerned, represented by Maurice
Williams

declares that the goods described above are Community goods.

At Liverpool   on 18.4.19..
(Place of signature)   (Date)

(Signature)

C. 1126   F. 3817 (Jan. 1978)

Exhibit 12 **Consular invoice**

FC-8

REPUBLICA DE COLOMBIA   **C**   № 051544

1) **FACTURA CONSULAR No.**

Página No.

2) — País de venta: United Kingdom
3) — País de origen: United Kingdom
4) — Lugar de embarque: 12.3.19....
5) — Nombre del barco o Compañía Aérea: m.v. Percador,Atlantis Lynes
6) — Consignatario: Nombre y dirección: Cobbrah Co London
7) — Destinatario: Nombre y dirección: Jose Ferru Mompos
8) — Remitente: Nombre y dirección:
9) — Número de páginas: 28
10) — Número de conocimiento o guía: 17
11) — Aduana de destino: Barranquilla

ESTAMPILLAS
US $ 5.00

12) Cantidad y clase de bultos	13) Marca y números	14) PESO EN KILOS		15) No. de unidades	16) DENOMINACION COMERCIAL DE LA MERCANCIA	17) PRECIO DE LA MERCANCIA
		Bruto	Neto			
28 cases	1/28	1,972	1,750	56	Knitting machines – Cobbrah 14	U.S.$ 16,850

18) — Total en pesos colombianos $

SUMAN

Registro de importación No.				U.S.$	16,850
Oficina expedidora:					
Cantidad autorizada: US $					
Cantidad despachada: "					
Cantidad por despachar: "					

Lugar y fecha

Firma y sello del Cónsul

Exhibit 13 **Legalised invoice**

INVOICE	FACTURE FACTURA	RECHNUNG FACTUUR		

Seller (Name, Address, VAT Reg. No.)		Brussels Tariff No. 9468

MONOSTATICS EXPORT LTD
RANGERS LANE
SLOUGH TRADING ESTATE. BUCKS

Invoice No. and Date (Tax Point)	Seller's Reference
19976 1.9.19..	JJ34-189/44

Buyer's Reference
5/45YSR/33-9

Consignee
PATEL DISTRIBUTIONS
24 ASRAF STREET
BHERANI   LUNDY

Buyer (if not Consignee)

Country of Origin of Goods
United Kingdom

Terms of Delivery and Payment
C & F Bherani Payment 30 days
sight D/A.

Vessel/Aircraft etc.	Port of Loading
BEN LIMMER	LONDON

Port of Discharge
BHERANI

Marks and Numbers; Number and Kind of Packages; Description of Goods	Quantity	@	Amount (State Currency)
TRD			
1-8 8 Cases Car radio-phones			
BHERANI HS/3446 mark 6g	32	$194	US$6,208

TOTAL US$ 6,208		
Gross Weight(Kg) 128kg	Cube (M3) 0.10	

Name of Signatory
I.J.Johnson

Place and Date of Issue
Slough 1.8.19..

Signature/

It is hereby certified that this invoice shows the actual price of the goods described, that no other invoice has been or will be issued, and that all particulars are true and correct.

Exhibit 14 **Combined invoice and certificate of origin** *(first sheet)*

	INVOICE	FACTURE FACTURA	RECHNUNG FACTUUR	
			C.C.C.N No. 8448	

Seller (Name, Address, VAT Reg. No.)
SITPRO Export Ltd
High Street
Burton on Trent   DE15 1YZ
England   VAT No. 241 8235 77

Invoice No. and Date (Tax Point)
87982 – 8 Jul 1981

Seller's Reference
566 – 12353 CD

Buyer's Reference
NG 3421

Consignee
NITPRO
103 Lewis St PMB 12776
Lagos
NIGERIA

Buyer (if not Consignee)
As Consignee

Country of Origin of Goods
United Kingdom

Terms of Delivery and Payment
C & F Lagos. Payment by confirmed
Irrevocable Doc.Credit through British
International Bank, Burton.

Vessel/Aircraft etc.
UKWAL Vessel

Port of Loading
Liverpool

Port of Discharge
Lagos

Marks and Numbers; Number and Kind of Packages; Description of Goods	Quantity	@	Amount (State Currency)
NITPRO 10 Cases NG3421 Machine Tool Parts Lagos 1/10			

TOTAL
GBP £9704.00.

Gross Weight(kg) 5105   **Cube (m³)** 8.720

Totals as per attached
continuation sheet:

FOB Value: 9435.00
Freight: 269.00
C&F Total £9704.00.
Manufactured by SITPRO Export Ltd

Name of Signatory
H J Helliar, Chief Clerk

Place and Date of Issue
Burton 3 Jul 1981

Signature

It is hereby certified that this invoice shows the actual price of the goods described,
that no other invoice has been or will be issued, and that all particulars are true and
correct.

Exhibit 14 **Combined invoice and certificate of origin** *(second sheet)*

In accordance with Nigerian Government Notice 1989 of 1970.

NIGERIA

Combined Certificate of Value and of Origin and Invoice of Goods for
Exportation to Nigeria

CERTIFICATE OF VALUE

I, ...

SITPRO

of . . . .

*Manufacturers/Suppliers/Exporters of the goods enumerated in this invoice amounting to . . . .

hereby declare that I have the authority to make and sign this certificate on behalf of the aforesaid *Manufacturers,
Suppliers/Exporters and that I have the means of knowing and I do hereby certify as follows:—
(1) That this invoice is in all respects correct and contains a true and full statement of the price actually paid or to
be paid for the said goods, and the actual quantity thereof.
(2) That no different invoice of the goods mentioned in the said invoice has been or will be furnished to anyone.
(3) That no arrangement or understanding affecting the purchase price of the said goods has been or will be made
or entered into between the said exporter and purchaser or by anyone on behalf of either of them either by way of
discount, rebate, compensation or in any manner whatever other than as fully shown on this invoice.

CERTIFICATE OF ORIGIN

(1) That all the goods mentioned in this invoice have been wholly produced or manufactured in . . . .

(2) That all the goods mentioned in this invoice have been either wholly or partially produced or manufactured in

(3) That as regards those goods only partially produced or manufactured,
(a) the final process or processes of manufacture have been performed in . . . .

(b) the expenditure in material produced and/or labour performed in . . . . calculated
subject to qualifications hereunder, in the case of all such goods is not less than 25 per cent of the factory or works
costs of all such goods in their finished state.   *See note below.
(4) That in the calculation of such proportion of material produced and/or labour performed none of the following
items has been included or considered:—

Manufacturer's profit, or remuneration of any trader, agent, broker or other person dealing in the goods in their
finished condition; royalties; cost of outside packages, or any cost of packing the goods thereinto; any cost of conveying, insuring, or shipping the goods subsequent to their manufacture.

Dated at . . . . this . . . . day of . . . . 19 . . .

(Signature) . . . . *HJ Hellier* . . . . (Signature of Witness) . . . .

Note: (1) The person making the declaration should be the principal or a manager, chief clerk, secretary, or responsible
employee.
(2) The place or country of origin of imports is that in which the goods were produced or manufactured and, in
the case of partly manufactured goods, the place or country in which any final operation, has altered to any
appreciable extent the character, composition and value of goods imported into that country.
(3) In the case of goods which have at some stage entered into the commerce of, or undergone a process of
manufacture in a foreign country, only that labour and material which are expected in or added to the goods
after their return to the exporting territory, shall be regarded as the produce or manufacture of the territory
in calculating the proportion of labour and material in the factory or works cost of the finished article.
(4) *Delete the inapplicable.

Enumerate the following charges and state whether each amount has been included in or excluded from the above selling price to purchaser:-	Amount in currency of exporting country	State if included in above selling price to purchaser
(1) Cartage to rail and/or docks . . .		
(2) Inland freight (rail or canal) and other charges to the dock area, including inland insurance . . .		
(3) Labour in packing the goods into outside packages . . .		
(4) Value of outside packages . . .		
(5) If the goods are subject to any charge by way of royalties . . .		
(6) OCEAN FREIGHT . . .		
(7) OCEAN INSURANCE . . .		
(8) Commission, establishment and other charges of a like nature . . .		
(9) Other costs, dues, charges and expenses incidental to the delivery of the articles		

State full particulars of Royalties below :—

Exhibit 15   **Chamber of Commerce certificate of origin**

Consignor: (Expéditeur:)				B 644905
MacAlasdair James & Co. Ltd. Dundee				**COPY**

EUROPEAN COMMUNITIES
(Communautes Europeennes)

Consignee: (Destinataire:)

Einzig Behr GmbH

Hamburg

CERTIFICATE OF ORIGIN
(Certificat d'origine)

Consignment by: (Expédition prévue par:)

Truck

THE LONDON CHAMBER OF COMMERCE AND INDUSTRY

THE UNDERSIGNED AUTHORITY certifies that the goods shown below
(L'AUTORITE SOUSSIGNEE certifie que les marchandises désignées ci-dessous)

Serial No.	Packages		Description of goods	Weight (1)	
	Number and kind	Marks and numbers		gross	net
3	10 cases	MAJ HAMBURG 1.- 10	Metal caps for beer bottles	950Kilos	821Kilos

originated in:

(sont originaires de:)   UNITED KINGDOM

London 1.10.19..

(Place and date of issue)

The London Chamber of Commerce and Industry

(Name, signature and stamp of competent authority)

(1) This entry may, where appropriate, be replaced by others allowing identification of the goods.
DTI/XP/1302.

Netherton and Worth Limited, Truro, Cornwall.

Exhibit 16   **Blacklist certificate**

Frank C. Strick & Company Ltd.,
12/20 Camomile Street
London EC3A 7HB

TO WHOM IT MAY CONCERN

THE S.S. NURMAHAL IS NOT SCHEDULED OR INTENDED TO CALL
AT ANY ISRAELI PORTS WHILST ON HER PRESENT VOYAGE.

WE ARE ADVISED BY HER OWNERS THAT THIS VESSEL IS NOT
ISRAELI OWNED.

TO THE BEST OF OUR KNOWLEDGE AND BELIEF THIS VESSEL
IS NOT INCLUDED IN THE ARABIAN BOYCOTT OF ISRAEL BLACKLIST.

FOR FRANK C. STRICK & COMPANY LTD.
LOADING BROKERS

Exhibit 17 **Veterinary certificate**

Export of dogs/cats to the
Federal Republic of Germany from Great Britain
Ausfuhr von Hunden/Katzen aus Gross Britannien
nach der Deutschen Bundesrepuplik

APPENDIX A

VETERINARY CERTIFICATE
TIERARZTLICHE BESCHEINIGUNG

Issued by an authorised Local Veterinary
Inspector of the Ministry
Ausgestellt von einem bevollmachtigten ortlichen
Tierarztlichen Inspektor des Ministeriums

I. Number and Identification of the animals
Zahl und Identifizierung der Tiere

Breed	Sex	Age or date of birth	Identification Marks
Rasse	Geschlecht	Alter oder Geburtsdatum	Kennzeichen
Bulldog	Male	2 years	

II. Origin of the animals
Herkunft der Tiere

1) Name and address of exporter
   Name und Anschrift des exporteurs ....LAMBERT'S DOG KENNEL.........
   GODALMING

2) Address of premises where animals ..KING'S CROSS HOUSE...........
   were examined. ....
   Anschrift der Gebaude, in denen
   die Tiere untersucht wurden

3) Name of owner MARGARET SHEEHAN...........
   Name des Eigentumers ....

III. Health Certificate
Gesundheitsbescheinigung

I HEREBY CERTIFY THAT on ...1st APRIL 19.... I examined the animal(s)
described above and found it/them to be free from signs or symptoms of
infectious or contagious disease and that I have no reason to suspect
the presence of disease.

ICH BESCHEINIGE HIERMIT DASS ich am .... das (die) oben
boschriebene(n) Tier(e) untersucht habe und dass ich es (sie) frei von
Anzeichen oder Symptomen einer anstechenden oder übertragaren Krankheit
fand und dass ich keinen Grund habe, das Vorhandensein einer Krankheit
zu vermuten.

Signature .... RCVS
Unterschrift

Name in block letters .HENRY HUTSON........
Name in Druckschrift ....

STAMP OF LOCAL   Local Veterinary Inspector
VETERINARY INSPECTOR   Ministry of Agriculture, Fisheries and Food.
Siegel des Ortlichen   Ortlicher Tierarztlicher Inspektor
Tierarztlichen Inspektors. Ministerium fur Landwirtschaft, Fischerei
                            und Nahrungsmittel
                            Address 17th DRAPERS GARDENS, LONDON.
                            Anschrift ....
Date of issue ..1.4.19.... ....
Tag der Ausfertigung

Exhibit 18   **Letter of insurance**

JIM ROBINSON (BROKERS) LTD.,   9th August 19....
1 HEYCORSE
HARTSHILL.

To whom it may concern.

LETTER OF INSURANCE

No. 44537   £389.66

Dear Sirs,

We hereby confirm that we have declared the sum of £389.66 .... under Policy .... effected
with Trevor Fielding Insurance Company Ltd.,

on a shipment of paper clips - 15 cartons

Marks and Nos.   C.V.B.
                  166 - 180
                  BARCELONA

per S.S. Rainbow
At and from London to Barcelona

We undertake to hold the amount recovered on the Policy and/or Policies, so far as any claim on
the above mentioned interest is concerned, at the disposal of the Holder of this letter, upon its being
surrendered to us, duly endorsed.

In the event of accident whereby loss or damage may result in a claim on Underwriters the Assured
are requested to communicate at once with the nearest Lloyd's Agents.
 Jim Robinson (Brokers) Ltd
Yours faithfully, *Stewart Graham*

Exhibit 19 **Insurance company's open cover certificate** *(front)*

Exporter's Reference 679-004 SPD

Norwich Union Fire Insurance Society Ltd.
Maritime Insurance Company Ltd.

NORWICH HOUSE, WATER STREET, LIVERPOOL L2 8UP.

INSURANCE CERTIFICATE No. A.R./ CODE No. 66/KK/

This is to Certify that have been issued with an Open Policy and this certificate conveys all rights of the policy (for the purpose of collecting any loss or claim) as fully as if the property were covered by a special policy direct to the holder of this certificate but if the destination of the goods is outside of the United Kingdom this certificate may require to be stamped within a given period in order to comply with the Laws of the country of destination. Notwithstanding the description of the voyage stated herein, provided the goods are at the risk of the Assured this insurance shall attach from the time of leaving the warehouse, premises or place of storage in the interior.

Conveyance: Triangle Vessel
From: Felixstowe
Via/To: Gothenburg
To: Stockholm
Insured Value / Currency: £9874.00 so valued

Marks and Numbers / Interest

1 x 12m TILT Trailer holding:

1) 6749
1/200 200x25 kg net polythene lined steel drums ANTIMONY TRICHLORIDE Class 8 UN No 1956

2) 6749
201/400 200x25 kg net polythene lined steel drums HYDROFLUORIC ACID SOLUTION 50% W/W Class 8 UN No 1974

SPECIMEN

CONDITIONS:— ALL RISKS as per current Institute Cargo Clauses. (All Risks)
Subject to Institute Replacement Clause. (as applicable)
Including War, Strikes, Riots and Civil Commotions as per current Institute Clauses.
Refer to Clauses as over.

SURVEY CLAUSE:— In the event of loss or damage which may give rise to a claim under this certificate, notice must be given immediately to to the undernoted agent/s so that he/they may appoint a Surveyor if he/they so desire.

Agents at .... are ....

....

CLAIMS In the event of a claim arising under this Certificate it is agreed that it shall be settled in accordance with English Law and Custom and shall be so settled in Liverpool or at ....

by ....

Liverpool Marine Underwriter

This Certificate Requires Endorsement.

Dated Stoke 4 July 19..

Signed

The original Certificate must be produced when claim is made and must be surrendered on payment.

Exhibit 19 **Insurance company's open cover certificate** *(back)*

<u>IMPORTANT</u>

**PROCEDURE IN THE EVENT OF LOSS OR DAMAGE FOR WHICH
UNDERWRITERS MAY BE LIABLE**

<u>LIABILITY OF CARRIERS, BAILEES OR OTHER THIRD PARTIES</u>

It is the duty of the Assured and their Agents, in all cases, to take such measures as may be reasonable for the purpose of averting or minimising a loss and to ensure that all rights against Carriers, Bailees or other third parties are properly preserved and exercised. In particular, the Assured or their Agents are required:—

1. To claim immediately on the Carriers, Port Authorities or other Bailees for any missing packages.

2. In no circumstances, except under written protest, to give clean receipts where goods are in doubtful condition.

3. When delivery is made by Container, to ensure that the Container and its seals are examined immediately by their responsible official.

   If the Container is delivered damaged or with seals broken or missing or with seals other than as stated in the shipping documents, to clause the delivery receipt accordingly and retain all defective or irregular seals for subsequent identification.

4. To apply immediately for survey by Carriers' or other Bailees' Representatives if any loss or damage be apparent and claim on the Carriers or other Bailees for any actual loss or damage found at such survey.

5. To give notice in writing to the Carriers or other Bailees within three days of delivery if the loss or damage was not apparent at the time of taking delivery.

NOTE.—The Consignees or their Agents are recommended to make themselves familiar with the Regulations of the port Authorities at the port of discharge.

SURVEY AND CLAIM SETTLEMENT

In the event of loss or damage which may involve a claim under this insurance, immediate notice of such loss or damage should be given to and a Survey Report obtained from the Office or Agent nominated herein.

In the event of any claim arising under this insurance, request for settlement should be made to the Office or Agent nominated herein.

DOCUMENTATION OF CLAIMS

To enable claims to be dealt with promptly, the Assured or their Agents are advised to submit all available supporting documents without delay, including when applicable:—

1. Original policy or certificate of insurance.

2. Original or copy shipping invoices, together with shipping specification and/or weight notes.

3. Original Bill of Lading and/or other contract of carriage.

4. Survey report or other documentary evidence to show the extent of the loss or damage.

5. Landing account and weight notes at final destination.

6. Correspondence exchanged with the Carriers and other Parties regarding their liability for the loss or damage.

The Institute clauses stated herein are those current at the date of printing of this certificate but where such clauses are revised the Institute clauses current at the time of commencement of the risk hereunder are deemed to apply.

Exhibit 20 **Lloyd's open cover certificate** *(front)*

COPY ONLY
Lloyd's Agent at ..... BOMBAY
is authorised to adjust and settle on behalf
of the Underwriters, and to purchase on
behalf of the Corporation of Lloyd's, in
accordance with Lloyd's Standing
Regulations for the Settlement of Claims
Abroad, any claim which may arise on this
Certificate.

LLOYD'S

Exporters
Reference

THIS CERTIFICATE
REQUIRES ENDORSEMENT

SL3/80/0471.

Certificate of Insurance No. C 1473/ 111344

This is to Certify that there has been deposited with the Committee of Lloyd's an Open Cover effected by *Sedgwick Forbes Marine Limited, of Lloyd's, acting on behalf of Glaxo Holdings Ltd., and/or their Subsidiary and/or Associated Companies,* with Underwriters at Lloyd's, dated the *First* day of *July,* 1977, and that the said Underwriters have undertaken to issue to *Sedgwick Forbes Marine Limited,* Policy/Policies of Marine Insurance at Lloyd's to cover, up to *£500,000* or *U.S. $1,000,000* (but £500,000 in respect of transit warehouse Colon Free Zone, Panama) *(or equivalent in other currencies)* in all by any one steamer *and/or motor vessel and/or craft or sending by air and/or post and/or conveyances, Interest in accordance with the Assured's Business on or under deck,* to be shipped on or before the Thirtieth day of *June, 1981,* from any port or ports, place or places in *the World (excluding shipments and/or sendings within the United Kingdom)* to any port or ports, place or places in *the World;* and that *Glaxo Holdings Ltd., and/or their Subsidiary and/or Associated Companies* are entitled to declare against the said Open Cover the shipments attaching thereto.

Item No. 765

Dated at Lloyd's, London, 30th October, 1978.

This document being a copy is unsigned, but the original Certificate and the duplicate thereof is here signed on behalf of the Committee of Lloyd's.

Conveyance	City of Gloucester	From	Consignor's warehouse or Domicile U.K.	
Via/To	Berkenhead	To	Consignee's warehouse anywhere in India.	INSURED VALUE/Currency: £1155.00 Sterling.

Marks and Numbers   Interest

GLAXO

BOMBAY

LETTER OF CREDIT NO. DCBOM790135

IMPORT LICENCE NO. P/D/1436502

Nos. 4181/4187G.

7 Fibre kegs.

LECITHIN SPECIAL GRADE TYPE 4213.

Marine & War £1155.00

Covering all risks whatsoever for C.I.F. value plus 10% uplift.

Cover to include Institute Cargo Clauses (All Risks), Institute War Clauses and Institute Strikes Riots and Civil Commotions Clauses.
Cover to also include theft, pilferage non-delivery, from the Consignor's warehouse to any of the Consignee's warehouse anywhere in India.

We hereby declare for Insurance under the said Cover interest as specified above so valued subject to the terms of the Standard Form of Lloyd's Marine Policy providing for the settlement of claims abroad and to the special conditions stated below and on the back hereof.

Institute Cargo Clauses (All Risks) (1.1.63) including damage by weevil but air sendings subject to Institute Air Cargo Clauses (All Risks) (excluding sendings by Post) (15.6.65) (Clause 10 deleted) as applicable including damage by weevil.
Institute War Clauses (1.7.76) or Institute War Clauses (including on-carriage by Air) (1.7.76) or Institute War Clauses (Air) (excluding sendings by Post) (1.1.71) or Institute War Clauses for the insurance of sendings by Post (1.1.71) as applicable.
Institute Strikes Riots and Civil Commotions Clauses (1.1.63) where applicable.

FURTHER CONDITIONS OVERLEAF.

Underwriters agree losses, if any, shall be payable to the order of.................. ORDER .... on surrender of this Certificate.

In the event of loss or damage which may result in a claim exceeding £150 under this Insurance, immediate notice should be given to the Lloyd's Agent at the port or place where the loss or damage is discovered in order that he may examine the goods and issue a survey report.

(Survey fee is customarily paid by claimant and included in valid claim against Underwriters.)

This Certificate not valid unless the Declaration be signed by
GLAXO HOLDINGS LTD. and/or their Subsidiary
and/or Associated Companies.

Dated at   LONDON 16th March, 1979.

For: GLAXO HOLDINGS LIMITED.
Signed

Brokers: Sedgwick Forbes Marine Limited,
Sedgwick Forbes House, 33, Aldgate High Street, London, EC3N 1AJ.

12759·0

Exhibit 20   **Lloyd's open cover certificate** *(back)*

Postal Sendings:— Institute Cargo Clauses (All Risks) (1.1.63) from time of leaving office of sender and until safely delivered as addressed
Liquid cover interests contained in barrels, casks, kegs or similar containers:— Claims for shortage or leakage, subject to an excess of 1% each container
Including risk of transhipment if any
Including risk to from and whilst at packers
Including risk from interior until finally delivered at destination
Including risk during storage prior to shipment and after arrival at destinations, including during installation
Including risk during any delay or storage during transit
Including risk at exhibitions abroad and during incidental transits
No survey required in respect of loss and/or damage not exceeding £150

■LAYS HOLDINGS LIMITED

General Average and Salvage Charges payable as provided in the contract of affreightment. In the event of the contributory value for the purpose of contribution to General Average or Salvage Charges exceeding the insured value, it is agreed that such amount shall be paid in full by Underwriters hereunder. General Average deposits payable on production of General Average deposit receipts.

UNDISCLOSED DAMAGE
It is agreed that any loss or damage discovered on opening cases and/or packages shall be deemed to have occurred during the transit insured hereunder (and irrespective of attachment of Assured's Interest) and shall be paid for accordingly unless proof conclusive to the contrary be established, it being understood that any cases and/or packages showing visible signs of damage must be opened immediately on the cessation of risk hereunder.

INSTITUTE LOCATION CLAUSE (1.1.30)
In case of loss and/or damage before shipment to the insured interest in any one locality, the Underwriter, notwithstanding anything to the contrary contained in this contract, shall not be liable in respect of any one accident or series of accidents arising out of the same event for more than his proportion of an amount up to, but not exceeding, the sum of £500,000 or U.S. $1,000,000 (or equivalent in other currencies). The conveyance of the insured interest upon interior waterways or by land transit shall not be deemed to be shipment within the meaning of this clause.

"The Institute Clauses printed or referred to herein are those current at the date of printing of this Certificate but where such Clauses are subsequently revised then the revised Institute Clauses shall apply if this insurance attaches on or after the date of the revised Clauses."

DOCUMENTATION OF CLAIMS

To enable claims to be dealt with promptly, the Assured or their Agents are advised to submit all available supporting documents without delay, including when applicable:—

1. Original policy or certificate of insurance.
2. Original or copy shipping invoices, together with shipping specification and/or weight notes.
3. Original Bill of Lading and/or other contract of carriage.
4. Survey report or other documentary evidence to show the extent of the loss or damage.
5. Landing account and weight notes at final destination.
6. Correspondence exchanged with the Carriers and other Parties regarding their liability for the loss or damage.

IMPORTANT
LIABILITY OF CARRIERS, BAILEES OR OTHER THIRD PARTIES
It is the duty of the Assured and their Agents, in all cases, to take such measures as may be reasonable for the purpose of averting or minimising a loss and to ensure that all rights against Carriers, Bailees or other third parties are properly preserved and exercised. In particular, the Assured or their Agents are required:—
1. To claim immediately on the Carriers, Port Authorities or other Bailees for any missing packages.
2. In no circumstances, except under written protest, to give clean receipts where goods are in doubtful condition.
3. When delivery is made by Container, to ensure that the Container and its seals are examined immediately by their responsible official. If the Container is delivered damaged or with seals broken or missing or with seals other than as stated in the shipping documents, to clause the delivery receipt accordingly and retain all defective or irregular seals for subsequent identification.
4. To apply immediately for survey by Carriers' or other Bailees' Representatives if any loss or damage be apparent and claim on the Carriers or other Bailees for any actual loss or damage found at such survey.
5. To give notice in writing to the Carriers or other Bailees within 3 days of delivery if the loss or damage was not apparent at the time of taking delivery.
Note.—The Consignees or their Agents are recommended to make themselves familiar with the Regulations of the Port Authorities at the port of discharge.

NOTE.—It is necessary for the Assured when they become aware of an event which is "held covered" under this insurance to give prompt notice to Underwriters and the right to such cover is dependent upon compliance with this obligation.

Printed by Lloyd's of London Printing Services Ltd.

Exhibit 21   **Insurance policy** *(front)*

Maritime Insurance Company Limited
ESTABLISHED 1864

NORWICH HOUSE   12 WATER STREET   LIVERPOOL L2 8UP
CABLES MARITIME LIVERPOOL   TELEX 629664

POLICY No.
7736MC79999

£1,950

SURVEY CLAUSE:

In the event of loss or damage which may give rise to a claim under this policy notice must be given immediately to the under-noted Agent/s so that he/they may nominate a Surveyor.

Agents at

AUCKLAND

are **A.N. Other Pty,**

21, Abercrombie

Square.

In the event of a claim arising under this policy it is agreed that it shall be settled in accordance with English Law and Custom and shall be so settled at

by...............................

AS ABOVE

INSTITUTE DANGEROUS DRUGS CLAUSE.

"It is understood and agreed that no claim under this policy will be paid in respect of drugs to which the various International Conventions relating to Opium and other dangerous drugs apply unless

(1) the drugs be expressly declared as such in the policy and the name of the country from which and the name of the country to which they are consigned shall be specifically stated in the policy

and

(2) the proof of loss is accompanied either by a licence, certificate or authorization issued by the Government of the country to which the drugs are consigned showing that the importation of the consignment into that country has been approved by that Government, or, alternatively, by a licence, certificate or authorization issued by the Government of the country from which the drugs are consigned showing that the export of the consignment to the destination stated has been approved by that Government;

and

(3) the route by which the drugs were conveyed was usual and customary"

Ref. No. 66/KK/ 499   CR

Examiner ....

WHEREAS it hath been proposed to the **Maritime Insurance Company Limited** by

XYZ Company Limited

as well in   **their**   own name as for and in the name and names of all and every other person or persons to whom the subject matter of this Policy does may or shall appertain in part or in all to make with the said Company the Insurance hereinafter mentioned and described. **Now this Policy Witnesseth** that in consideration of the said person or persons effecting this Policy promising to pay the said Company a Premium at and after the rate of

"as arranged"

per cent. for such Insurance the said Company takes upon itself the burthen of such Insurance to the amount of **One thousand, nine hundred and fifty pounds** and promises and agrees with the Insured their Executors Administrators and Assigns in all respects truly to perform and fulfil the Contract contained in this Policy. **And** it is hereby agreed and declared that the said Insurance shall be and is an Insurance (lost or not lost) from **Birmingham via Liverpool**

to **Auckland.**

ALL RISKS Subject to Institute Cargo Clauses as over.

Subject to the Replacement Clause as over, as applicable.
Including War, S.R. & C.C. Risks as per current Institute Clauses.

And it is also agreed and declared that the subject matter of this Policy as between the Insured and the said Company so far as concerns this Policy shall be and is as follows upon

62 Cases Textile Machinery.

Valued at £1950.

XYZ
AUCKLAND
1 - 62

in the Ship or Vessel called the **"Florence Nightingale" and conveyances.** whereof   is at present Master or whoever shall go for Master in the said Ship or Vessel. **And** the said Company promises and agrees that the Insurance aforesaid shall commence from the time when the Goods and Merchandise shall be laden on board the said Ship or Vessel Craft or Boat as above and continue until the said Goods and Merchandise be discharged and safely landed at as above. **And** that it shall be lawful for the said Ship or Vessel in the Voyage so Insured as aforesaid to proceed and sail to and touch and stay at any ports or places whatsoever without prejudice to this Insurance. **And** touching the Adventures and Perils which the said Company is contented to bear and does take upon itself in the Voyage so Insured as aforesaid they are of the Seas Men of War Fire Enemies Pirates Rovers Thieves Jettisons Letters of Mart and Countermart Surprisals Takings at Sea Arrests Restraints and Detainments of all Kings Princes and People of what Nation Condition or Quality soever Barratry of the Master and Mariners and of all other Perils Losses and Misfortunes that have or shall come to the Hurt Detriment or Damage of the aforesaid subject matter of this Insurance or any part thereof. **And** in case of any Loss or Misfortune it shall be lawful to the Insured their Factors Servants and Assigns to sue labour and travel for in and about the Defence Safeguard and Recovery of the aforesaid subject matter of this Insurance or any part thereof without prejudice to this Insurance the charges whereof the said Company will bear in proportion to the sum hereby Insured. **And** it is expressly declared and agreed that the acts of the Insurer or Insured in Recovering Saving or Preserving the Property Insured shall not be considered a waiver or acceptance of abandonment. **And** it is declared and agreed that Corn Fish Salt Fruit Flour and Seed are warranted free from average unless general or the ship be stranded sunk or burnt and that Sugar Tobacco Hemp Flax Hides and Skins are warranted free from average under Five Pounds per centum and that all other Goods are warranted free from average under Three Pounds per centum unless general or the ship be stranded sunk or burnt.

1. Warranted free of capture, seizure, arrest, restraint or detainment, and the consequences thereof or of any attempt thereat; also from the consequences of hostilities or warlike operations, whether there be a declaration of war or not; but this warranty shall not exclude collision, contact with any fixed or floating object (other than a mine or torpedo), stranding, heavy weather or fire unless caused directly (and independently of the nature of the voyage or service which the vessel concerned or, in the case of a collision, any other vessel involved therein, is performing) by a hostile act by or against a belligerent power; and for the purpose of this warranty "power" includes any authority maintaining naval, military or air forces in association with a power.

Further warranted free from the consequences of civil war, revolution, rebellion, insurrection, or civil strife arising therefrom or piracy.

2. Warranted free of loss or damage
    (a) caused by strikers, locked-out workmen or persons taking part in labour disturbances, riots or civil commotions;
    (b) resulting from strikes, lock-out labour disturbances, riots or civil commotions.

3. (a) Should the risks excluded by Clause 1 (F.C. & S. Clause) be reinstated in this policy by deletion of the said clause or should the risks or any of them mentioned in that clause or the risks of mines, torpedoes, bombs or other engines of war be insured under this policy, Clause (b) below shall become operative and anything contained in this contract which is inconsistent with Clause (b) or which affords more extensive protection against the aforesaid risks than that afforded by the Institute War Clauses relevant to the particular form of transit covered by this insurance is null and void.
    (b) This policy is warranted free of any claim based upon loss of, or frustration of, the insured voyage or adventure caused by arrests restraints or detainments of Kings Princes Peoples Usurpers or persons attempting to usurp power.

In Witness whereof the undersigned on behalf of the said Company has hereunto set his hand in **LIVERPOOL**

the   **twelfth**   day of   **July**   19 **77**

.... UNDERWRITER

DELETED

Exhibit 21 **Insurance policy** *(back)*

REPLACEMENT CLAUSE.

In the event of loss of or damage to any part or parts of an insured machine or article caused by a peril covered by the Policy the sum recoverable shall not exceed the cost of replacement or repair of such part or parts plus charges for forwarding and refitting, if incurred, but excluding duty unless the full duty is included in the amount insured, in which case loss, if any, sustained by payment of additional duty shall also be recoverable. Provided always that in no case shall the liability of Underwriters exceed the insured value of the complete machine or article.

IMPORTANT

PROCEDURE IN THE EVENT OF LOSS OR DAMAGE FOR WHICH UNDERWRITERS MAY BE LIABLE

LIABILITY OF CARRIERS, BAILEES OR OTHER THIRD PARTIES

It is the duty of the Assured and their Agents, in all cases, to take such measures as may be reasonable for the purpose of averting or minimising a loss and to ensure that all rights against Carriers, Bailees or other third parties are properly preserved and exercised. In particular, the Assured or their Agents are required:—

1. To claim immediately on the Carriers, Port Authorities or other Bailees for any missing packages.

2. In no circumstances, except under written protest, to give clean receipts where goods are in doubtful condition.

3. When delivery is made by Container, to ensure that the Container and its seals are examined immediately by their responsible official. If the Container is delivered damaged or with seals broken or missing or with seals other than as stated in the shipping documents, to clause the delivery receipt accordingly and retain all defective or irregular seals for subsequent identification.

4. To apply immediately for survey by Carriers' or other Bailees' Representatives if any loss or damage be apparent and claim on the Carriers or other Bailees for any actual loss or damage found at such survey.

5. To give notice in writing to the Carriers or other Bailees within three days of delivery if the loss or damage was not apparent at the time of taking delivery.

NOTE.—The Consignees or their Agents are recommended to make themselves familiar with the Regulations of the port Authorities at the port of discharge.

SURVEY AND CLAIM SETTLEMENT

In the event of loss or damage which may involve a claim under this insurance, immediate notice of such loss or damage should be given to and a Survey Report obtained from the Office or Agent nominated herein.

In the event of any claim arising under this insurance, request for settlement should be made to the Office or Agent nominated herein.

DOCUMENTATION OF CLAIMS

To enable claims to be dealt with promptly, the Assured or their Agents are advised to submit all available supporting documents without delay, including when applicable:—

1. Original policy or certificate of insurance.

2. Original or copy shipping invoices, together with shipping specification and/or weight notes.

3. Original Bill of Lading and/or other contract of carriage.

4. Survey report or other documentary evidence to show the extent of the loss or damage.

5. Landing account and weight notes at final destination.

6. Correspondence exchanged with the Carriers and other Parties regarding their liability for the loss or damage.

1/1/63

INSTITUTE CARGO CLAUSES (ALL RISKS).

(Transit Clause — Incorporating Warehouse to Warehouse Clause.)

1. This insurance attaches from the time the goods leave the warehouse or place of storage at the place named in the policy for the commencement of the transit, continues during the ordinary course of transit and terminates either on delivery
   (a) to the Consignees' or other final warehouse or place of storage at the destination named in the policy,
   (b) to any other warehouse or place of storage, whether prior to or at the destination named in the policy, which the Assured elect to use either
      (i) for storage other than in the ordinary course of transit
      or (ii) for allocation or distribution,
   or (c) on the expiry of 60 days after completion of discharge overside of the goods hereby insured from the overseas vessel at the final port of discharge,
   whichever shall first occur.
   If, after discharge overside from the overseas vessel at the final port of discharge, but prior to termination of this insurance, the goods are to be forwarded to a destination other than that to which they are insured hereunder, this insurance, whilst remaining subject to termination as provided for above, shall not extend beyond the commencement of transit to such other destination.
   This insurance shall remain in force (subject to termination as provided for above and to the provisions of Clause 2 below) during delay beyond the control of the Assured, any deviation, forced discharge, reshipment or transhipment and during any variation of the adventure arising from the exercise of a liberty granted to shipowners or charterers under the contract of affreightment.

(Termination of Adventure Clause.)

2. If owing to circumstances beyond the control of the Assured either the contract of affreightment is terminated at a port or place other than the destination named therein or the adventure is otherwise terminated before delivery of the goods as provided for in Clause 1 above, then, subject to prompt notice being given to Underwriters and to an additional premium if required, this insurance shall remain in force until either
   (i) the goods are sold and delivered at such port or place, or, unless otherwise specially agreed, until the expiry of 60 days after completion of discharge overside of the goods hereby insured from the overseas vessel at such port or place, whichever shall first occur,
   or (ii) if the goods are forwarded within the said period of 60 days (or any agreed extension thereof) to the destination named in the policy or to any other destination, until terminated in accordance with the provisions of Clause 1 above.

(Craft, &c. Clause.)

3. Including transit by craft raft or lighter to or from the vessel. Each craft raft or lighter to be deemed a separate insurance. The Assured are not to be prejudiced by any agreement exempting lightermen from liability.

(Change of Voyage Clause.)

4. Held covered at a premium to be arranged in case of change of voyage or of any omission or error in the description of the interest vessel or voyage.

(All Risks Clause.)

5. This insurance is against all risks of loss of or damage to the subject-matter insured but shall in no case be deemed to extend to cover loss damage or expense proximately caused by delay or inherent vice or nature of the subject-matter insured. Claims recoverable hereunder shall be payable irrespective of percentage.

(Constructive Total Loss Clause.)

6. No claim for Constructive Total Loss shall be recoverable hereunder unless the goods are reasonably abandoned either on account of their actual total loss appearing to be unavoidable or because the cost of recovering, reconditioning and forwarding the goods to the destination to which they are insured would exceed their value on arrival.

(G.A. Clause.)

7. General Average and Salvage Charges payable according to Foreign Statement or to York-Antwerp Rules if in accordance with the contract of affreightment.

(Seaworthiness Admitted Clause.)

8. The seaworthiness of the vessel as between the Assured and Underwriters is hereby admitted.
   In the event of loss the Assured's right of recovery hereunder shall not be prejudiced by the fact that the loss may have been attributable to the wrongful act or misconduct of the shipowners or their servants, committed without the privity of the Assured.

(Bailee Clause.)

9. It is the duty of the Assured and their Agents, in all cases, to take such measures as may be reasonable for the purpose of averting or minimising a loss and to ensure that all rights against carriers, bailees or other third parties are properly preserved and exercised.

(Not to Inure Clause.)

10. This insurance shall not inure to the benefit of the carrier or other bailee.

("Both to Blame Collision" Clause.)

11. Where the Assured are liable to indemnify the Assured against each proportion of liability under the contract of affreightment "Both to Blame Collision" Clause as is in respect of a loss recoverable hereunder, the Underwriters agree to notify the Assured under this said Clause the Underwriters agree to defend the Assured against such claim.

(F.C. & S. Clause.)

12. Warranted free of capture, seizure, arrest, restraint or detainment, and the consequences thereof or of any attempt thereat; also from the consequences of hostilities or warlike operations, whether there be a declaration of war or not; but this warranty shall not exclude collision, contact with any fixed or floating object (other than a mine or torpedo), stranding, heavy weather or fire unless caused directly (and independently of the nature of the voyage or service which the vessel concerned or, in the case of a collision, any other vessel involved therein, is performing) by a hostile act by or against a belligerent power; and for the purpose of this warranty "power" includes any authority maintaining naval, military or air forces in association with a power.
   Further warranted free from the consequences of civil war, revolution, rebellion, insurrection, or civil strife arising therefrom, or piracy.
   Should Clause No. 12 be deleted, the relevant current Institute War Clauses shall be deemed to form part of this Insurance.

(F.S.R. & C.C. Clause.)

13. Warranted free of loss or damage
   (a) caused by strikers, locked-out workmen, or persons taking part in labour disturbances, riots or civil commotions;
   (b) resulting from strikes, lock-outs, labour disturbances, riots or civil commotions.
   Should Clause No. 13 be deleted, the relevant current Institute Strikes Riots and Civil Commotions Clauses shall be deemed to form part of this insurance.

(Reasonable Despatch Clause.)

NOTE.—It is necessary for the Assured when they become aware of an event which is "held covered" under this insurance to give prompt notice to Underwriters and the right to such cover is dependent upon compliance with this obligation.

Exhibit 22   **Air waybill/air consignment note**

125- 8195 0411	Airport of Departure	Execution Date	TC			For Carrier use only		125- 8195 0411	
HR						Flight/Day	Flight/Day		

Airport of Departure (Address of First Carrier) and Requested Routing	Airport of Destination	Flight/Day	Flight/Day	**Air Waybill**
LONDON	CARACAS			(Air Consignment note)

Not negotiable

By First Carrier	To	By	To	By	Consignee's Name and Address

British airways
Issued by British Airways
Member of IATA

Copies 1, 2 and 3 of this Air Waybill are originals and have the same validity.

JOSE MARTINEZ EGA
CALLE FLORIDA 6
CARACAS
VENEZUELA

It is agreed that the goods described herein are accepted in apparent good order and condition (except as noted) for carriage **subject to the conditions of contract on the reverse hereof. The shipper's attention is drawn to the notice concerning carriers' limitation of liability.** Shipper may increase such limitation of liability by declaring a higher value for carriage and paying a supplemental charge if required.

Shipper's Account Number	Shipper's Name and Address
557P	

The shipper certifies that the particulars on the face hereof are correct. The shipper also certifies that the contents of this consignment are properly described by name and have no **hazardous characteristics** as defined in the International Air Transport Association's Restricted Articles Regulations.

C. Graham

Signature of Shipper or his Agent

P. PUGH TEXTILES LTD
555 KING STREET
MANCHESTER

The shipper certifies that the particulars on the face hereof are correct, and that insofar as any part of the consignment contains **restricted articles,** such part is properly described by name and is in proper condition for carriage by air according to the International Air Transport Association's Restricted Articles Regulations.

C. Graham

Signature of Shipper or his Agent

Issuing Carrier's Agent, Account No.	Issuing Carrier's Agent, Name and City
884332DFT	

Signature of Issuing Carrier or its Agent

Agent's IATA Code	BA HEATHROW

Date	Place
5.5.19	LONDON

Currency	Declared Value for Carriage	Declared Value for Customs

Weight Charge and Valuation Charge		All Other Charges at Origin		Accounting Information
Prepaid	Collect	Prepaid	Collect	

No. of Packages RCP	Actual Gross Weight	kg lb	Rate Class / Commodity Item No.	Chargeable Weight	Rate/Charge	Total	Nature and Quantity of Goods (Incl. Dimensions or Volume)
6	131Kgs		9969	150Kgs	1.40	210.00	SIX PARCELS COTTON PIECE GOODS (GENEROS DE ALGODON)
						210.00	

	Prepaid Weight Charge	Prepaid Valuation Charge	Due Carrier	Total other Prepaid Charges	Due Agent	Total Prepaid	For Carrier's Use Only at Destination
PREPAID				10.50		10.50	

AWB Fee and Code	Clearance and Handling	Cartage	Other Charges (except Weight Charge and Valuation Charge) →	Collect Charges in Destination Currency

Disbursements	Disbursement Fee		Total Charges

	Collect Weight Charge	Collect Valuation Charge	Due Carrier	Total Other Collect Charges	Due Agent		Total Collect
COLLECT							210.00

CA Number	Attached EEC Transit Documents	Type	Customs Reference Number	In Envelope
				Yes / No

Handling Information

T327(15th)

Original 3 - (For Shipper)   125- 8195 0411

Exhibit 23   **Parcel post document** *(1)*

	Serial or Origin Number (if any)	FULL NAME AND ADDRESS AS SHOWN ON THE PARCEL	Postage Paid
1		*UNITED OVERSEAS BANKING CORPORATION*	
2		*LTD.,*	
3	0396	*SELEGIE ROAD*	
4	GREAT YARMOUTH 9	*SINGAPORE 17*	
5		*A/c ISLAND ENGINE TRADERS*	
6	0397	1 PARCEL R 5448/1	3.45
7	GREAT YARMOUTH 9	1 — " — R — " — 2	3.45
8		1 — " — R — " — 3	3.45
9	0398	1 — " — R — " — 4	3.45
0	GREAT YARMOUTH 9	1 — " — R — " — 5	3.45
1		1 — " — R — " — 6	3.45
2	0399		
3	GREAT YARMOUTH 9		
4			
5	0400		
6	GREAT YARMOUTH 9	MARKED :-	
7		IET	
8	0401	720 - 725	
9	GREAT YARMOUTH 9	SINGAPORE	
0		MADE IN U.K.	

Exhibit 24 **Parcel post document** *(2)*

To be used for packages for which the NON-ADHESIVE form of customs declaration is required. The corresponding customs declaration must be attached to the packages in such a way as to be readily available for inspection at the Post Office of posting.

VALUE ADDED TAX
Certificate of Posting of Goods Exported

VAT 443

1. Name and Address of sender	2. Sender's reference, if any
Vincent, Neville & Dewberry Ltd 117 Fox Lane London EC2P 2AH	345/UPU

3. Consignee	4. Insert 'X' if the contents are a gift ☐ a sample of merchandise ☐
Tireni Johnson Books Main Street George Town Grand Cayman B.W.I.	5. The undersigned certifies that the particulars given in this declaration are correct. 6. Place and date London 27.3.19...

7. Observations	8. Signature *A Green.*
	9. Country of origin of the goods UK	10. Country of destination Grand Cayman
		11. Total Gross weight 3.8 kilos

12. Number of items	13. Detailed description of contents	14. Tariff No.	15. Net weight Kg / g	16. Value
Three	30 x Life among the conch		3 / 500	

All unused space in columns 12 to 16 to be ruled through before presentation to the Post Office clerk.

CERTIFICATE OF POSTING

...Three...............(number in words) parcel(s) bearing a Declaration as above and the approved label form VAT 444 "Value Added Tax—Goods Exported by Post" *has/have this day been posted for despatch *abroad/to the Channel Islands/to the Republic of Ireland.

*Delete as necessary

Stamp of Office of Posting

LONDON 15 6 9 APR

Initialled .../K.G.H........................

(Officer of the Post Office)

Exhibit 25   **FIATA-FCR forwarder's certificate of receipt**

Suppliers or Forwarders Principals	FIATA FCR	
Karalex & Co Ltd Benders Court Priestly Road Leeds	Emblem of National Association	**No.** 25 Country Code
	Forwarders Certificate of Receipt	
	ORIGINAL	Forw. Ref.

Consignee

Magma Stemigan
Vesterkirke Gade
Copenhagen
Denmark

Marks and number	Numbers and kind of packages	Description of goods	Gross weight	Measurement
MS COPENHAGEN 335-337	THREE CRATES	SYLOMITE RESIN	45 kg	

Contents, weight and measurement according to senders declaration

We certify having assumed control of the above mentioned consignment in external apparent good order and condition

      at the disposal of the consignee ☐

with irrevocable instructions*

      to be forwarded to the consignee ☒

* Forwarding instructions can only be cancelled or altered if the original Certificate is surrendered to us, and then only provided we are still in a position to comply with such cancellation or alteration.

Instructions authorizing disposal by a third party can only be cancelled or altered if the original Certificate of Receipt is surrendered to us, and then only provided we have not yet received instructions under the original authority.

Special remarks

Instructions as to freight and charges   Prepaid

Place and date of issue

Leeds 9.6.19..

Stamp and authorized signature
East Riding Forwarders Ltd

Taylor

Exhibit 26 **FIATA-FCT forwarder's certificate of transport**

The goods and instructions are accepted and dealt with subject to the General Conditions printed overleaf.

COPYRIGHT FIATA / Zurich - Switzerland 1.79

Text authorized by FIATA.

Suppliers or Forwarders Principals: Gillian Fashion House 62a Bond Street London	**FIATA FCT** Emblem of National Association **Forwarders** No. 26 Country Code **Certificate of Transport** **ORIGINAL** Forw. Ref.

Consigned to order of:

Mireille
3 Place du Tetre
Montmarte Paris

Notify address:

Conveyance: TWC vehicle **from/via:** London

Destination: Paris

Marks and numbers	Numbers and kind of packages	Description of goods	Gross weight	Measurement
GFH PARIS 1-2	Two cases	Fashion goods	12kg	0.025

specimen

Contents, weight and measurement according to senders declaration

Acceptance of this document or the invocation of rights arising therefrom acknowledges the validity of the following conditions, regulations and exceptions also of the trading conditions printed overleaf, except where the latter conflict with conditions 1-6 below.
1. The undersigned are authorized to enter into contracts with carriers and others involved in the execution of the transport subject to the latter's usual terms and conditions.
2. The undersigned do not act as Carriers but as Forwarders. In consequence they are only responsible for the careful selection of third parties, instructed by them, subject to the conditions of Clause 3 hereunder.
3. The undersigned are responsible for delivery of the goods to the holder of this document through the intermediary of a delivery agent of their choice. They are not responsible for acts or omissions of Carriers involved in the execution of the transport or of other third parties. The undersigned Forwarders will, on request, subrogate their claims against Carriers and other parties.
4. Insurance of the goods will only be effected upon express instructions in writing.
5. Unforeseen and/or unforeseeable circumstances entitle the undersigned to deviate from the envisaged route and/or method of transport.
6. Unforeseen and/or unforeseeable disbursements and charges are for the account of the goods.

Insurance through the intermediary or the undersigned Forwarders

☒ Not covered

☐ Covered according to the attached Insurance Policy/Certificate.

All disputes shall be governed by the law and within the exclusive jurisdiction of the courts at the place of issue.

For delivery of the goods please apply to:

Speditions S.A.

Freight and charges prepaid to: Paris

thence for account of goods, lost or not lost.

We, the Undersigned Forwarders in accordance with the instructions of our Principals, have taken charge of the abovementioned goods in good external external condition at: London ....

for despatch and delivery as stated above or order against surrender of this document properly endorsed.

In witness thereof the Undersigned Forwarders have signed .... originals of this FCT document, which are of this tenor and bear the same date. When one of these has been accomplished, the others will lose their validity.

Place and date of issue

London 5.5.19..

Stamp and authorized signature

City Forwarders Ltd

Exhibit 27 **FIATA–combined transport bill of lading** *(front)*

Shipper			
P. Spiro Associates Limited	Emblem of National Association	**FBL** **No.** 27	Country Code
		NEGOTIABLE FIATA COMBINED TRANSPORT BILL OF LADING issued subject to ICC Uniform Rules for a Combined Transport Document (ICC publication 298).	**ICC**

Consigned to order of

Graham Harmonics (Pty) Limited

Notify address

Place of Receipt

CANTERBURY

Place of Delivery

SYDNEY

Marks and numbers	Number and kind of packages	Description of goods	Gross weight	Measurement
FIT CHAPS 1 - 10	10 cases Musical instruments		90 kg	

specimen

according to the declaration of the merchant

The goods and instructions are accepted and dealt with subject to the Standard Conditions printed overleaf.

Taken in charge in apparent good order and condition, unless otherwise noted herein, at the place of receipt for transport and delivery as mentioned above.

One of these Combined Transport Bills of Lading must be surrendered duly endorsed in exchange for the goods. In Witness whereof the original Combined Transport Bills of Lading all of this tenor and date have been signed in the number stated below, one of which being accomplished the other (s) to be void.

Freight amount		Freight payable at Origin	Place and date of issue LONDON 26.2.19..
Cargo Insurance through the undersigned ☒ not covered ☐ Covered according to attached Policy		Number of Original FBL's TWO	Stamp and authorized signature Kent Coast Forwarding Ltd
For delivery of goods please apply to:	Tierney Carriers Sydney		

Exhibit 27 FIATA– combined transport bill of lading *(back)*

Standard Conditions (1978) governing FIATA COMBINED TRANSPORT BILLS OF LADING

Definitions «Merchant» means and includes the Shipper, the Consignor, the Consignee, the Holder of this Bill of Lading, the Receiver and the Owner of the Goods. «The Freight Forwarder» means the issuer of this Bill of Lading as named on the face of it.

The headings set forth below are for easy reference only.

CONDITIONS

1. **Applicability**
Notwithstanding the heading «Combined Transport Bill of Lading», the provisions set out and referred to in this document shall also apply if the transport as described on the face of the Bill of Lading, contrary to the original intention of the parties, is performed by one mode of transport only.

2. **Issuance of the «Combined Transport Bill of Lading»**

2.1 By the issuance of this «Combined Transport Bill of Lading», the Freight Forwarder:
a) undertakes to perform and/or in his own name to procure the performance of the entire transport, from the place at which the goods are taken in charge to the place designated for delivery in this Bill of Lading.
b) assumes liability as set out in these Conditions.

2.2 For the purposes and subject to the provisions of this Bill of Lading, the Freight Forwarder shall be responsible for the acts and omissions of any person of whose services he makes use for the performance of the contract evidenced by this Bill of Lading.

3. **Negotiability and title to the goods**

3.1 By accepting this Bill of Lading the Merchant and his transferees agree with the Freight Forwarder that, unless it is marked «non-negotiable», it shall constitute title to the goods and the holder, by endorsement of this Bill of Lading, shall be entitled to receive or to transfer the goods herein mentioned.

3.2 This Bill of Lading shall be prima facie evidence of the taking in charge by the Freight Forwarder of the goods as herein described. However, proof to the contrary shall not be admissible when this Bill of Lading has been negotiated or transferred for valuable consideration to a third party acting in good faith.

4. **Dangerous Goods and Indemnity**

4.1 The Merchant shall comply with rules which are mandatory according to the national law or by reason of international Convention, relating to the carriage of goods of a dangerous nature, and shall in any case inform the Freight Forwarder in writing of the exact nature of the danger, before goods of a dangerous nature are taken in charge by the Freight Forwarder and indicate to him, if need be, the precautions to be taken.

4.2 If the Merchant fails to provide such information and the Freight Forwarder is unaware of the dangerous nature of the goods and the necessary precautions to be taken and if, at any time, they are deemed to be a hazard to life or property, they may at any place be unloaded, destroyed or rendered harmless, as circumstances may require, without compensation, and the Merchant shall be liable for all loss, damage, delay or expenses arising out of their being taken in charge, or their carriage, or of any service incidental thereto.
The burden of proving the Freight Forwarder knew the exact nature of the danger constituted by the carriage of the said goods shall rest upon the person entitled to the goods.

4.3 If any goods shipped with the knowledge of the Freight Forwarder as to their dangerous nature shall become a danger to the vehicle or cargo, they may in like manner be unloaded or landed at any place or destroyed or rendered innocuous by the Freight Forwarder, without liability on the part of the Freight Forwarder, except to General Average, if any.

5. **Description of Goods and Merchant's Packing**

5.1 The Consignor shall be deemed to have guaranteed to the Freight Forwarder the accuracy, at the time the goods were taken in charge by the Freight Forwarder, of the description of the goods, marks, number, quantity, weight and/or volume as furnished by him, and the Consignor shall indemnify the Freight Forwarder against all loss, damage and expenses arising or resulting from inaccuracies in or inadequacy of such particulars. The right of the Freight Forwarder to such indemnity shall in no way limit his responsibility and liability under this Bill of Lading to any person other than the Consignor.

5.2 Without prejudice to Clause 6 (A) (2) (c), the Merchant shall be liable for any loss, damage or injury caused by faulty or insufficient packing of goods or by faulty loading or packing within containers and trailers and on flats when such loading or packing has been performed by the Merchant or on behalf of the Merchant by a person other than the Freight Forwarder, or by the defect or unsuitability of the containers, trailers or flats, when supplied by the Merchant, and shall indemnify the Freight Forwarder against any additional expenses so caused.

6. **Extent of Liability**

A. 1) The Freight Forwarder shall be liable for loss of or damage to the goods occurring between the time when he takes the goods into his charge and the time of delivery.

2) The Freight Forwarder shall, however, be relieved of liability for any loss or damage if such loss or damage was caused by:
a) an act or omission of the Merchant, or person other than the Freight Forwarder acting on behalf of the Merchant or from whom the Freight Forwarder took the goods in charge;
b) insufficiency or defective condition of the packaging or marks and/or numbers;
c) handling, loading, stowage or unloading of the goods by the Merchant or any person acting on behalf of the Merchant;
d) inherent vice of the goods;
e) strike, lockout, stoppage or restraint of labour, the consequences of which the Freight Forwarder could not avoid by the exercice of reasonable diligence;
f) any cause or event which the Freight Forwarder could not avoid and the consequences whereof he could not prevent by the exercise of reasonable diligence;
g) a nuclear incident if the operator of a nuclear installation or a person acting for him is liable for this damage under an applicable international Convention or national law governing liability in respect of nuclear energy.

3) The burden of proving that the loss or damage was due to one or more of the above causes or events shall rest upon the Freight Forwarder.
When the Freight Forwarder establishes that, in the circumstances of the case, the loss or damage could be attributed to one or more of the causes or events specified in b) to d) above, it shall be presumed that it was so caused. The claimant shall, however, be entitled to prove that the loss or damage was not, in fact, caused wholly or partly by one or more of these causes or events.

B. When in accordance with clause 6. A.1 the Freight Forwarder is liable to pay compensation in respect of loss or damage to the goods and the stage of transport where the loss or damage occurred is known, the liability of the Freight Forwarder in respect of such loss or damage shall be determined by the provisions contained in any international Convention or national law, which provisions
(i) cannot be departed from by private contract, to the detriment of the claimant, and
(ii) would have applied if the Claimant had made a separate and direct contract with the Freight Forwarder in respect of the particular stage of transport where the loss or damage occurred and received as evidence thereof any particular document which must be issued in order to make such international convention or national law applicable.

7. **Paramount Clause**
The Hague Rules contained in the International Convention for the unification of certain rules relating to Bills of Lading, dated Brussels 25th August 1924, or in those countries where they are already in force the Hague-Visby Rules contained in the Protocol of Brussels, dated February 23rd 1968, as enacted in the Country of Shipment, shall apply to all carriage of goods by sea and, where no mandatory international or national law applies, to the carriage of goods by inland waterways also, and such provisions shall apply to all goods whether carried on deck or under deck.

8. **Limitation Amount**

8.1 When the Freight Forwarder is liable for compensation in respect of loss of or damage to the goods, such compensation shall be calculated by reference to the value of such goods at the place and time they are delivered to the Consignee in accordance with the contract or should have been so delivered.

8.2 The value of the goods shall be fixed according to the current commodity exchange price, or, if there be no such price, according to the current market price, or, if there be no commodity exchange price or current market price, by reference to the normal value of goods of the same kind and quality.

8.3 Compensation shall not, however, exceed 30 Francs («Franc» meaning a unit consisting of 65,5 mgs of gold of millesimal fineness 900) per kilo of gross weight of the goods lost or damaged, unless, with the consent of the Freight Forwarder, the Merchant has declared a higher value for the goods and such higher value has been stated in the CT Bill of Lading, in which case such higher value shall be the limit. However, the Freight Forwarder shall not, in any case, be liable for an amount greater than the actual loss to the person entitled to make the claim.

9. **Delay, Consequential Loss, etc.**
Arrival times are not guaranteed by the Freight Forwarder. If the Freight Forwarder is held liable in respect of delay, consequential loss or damage other than loss of or damage to the goods, the liability of the Freight Forwarder shall be limited to double the freight for the transport covered by this Bill of Lading, or the value of the goods as determined in Clause 8, whichever is the less.

10. **Defences**

10.1 The defences and limits of liability provided for in these Conditions shall apply in any action against the Freight Forwarder for loss of or damage or delay to the goods whether the action be founded in contract or in tort.

10.2 The Freight Forwarder shall not be entitled to the benefit of the limitation of liability provided for in paragraph 3 of Clause 8 if it is proved that the loss or damage resulted from an act or omission of the Freight Forwarder done with intent to cause damage or recklessly and with knowledge that damage would probably result.

11. **Liability of Servants and Sub-contractors**

11.1 If an action for loss of or damage to the goods is brought against a person referred to in paragraph 2 of Clause 2, such person shall be entitled to avail himself of the defences and limits of liability which the Freight Forwarder is entitled to invoke under these Conditions.

11.2 However, if it is proved that the loss or damage resulted from an act or omission of this person, done with intent to cause damage or recklessly and with knowledge that damage would probably result, such person shall not be entitled to benefit of limitation of liability provided for in paragraph 3 of Clause 8.

11.3 Subject to the provisions of paragraph 2 of Clause 10 and paragraph 2 of this Clause, the aggregate of the amounts recoverable from the Freight Forwarder and the persons referred to in paragraph 2 of Clause 2 shall in no case exceed the limits provided for in these Conditions.

12. **Method and Route of Transportation**
The Freight Forwarder reserves to himself a reasonable liberty as to the means, route and procedure to be followed in the handling, storage and transportation of goods.

13. **Delivery**
If delivery of the goods or any part thereof is not taken by the Merchant, at the time and place when and where the Freight Forwarder is entitled to call upon the Merchant to take delivery thereof, the Freight Forwarder shall be entitled to store the goods or the part thereof at the sole risk of the Merchant, where upon the liability of the Freight Forwarder in respect of the goods or that part thereof stored as aforesaid (as the case may be) shall wholly cease and the cost of such storage (if paid by or payable by the Freight Forwarder or any agent or sub-contractor of the Freight Forwarder) shall forthwith upon demand be paid by the Merchant to the Freight Forwarder.

14. **Freight and Charges**

14.1 Freight shall be paid in cash without discount and, whether prepayable or payable at destination, shall be considered as earned on receipt of the goods and not to be returned or relinquished in any event.

14.2 Freight and all other amounts mentioned in this Bill of Lading are to be paid in the currency named in the Bill of Lading or, at the Freight Forwarder's option in the currency of the country of dispatch or destination at the highest rate of exchange for bankers sight bills current for prepayable freight on the day of dispatch and for freight payable at destination on the day when the Merchant is notified of arrival of the goods there or on the date of withdrawal of the delivery order, whichever rate is the higher, or at the option of the Freight Forwarder on the date of the Bill of Lading.

14.3 All dues, taxes and charges or other expenses in connection with the goods shall be paid by the Merchant.

14.4 The Merchant shall reimburse the Freight Forwarder in proportion to the amount of freight for any costs for deviation or delay or any other increase of costs of whatever nature caused by war, warlike operations, epidemics, strikes, government directions or force majeure.

14.5 The Merchant warrants the correctness of the declaration of contents, insurance, weight, measurements or value of the goods but the Freight Forwarder reserves the right to have the contents inspected and the weight, measurements or value verified. If on such inspection it is found the declaration is not correct it is agreed that a sum equal either to five times the difference between the correct figure and the freight charged, or to double the correct freight less the freight charged, whichever sum is the smaller, shall be payable as liquidated damage to the Freight Forwarder for his inspection costs and losses of freight on other goods notwithstanding any other sum having been stated on the Bill of Lading as freight payable.

15. **Lien**
The Freight Forwarder shall have a lien on the goods for any amount due under this Bill of Lading including storage fees and for the cost of recovering same, and may enforce such lien in any reasonable manner which he may think fit.

16. **General Average**
The Merchant shall indemnify the Freight Forwarder in respect of any claims of a General Average nature which may be made on him and shall provide such security as may be required by the Freight Forwarder in this connection.

17. **Notice**
Unless notice of loss of or damage to the goods and the general nature of it be given in writing to the Freight Forwarder or the persons referred to in paragraph 2 of Clause 2, at the place of delivery before or at the time of the removal of the goods into the custody of the person entitled to delivery thereof under this Bill of Lading, or if the loss or damage be no apparent, within seven consecutive days thereafter, such removal shall be prima facie evidence of the delivery by the Freight Forwarder of the goods as described in this Bill of Lading.

18. **Non delivery**
Failure to effect delivery within 90 days after the expiry of a time limit agreed and expressed in a CT Bill of Lading or, where no time limit is agreed and so expressed, failure to effect delivery within 90 days after the time it would be reasonable to allow for diligent completion of the combined transport operation shall, in the absence of evidence to the contrary, give to the party entitled to receive delivery, the right to treat the goods as lost.

19. **Time Bar**
The Freight Forwarder shall be discharged of all liability under the rules of these Conditions, unless suit is brought within nine months after
(i) the delivery of the goods, or
(ii) the date when the goods should have been delivered, or
(iii) the date when in accordance with Clause 18, failure to deliver the goods would, in the absence of evidence to the contrary, give to the party entitled to receive delivery, the right to treat the goods as lost.

20. **Jurisdiction**
Actions against the Freight Forwarder may only be instituted in the country where the Freight Forwarder has his principal place of business and shall be decided according to the law of such country.

Exhibit 28   **House bill of lading** *(front)*

SHIPPED by or RECEIVED for shipment from in apparent good order and condition, except as noted in the Particulars.

Shipper

Marshall & Co. Limited

(hereinafter called the Shipper)

Consignee (If 'Order' State Notify Party and Address)

Carl Delicat AG
Frederick Ebert Anlage 46
Frankfurt AM
West Germany

Notify Party and Address (leave blank if stated above)

Customs Assigned No.	B/Lading Number
	28

Shipper's Reference

3//49M

Forwarder's Reference

BG39776a

Conveyance	Point of Loading
	DUDLEY
Point of Discharge	Destination
FRANKFURT AM	FRANKFURT AM

HOUSE BILL OF LADING

Contents, weight, value and measurement according to sender's declaration

Marks, Nos. and Container No.	No. and Kind of Packages; Description of Goods	Gross Weight (Kg)	Cube (M³)
M & C 1 - 40 Container 669	40 cartons dental supplies	756kg	

S P E C I M E N

This House Bill of Lading shall have effect subject to the Standard Trading Conditions of the Institute of Freight Forwarders Ltd, as printed overleaf, and to the following:—

1. The Company is authorised to enter into contracts with Carriers and others involved in the execution of the transport subject to the latter's terms and conditions.

2. The Company does not act as Carriers but as Forwarding Agents. In consequence they are only responsible for the careful selection of third parties, instructed by them, subject to the conditions of Clause 3 hereunder.

3. The Company is responsible for delivery of the goods to the holder of this document through the intermediary of a delivery correspondent of their choice, subject to Clause 18 overleaf. The Company is not responsible for acts or omissions of Carriers involved in the execution of the transport or of other third parties.

4. No claims shall in any circumstances attach to the Company for failure to notify Consignees or Receivers of arrival of the goods.

5. Claims in respect of loss or damage must be notified within seven days of delivery.

IN WITNESS whereof the Undersigned have signed the number of Bills of Lading shown all of this tenor and date. One Bill of Lading, duly endorsed, is to be given up in exchange for the goods or for a delivery order for same upon which the other Bills of Lading contained in the set shall be void.

Freight Payable at	Place and Date of Issue
ORIGIN	BIRMINGHAM 17.6.19..
Number of Original Bs/Lading	
TWO	

For particulars of delivery apply with this Bill of Lading to

Kruse GmbH
Mainzer Landstrasse 197
Frankfurt AM

For and on behalf of
MIDLAND FORWARDERS LTD

IFF
H-B/L
4-77
762

Printed by Systemforms Ltd 01-505 6125/6

Approved by SITPRO
Recommended by the Institute of Freight Forwarders

Exhibit 28 **House bill of lading** *(back)*

STANDARD TRADING CONDITIONS — 1981 EDITION

THE INSTITUTE OF FREIGHT FORWARDERS LTD.   COPYRIGHT © 1981

SECTION I

1. All and any business undertaken, including any advice, information or service provided whether

   gratuitously or not by:

   (hereinafter called "the Company") is transacted subject to the Conditions hereinafter set out. All other terms and conditions are hereby excluded. Should the Customer wish to contract with the Company otherwise than subject to these Conditions special arrangements can be made and revised prices quoted, provided that such arrangements shall only apply if reduced to writing and signed by a Director or the Secretary of the Company. Save as aforesaid no agent or employee of the Company has the Company's authority to waive or vary these conditions.

2. The Company is a Forwarding Agent and, except in the special circumstances to which Sections II and III of these Conditions apply, acts solely as agent in performing and securing services for the Customer and entering into contracts on the Customer's behalf with other persons. Except in the special circumstances to which Section III of these Conditions apply the Company is not a carrier and does not make or purport to make any contract for the carriage, storage, packing or handling of goods with the Customer. The Company is not a common carrier.

3. The Company shall be entitled to enter into contracts
   (a) for the carriage of goods by any route or by any means;
   (b) for the storage, packing or handling of the goods by any persons at any place or places and for any length of time;
   and to do such acts as may be necessary or incidental thereto at the absolute discretion of the Company, and to depart from the Customer's instructions in any respect if in the opinion of the Company it is necessary or desirable to do so in the Customer's interests.

4. The Company expressly authorises the Company to do such acts and enter into such contracts as are referred to in Condition 3 on behalf of the Customer so as to bind the Customer by such acts and contracts in all respects, notwithstanding any departure from the Customer's instructions as aforesaid.

5. The Customer warrants that he is either the owner or the authorised agent of the owner of the goods (including any containers or equipment) to which any business relates, and further warrants that he is authorised to accept and is accepting these Conditions not only for himself but also as agent for and on behalf of the owner of the goods and all other persons who are or may hereafter become interested in the goods (all such persons being hereinafter called "the Owner").

6. The Company shall be entitled to perform any of its obligations hereunder by itself or by its parent, subsidiary or associated companies, or by any other person, firm or company carrying out the functions of Forwarding Agent. Any contract to which these Conditions apply is made by the Company on their own behalf, and also as agent for and on behalf of any such parent, subsidiary or associated company, and any such company shall be entitled to the benefit of these Conditions. The Customer will not seek to impose upon any such company a liability greater than that accepted by the Company under these Conditions.

7. Estimates and quotations are given on the basis of immediate acceptance and are subject to withdrawals or revisions. Further unless otherwise agreed in writing the Company shall be after acceptance at liberty to revise quotations or charges with or without notice in the event of changes occurring in currency exchange rates, rates of freight, insurance premiums or any charges applicable to the goods.

8. The Customer warrants that the description and particulars of any consignments furnished by or on behalf of the Customer are accurate.

9. (i) The Company shall not be obliged to make any declaration for the purpose of any statute or convention or contract as to the nature or value of any goods or as to any special interest in delivery, unless expressly instructed by the Customer in writing.

   (ii) Where there is a choice of rates according to the extent or degree of the liability assumed by carriers, warehousemen or others, goods will be forwarded, dealt with etc., at Customer's risk or other minimum charge and no declaration of value (where optional) will be made; unless express instructions in writing to the contrary have previously been given by the Customer.

10. The Company shall not be obliged to arrange for the goods to be carried, stored or handled separately from the goods of other Customers.

11. The Company shall be entitled to retain and be paid all brokerages, commissions, allowances and other remunerations customarily retained by or paid to Forwarding Agents and insurance brokers.

12. No insurance will be effected except upon express instructions given in writing by the Customer and all insurances effected by the Company are subject to the usual exceptions and conditions of the policies of the insurance company or underwriters taking the risk. The Company shall not be under any obligation to effect a separate insurance on each consignment but may declare it on any open or general policy. Should the insurers dispute their liability for any reason the insured shall have recourse against the insurers only and the Company shall not be under any responsibility or liability whatsoever in relation thereto notwithstanding that the premium upon the policy may not be at the same rate as that charged by the Company or paid to the Company by its Customer.

13. Except under special arrangements previously made in writing the Company will not accept or deal with any noxious, dangerous, hazardous or inflammable or explosive goods or any goods likely to cause damage. Should any Customer nevertheless deliver any such goods to the Company or cause the Company to handle or deal with any such goods otherwise than under special arrangements previously made in writing, he shall be liable for all loss or damage whatsoever caused by or to or in connection with the goods however arising and shall indemnify the Company against all penalties, claims, damages, costs and expenses whatsoever arising in connection therewith and the goods may be destroyed or otherwise dealt with at the sole discretion of the Company or any other person in whose custody they may be at the relevant time. If such goods are accepted under arrangements previously made in writing, they may nevertheless be so destroyed or otherwise dealt with on account of risk to other goods, property, life or health. The expression "goods likely to cause damage" includes goods likely to harbour or encourage vermin or other pests.

14. Except under special arrangements previously made in writing the Company will not accept or deal with bullion, coins, precious stones, jewellery, valuables, antiques, pictures, livestock or plants. Should any Customer nevertheless deliver any such goods to the Company or cause the Company to handle or deal with any such goods otherwise than under special arrangements previously made in writing the Company shall be under no liability whatsoever for or in connection with the goods however caused.

15. The Company shall be entitled at the expense of the Customer to sell or dispose of
   (a) on 21 days' notice in writing to the Customer or, where the Customer cannot be traced, after the goods have been held by the Company for 90 days, all goods which in the opinion of the Company cannot be delivered either because they are insufficiently or incorrectly addressed or because they are not collected or accepted by the consignee or for any reason, and
   (b) without notice perishable goods which are not taken up immediately on arrival or which are insufficiently or incorrectly addressed or marked or which in the opinion of the Company would be likely to perish in the course of the carriage, storage or handling.

16. The Company shall have a general lien on all goods or documents relating to goods in its possession for all sums due at any time from the Customer or Owner, and shall be entitled to sell or dispose of such goods or documents at the expense of the Customer and apply the proceeds in or towards the payment of such sums on 28 days' notice in writing to the Customer.

17. (i) When goods are accepted or dealt with upon instructions to collect freight, duties, charges or other expenses from the consignee or any other person the Customer shall remain responsible for the same if they are not paid by such consignee or other person immediately when due.

   (ii) Without prejudice to Condition 5 the Company shall have the right to enforce any liability of the Customer under these Conditions or to recover any sums to be paid by the Customer under these Conditions not only against or from the Customer but also if it thinks fit against or from the sender and/or consignee and/or Owner.

   (iii) All sums shall be paid to the Company in cash immediately when due without deduction and payment shall be withheld or deferred on account of any claim, counterclaim or set-off.

18. The Company shall not be liable to the Customer or Owner
   (a) for loss or damage caused by any failure to carry out or negligence in carrying out the Customer's or Owner's instructions, or by any failure to perform or negligence in performing the Company's obligations (whether such obligations arise by contract or otherwise), unless such loss or damage is due to the wilful neglect or default of the Company or its own servants;
   (b) for consequential loss or loss of market or delay or deviation however caused.

19. In no case whatsoever shall any liability of the Company, however arising, and notwithstanding that the cause of loss or damage be unexplained, exceed
   (a) the value of the relevant goods, or
   (b) a sum at the rate of £800 per tonne of 1000 kilos on the gross weight of the goods, or
   (c) £15,000 in respect of any one claim
   whichever shall be the least.

20. Without prejudice to Condition 18, any claim by the Customer or Owner against the Company shall be made in writing and notified to the Company
   (a) in the case of damage to the goods within 7 days after the end of the transit where the transit ends in the British Isles and within 14 days after the end of the transit where the transit ends outside the British Isles,
   (b) in the case of delay in delivery or non-delivery within 14 days of the date when the goods should have been delivered, and
   (c) in any other case within 14 days of the event giving rise to the claim.
   Any claim not made and notified as aforesaid shall be deemed to be waived and absolutely barred.

21. No claim of any kind shall be made against any servant or agent of the Company on any ground whatsoever. No claim of any kind shall be made against any parent, subsidiary or associated company of the Company, or against any forwarding agent employed by the Company in pursuance of Condition 6, or against any of their respective servants or agents on any ground whatsoever.

22. The Customer shall indemnify the Company against all duties, taxes, payments, fines, expenses, losses, damages (including physical damage) and liabilities, whether or not arising out of the negligence of the Company, their servants or agents, suffered or incurred by the Company in the performance of their obligations under any contract to which these conditions apply, including any liability to indemnify any other person against claims made against such other person by the Customer or by the Owner.

SECTION II

23. Where in any circumstances the Company acts as principal in entering into a contract with any other person for the carriage, storage, packing or handling of the goods by Sea Act, 1971, The Carriage by Air Act, 1961, The for the purpose of the Carriage of Goods by Sea Act, 1971, The Carriage by Air Act, 1961, The Carriage by Air (Supplementary Provisions) Act, 1962, The Carriage of Goods by Road Act, 1965, or for any other purpose, nor does it make or purport to make any contract for the carriage, storage, packing or handling of any goods with the Customer. The Company's sole obligation is to procure contracts for the carriage, storage, packing or handling of goods by other persons.

24. Without prejudice to the exceptions and limitations contained herein, the Company shall be entitled to the benefit of all exceptions and limitations in favour of the carrier or other person storing or handling the goods (such other person together with the carrier being hereinafter called "the Carrier"), contained in the Company's contract with the Carrier. The Customer will not seek to impose on the Carrier any liability greater than that accepted by the Carrier under such contract.

25. The liberties contained in Condition 3 and the provisions, exceptions and limitations contained in Conditions 1 and 5 to 22 shall apply to this Section of these Conditions.

SECTION III

26. Notwithstanding the provision of Sections 1 and 11 of these Conditions, the Company shall be entitled to perform all or part of the carriage, storage, packing or handling of the goods by themselves or by their subsidiary or associated companies. This Section of these Conditions shall apply to any such case, and also to any case where, notwithstanding Condition 23, the Company is deemed to be the Carrier or otherwise to be in possession of the goods. This Section of these Conditions shall apply only so long as and to the extent that the Company is or is deemed to be the Carrier or in possession of the goods as aforesaid and no further.

27. The Company shall be entitled
   (a) to carry the goods by any route or by any means, and
   (b) to store, pack or handle the goods at any place or places and for any length of time
   and to do all such other acts as may be necessary or incidental thereto at the absolute discretion of the Company and to depart from the Customer's instructions if in the opinion of the Company it is necessary or desirable to do so in the Customer's interests.

28. The Company shall not be liable to the Customer or Owner for loss of or damage to the goods resulting from:-
   (a) fire;
   (b) any other cause, unless such loss or damage is proved to be due to wilful neglect or default of the Company or its servants.

29. Without prejudice to Condition 28, the liberties contained in Condition 3 and the provisions, exceptions and limitations contained in Conditions 1 and 5 to 22 shall apply to this Section of these Conditions.

30. Where the Company is or is deemed to be the Carrier under a contract subject to legislation compulsorily applicable thereto the Company shall be entitled to all the rights, immunities, exceptions and limitations conferred on the Carrier by virtue of such legislation, and these Conditions shall be void to the extent that they are inconsistent with such rights, immunities, exceptions and limitations, but no further.

SECTION IV

31. Where in these Conditions any matter is to be determined in accordance with the opinion of the Company, the certificate of a Director or the Secretary of the Company for the time being shall be conclusive evidence as to any matter so certified.

32. These Conditions, and any act or contract to which they apply, shall be governed by English Law, and any dispute arising out of any such act or contract shall be within the exclusive jurisdiction of the English Courts.

February 1981

Exhibit 29 **Rail consignment note**

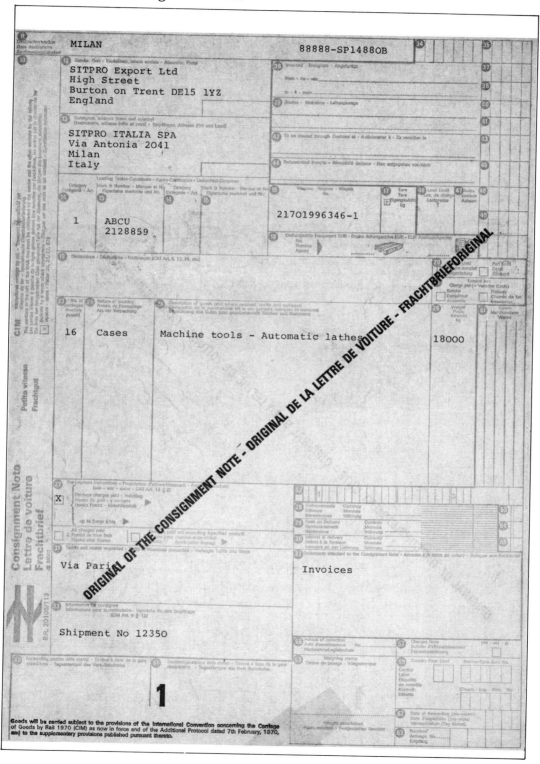

Exhibit 30 **Road waybill (CMR)**

SITPRO FTA 1980 LETTRE DE VOITURE INTERNATIONALE	(CMR)	INTERNATIONAL CONSIGNMENT NOTE

Sender (Name, Address, Country) Expéditeur (Nom, Adresse, Pays)	Customs Reference/Status 88888-SP14879A
SITPRO Export Ltd High Street Burton-on-Trent DE15 1YZ England	Senders/Agents Reference 380-12347-47 SP14879A
Consignee (Name, Address, Country) Destinataire (Nom, Adresse, Pays) SITPRO ITALIA SPA Via Antonia 2041 Milan Italy	Carrier (Name & Address) Transporteur (Nom et Adresse) Burton Forwarding Limited High Street Burton England
	Successive Carriers Transporteurs successifs
Place & date of taking over the goods (place, country, date) Lieu et date de la prise en charge des marchandises (Lieu, pays, date) 5 October 1981 Burton-on-Trent	None
Place designated for delivery of goods (place, country) Lieu prévu pour la livraison des marchandises (lieu, pays) Milan, Italy	This carriage is subject, notwithstanding any clause to the contrary, to the Convention on the Contract for International Carriage of Goods by Road (CMR) Ce transport est soumis, monobstant toute clause contraire à la Convention Relative au Contrat de Transport Internationale de Marchandise par Route (CMR)

NB FOR DANGEROUS GOODS INDICATE 1 CORRECT TECHNICAL NAME (PROPER SHIPPING NAME) 2 HAZARD CLASSIFICATION 3 UN NUMBER 4 FLASHPOINT (IF ANY) IN °C	Marks & Nos. No & Kind of Packages, Description of Goods Marques et Nos. No et nature des colis. Désignation des marchandises ESITALIA 12347 MILAN 1/2	2 Cartons Ethical Pharmaceuticals Non Hazardous	Gross weight (kg) or Quantity Poids Brut (kg) ou Quantité 131 kg

Carriage Charges Prix de transport	Senders Instructions for Customs, etc Instructions de l'Expéditeur (optional) Clear Customs Milan
Reservations	Documents attached Documents Annexes (optional) Invoices
	Special agreements Conventions particulières (optional)
Goods Received Marchandises Reçues	Signature of Carrier Signature du transporteur	Company completing this note SITPRO Export Ltd 0283-41835
		Place and Date Lieu et date Burton 5 October 1981

Exhibit 31 **Common short form bill of lading**

© GCBS 1979

| Shipper | COMMON SHORT FORM BILL OF LADING | UK Customs Assigned No 99999 | B/L No 31 |

Shipper
SITPRO Export Ltd
High Street
Burton on Trent DE15 1YZ
England
VAT No. 24182357

COMMON SHORT FORM BILL OF LADING

UK Customs Assigned No
99999

B/L No 31

Shipper's Reference
862 – 12351CD

F/Agent's Reference
12479

Consignee (if "Order" state Notify Party and Address)
Laboratorios FRANKENSTEIN S A
Rua Primera 1
Caracas
VENEZUELA

Name of Carrier
Lennon Line Ltd

Notify Party and Address (leave blank if stated above)

The contract evidenced by this Short Form Bill of Lading is subject to the exceptions limitations conditions and liberties (including those relating to pre carriage and on carriage) set out in the Carrier's Standard Conditions applicable to the voyage covered by this Short Form Bill of Lading and operative on its date of issue
If the carriage is one where the provisions of the Hague Rules contained in the International Convention for unification of certain rules relating to Bills of Lading dated Brussels on 25th August 1924 as amended by the Protocol signed at Brussels on 23rd February 1968 (the Hague Visby Rules) are compulsorily applicable under Article X the said Standard Conditions contain or shall be deemed to contain a Clause giving effect to the Hague Visby Rules Otherwise except as provided below the said Standard Conditions contain or shall be deemed to contain a Clause giving effect to the provisions of the Hague Rules
The Carrier hereby agrees that to the extent of any inconsistency the said Clause shall prevail over the exceptions limitations conditions and liberties set out in the Standard Conditions in respect of any period to which the Hague Rules or the Hague Visby Rules by their terms apply Unless the Standard Conditions expressly provide otherwise neither the Hague Rules nor the Hague Visby Rules shall apply to this contract where the goods carried hereunder consist of live animals or cargo which by this contract is stated as being carried on deck and is so carried
Notwithstanding anything contained in the said Standard Conditions the term Carrier in this Short Form Bill of Lading shall mean the Carrier named on the front thereof
A copy of the Carrier's said Standard Conditions applicable hereto may be inspected or will be supplied on request at the office of the Carrier or the Carrier's Principal Agents

Applicable only when document used as a Through Bill of Lading

Pre-Carriage by*	Place of Receipt by Pre-Carrier*
Lennon Vehicle	Burton on Trent
Vessel	Port of Loading
Voyager	Liverpool
Port of Discharge	Place of Delivery by On-Carrier*
La Guaira	Caracas

Particulars declared by Shipper

Marks and Nos; Container No.	Number and kind of packages, Description of Goods	Gross Weight	Measurement
FRANKENSTEIN ED1814 CARACAS VIA LA GUAIRA	2 Cartons Ethical Pharmaceuticals (Non-dangerous) Productos farmaceuticos I/L 80/9999999	160kg	0.250m3

Freight Details; Charges etc.

RECEIVED FOR CARRIAGE as above in apparent good order and condition, unless otherwise stated hereon, the goods described in the above particulars.

IN WITNESS whereof the number of original Bills of Lading stated below have been signed, all of this tenor and date, one of which being accomplished the others to stand void.

GCBS
CSF
BL
1979

710

Ocean Freight Payable at	Place and Date of Issue
Origin	
Number of Original Bs/L	Signature for Carrier; Carrier's Principal Place of Business
1	

Authorised and Licensed by the

Exhibit 32 **Bill of lading (liner)** *(front)*

Shipper	**BILL OF LADING**
Wyatt Porter Limited	UK Customs Assigned No. — B/L No. 32
	Shipper's Ref.
	F/Agent's Ref.

Consignee (If 'Order' state Notify Party and Address)

Jose Martinez & Cia

BLUE STAR LINE
HOULDER LINE
LAMPORT + HOLT LINE
ROYAL MAIL LINES

JOINT SERVICE
SOUTHBOUND
BRAZIL AND RIVER PLATE

Notify Party and Address (leave blank if stated above)

Pre-Carriage By*	Place of Receipt by Pre-Carrier*
Vessel HAINES	Port of Loading SOUTHAMPTON
Port of Discharge SAO PAULO	Place of Delivery by On-Carrier*

Marks and Nos; Container No;	Number and kind of packages; description of goods	Gross Weight	Measurement
Blue Flash	1600 bundles tempered steel rods	874,277	

The Shipper must declare the nature and the value of the goods prior to the issue of this Bill of Lading before shipment and insert such particulars herein paying the corresponding additional freight of 4% ad valorem in consideration of which the carrier shall respond for the total value of the goods. In the event that the value of the goods is not declared by the shippers prior to the issue of this Bill of Lading, and that the additional ad valorem freight be not paid, the value of the cargo shall be deemed not to exceed that monetary limitation provided for in the Hague Rules or the Hague Visby Rules whichever is applicable to this shipment by clause 1 overleaf.

Freight details, charges, etc.

S H I P P E D in apparent good order and condition (unless otherwise stated herein) on board (the local vessel if named above but otherwise on board) the ocean vessel at the port of loading thereof the goods described above as declared by the shipper to be carried therefrom and delivered (such carriage and delivery being subject to the exceptions, limitations, conditions and liberties herein agreed) in the like order and condition at the port of discharge or place of delivery (as the case may be) or so near thereto as the carrying vessel may safely always afloat unto the consignee or his or their assigns.

IN WITNESS whereof the master or agent of the ocean vessel has signed the number of original Bills of Lading stated below all of this tenor and date, one of which being accomplished, the others shall stand void.

Ocean Freight Payable at DESTINATION	Place and date of issue SOUTHAMPTON 30.3.19..
Number of Original Bs/L THREE	Signature FOR THE MASTER

ICS
B/L
1 Jan. 72   SHIPPERS SIGNATURE
710

*Applicable only when document used as a Through Bill of Lading

ORIGINAL

Exhibit 32 **Bill of lading (liner)** *(back)*

1. It is mutually agreed that this Bill of Lading shall have effect subject to the provisions of the International Convention relating to Bills of Lading dated Brussels 25th August 1924 (hereinafter called the Hague Rules) except where legislation giving effect to the Hague Rules as amended by the Protocol signed at Brussels 23rd February 1968 (hereinafter called the Hague Visby Rules) is compulsorily applicable in which case the Bill of Lading shall have effect subject to the provisions of such legislation. If anything contained herein is inconsistent with or repugnant to the said legislation or rules, it shall be null and void to the extent of such inconsistency or repugnance but no further. Neither the Hague Rules nor the Hague Visby Rules shall apply to the contract where the goods carried consist of live animals or plants or of cargo which by the contract is stated as being carried on deck and is so carried.

Nothing herein contained shall prevent the Carrier from claiming in the Courts of any Country the benefit of, or derogate in any way from any statutory protection or limitation of liability afforded to Shipowner or Carrier by the laws of such Country or by the laws of the Country in which the goods were shipped. In this Bill of Lading "the vessel" means any vessel carrying the goods other than one by which the goods are forwarded under Clause 4.

It is hereby expressly agreed that no servant or agent of the Carrier (including every independent contractor from time to time employed by the Carrier) shall in any circumstances whatsoever be under any liability whatsoever to the Shipper, Consignee or Owner of the goods or to any holder of this Bill of Lading for any loss, damage or delay of whatsoever kind arising or resulting directly or indirectly from any act, neglect or default on his part while acting in the course of or in connection with his employment and, without prejudice to the generality of the foregoing provisions in this Clause, every exemption, limitation, condition and liberty herein contained and every right, exemption from liability, defence and immunity of whatsoever nature applicable to the Carrier or to which the Carrier is entitled hereunder shall also be available and shall extend to protect every such servant or agent of the Carrier acting as aforesaid and for the purpose of all the foregoing provisions of this Clause the Carrier is or shall be deemed to be acting as agent or trustee on behalf of and for the benefit of all persons who are or might be his servants or agents from time to time (including independent contractors as aforesaid) and all such persons shall to this extent be or be deemed to be parties to the contract in or evidenced by this Bill of Lading.

The Carrier shall be entitled to be paid by the Shipper, Consignee, Owner of the goods and/or Holder of this Bill of Lading (who shall be jointly and severally liable to the Carrier therefore) on demand any sum recovered or recoverable by either such Shipper, Consignee, Owner of the goods and/or Holder of this Bill of Lading or any other from such servant or agent of the Carrier for any such loss, damage, delay or otherwise.

2. *(a)* Neither the Carrier, his agents, servants nor the vessel shall be liable for any loss, detention or damage of or to the goods or any part thereof howsoever caused prior to loading on or subsequent to discharge from the ocean vessel even though such loss, detention or damage be caused by the negligence of the Carrier, his agents or servants or other persons for whom the Carrier is responsible, or by the unseaworthiness or unfitness of any ship, craft or conveyance at the time the goods or any part thereof are placed therein or at any time thereafter, and even though the goods or any part thereof are in the custody of the Carrier, his agents or servants as warehousemen or otherwise howsoever, and the goods or any part thereof prior to loading or subsequent to discharge as aforesaid are at the sole risk of the Owner of the goods.

(b) (i) In respect of goods which in this Bill of Lading are stated as being carried on deck and are so carried, the Carrier, whether in his capacity as Carrier or otherwise, shall not be liable for any loss, damage or delay whatsoever and wheresoever arising, and even though caused by the negligence of the Carrier, his agents or servants, or by the unseaworthiness or unfitness at any time of the vessel or of any ship, craft, conveyance or place.

(ii) Freight on livestock shall be paid (ship lost or not lost) on the number shipped without regard to and irrespective of the number and condition of those landed. Neither the Hague Rules nor the Hague Visby Rules shall govern the contract as set out in this Bill of Lading as regards cargo which is stated in this Bill of Lading as being carried on deck and is so carried and/or as regards live animals and plants. Such cargo and live animals and plants are carried entirely at the risk of the shipper, consignee, owner of the goods, and the holder of the Bill of Lading, the Carrier being under no liability whatsoever therefore notwithstanding unseaworthiness or unfitness of the ship or negligence on the part of the Carrier or on the part of any person for whose negligence apart from this clause the Carrier would have been responsible. In other respects the terms and conditions hereof shall apply to any such deck cargo, live animals and plants. Live animals, plants and deck cargo to be taken by the consignee immediately on vessel's arrival otherwise the Carrier is at liberty to land such at the sole risk and expense of the shipper, consignee or owner.

3. *(a)* The vessel is at liberty to proceed by any route, to proceed to return to and stay at any port or ports whatsoever (including the loading port) in any order in or out of the route or in a contrary direction to or beyond the port of discharge once or oftener for taking on board bunkers or supplies or loading or discharging cargo or embarking or disembarking passengers whether in connection with the present or prior or subsequent voyage, or for any other purpose whatsoever, and after arrival at the port of discharge herein provided to leave such port and with the like liberties as aforesaid to return to and discharge the said cargo at such port. The exercise of any liberty in this clause shall form part of the agreed voyage.

(b) The vessel may sail with or without pilots and may adjust compasses and make trial trip with or without cargo on board and may tow and be towed and tow and assist vessels or aircraft in all situations, and may put into and remain at or delay sailing from any port or ports for repairing or dry docking with or without cargo on board or for any other purpose whatsoever should circumstances in the opinion of the Carrier, Master or Agents render this desirable all as part of the agreed voyage.

(c) The Carrier may carry the goods to or from the vessel in any ship, craft or land conveyance, and the Carrier shall not be liable for any loss of or damage or delay to the goods while in such ship, craft or land conveyance, even though caused by negligence of the Carrier, his agents or servants or by the unseaworthiness or unfitness of any such ship, craft or land conveyance or otherwise howsoever.

(d) The goods or part thereof may be carried by the named or other Vessels, whether belonging to the Line or others, and should circumstances in the opinion of the Carrier, Master or Agent render transhipment desirable or expedient may be transhipped at any port or ports, place or places whatsoever, and while in course of transhipment may be placed or stored in craft or ashore and may be re-shipped or forwarded or returned by land and/or water and/or air at Carrier's option and expense, all as part of the contract voyage and all the provisions of this Bill of Lading shall continue to apply.

(e) If the voyage to or entering of the port of discharge or if the ship or cargo operations thereat or if the departure therefrom shall be or shall at any time appear likely to be prohibited or prevented or delayed by any of the following matters or events (whether existing or anticipated): ice, weather; blockade, interdict; quarantine; strikes, lock-outs or labour troubles (whether the Carrier or his servants or agents are or are likely to be parties thereto or not); civil commotions; riot; or any other disturbances; epidemic; fever or other illnesses, congestion; obstruction, or any other cause whatsoever beyond the Carrier's control, or shall be considered by the Carrier, Master or Agents (whose decision shall be absolute and binding on all parties) to be unsafe or likely to prejudice the interests of the vessel (including her future engagements) or her cargo whether by delay or otherwise howsoever; then the goods may at the Carrier's option be landed or put into lighters there or at such other port or place as the Carrier, Master or Agents shall in his or their absolute discretion select and there discharged, or they may be carried back in the same vessel to the country of shipment and either discharged there or returned (subject to the foregoing options if any of the foregoing events shall recur) to the port of discharge and there discharged all as part of the agreed voyage, and until the goods are discharged as aforesaid all the provisions of this Bill of Lading shall continue to apply. In the case of a strike or Lock-out (whether the Carrier, his agents or servants are parties thereto or not) at an intermediate port on either the original voyage or return voyage from the country of shipment preventing the sailing of the vessel when ready to proceed to the port of discharge, the Carrier may discharge the goods at the intermediate port. The Carrier is hereby expressly permitted to discharge at any such port whether intermediate or otherwise as aforesaid notwithstanding that such discharge would delay, defeat or frustrate in whole or in part the object for which the goods were shipped. In any case where discharge is effected under provision of this clause the Carrier's responsibility shall cease on such discharge the goods being thereafter at the risk of the Owner of the goods, and such discharge shall, notwithstanding anything contained in this Bill of Lading, constitute due delivery of the goods under this Bill of Lading, and the Holder of the Bill of Lading the Owner of the goods and the Consignee shall be jointly and severally liable for all charges and expenses incurred in consequence of such discharge, the Carrier, Master and Agents acting solely as agents of the Consignee and/or Owner of the goods after completion of discharge. The Carrier will so far as practicable give immediate notice of such discharge to the Consignee of the goods, if known, but shall incur no liability for failure so to do.

(f) The vessel may carry cargo of all kinds, dangerous or otherwise. The Carrier may stow the goods in poop, forecastle, deckhouse, shelter deck, passenger space, bunker space or any other covered in space, and unless stated as being carried on deck such goods shall be deemed for all purposes (including general average) to be stowed under deck. The goods may also be stowed by the Carrier or his agents or servants in containers, and containers whether stowed as aforesaid or received fully stowed from the Shippers may be carried on or under deck without notice to the Shipper, and, if they are so carried, the Hague Rules or the Hague Visby Rules as incorporated herein shall be applicable notwithstanding carriage on or under deck, and the goods and/or containers shall contribute to general average, whether carried on or under deck.

(g) In the event of the imminence or existence of any of the following – War between any nations, hostilities, war like operations, rebellion or civil war, prohibition, restriction or control by any Government of intercourse, commercial or otherwise with any country from at or to which the vessel normally proceeds or calls, control or direction by any government or other Authority of the use or movements of the vessel or the insulated or other space in the vessel, the Carrier and/or his Agents and/or the Master, if he or they consider there to be any risk that the vessel or her Master, Officers, Crew, Passengers or any of them or cargo or any part thereof could be subject to loss, damage, injury, detention or delay in consequence of the said war, hostilities, war like operations, rebellion, civil war, prohibition, restriction, control or direction, may at any time before or after the commencement of the voyage, alter or vary or depart from the proposed or advertised or agreed or customary route or voyage (including the right to omit ports or places not directly affected by any of the matters aforesaid) and/or delay or detain the vessel and/or discharge the cargo (for delivery or storage or transhipment) at or off any port or ports, place or places without being liable for any loss or damage whatsoever directly or indirectly sustained by the Owner of the goods. If and when the goods are so discharged at such port or ports, place or places, they shall be landed or put into craft or vessels at the expense and risk of the Owner of the goods and the Carrier's responsibility shall cease on discharge, the Carrier, Master or Agents giving notice of such discharge to the Consignee of the goods so far as he is known. The vessel, in addition to any liberties expressed or implied herein, shall have liberty to comply with any orders or directions as to departure, arrival, route, voyage, ports of call, delay, detention, discharge (for delivery or storage or transhipment) or otherwise howsoever, given by any Government or any Department thereof, or any person acting or purporting to act with the authority of any Government or of any Department thereof, or by any Committee or person having under the terms of the War Risks Insurance on the vessel the right to give such orders or directions, and if by reason of or in compliance with any such orders or directions or by reason of the exercise by the Carrier of any other liberty mentioned in this Clause anything is done or is not done the same shall be within this contract. Discharge under any liberty mentioned in this clause shall, notwithstanding anything contained in this Bill of Lading constitute due delivery of the goods under this Bill of Lading and the Owner and/or Consignee of the goods shall bear and pay all charges and expenses resulting from such discharge, and the full freight stipulated herein, if not prepaid, shall on such discharge become immediately due and payable by the Owner and/or Consignee of the goods, and if freight has been prepaid the Carrier shall be entitled to retain the same. The vessel is free to carry contraband, explosives, munitions or war like stores, and may sail armed or unarmed.

4. If this Bill of Lading provides for the goods to be transhipped at a port or place in South America and to be forwarded thence, the Carrier shall be under no obligation himself to deliver the goods at the port or place of delivery, but on arrival of the vessel at the named port of transhipment or at such other port or place which the Carrier may elect as the port or place of transhipment the Carrier shall at his own expense (unless otherwise herein provided for) discharge and tranship or land or store the goods (either ashore or afloat) at such port or place and with all reasonable despatch forward them by sea or inland waterways or by land or by air by any route to the port or place of delivery. The Carrier has the right to forward in lots or parts. On discharge from the vessel at such port or place of transhipment the Carrier's responsibility shall cease, and neither he nor the vessel shall be liable in any circumstances for any loss or detention of or damage to the goods howsoever caused occurring after such discharge. In respect of the on-carriage of goods from such port or place of transhipment to the port or place of delivery, and of the storage, transport and transhipment of the goods while not on board the vessel, the Carrier acts as forwarding agent only, making a contract for such storage, transport, transhipment and on-carriage on the terms and subject to the provisions of the contract in use by the person or on-carrier with whom such contract is made and not making any declaration of value unless expressly instructed by the Shipper, and paying the expenses of such operations but incurring no responsibility as carrier or custodian of the goods or otherwise for any loss, damage or detention howsoever caused; in respect of such on-carriage, the goods shall be subject to all the liberties (including the liberty to carry the goods on deck), conditions and exceptions of the on-carrier conveying them beyond the port or place of transhipment, and the Shipper will have the benefit of any obligations of any such on-carrier (by sea and/or inland waterways and/or land and/or air) or of any warehouseman, lighterman or others under their respective contracts with the on-Carrier. If for any cause whatsoever the goods shall be delayed at the port or place of transhipment beyond the period which would elapse before transhipment in normal circumstances the storage and other charges upon the goods after the expiration of the normal period shall be borne by the Consignee or Owner of the goods.

5. Freight shall be payable by the shippers in full without discount or abatement at the port of shipment in exchange for Bill of Lading and shall be deemed to have been earned on shipment, ship and/or goods lost or not lost. The freight payable as herein has been calculated and based upon the description and particulars of the goods declared by the Shipper to the Carrier. The Carrier shall be entitled to re-weigh or re-measure any goods, and freight shall be paid on the excess weight or measurement (if any), so ascertained. The expense incident to re-weighing or re-measuring shall be borne by the Carrier if the weights or measurements as furnished by the Shipper are found to be correct, but otherwise such expenses shall be borne and paid by the Owner or Consignee of the goods. If the description or (in cases where the value has been stated) the value of the goods has been mis-stated by the Shipper, double the amount of such freight shall be paid as liquidated damages by the Shipper, Consignee and/or Owner of the goods as would have been charged if the goods had been accurately described and valued and a certificate signed by the Carrier or his Agents shall be conclusive evidence of the amount that would have been so charged.

6. The Shipper, Consignee and/or Owner of the goods shall bear and pay the cost of labour and material for mending, baling, bagging, packing, cooperage and repairs to and renewals of packages, boxes, crates, wrappers, bales, bags or barrels resulting from insufficiency of packing or from excepted perils.

7. The Carrier shall have a lien over the goods, and the right to sell the same by public auction or otherwise for all freight, primage, charges (including additional freight or double freight and/or expenses under Clause 6 payable on corrected weight or measurement), demurrage, damages for detention, and for all payments made and liabilities incurred in respect of charges, expenditure, damages (including damage to the vessel or other cargo), costs and expenses (including the costs and expenses of exercising such lien and of such sale), and for the interest (if any) payable which under this Bill of Lading are to be borne and paid by the Shipper, Consignee or Endorsee of the Bill of Lading, or Receiver of the goods. If on a sale of the goods the proceeds fail to cover the amount for which the Carrier has a lien on the goods and the costs and expenses of exercising such lien and of the sale, the Carrier shall be entitled to recover the difference from the Shipper, Consignee and/or Owner of the goods.

8. *(a)* Delivery of the goods shall be taken immediately the vessel is ready to discharge, berthed or not berthed, and continuously as fast as vessel can deliver, and the Carrier shall be at liberty to discharge continuously day and night, Sundays and holidays included, on to quay or into craft, all extra expense to be for account of the Consignee, the Owner of the goods and the Holder of the Bill of Lading jointly and severally. The Carrier shall be under no liability to notify the Consignee or any other party of the arrival of the goods, notwithstanding any custom of the port to the contrary or any written request in this Bill of Lading or otherwise. If the Consignee, the Owner of the goods or the Holder of the Bill of Lading requires delivery before or after usual hours he shall pay on demand any extra expense incurred.

(b) If delivery is not taken as aforesaid the Shipper, the Consignee, the Owner of the goods and the Holder of the Bill of Lading shall be jointly and severally liable to pay the Carrier, by way of liquidated damages, a sum calculated at the rate of 24 U.S. cents per gross register ton of the vessel's tonnage for each day or part of a day during which there is delay in taking delivery and such damages shall be due daily and payable on demand. Also the Carrier may at his option and at the expense of the goods discharge all or any part of the goods and/or sort and/or stack and/or store them in shed, store or craft or land conveyance, subject to the Carrier's liens and to the provisions of Clause 2 hereof, and without prejudice to the Carrier's right to the said damages for any periods prior to such discharge. The Carrier in addition to his other rights under this paragraph, may shift, re-stow, land and re-ship any goods which in the opinion of the Carrier are delaying the prompt discharge of other goods and the expense of so doing and of labour standing by onship and/or quay and any other expenses incurred by the Carrier during the period of delay in the reception of any goods shall be due and payable on demand by the Consignee, the Owner of the goods and the Holder of the Bill of Lading jointly and severally and the Carrier's decision regarding the amount of such expenses shall be conclusive.

(c) The current landing, overside and/or reception charges, including lighterage if any and also the current charges for sorting and stacking cargo on wharf or in shed, shall be for account of the goods notwithstanding any custom of the port to the contrary. The Shipper, the Consignee, the Owners of the goods and the Holder of the Bill of Lading shall jointly and severally indemnify the Carrier against all loss, liability or expense caused owing to Customs, Consular or other regulations not being complied with, or to Customs permit and/or other necessary papers not being lodged within twenty-four hours after vessel's entry at the Customs or when required, or to importation of the goods being prohibited, and the Carrier shall be at liberty to return the goods to the port of shipment, or to discharge them at any other port and such discharge shall constitute due delivery under this Bill of Lading, and in either case at the expense of the Shipper, the Consignee, the Owner of the goods and the Holder of the Bill of Lading, who shall be liable jointly and severally for all charges, freights and forwarding expenses thereon, and the Carrier shall have a lien on the goods for all such loss, liability, expense, charges, freights and forwarding expenses.

9. The Carrier undertakes that vessel is fully classed and holds a Refrigerating Machinery Certificate and that before loading cargo in any insulated space or spaces or insulated containers a survey shall be held and a Loading Certificate issued by a competent surveyor that the insulation, dunnage, battens, refrigerating machinery and appliance are in good and satisfactory order, and the existence of said Class and the production of the Certificate shall be conclusive evidence against the Shipper, Consignee and Endorsee of this Bill of Lading that the Carrier has exercised due diligence at the date of the said survey to make the vessel in respect of the matters mentioned in the said Certificate fit and safe for the reception, carriage and preservation of the goods and has exercised due diligence to make the vessel in all the said respects seaworthy and properly equipped and supplied.

10. The Carrier and his Agents shall have the right of nominating the berth or berths for loading and discharging at all ports and places whatsoever, any custom to the contrary notwithstanding.

11. The Carrier will not be accountable for goods of any description in respect of any one package or unit for an amount beyond the sum stipulated in the provisions of the said legislation or Act and Rules (as the case may be) referred to in Clause 1 hereof, unless the value thereof shall have been stated in writing both on the Broker's Order, which must be obtained before shipment, and on the Shipping Note presented on shipment, and extra freight agreed upon and paid, and Bills of Lading signed with a declaration of the nature and value of the goods appearing thereon. When the value is declared and extra freight agreed as aforesaid, the carrier's liability shall not exceed such value, or *pro rata* on that basis in the event of partial loss or damage.

12. In the event of the Carrier being liable for damage to or loss of any goods carried by the vessel, all claims in respect of such loss or damage shall be deemed to be waived unless notice of claim is made in writing to the Carrier or his Agents at the final port of discharge of the goods in respect of which the claim is made within three days after such goods were or should have been discharged from the vessel.

13. In the event of accident, danger, damage or disaster, before or after the commencement of the voyage, resulting from any cause whatsoever, whether due to negligence or not, for which, or for the consequence of which the Carrier is not responsible, by Statute, contract, or otherwise, the goods, Shipper, Consignee or Owner of the goods shall contribute with the Carrier in general average to the payment of any sacrifices, losses, or expenses of a general average nature that may be made or incurred, and shall pay salvage and special charges incurred in respect of the goods.

General average shall be adjusted according to York Antwerp Rules, 1974. Adjustments shall be prepared at such port as shall be selected by the Carrier. Such deposit as the Carrier or his Agents may deem sufficient to cover the estimated contribution of the goods and any special charges thereon shall, if required, be paid to the Carrier or his Agents previously to the delivery of the goods. Should salvage services be rendered to the cargo by any other vessel or vessels belonging wholly or in part to or chartered by the same ownership or Line, such salvage services shall be paid for as fully as if they had been rendered by a vessel or vessels entirely the property of different ownerships or Lines.

14. If the vessel comes into collision with another ship as a result of the negligence of the other ship and any act, neglect or default of the master, mariner, pilot or the servants of the Carrier in the navigation or in the management of the vessel, the Owner of the goods carried hereunder will indemnify the Carrier against all loss or liability to the other or non-carrying ship or her Owners in so far as such loss or liability represent loss of, or damage to or any claim whatsoever of the Owner of the said goods, paid or payable by the other or non-carrying ship or her Owners to the Owner of the said goods and setoff, recouped or recovered by the other or non-carrying ship or her Owners as part of their claim against the carrying vessel or Carrier. The foregoing provisions shall also apply where the Owners, Operators or those in charge of any ship or ships or objects other than, or in addition to, the colliding ships or objects are at fault in respect to a collision or contact.

15. If the vessel is not owned by or chartered by demise to the Company or Line by whom this Bill of Lading is issued (as may be the case notwithstanding anything that appears to the contrary) this Bill of Lading shall take effect only as a contract with the Owner or Demise Charterer as the case may be as Principal made through the agency of the said Company or Line who act as Agents only and shall be under no personal liability whatsoever in respect thereof.

16. The contract evidenced by this Bill of Lading shall be governed by the law of England.

(DESPACHO DIRECTO AT BUENOS AIRES AND ROSARIO)

17. If upon the Ship's arrival at destination no discharging berth alongside the quay is available Consignees of despacho directo cargo are to provide lighters to receive their cargo as soon as same is to hand, in default of which the Ship is to be at liberty to engage lighters according to the Tariff of the Buenos Aires Centro de Lancheros and, in the case of Rosario, according to the customary Tariff of the port, and to discharge the same into such lighters by day and by night at the exclusive risk and expense of Shippers, Consignees and Receivers, who shall pay the cost of engaging such lighters and any eventual demurrage thereon, and the Ship and her Owners shall have a lien on such cargo until such expense and demurrage has been paid. Once the Ship is berthed alongside the quay the Consignees and Receivers of such despacho directo goods shall take delivery of same as soon as they are to hand at the minimum rate of 60 tons per day per hatch for Iron and 100 tons per day per hatch for cargo other than iron. In the event of any breach at any time of this obligation the Owners shall be entitled immediately upon such breach to discharge the balance of such cargo into lighters by day and by night at the risk and expense of the Shippers, Consignees and Receivers, and the Owners shall have a lien on the cargo so discharged until such expense and any demurrage on lighters has been paid. All responsibility of the ship and her Owners in respect of such cargo shall cease on the said goods leaving the Ship's rail.

(JOINT SURVEYS AT ARGENTINE PORTS)

18. In case of apprehended loss and/or damage to the cargo, the Carrier and Consignee mutually bind themselves to hold a private survey, alongside ship or in the adjacent shed not later than twenty-four hours after discharge with all the effects of a judicial survey (see Article 1079/80 of the Argentine Code of Commerce). Should the Consignee and/or Underwriters apply for a judicial survey without first obtaining a written refusal from the carrier to hold a private survey, all the expenses thereof shall be for account of the party who applied for the same, without any right of recovery (Article 3 Clause 6 of the Brussels Convention, 1924-Law 15.787).

19. Should the cargo be of a nature which according to the Regulation of the Port Authorities must be received in Boca or Barracas or other place specified in the Regulations, and should the vessel not discharge in Boca or Barracas or other such specified place, the cargo shall be taken thither from alongside vessel in lighters provided by the Consignees, or if not provided by the Consignees in lighters provided by the ship, but in any event the lighterage shall always be at the expense and risk of Consignees and Vessel's liability shall accordingly cease as soon as the cargo crosses the Ship's rail.

20. Goods for Buenos Aires are to be delivered on arrival of the ship at Buenos Aires free of lighterage expense at a wharf in the Darsena or Docks of Buenos Aires but if from any cause whatever the ship should be unable to get to the wharf and obtain a berth where she can immediately discharge into the Warehouse of the Docks or should the goods not be admitted into the Warehouse the Agents of the ship may effect the discharge by lighters, the lighterage and all wharfage dues being for account of the cargo. Save insofar as they are expressly contradicted by this clause the delivery of the goods to Buenos Aires is also to be subject to all exceptions and conditions of this Bill of Lading.

21. Additional to the freight for the renewal of the Brazilian Merchant Marine (Law Decree No. 1801 of 18.8.80) equivalent to 20% of the freight to be paid by the Consignee(s) to the Carrier's Agent at port of destination in cruzeiros at the rate of exchange published by SUNAMAM for this purpose. In default of such payment by or on behalf of the Consignee(s) or other Owner(s) of the goods within seven days of the arrival of the vessel at port of destination, the Carrier shall have the right of recourse against Shippers and be entitled to recover from them the amount of any of this additional unpaid.

22. Argentine freight tax instituted by present law or any future law is payable by the importers.

23. All expenses and charges up to Ship's rail at port of loading and expenses and charges after Ship's rail at port of discharge are for the account of cargo.

24. Carrier cannot accept any responsibility for non-compliance with packing requirements as established under ruling 14/80 of Capitania de Puerto de Buenos Aires. Any consequencas financial or otherwise resulting from non-compliance with this ruling to be for the account of the cargo.

25. In accepting this Bill of Lading the shipper, Consignee and/or Owners of the goods and the holder of this Bill of Lading, expressly accept and agree to all its stipulations, conditions and exceptions whether written, printed, stamped or incorporated on the front or back hereof, as fully as if they were all signed by such shipper, consignee, owner or holder. This Bill of Lading shall be construed and governed by English Law, and shall apply from the time the goods are received for shipment until delivery, but always subject to the conditions and exceptions of the carrying conveyance; it shall be given up, duly endorsed, in exchange for delivery order if required.

N.B. Clause 21—
Reference to 20% is to be read as 30%.

Exhibit 33 **Sea waybill**

© GCBS 1979	

NON-NEGOTIABLE SEA WAYBILL

UK Customs Assigned No.   SWB No. 33
99999
Shipper's Reference
566 – 12353 CD
F/Agent's Reference

Shipper
SITPRO Export Ltd
High Street
Burton on Trent   DE15 1YZ
England   VAT No. 241 8235 77

Consignee
NITPRO
103 Lewis St PMB 12776
Lagos
NIGERIA

Name of Carrier
UKWAL Vessel

Notify Party and Address (leave blank if stated above)

The contract evidenced by this Waybill is subject to the exceptions, limitations, conditions and liberties (including those relating to pre-carriage and on-carriage) set out in the Carrier's Standard Conditions of Carriage applicable to the voyage covered by this Waybill and operative on its date of issue; if the carriage is one where had a Bill of Lading been issued the provisions of the Hague Rules contained in the International Convention for unification of certain rules relating to Bills of Lading dated Brussels, 25th August 1924, as amended by the Protocol signed at Brussels on the 23rd February 1968 (the Hague Visby Rules) would have been compulsorily applicable under Article X of the said Standard Conditions contain or shall be deemed to contain a Clause giving effect to the Hague Visby Rules. Otherwise the said Standard Conditions contain or shall be deemed to contain a Clause giving effect to the provisions of the Hague Rules. In neither case shall the proviso to the first sentence of Article V of the Hague Rules or the Hague Visby Rules apply. The Carrier hereby agrees: (i) that to the extent of any inconsistency the said clause shall prevail over the said Standard Conditions in respect of any period to which the Hague Rules or the Hague Visby Rules by their terms apply; and (ii) that for the purpose of the terms of this Contract of Carriage this Waybill falls within the definition of Article 1(b) of the Hague Rules and the Hague Visby Rules.
The Shipper accepts the said Standard Conditions on his own behalf and on behalf of the Consignee and the owner of the goods and warrants that he has authority to do so. The Consignee by presenting this Waybill and/or requesting delivery of the goods further undertakes all liabilities of the Shipper hereunder such undertaking being additional and without prejudice to the Shipper's own liability. The benefit of the contract evidenced by this Waybill shall thereby be transferred to the Consignee or other persons presenting this Waybill.
Notwithstanding anything contained in the said Standard Conditions, the term Carrier in this Waybill shall mean the Carrier named on the front thereof.
A copy of the Carrier's said Standard Conditions applicable hereto may be inspected or will be supplied on request at the office of the Carrier or the Carrier's Principal Agents.

Pre-Carriage by*
UKWAL

Place of Receipt by Pre-Carrier*
Birmingham

Vessel
UKWAL Vessel

Port of Loading
Liverpool

Port of Discharge
Lagos

Place of Delivery by On-Carrier*
Lagos

Marks and Nos; Container No.	Number and kind of packages; Description of Goods	Gross Weight	Measurement
NITPRO NG3421 Lagos 1/10	10 Cases Machine Tool Parts	5105kg	8.720m3

Freight Details; Charges etc.

RECEIVED FOR CARRIAGE as above in apparent good order and condition, unless otherwise stated hereon, the goods described in the above particulars.

GCBS
SWB
1979

711

Ocean Freight Payable at
Origin

Place and Date of Issue

Signature for Carrier; Carrier's Principal Place of Business

Exhibit 34 **Mate's receipt**

H S K

HANSEATISCHES SEEFRACHTENKONTOR G.M.B.H. HAMBURG

Durchwahl Nr. 334/336   13.Juni 19..

G O O D S   R E C E I P T

Received in apparent good order and condition on board
the MV "BORCHNUNG" the undermentioned goods for shipment
from Hamburg to Istanbul.

Received from Firma Kunzchemie, Hamburg

K.C.H.
Istanbul
1/20   20 drums   Potassium Ferricyanide 1100 kos

Hochachtungsvoll
Hanseatisches Seefrachtenkontor
G.m.b.H.

P.Strauss

Exhibit 35 **Bill of exchange drawn in foreign currency and payable at sight**
(front)

EXCHANGE FOR U.S. $5,000.00   16th May   19

At   sight   *pay this* first *Bill of Exchange*
                                                          to the Order of
second unpaid

ourselves

the sum of United States dollars five thousand only

Value   received   *which place to Account*
To   Hans Loyler Inc.   per pro Jones Diceheart Ltd
          New York   Secretary

Foreign B/X. Printed & Sold by Waterlow & Sons Ltd., London, E.C.1.

(back)

per pro Jones Diceheart Ltd
         Secretary

Exhibit 36   **Bill of exchange drawn in sterling and payable at 60 days date** *(front)*

EXCHANGE FOR £720.00   17th May   19

At   60 days date   *pay this* first *Bill of Exchange*

second unpaid   *to the Order of*

ourselves

the sum of seven hundred and twenty pounds only

Value   received   *which place to Account*

To   Bruce Sistersohn   Fife's Pipes Co.
     Zurich Switzerland   T.W. Waterhouse.
                                              Director

(Foreign B/X. Printed & Sold by Waterlow & Sons Ltd., London, E.C.2.)

(back)

Fife's Pipes Co
Director
T. W. Waterhouse.

Exhibit 37   **Bill of exchange accepted payable at 30 days' sight** *(front)*

EXCHANGE FOR £1,600.00   1st June   19

At   30 days sight   *pay this* sole L^D *Bill of Exchange*
                                                              to the Order of

Sanderson Witt & Smiths

One thousand six hundred pounds only

Accepted 4th June 19.
Payable 6th July 19.
Journal Barkley
Secretary Sillick & Sons
Barkley, Sillick & Sons

Value   received   *which place to Account*

To   Barkley, Sillick & Sons Ltd.,   For Sanderson Witt & Smiths
       London   Director

(back)

                    For Sanderson Witt & Smiths
                              Director

Exhibit 38 **Promissory note**

PROMISSORY   NOTE

London 28th May 19..

£5213.00

On the 28th August 19.. fixed by the Promissory Note
we promise to pay N.Y.C. Ingafielf A/S or order at their offices
in Oslo the sum of five thousand two hundred and thirteen pounds
sterling.

For and on behalf of

Sithers Johnson Ltd.

Exhibit 39 **Inspection and sampling order**

No. 219   25th April   19

To The Superintendent of Brown's Warehouse, Wapping.

PLEASE ~~XXXXXXXXXX~~ ~~XXXXXXXXX~~ grant inspection facilities to   ~~XXXXXXX~~
the bearer for the purpose of examining
the undermentioned Goods,

ex Ship Robert Dove   Rotation No. 96335

Charges to be paid by us

Marks and Numbers	Quantity	Description
Q.A.T. 4 - 17	fourteen	Carpets

OFFICE COPY

SPECIMEN

Per pro
NATIONAL WESTMINSTER BANK LIMITED

Caravelle

Office or Branch
Manager

430-1-9 69

Exhibit 40   **Delivery order**

DELIVERY ORDER

No. 107   4th July   19

To The Superintendent of London Warehouses Ltd.

PLEASE DELIVER TO Alexander Productions   or Order

the undermentioned Goods,

ex Ship Mustansir   Rotation No.   6640L

Charges to be paid by consignee

Marks and Numbers	Quantity	Description
M M M M M M	One case	Photographic spools

S P E C I M E N

Per pro
NATIONAL WESTMINSTER BANK LIMITED

Chesil Beach
....
Office or Branch
....
Manager

430-1-9-69

Exhibit 41   **Warehouse receipt**

SIVEWRIGHT TRANSPORT & STORAGE LIMITED

SPECIMEN ONLY OF   ADVICE OF GOODS RECEIVED

R 8067
R 8067

Into...... Morpeth Tongue ....WAREHOUSE, BIRKENHEAD.

On (date)...... 25th June, 1977 ....   I. No........ 12554 ....

Sender or Ex......ex. 'TOKIO EXPRESS' ......   M/C No.......................................

A/c............ Messrs. Black & Sons Ltd., ...

Senders Ref.	Marks and or Numbers	Quantity of Packages	Tons	Cwts.	Qts.	Lbs.	WEIGHTS, Descriptions or other particulars (provided by senders)	Remarks
1231	BLACK/BLUE	4	400	Kilos			Pallets Empty Glass Ink Bottles.	
							A number of bottles broken.	
							UNEXAMINED	
	TOTALS	(−4−) FOUR						

OBSERVATIONS.   E. & O. E., and subject to our Conditions of Storage.

For SIVEWRIGHT TRANSPORT & STORAGE LTD.

Exhibit 42 **Trust receipt** *(front)*

NWB1044 Trust Certificate

To Rimmer Glendz & Co
9, Trottingham Park
London E. 1.

The Customer

3rd May   19___

Dear Sir,

We hand you herewith the undermentioned documents of title to the undermentioned goods (now in pledge to us as security for advances) on the following terms and conditions:—

You undertake to hold the documents of Title and the said goods when received (and the proceeds thereof when sold) as trustees for NATIONAL WESTMINSTER BANK LIMITED (the Bank).

(a) (b) (c)
one or more of
these to be deleted.

(a) As you require the said documents in order to obtain delivery of the said goods you undertake to warehouse them in the name of the Bank and to hand us the Warrants forthwith; also to insure the goods against all risks to their full insurable value and to hold the policies on our behalf and in case of loss to pay the Insurance moneys to us in the same manner as proceeds of sales.

(b) As you require the said goods in order to despatch the same to your agents for the purpose of sale or for processing printing or for the further preparation of the said goods in any manner whatsoever for immediate or eventual sale you undertake to hand us the receipts of your agents for the said goods and at all times to keep the goods fully insured against all risks however caused and to hold the policies on our behalf and in case of loss to pay the Insurance money to us in the same manner as proceeds of sales.

Insert number
of days

(c) As you require the said goods in order to deliver the goods to the Buyers you undertake to pay us the proceeds of sales without deduction of any expenses and immediately upon the receipt thereof or of each portion thereof, as the case may be within 15 days days from the date hereof and to give us on request full authority to receive from any person or persons the purchase moneys of such goods or any of them and in the meantime to hold the goods in trust for us.

You undertake also to keep this transaction separate from all other transactions.

We authorise you to take delivery of the goods on our behalf and to act as our trustees in the custody and realisation of the same and we request you to pay the proceeds of all sales to us immediately and specifically as received by you and to act on the above terms.

Yours faithfully,

NATIONAL WESTMINSTER BANK LIMITED

PRINCES STREET OFFICE
_____ Branch

_____ Manager

Exhibit 42 **Trust receipt** *(back)*

The Schedule of Documents and Goods

Description of Documents	Description of Goods	Vessel	Name of Buyer	Invoice Price
3/3 B/Ls Insurance Pol. Invoice in trip	Tinned peaches	Flemmington	Andrew Sprite & Son	£2,400

To The Manager,   7th May   19___

National Westminster Bank Limited

PRINCES STREET OFFICE

1, PRINCES STREET, E.C.2.   Branch

Dear Sir,

I/We acknowledge receipt of the above-mentioned documents relating to the above-mentioned goods of the Bank which I/we receive and/or will deal with upon the above terms and conditions giving as I/we do hereby all the undertakings mentioned above.

(*)to be deleted if (c) above is deleted

(*) I/We hereby declare that I am/ we are not indebted to the Buyers of the goods.

Yours faithfully,

For & on behalf of
Rimmer Gleadz & Co.

Secretary

PAST EXAMINATION QUESTIONS

1   Explain the following types of bills of lading:
a   clean
b   short form, and
c   charter party
     Why is type *c* normally unacceptable to banks for tender under credits?

(Institute of Export)

2   Explain the following terms when applied to bills of lading:
a   liner
b   through
c   forwarding agent's bill
d   received for shipment
     Which of the above would not be acceptable to banks as tender under a documentary credit, and why?

(Institute of Freight Forwarders)

3   What are the principal documents usually called for under a documentary credit: what are the main purposes of each, and what are the particular details in them to which a bank pays special attention when effecting payment under the credit?

(Institute of Bankers)

A fundamental knowledge of shipping documents is required in order to answer a number of questions involving collections and documentary credits. The above are typical and probably demand a greater knowledge of documentation than the settlement system of documentary credits to which they refer (see Chapter 5 on documentary credits).

CHAPTER FOUR

Collections

1. INTRODUCTION

Collections provide the trading parties, buyer and seller, with a compromise between open account terms and payment in advance for the settlement of their transactions.

An exporter who wants the proceeds of a sale of goods or services collected from the overseas buyer and credited to his bank account will give instructions to his bank to do this for him. The exporter has to initiate the act of collection by drawing a bill of exchange on his overseas buyer with or without documents attached and giving it to his bank with the appropriate collection instructions. In some cases the presentation of documents may be without a draft. The remitting bank will use the services of a branch or another bank in the buyer's country to call upon the importer to make payment. This is done in accordance with the specified instructions and, if all goes well, the collecting bank will be able to transfer the proceeds to the remitting bank which, in turn, will credit its customer's account.

Some of the technical expressions used are explained in section 14 in this chapter. Banks in the UK and some 80 other countries apply these 'rules' to all collections.

The collection service offered by banks is a means by which a creditor in one country may obtain settlement from a debtor in another through banking channels at a minimum cost. A documentary collection can offer the exporter a degree of security in the transaction, which is not inherent in a clean collection or open account method, provided all the documents of title are handled by the banks. The banks will therefore have constructive control over the goods through the title documents and can arrange for release of such title only against payment. In the event of non-payment, the banks, if they have constructive control over the goods, can arrange for their release/protection/warehousing or re-shipment on behalf of the unpaid exporter and in accordance with his instructions.

The bills department of a large bank will usually have three main sections:

a   *Outward collections*: the bank acts as the remitting bank by sending documents abroad and obtaining payment through its agents.

b   *Inward collections*: the bank acts as a collecting bank and receives documents and instructions from banks abroad on whose behalf it endeavours to collect money from UK importers, remitting the proceeds to its principals, the remitting banks abroad.

c   *Bills for sale*: this section provides finance and is dealt with later in this chapter.

2.   PARTIES INVOLVED IN A COLLECTION

A Correct bills terminology	B Other names of parties
The principal ↓	Exporter or seller or drawer or a bank collecting on its own behalf
The remitting bank ↓	Principal's bank
The collecting bank ↓	Correspondent or agent of the remitting bank
The presenting bank	The bank actually presenting to the drawee

Column A shows the direction in which the documents move between the parties, here described in correct terminology. The words in column B are synonymous with those in column A. In the event of any difficulty arising in a transaction, such as non-payment, the principal may have an agent in the drawee's country who will look after things for him. This agent is known as the 'case of need' and it is essential that the principal advises the remitting bank of the powers of his agent.

The procedure of events under a collection is as follows: the principal ships his goods and may:

● present the shipping documents to his bank, or
● send them direct to the drawee

Under the first procedure the remitting bank will receive from its customer a clean bill of exchange, a bill of exchange accompanied by documents, or documents alone without a bill of exchange. In each case the presentation to the remitting bank will be accompanied by the customer's instructions in the form of a collection order (see section 6 of this chapter). The remitting bank will forward the documents and/or bills of exchange to a collecting bank, usually in the drawee's centre with corresponding instructions. The collecting bank may effect the presentation to the drawee directly or may use the services of another bank – the presenting bank. In either case the collection will be discharged only after settlement in the manner prescribed by the principal. The collecting bank will either account to the remitting bank for the proceeds, if paid, or report non-payment. The remitting bank will thus report the fate of the collection to the principal, making the proceeds available to him.

3.   CLEAN COLLECTIONS

A clean collection is one which consists of one or more bills of exchange or promissory notes (or cheques, or receipts, or other similar financial documents for obtaining the payment of money), there being no commercial documents attached, such as invoices, shipping documents, etc.

a   An exporter may draw a bill of exchange on the importer, which he hands to his bank for collection of the proceeds. The shipping documents to which the bill relates will probably have been sent to the buyer already. This therefore is a similar means of settlement to open account trade, except the buyer is prompted to pay under a collection by the presentation of a bill of exchange whereas on open account terms the buyer agrees to settle at a predetermined time.

b   The payee of a cheque drawn by someone abroad will require his bank, the remitting bank, to remit the cheque abroad for payment by the foreign bank on which it is drawn. Assuming that funds are available and may be transferred to the UK, the cheque will be paid, and the payee will receive payment as soon as his bank, the remitting bank, is paid.

c   Travellers' cheques issued by foreign banks abroad and encashed in the UK are sent for collection to the bank abroad by which they were issued. The remitting bank normally collects these items for its own account, having previously paid the presenter (see section 17 of this chapter).

d   Promissory notes are seen less frequently than, say, bills of exchange. The payee or holder of a note will present it to his bank for collection of the proceeds from the overseas maker. Under special finance arrangements (see Chapter 6), promissory notes held by the lending bank, usually under medium- or long-term facilities, as part of their security will be sent for collection and payment near to their maturity dates. Having financed the item the remitting banker will forward it for collection for his own account.

4.   SIGHT AND TERM BILLS OF EXCHANGE

Bills of exchange drawn at sight are payable by the drawee on presentation.

Term bills of exchange drawn to mature for payment at a fixed or future determinable time provide the drawee (buyer) with time to pay. The drawee is normally expected to accept term bills drawn on him, thereby giving his undertaking to make payment at the time specified in the bill of exchange.

Term or tenor bills may be sent by the remitting bank to the collecting bank *i* for acceptance by the drawee and return to the remitting bank, or *ii* for acceptance by the drawee and then to be held by the collecting bank for eventual payment. When a bill of exchange is despatched on an 'acceptance and return' basis, the accepted bill, being the property of the drawer (principal), is usually sent to the drawer when it is received back by his bank. Near to the maturity date of the bill the drawer returns it to his bank, this time to send it for collection payable on the maturity date. While the majority of collecting banks throughout the world will hold accepted bills on behalf of the remitting banks, pending re-presentation for payment at maturity, there are some that have no facilities to do this and will return an accepted bill automatically. *The vast majority of term bills are held abroad after acceptance, pending payment at maturity,* and the few that are returned to the drawer's country are normally required as *security for special export lending* (see Chapter 6). Principals are usually reluctant to pay double collection charges for handling a bill twice, as well as having to hold an accepted bill in the meantime and arrange for its re-presentation for payment.

5. DOCUMENTARY COLLECTIONS

Documentary collections may be described as financial documents accompanied by commercial documents, or commercial documents not accompanied by financial documents: these terms are defined in section 14 of this chapter. The documents presented may represent the full title to the goods, or on the other hand may provide evidence that the buyer has obtained, or is likely to be able to obtain, the goods without necessarily requiring the documents submitted through the banks for collection. Where title documents are presented, or where goods have been consigned to the collecting bank directly, the collecting bank is able to exercise control over the goods on behalf of the remitting bank.

Release of the documents to the buyer (drawee) which will enable him to obtain the goods, if he has not done so already, may be made as follows:

Sight bill	Term bill
Against payment (D/P)	Against acceptance (D/A documents against acceptance)
	or
	Against payment (D/P documents against payment)

Further details of D/A and D/P are provided under sections 7 and 8 of this chapter.

What points should the remitting bank look for when receiving a customer's documents prior to sending them abroad for payment? Remitting banks have a moral, though not a legal, responsibility to examine cursorily their customers' documents to identify factors that would either cause unnecessary delay in payment or result perhaps in non-payment altogether: moreover in so doing they may well save themselves trouble later. The points to look for include:

i   Correct endorsements on bills of lading, insurance documents, and bills of exchange.

ii   Complete set of shipping documents; if one is missing it is important for the bank to query this fact with the customer. If documents are missing, such as an original bill of lading, it is important for the collecting bank to know whether or not it has control over the goods and, in the event of non-payment, can protect itself as instructed. The missing bill may have been sent directly to the buyer, or may have been retained by the drawer, or could be lost.

iii   The bill of exchange must be properly drawn since it is on this document that payment is to be made, finance provided, or action taken in the event of default by the drawee.

iv   Under C & F or CIF contracts (evidenced by the invoices), when accompanied by a document of movement such as a bill of lading, the document of movement must be marked 'freight paid'.

v   Under CIF contracts an insurance document should be presented showing goods insured for at least the amount of the invoice.

vi   The documentary requirements of the importing authorities of the drawee's country must be met, otherwise the goods will not be cleared by the customs in that country, or the buyer may get the goods but will have to pay a higher rate of import duty than he need. As regulations differ from country to country, and alterations to documentary requirements are common, it is necessary for exporters and freight forwarders, and customary for bankers, to have up to date sources of information. The Department of Trade, the embassy of the importer's country, and Croner's *Handbook for Exporters* (which is up-dated monthly), are the most popular sources.

The degree to which individual banks check points *i–vi* above may vary, particularly as Article 2 of *Uniform Rules for Collections* (section 14, below) states that there is no obligation to examine the documents except to verify that those listed in the collection order have been received.

6. THE COLLECTION ORDER

The exporter requiring his bank to collect the proceeds of a documentary collection must give complete and precise instructions to the remitting bank. The remitting bank must act in accordance with those instructions, most of which will be passed on to the overseas collecting bank to effect. An example of a collection order appears at the end of this section. The following information is required by banks handling collections:

i To which bank should the collection be sent? If the drawer has not been asked by the drawee to have the collection presented through the drawee's own bank the remitting bank will probably be given the opportunity to forward the collection to a collecting bank of its choice (see section 14, Article 3 in this chapter).

ii When a term bill accompanies a documentary collection the collecting bank must know whether the documents may be released to the drawee against his acceptance or only against payment of the bill. In the absence of instructions, commercial documents will be released only against payment.

iii Buyers in many countries abroad are in the habit of deferring payment or acceptance of the bills until arrival of the carrying steamer. The collecting bank however will, unless otherwise instructed, present the collection immediately it is received for payment or acceptance.

iv The collecting bank should be told how to remit the proceeds obtained, by airmail, cable or SWIFT. The amount is usually a significant factor, as exporters will probably require that larger sums be cabled or sent by an urgent SWIFT message. Smaller payments might not justify the additional cost of a cable remittance.

v Banks make charges for their collection services which must be paid either by the principal or drawee; occasionally payment is shared between the two parties.

Remitting bank charges paid by	Collecting bank charges paid by	Collecting bank claims from drawee	Remitting bank receives from collecting bank
a Drawee	Drawee	Bill amount plus all bank charges	Bill amount plus its own charges. Principal gets bill amount
b Principal	Principal	Bill amount only	Bill amount less collecting bank's charges. Principal gets bill amount less all bank charges
c Principal	Drawee	Bill amount plus own charges only	Bill amount. The principal gets the bill amount less remitting bank's charges

The action to be taken in the event of charges being refused by the drawee is covered in section 14 (Articles 22 and 23) of this chapter. An example of a collection order is reproduced on page 119.

vi Instruction should be given as to whether, and in what circumstances, the bill is to be protested (or other legal process taken in lieu of that). Further information on this subject is given in section 10 of this chapter.

vii   In the event of default or delayed payment, the exporter's agent in the importer's country may be asked to assist in obtaining settlement. This agent is known as the 'case of need'. It is necessary for the collecting bank to have the full name and address of the case of need to advise him in accordance with the instructions given. The collecting bank also needs to know the precise powers of the case of need since these may range from merely keeping an eye on things to taking delivery of the goods and disposing of them. Unconditional powers will entitle the case of need to demand the title documents from the collecting bank without payment. If such powers are accorded and implemented the collecting bank will deliver all documents against the case of need's simple receipt.

viii   What action the collecting bank should take to protect the goods is discussed in section 9 of this chapter.

A final but most important aspect of the collection order is the disclaimer of liability clause. The drawer is required to sign the form to signify his agreement to the terms as stated therein. Since this includes the fact that the collection is subject to ICC *Uniform Rules*, this incorporates automatically the disclaimer of liability clauses contained in Articles 3, 4, 5 and 19 of those rules. The form may also include further clauses in the case of individual banks. In some instances banks may be prepared to take a specific general disclaimer document to cover all collections handled.

7.   ADVANTAGES AND DISADVANTAGES TO THE EXPORTER

Advantages

i   In order to ascertain whether a collection is an appropriately safe method of obtaining settlement, the exporter should have obtained (*a*) a good, recent status report on the buyer, and (*b*) a satisfactory economic/political report on the buyer's country. Credit insurance cover may protect the exporter to a certain extent (see Chapter 6).

ii   Finance may be provided through the following facilities:
  * negotiations (see this chapter, section 17)
  * advances against outward collections (see this chapter, section 18)
  * acceptance credits (see this chapter, section 20)
  * special ECGD-backed export loans (see Chapter 6)

iii   The exporter may obtain a measure of protection for his goods if control over them is vested in the collecting bank, either by its having possession of the full set of documents as collecting agents for the exporter, or by virtue of the goods having been consigned, with the collecting bank's consent, to the order of the collecting bank as agent for the exporter.

iv   A reputable collecting bank will on the drawer's behalf press for payment and often succeed in obtaining it from drawees who wish to defer paying.

v   Where title documents are to be released only against payment the exporter's position is more secure than in the case of open account terms, clean collections, or where documents may be released against the drawee's acceptance of the bill.

vi   The system of settlement is cheaper than under a documentary credit.

Collection order

FOREIGN BILL AND/OR DOCUMENTS FOR COLLECTION

Drawer/Exporter	Drawer's/Exporter's Reference(s) (to be quoted by Bank in all correspondence)
Smith, Jones & Robinson Limited 116 Fox Lane London EC1A 1BB	123/81

Consignee	Drawee (If not Consignee)
South Denmark Import Corporation Kastelsvej 16-18 DK 2100 Copenhagen Denmark	South Denmark Import Corporation Nyhavnsgade 12 Ringsted Denmark

To (Bank)	For Bank use only
City of London Bank Limited 2002 London Wall London EC2N 4FT	

FORWARD DOCUMENTS ENUMERATED BELOW BY AIRMAIL. FOLLOW SPECIAL INSTRUCTIONS AND THOSE MARKED X

Bill of Exchange	Comm'l. Invoice	Cert'd./Cons. Inv.	Cert. of Origin	Ins'ce Pol./Cert.	Bill of Lading	Parcel Post Rec'pt.	Air Waybill
1	3			1	2/2		

Combined Transport Doc.	Other Documents and whereabouts of any missing Original Bill of Lading
	1/2 Bills of lading sent direct to consignee

	ACCEPTANCE	PAYMENT		Protest	Do Not Protest
RELEASE DOCUMENTS ON	X		If unaccepted →		X
If documents are not taken up on arrival of goods	Warehouse Goods X	Do Not Warehouse	and advise reason by	Cable X	Airmail
	Insure Against Fire X	Do Not Insure	If unpaid →	Protest X	Do Not Protest
Collect ALL Charges		X	and advise reason by	Cable X	Airmail
Collect Correspondent's Charges ONLY			Advise acceptance and due date by	Cable	Airmail X
Return Accepted Bill by Airmail			Remit Proceeds by	Cable X	Airmail

In case of need refer to	For Guidance	Accept their Instructions
Fred Petersen, 18 Forbindelsesvej, 2100 Copenhagen	X	

SPECIAL INSTRUCTIONS: 1. Represent on arrival of goods if not honoured on first presentation.

Date of Bill of Exchange 16 May 1981	Bill of Exchange Value/Amount of Collection
Tenor of Bill of Exchange 60 days sight	GBP 7600
Bill of Exchange Claused:—	Please collect the above mentioned Bill and/or Documents subject to the Uniform Rules for Collections 1978 Revision ICC publication no 322. I/We agree that you shall not be liable for any loss, damage, or delay however caused which is not directly due to the negligence of your own officers or servants. Date and Signature London 16 May 1981

447

Transart Copier Systems Software 1977

Disadvantages

i The exporter will not be paid until funds are received by his bank (the remitting bank) in settlement, unless finance is provided by a method listed under *ii* above, and this could prove expensive.

ii The security of payment is not as good as that offered by settlement in advance of goods exported, or even against a documentary credit.

iii The goods, if not taken up by the buyer, will probably incur demurrage or warehouse charges, may have to be re-shipped, and, of course, might never be sold at all. Further insurance costs, and perhaps agents' fees, will add to the potential liability the exporter faces. Whilst he can insure against loss or damage to his goods, he will have to bear a percentage of the risk of losses otherwise covered by credit insurance (see Chapter 6).

8. ADVANTAGES AND DISADVANTAGES TO THE IMPORTER

Advantages

i Collections tend to favour the buyer rather than the seller. The buyer usually wants the goods before paying for them. A clean collection where documents have been sent in advance is as satisfactory to the buyer as open account terms. Documents against acceptance have the same advantages. The buyer can take delivery of the goods and examine them and check that they are what he had ordered before he pays. However, if he has accepted a bill of exchange he still has the legal liability indicated under 'disadvantages' (see below).

ii Deferred credit terms – ie, trade credit – may be obtained by way of term bills of exchange.

iii It is more convenient than going to the trouble of having a documentary credit established, and cheaper.

iv If, and only if, the collection order specifically authorises it, payment and/or acceptance may be deferred until the arrival of the goods.

It may also be noted that direct finance may be obtained by the importer to settle the debt due to the overseas exporter under the collection by obtaining any of the following facilities:

● an overdraft/loan
● a loan against the goods as security
● an acceptance credit facility

Disadvantages

i D/A collections make the importer legally liable on an accepted bill of exchange on which action may be taken in the event of default, quite independently of the underlying contract of sale.

ii D/P collections must be paid on presentation; this may take place before the arrival of the goods, which may perhaps not be what the importer ordered.

9. PROTECTION OF GOODS

Despite the fact that banks have no obligation to take any action in respect of the goods, instructions conveyed in the collection order should be given to the collecting bank as to the care and disposal of goods (in the event of dishonour). Advice of dishonour must be sent to the remitting bank as instructed without delay, and the presenting bank should endeavour to discover and notify the remitting bank of the reasons. The latter may then communicate any further instructions that may be obtained from the exporter. In the meantime the goods should if possible be looked after in accordance with the instructions appearing in the collection order; sometimes the collecting bank is asked to warehouse the goods and insure at least against fire. A port may have no warehouse facilities suitable for the goods in question, and it may not be possible for them to be stored, despite instructions to do so having been given in the remitting schedule. In addition to the risk of fire there are risks of theft, damage by rain, etc, which, unless covered by an extension to the marine insurance policy, may result in the exporter suffering a total loss. Customs formalities at the port of discharge may require that duty be paid and, if subsequently the goods are re-shipped to the seller's country or to an alternative buyer elsewhere, that duty may not necessarily be refunded. Some customs authorities prohibit re-shipment.

All this can cost the seller money that he will probably not be able to recover by a resale. Should the exporter have a suitable agent in the buyer's country who can be relied upon to look after his principal's interests, such agent may be nominated the 'case of need'. Depending on the mandate given to him, the case of need should be able to keep the exporter's disbursements to a minimum, and possibly even find an alternative buyer.

Croner's *Handbook for Importers* provides up to date documentary and other regulations concerning imports of goods into the UK.

10. PROTEST

The reasons/purposes for protest instructions to be given are:
* to retain the right of recourse against prior endorsers and the drawer – which is essential when a bill may have been discounted or negotiated, and
* as a prelude to legal action in order to provide proof of presentation.

A bill is dishonoured when (a) a sight bill is unpaid on presentation to the drawee or (b) a term bill is not accepted on presentation or is unpaid at maturity.

In many countries, including the UK, a drawer may wish to take legal action to recover money due to him by a defaulting drawee, in which case the dishonoured bill must be protested, an action which provides the court with acceptable evidence that the bill has in fact been presented and was dishonoured for reasons stated in the deed of protest. Usually a notary public will protest a bill of behalf of the drawer by calling on the drawee and demanding payment or acceptance. If the bill remains dishonoured the notary will record the reasons, if any, given by the drawee. This information is included in a formal document, the deed of protest, and may be presented in court as evidence of dishonour. A general point is that it is important to keep the drawer advised of what is happening to his collection.

The following paragraph dealing with unpaid bills is taken from a lecture on the subject of 'Collections and Negotiations' given in 1928: such bizarre advices are still received today.

'Customers sometimes express annoyance that a bill has been returned unpaid with no reason given. It is annoying but quite a common thing in many countries. We always endeavour to get our correspondent to obtain a reason and we sometimes get rather startling ones. A few specimens may amuse you. In one case, a letter from a correspondent in central America stated: "This bill returned unpaid. Reason – drawee in prison for murder." A few others are: "Drawee has gone to races and hopes to pay tomorrow." "Will pay when the seeds germinate." "Refuse acceptance but will pay at maternity." A really complicated one was the following: "Drawee has been declared bankrupt and the liquidator appointed has been put in prison for homicide." '

The action of protesting a bill can completely ruin a drawee's business reputation in certain countries abroad where it is taken to be tantamount to an act of bankruptcy. Although occasionally there are genuinely good and sound reasons for dishonouring a bill, such as the seller not complying with the contract, or errors in documentation, it has to be recognised that such action may have serious consequences for the buyer yet yield no financial satisfaction to the seller. How effective then is the act of protesting a dishonoured bill? The threat of protesting a bill may be sufficient to ensure payment, and the act of protesting may in some cases frighten the drawee into paying before the action gets to court. However, the main problem is that when a bill is dishonoured and then protested it is quite possible:
- that the drawee cannot be found to be sued
- that he has no money anyway
- that he has good contractual reasons for *not* accepting or paying

This would mean that the principal would:
- not be able to recover from the drawee
- be wasting money on the deed of protest and then the ensuing action

In many countries, including the UK, there is a statutory limitation to the time within which a dishonoured accepted bill must be protested for non-payment. This time varies according to local legal regulations in different countries. Despite the fact that section 51 of the Bills of Exchange Act 1882 states that a foreign bill must be protested if dishonoured, and that failure to do so will discharge the drawer and endorsers from liability on the bill, the collecting bank acts upon the instructions it has been given and is not concerned with the UK law on the subject because it is acting on behalf of an overseas correspondent.

Under English law, a system may be carried out of 'noting' inward bills that are dishonoured. Noting is a preliminary step to protesting. It is cheaper than protesting and holds open the right to protest formally at a later time should it be considered necessary. If the services of a notary cannot be obtained at the place where the bill is dishonoured, a 'householder's protest' is sufficient. This is a certificate of presentation and an attestation of dishonour, made by a householder or a substantial resident of that place, in the presence of two witnesses, and signed by them all. A bill must be presented at the proper place. When a place of payment is specified in the bill or, when it is accepted payable at a particular place (such as at a bank), presentation must be made at that place and, in the event of dishonour, a foreign bill must be noted or protested at that same place. Outside England, the process of noting is possible in a few Commonwealth countries only. This particular paragraph deals solely with English law.

11. CLAUSES ON BILLS OF EXCHANGE

Clausing a bill of exchange may enable the drawer to fix precisely the amount he will receive in his own currency. Such clauses are:

i   *Payable at the collecting banker's selling rate for demand drafts on London.* The drawee must accept the rate of exchange quoted by the collecting bank. The drawer will obtain the bill amount less collection charges and foreign stamp duty if applicable. The clause relates to bills drawn in sterling only.

ii *Payable at the current rate of exchange for demand drafts on London together with all bank charges*. The drawee must pay the bill amount plus all charges. The drawer receives the face amount of the bill.

iii *Payable at the current rate of exchange for demand drafts on . . ., plus interest at . . . per cent from the date hereof until the approximate date of arrival of return remittance in . . .* The first and third gaps in the above clause will have the name of a city inserted – eg, 'London' or 'New York'. If 'London' appears the bill should be in sterling; if 'New York', dollars, etc. The drawer will receive interest in addition to the bill amount. This clause is often seen although it renders the document invalid as a bill of exchange because the amount in money is not certain as the interest period cannot be determined precisely – eg, the *approximate* date of arrival of the return remittance. It could be argued that this date might never arrive; in any event it has to be *estimated* and therefore does not conform to section 3(i) of the Bills of Exchange Act 1882 as being a *sum certain* in money. If interest were to run to the date of payment, or to any other determinable date, it would most certainly conform to sections 3(i) and 9(i)(a) and be a valid instrument under the Act.

iv *Payable in sterling effective*. This clause is required for certain European countries. The drawee must make payment in sterling which, by local exchange control regulations, may be freely transferred to the UK. He must therefore have obtained the necessary approval by the time of payment. Articles 11 and 12 of *Uniform Rules for Collections* refer.

v *Exchange as per endorsement*. This clause is used for the negotiation of sterling bills, usually confined to trade between the UK and South Africa and the UK and East Africa. The UK negotiating bank (see sections 17 and 19 in this chapter) pays the drawer the full amount of the sterling bill, then calculates the gross amount due from the foreign drawee in his own currency to include all the bank's charges and interest between the time the drawer is paid in the UK and the time that the drawee settles abroad. The negotiating bank puts the foreign currency amount and rate of exchange on the bill or collection order and the drawee must pay the sum demanded. From the principal's point of view it is a sterling bill; from the drawee's point of view it is a bill in his own currency, but he runs an exchange risk as the conversion exchange rate is inserted by the UK remitting bank (see Chapter 8).

12. COLLECTIONS IN FOREIGN CURRENCY

a Outward collections

Foreign currency proceeds received on behalf of a UK-resident principal may be bought by the remitting bank and the sterling equivalent credited to the principal's account. However, when the principal has a foreign currency account the proceeds may be paid direct into that account. The sale of foreign currency proceeds by the principal may be made when they arrive, as a spot transaction (see Chapter 8). On the other hand the proceeds may be applied against a forward contract which would enable the principal to determine in advance the exact amount of sterling to be credited to his account when the collection proceeds arrive.

The remitting bank will ask the collecting bank to remit foreign currency proceeds after collection in one of the following ways:

i   By crediting the remitting bank's *nostro* account, by mail, cable, telex or SWIFT advice to the remitting bank.

ii By airmail, telex, cable or SWIFT payment to another bank with which the remitting bank maintains a *nostro* account, again by advice to the remitting bank.

iii By airmailing a banker's draft drawn, in the foreign currency to be collected, on a bank in the country of the currency. An example might be a collection in US dollars on Brazil in which the Brazilian collecting bank is required to forward its draft on a bank in, say, New York. This draft, when received by the remitting bank, may be negotiated and sterling proceeds paid to the UK principal. Alternatively, if the principal has a dollar account this account could be credited with the dollar amount. In both cases the dollar draft would then be sent to New York for payment and crediting to the remitting bank's *nostro* account with its New York correspondent.

b Inward collections

Importers on whom bills in foreign currency are drawn may:

i   Buy the currency at the spot rate ruling on the due date of payment.

ii Buy the currency forward. This will fix the rate of exchange so that the importer knows what his sterling liability will be on the due date in the future. If he relies on a spot transaction the rates may well have altered to his detriment, causing the importer to pay more sterling for the same amount of foreign currency.

iii Pay the currency amount due to the debit of a foreign currency account if the importer has such an account.

iv Buy spot currency on the day the bill is accepted and place funds on a deposit account until maturity.

13. SPECIFIC REQUIREMENTS OF OVERSEAS IMPORTING AUTHORITIES

Each country has its own regulations concerning the documents required, licensing, insurance, marking of goods, etc. These regulations change from time to time according to economic variations or government policies. Exporters have to know the appropriate current regulations in force in the buyer's country to ensure that the goods exported will pass through the importer's customs with minimum formality. Considerable delay can occur when regulations are not complied with, and this can result in the authorities impounding or confiscating the goods. Two of the leading publications which provide information of this nature are Croner's *Handbook for Exporters* and *The Exporter's Yearbook*. Both publications are regularly updated with changes that may have taken place. Exporters are advised to contact the Department of Trade, and perhaps the commercial section of the importing country's embassy in the UK, for further information of this nature.

Although there is no responsibility placed on the remitting banker under *Uniform Rules for Collections*, nevertheless he should be able to advise exporting customers of the documentary requirements for any particular country. When for example a documentary collection is presented to the remitting bank and upon cursory examination it is noted that three invoices in English with facsimile signatures have been presented, whereas for this particular country four invoices in

Spanish, manually signed, are required, it would be advisable to inform the customer before despatching his documents to the collecting bank. The customer may have forwarded the documents directly; he may still have them and sent to his bank the wrong ones; or he may not have been aware of the current regulations.

14. 'UNIFORM RULES FOR COLLECTIONS'

International Chamber of Commerce Publication No. 322 (1978)

With effect from January 1979 this code of practice, drawn up by the International Chamber of Commerce, was adopted by the British Bankers Association and the Accepting Houses Committee. The rules set out, in precise and clear wording, definitions of terms used in collection work and procedures to be effected by all parties involved.

The Articles cover liabilities and responsibilities, presentation, payment, acceptance, promissory notes, receipts and other instruments, protest, case of need and protection of goods, advice of fate, and interest charges and expenses.

General provisions and definitions

A These provisions and definitions and the following Articles apply to all collections as defined in **B** below and are binding upon all parties thereto unless otherwise expressly agreed or unless contrary to the provisions of a national, state or local law and/or regulation which cannot be departed from.

B For the purpose of such provisions, definitions and articles:

1 *i* 'Collection' means the handling by banks, on instructions received, of documents as defined in *ii* below, in order to:
  (a) obtain acceptance and/or, as the case may be, payment, or
  (b) deliver commercial documents against acceptance and/or, as the case may be, against payment, or
  (c) deliver documents on other terms and conditions.

 ii 'Documents' means financial documents and/or commercial documents:
  (a) 'financial documents' means bills of exchange, promissory notes, cheques, payment receipts or other similar instruments used for obtaining the payment of money
  (b) 'commercial documents' means invoices, shipping documents, documents of title or other similar documents, or any other documents whatsoever, not being financial documents.

 iii 'Clean collection' means collection of financial documents not accompanied by commercial documents.

 iv 'Documentary collection' means collection of:
  (a) financial documents accompanied by commercial documents
  (b) commercial documents not accompanied by financial documents.

2 The 'parties thereto' are:
 i the 'principal', who is the customer entrusting the operation of collection to his bank
 ii the 'remitting bank', which is the bank to which the principal has entrusted the operation of collection
 iii the 'collecting bank', which is any bank, other than the remitting bank, involved in processing the collection order
 iv the 'presenting bank', which is the collecting bank making presentation to the drawee.

3   The 'drawee' is the one to whom presentation is to be made according to the collection order.

C   All documents sent for collection must be accompanied by a collection order giving complete and precise instructions. Banks are permitted to act only upon the instructions given in such collection order, and in accordance with these rules.

If any bank cannot, for any reason, comply with the instructions given in the collection order received by it, it must immediately advise the party from whom it received the collection order.

Liabilities and responsibilities

Article 1
Banks will act in good faith and exercise reasonable care.

Article 2
Banks must verify that the documents received appear to be as listed in the collection order and must immediately advise the party from whom the collection order was received of any documents missing.

Banks have no further obligation to examine the documents.

Article 3
For the purpose of giving effect to the instructions of the principal, the remitting bank will utilise as the collecting bank:
i   the collecting bank nominated by the principal, or, in the absence of such nomination,
ii   any bank, of its own or another bank's choice, in the country of payment or acceptance, as the case may be.

The documents and the collection order may be sent to the collecting bank directly or through another bank as intermediary.

Banks utilising the services of other banks for the purpose of giving effect to the instructions of the principal do so for the account of and at the risk of the latter.

The principal shall be bound by and liable to indemnify the banks against all obligations and responsibilities imposed by foreign laws or usages.

Article 4
Banks concerned with a collection assume no liability or responsibility for the consequences arising out of delay and/or loss in transit of any messages, letters or documents, or for delay, mutilation or other errors arising in the transmission of cables, telegrams, telex, or communication by electronic systems, or for errors in translation or interpretation of technical terms.

Article 5
Banks concerned with a collection assume no liability or responsibility for consequences arising out of the interruption of their business by acts of God, riots, civil commotions, insurrections, wars, or any other causes beyond their control or by any strikes or lockouts.

Article 6
Goods should not be dispatched direct to the address of a bank or consigned to a bank without prior agreement on the part of that bank.

In the event of goods being dispatched direct to the address of a bank or consigned to a bank for delivery to a drawee against payment or acceptance or upon other terms without prior agreement on the part of that bank, the bank has no obligation to take delivery of the goods, which remain at the risk and responsibility of the party dispatching the goods.

Presentation
Article 7

Documents are to be presented to the drawee in the form in which they are received, except that remitting and collecting banks are authorised to affix any necessary stamps, at the expense of the principal unless otherwise instructed, and to make any necessary endorsements or place any rubber stamps or other identifying marks or symbols customary to or required for the collection operation.

Article 8

Collection orders should bear the complete address of the drawee or of the domicile at which presentation is to be made. If the address is incomplete or incorrect, the collecting bank may, without obligation and responsibility on its part, endeavour to ascertain the proper address.

Article 9

In the case of documents payable at sight the presenting bank must make presentation for payment without delay.

In the case of documents payable at a tenor other than sight the presenting bank must, where acceptance is called for, make presentation for acceptance without delay, and where payment is called for, make presentation for payment not later than the appropriate maturity date.

Article 10

In respect of a documentary collection, including a bill of exchange payable at a future date, the collection order should state whether the commercial documents are to be released to the drawee against acceptance (D/A) or against payment (D/P).

In the absence of such statement, the commercial documents will be released only against payment.

Payment
Article 11

In the case of documents payable in the currency of the country of payment (local currency), the presenting bank must, unless otherwise instructed in the collection order, only release the documents to the drawee against payment in local currency which is immediately available for disposal in the manner specified in the collection order.

Article 12

In the case of documents payable in a currency other than that of the country of payment (foreign currency) the presenting bank must, unless otherwise instructed in the collection order, only release the documents to the drawee against payment in the relative foreign currency which can immediately be remitted in accordance with the instructions given in the collection order.

Article 13

In respect of clean collections partial payments may be accepted if and to the extent to which and on the conditions on which partial payments are authorised by the law in force in the place of payment. The documents will only be released to the drawee when full payment thereof has been received.

In respect of documentary collections partial payments will be accepted only if specifically authorised in the collection order. However, unless otherwise instructed, the presenting bank will release the documents to the drawee only after full payment has been received.

In all cases partial payments will be accepted only subject to compliance with the provisions of either Article 11 or Article 12 as appropriate.

Partial payment, if accepted, will be dealt with in accordance with the provisions of Article 14.

Article 14
Amounts collected (less charges and/or disbursements and/or expenses where applicable) must be made available without delay to the bank from which the collection order was received in accordance with the instructions contained in the collection order.

Acceptance
Article 15
The presenting bank is responsible for seeing that the form of the acceptance of a bill of exchange appears to be complete and correct, but is not responsible for the genuineness of any signature or for the authority of any signatory to sign the acceptance.

Promissory notes, receipts and other similar instruments
Article 16
The presenting bank is not responsible for the genuineness of any signature or for the authority of any signatory to sign a promissory note, receipt, or other similar instrument.

Protest
Article 17
The collection order should give specific instructions regarding protest (or other legal process in lieu thereof), in the event of non-acceptance or non-payment.

In the absence of such specific instructions the banks concerned with the collection have no obligation to have the documents protested (or subjected to other legal process in lieu thereof) for non-payment or non-acceptance.

Any charges and/or expenses incurred by banks in connection with such protest or other legal process will be for the account of the principal.

Case of need (principal's representative) and protection of goods
Article 18
If the principal nominates a representative to act as case of need in the event of non-acceptance and/or non-payment the collection order should clearly and fully indicate the powers of such case of need.

In the absence of such indication banks will not accept any instructions from the case of need.

Article 19
Banks have no obligation to take any action in respect of the goods to which a documentary collection relates.

Nevertheless in the case that banks take action for the protection of the goods, whether instructed or not, they assume no liability or responsibility with regard to the fate and/or condition of the goods and/or for any acts and/or omissions on the part of any third parties entrusted with the custody and/or protection of the goods. However, the collecting bank must immediately advise the bank from which the collection order was received of any such action taken.

Any charges and/or expenses incurred by banks in connection with any action for the protection of the goods will be for the account of the principal.

Advice of fate, etc
Article 20

Collecting banks are to advise fate in accordance with the following rules:

i   Form of advice – all advices or information from the collecting bank to the bank from which the collection order was received, must bear appropriate detail including, in all cases, the latter bank's reference number of the collection order.

ii   Method of advice – in the absence of specific instructions the collecting bank must send all advices to the bank from which the collection order was received by quickest mail but, if the collecting bank considers the matter to be urgent, quicker methods such as cable, telegram, telex, or communication by electronic systems, etc, may be used at the expense of the principal.

iii   (*a*)   Advice of payment – the collecting bank must send without delay advice of payment to the bank from which the collection order was received, detailing the amount or amounts collected, charges and/or disbursements and/or expenses deducted, where appropriate, and method of disposal of the funds.

    (*b*)   Advice of acceptance – the collecting bank must send without delay advice of acceptance to the bank from which the collection order was received.

    (*c*)   Advice of non-payment or non-acceptance – the collecting bank must send without delay advice of non-payment or advice of non-acceptance to the bank from which the collection order was received.

The presenting bank should endeavour to ascertain the reasons for such non-payment or non-acceptance and advise accordingly the bank from which the collection order was received.

On receipt of such advice the remitting bank must, within a reasonable time, give appropriate instructions as to the further handling of the documents. If such instructions are not received by the presenting bank within 90 days from its advice of non-payment or non-acceptance, the documents may be returned to the bank from which the collection order was received.

Interest, charges, and expenses
Article 21

If the collection order includes an instruction to collect interest which is not embodied in the accompanying financial document(s), if any, and the drawee refuses to pay such interest, the presenting bank may deliver the document(s) against payment or acceptance as the case may be without collecting such interest, unless the collection order expressly states that such interest may not be waived. Where such interest is to be collected the collection order must bear an indication of the rate of interest and the period covered. When payment of interest has been refused the presenting bank must inform the bank from which the collection order was received accordingly.

If the documents include a financial document containing an unconditional and definitive interest clause the interest amount is deemed to form part of the amount of the documents to be collected. Accordingly, the interest amount is payable in addition to the principal amount shown in the financial document and may not be waived unless the collection order so authorises.

Article 22

If the collection order includes an instruction that collection charges and/or expenses are to be for account of the drawee and the drawee refuses to pay them, the presenting bank may deliver the document(s) against payment or acceptance as the case may be without collecting charges and/or expenses unless the collection order expressly states that such charges and/or expenses may not be waived. When payment of collection charges and/or expenses has been refused the presenting bank must inform the bank from which the collection order was received accordingly. Whenever collection charges and/or expenses are so waived they will be for the account of the principal, and may be deducted from the proceeds.

Should a collection order specifically prohibit the waiving of collection charges and/or expenses then neither the remitting nor collecting nor presenting bank shall be responsible for any costs or delays resulting from this prohibition.

Article 23

In all cases where in the express terms of a collection order, or under these rules, disbursements and/or expenses and/or collection charges are to be borne by the principal, the collecting bank(s) shall be entitled promptly to recover outlays in respect of disbursements and expenses and charges from the bank from which the collection order was received and the remitting bank shall have the right promptly to recover from the principal any amount so paid out by it, together with its own disbursements, expenses and charges, regardless of the fate of the collection.

The copyright of Uniform Rules for Collections, *Publication No. 322 (1978), is held by the International Chamber of Commerce, and copies of the publication are available from the British National Committee of the ICC, Centre Point, 103 New Oxford Street, London WC1A 1QB, and from the Publications Division, ICC Headquarters, 38 Cours Albert 1er – 75008 Paris, or from the ICC's national committees in over 50 countries.*

15.   BANK CONSIDERATIONS WHEN REMITTING BILLS

Outward collections are undertaken on the customer's express agreement that the remitting bank when using a collecting bank does so for the account and risk of the principal. So long as the remitting bank acts in good faith and exercises reasonable care the effect of this agreement is to negate the vicarious liability of the remitting bank for the negligence of its agent (the collecting bank).

The remitting bank does not pay the principal until the proceeds have been effectively received by the remitting bank. Provided the remitting bank carries out its customer's instructions without delay, there is no risk of loss to the bank. The remitting bank is under no legal obligation to examine the documents or, in fact, to do anything other than as instructed by the customer. However, there is a moral obligation, which must attach to any good customer service, to draw to the customer's attention any major defects or conflicting instructions. The documents are therefore given a cursory examination for errors which could involve delay in the clearance of the goods and probably involve demurrage charges or protracted delay in payment. When constructive control over the goods has been vested in the remitting bank it must protect its customer's goods, in accordance with his instructions, through its collecting bank correspondent. Instructions regarding warehousing, insurance cover, release of documents to the drawee or other named party, or re-shipment of the goods, must be given by the principal, and the remitting bank is responsible for instructing the collecting bank to carry them out.

16. BANK CONSIDERATIONS WHEN COLLECTING BILLS

The collecting bank is the agent of the remitting bank and is responsible for handling the collection in accordance with the remitting bank's instructions, even though the drawee may be a customer of the collecting bank. Documents may be released to the drawee against either acceptance or payment, but presentation must take place before this. If the drawee's residence or place of business is some distance from the collecting bank the documents may be sent to the collecting bank's branch or directly to the drawee's own bank, if known, (either of which will be described as the 'presenting bank') for presentation for acceptance or payment. The drawee is advised where the documents are so that he may examine them in the presence of a banker in a bank situated nearby. If documents are released by the collecting bank to a customer of its own, who is the drawee and thought to be of 'undoubted' standing, with a request to honour the bill, and the bill is subsequently dishonoured and documents lost or misappropriated, then the collecting bank will have to account to the overseas remitting bank for non-compliance with specific instructions. Normally documents may be released with safety to another bank, but not to a customer, without the collecting bank incurring liability for risks of default. In practice, UK collecting banks will release documents to drawees whose integrity and financial standing are undoubted, accompanied by a letter of trust (not a trust receipt) which states that the documents have been presented for payment or acceptance and may be examined on the understanding that payment for the accepted bill, or all the documents presented plus reasons for dishonour, will be returned without delay to the collecting bank. If, however, the documents are lost, or misused or misappropriated by the drawee, the UK collecting bank remains liable to the remitting bank.

Goods imported on a consignment basis, or those which have not been taken up by the drawees, must be protected in accordance with the remitting bank's instructions. Consignments are transactions in which a seller exports his goods without having first obtained a firm sale contract. The goods may be taken under the control of a bank in the importing country and held to the bank's order in a warehouse pending inspection by prospective buyers. Carpets, for instance, are sometimes imported into the UK on this basis.

17. NEGOTIATION AS A MEANS OF FINANCE

There are several meanings of the word 'negotiation' (see section 22 of this chapter):

i   The general term as applied to arranging a contract or discussing the terms and conditions of a contract.

ii The legal connotation of the word, particularly in connection with inland cheques and bills of exchange.

iii Negotiation as a means of financing an outward collection or funding the payee of a cheque drawn and payable abroad.

This section refers to the meaning of the word in *iii* above.

When a bank negotiates an outward collection it is buying its customer's bill drawn on an overseas buyer at the time the collection is remitted abroad. It is a convenient method of providing the exporter with working capital. Thus, the exporter, of consumer goods in particular, may draw cash against the collection lodged at his bank for negotiation. The bank in buying the bill will look to the overseas buyer as a source of repayment. In the event of non-payment or delayed payment, the negotiating bank exercises the right of recourse to its customer, the drawer. Therefore, if payment does not arrive within a reasonable time, the negotiating bank will debit its customer's account with the amount advanced plus interest. The cost of negotiation is similar to loan interest when provided by a joint stock bank. When a bank negotiates, it pays its customer straightaway and sends the bill and/or documents for collection for its own account. So far as the collecting bank is concerned this is just an inward collection.

Under English law the negotiating bank may become a holder in due course of the bill of exchange when it negotiates, and as such is given a right of action against the drawer in the event of default by the drawee. Should instructions be given for the bill not to be protested, this right is lost; as a result negotiating banks rely for reimbursement, when a bill is unpaid, on the specific right of recourse signed by their customer.

Apart from bills of exchange relating to exports, other items such as cheques and travellers' cheques are regularly negotiated. Although travellers' cheques as a rule are encashed for non-customers whom the encashing banker will not see again, and therefore to whom no recourse may be exercised, the negotiating (encashing) bank can rely on the standing of the bank issuing the travellers' cheque to pay the instrument drawn on them. The usual recourse is taken when negotiating an ordinary cheque payable to a customer.

The terms 'negotiation' and 'discounting' are often confused. They relate to quite different facilities which may be differentiated as follows:

Discounting		Negotiation	
i	There must be a bill of exchange	*i*	There need not be a bill of exchange; it is possible to negotiate shipping documents, although some banks would consider such finance to be an 'advance' rather than a negotiation
ii	The bill must be a term bill	*ii*	The bill may be a term bill or a sight bill
iii	The bill must be accepted	*iii*	It is *extremely unlikely* that the bill will have been accepted at the time of negotiation
iv	The bill is normally re-discountable locally to a discount house or another bank	*iv*	There is no secondary market for negotiated paper (except forfaited items)
v	The bill may be held in portfolio, or re-discounted after discounting	*v*	The bill will be sent to the centre for payment (usually abroad) and *not* held by the negotiating bank
vi	The drawee/acceptor should have a marketable name in the discounting bank's locality	*vi*	The drawee/acceptor is a party abroad
vii	The bill is normally payable in the discounting bank's locality	*vii*	The bill is payable abroad
viii	The majority of foreign bills discounted in London are drawn on London banks under documentary acceptance credits, or acceptance credit lines	*viii*	The majority of bills negotiated in London are presented on a collection basis and are drawn on importers abroad
ix	The exact date of receipt of funds is known at the time of discounting; payable on the maturity date	*ix*	The date of the actual receipt of funds can only be estimated at the time of negotiation; in practice it is usually *after* the maturity date

The currency of the bill, be it sterling or US dollars, makes no difference to the situation, as either may be negotiated and it is possible to discount and to re-discount in London both sterling and foreign currency paper. Indeed the London discount houses are keen to develop a market for prime foreign currency bills. It is the *place of payment* and the standing of the acceptor which are of importance (see also Chapter 5, section 6).

18. ADVANCES AGAINST COLLECTIONS

This is a similar facility to a negotiation line, the right of recourse, the interest rate, and the periods of credit which may normally be financed, being the same. This facility is available to:

i The remitting bank, which may not wish to lend the full amount of the bill (ie, negotiate) but advance a proportion of each bill presented, leaving the exporter to finance the balance from his own resources.

ii The exporter, who may not wish to pay the interest on financing 100 per cent of his export bills under a negotiation facility if he himself has the liquidity to service part of the credit period granted.

An advance against a collection can be described as part collection, part negotiation. Banks tend to differentiate between the two facilities because the degree of liability involved differs, an advance against an outward collection representing only a proportion of the bill amount as a rule, with the bank not becoming a party to the bill itself. When the bank negotiates a bill it becomes a holder for value and can become a holder in due course. When advancing against a bill the bank will be a holder for value to the extent that it has a lien on the bill. In both cases the exporter's bank will take a general letter of hypothecation which pledges as security to the bank all bills held for the customer's account whether advanced against or not.

19. BANK CONSIDERATIONS WHEN NEGOTIATING BILLS

a Security in the transaction. When an exporting customer requires his bank to negotiate his bills, thereby providing him with working capital, the bank will consider the request in the light of factors common to all forms of bank lending. The customer's integrity, business acumen and ability, financial (balance sheet) standing, period of credit required, total amount of the facility, nature of the exporter's business, his past record of trading and banking relationship, conventional security held or offered, etc. If these basic lending criteria are satisfied the bank may provide a negotiation line of credit within which the exporter may present his bills for immediate finance. The source of repayment for a negotiated bill is the overseas drawee, and the credit periods granted to the overseas buyer are usually short-term facilities, generally less than one year. The negotiating bank relies on the right of recourse to its customer, the drawer, in the event of non-payment from the anticipated source.

This right of recourse may be taken once and held to cover all transactions negotiated, or it may be taken each time bills are presented by the customer signing the collection order containing a printed undertaking to repay on demand, in the event of payment not being received from abroad, the sum negotiated plus interest charges, etc. As financial circumstances sometimes change very rapidly it is just possible that after negotiation the buyer defaults and the drawer also goes into liquidation. The right of recourse is of little use in this event, if insufficient funds are available to pay all the creditors. A general letter of hypothecation may be taken provided it specifically includes a right to sell, which will enable the negotiating bank to dispose of the goods immediately without first making demand on the customer, so the bank can act quickly if necessary should it need to exercise the right to sell the goods. The bank might take the assignment of an ECGD comprehensive short-term guarantee which would cover 90–95 per cent of the risks of non-payment (see Chapter 6 for details). Status enquiries on the buyers will help to reduce the likelihood of negotiating bills which are subsequently dishonoured. Banks will not negotiate a bill drawn on a person who is known to have previously dishonoured a bill; nor will they be happy about negotiating bills payable in countries which have, or are likely to declare, a 'moratorium' (a legal deferment of payment, usually arising from extreme economic or political circumstances).

b   Individual items may be negotiated when it is inappropriate to establish a negotiation line with a revolving limit. Common items negotiated individually are: travellers' cheques that are drawn on and payable by a bank abroad, and ordinary cheques that are payable by a bank abroad, provided the drawer has the money and it may be transferred. Travellers' cheques are negotiated without recourse to the payee, who will probably be a non-customer. Ordinary cheques will only be negotiated with recourse to the payee, who is usually a customer of the bank. When cheques (other than Eurocheques) payable abroad are presented by a non-customer for encashment they are not normally negotiated but sent for collection.

c   Examination of documents presented for negotiation. The negotiating bank will be remitting the documents for collection and payment for its own account, and will examine the documents for the same points as it would under an ordinary collection on behalf of its customers. The prime security is the right of recourse to an undoubted customer. The bill must be correctly drawn, and documents presented must be endorsed where required (for further details, refer back to section 5 in this chapter). Entirely different considerations may apply when a bill is negotiated in the terms of an irrevocable negotiation credit (see Chapter 5).

d   The negotiation of bills drawn in foreign currency may result in the negotiating bank making foreign currency or sterling available to its customer. In either case, however, if the foreign currency item is unpaid and the negotiating bank does not receive the foreign currency anticipated from abroad, then the customer must bear any exchange loss incurred in placing the negotiating bank in foreign currency funds (see Chapter 8 on foreign exchange).

20. ACCEPTANCE CREDIT LINES

a   For the exporter

Under an agreed arrangement, drafts drawn by the exporter on the overseas buyer and accompanied by documents form the security and are handled as documentary collections by the bank. These documents are in fact pledged to the bank and are usually covered by an ECGD policy. The exporter then draws a draft on the bank for the agreed proportion of the face value of these documentary collections (eg, 85 per cent) to mature slightly later than the expected time of receipt of proceeds from the underlying commercial transactions. After acceptance by the bank, this draft is discounted and the proceeds paid to the exporter. The proceeds of the documentary collection should provide the bank with funds in time to meet its own acceptance. However, the bank has a right of recourse to the exporter in the event of an overseas buyer defaulting. If the proceeds from the underlying business are received after maturity of the financing bill the matter is usually dealt with as a cash advance at an agreed rate.

b   For the importer

When the importer is due to take up documents from his overseas supplier he can by arrangement draw his own draft on the bank at the required usance. Again, this financing bill is discounted after acceptance, and the proceeds provide the greater part of the remittance now sent to the overseas seller. In all probability a certificate of pledge will be required, together with deposit of the shipping documents, which may later be released to the importer, normally against a trust receipt, on the arrival of the goods.

The period of the financing bill should give the importer time to process and sell the goods, enabling him to place the bank in funds upon maturity of the bill.

c   The cost

The cost to the client is made up of two factors:
* the discount rate for fine bank bills, which will be found daily in the financial press, and
* the acceptance commission, usually about one per cent per annum.

The sterling lent by banks to the discount houses at call, being part of the liquidity requirement of a UK bank's statutory reserve assets (ERAs), normally attracts relatively low interest rates because of the facility for withdrawal by the banks. This 'cheap' source of funds enables the discount houses to buy first class bank paper at rates often more attractive than quoted by the clearers for overdrafts. Acceptance credit lines are used principally for the financing of trade. However, this type of financial paper may be used for other reasons when wholesale finance in sums of £100,000 or more are required, usually for periods of up to six months on a roll over basis.

Acceptance credits are by no means a complete monopoly of the accepting house merchant banks; the foreign banks and clearers also provide them. From time to time a major exporter or importer, of a size and a stability sufficient to justify a clean credit facility to very large figures, may take advantage of this type of finance to provide funds to continue its business. In such cases the size of the sum required calls for a syndicate of banks to supply it. A number of banks, perhaps led by a merchant bank, will be assembled for this purpose in a consortium that will usually include both merchant banks and others.

These facilities may be established in sterling or foreign currency. The words 'acceptance' and 'credit' are very common in trade-finance jargon. It is not surprising therefore that 'acceptance credit' is a name given to two entirely different facilities. The 'acceptance credit line' described above is a clean credit facility most commonly associated with the methods of settlement of open account, or on a collection basis. This facility should not be confused with the 'documentary acceptance credit' which is described in the next chapter and is only associated with the documentary credit as a means of settlement. Both are briefly described in the glossaries of terms in this chapter and Chapter 5.

21. A SET OF SHIPPING DOCUMENTS BEING SENT FOR COLLECTION

The illustrated examples which follow (see pages 137 to 145) constitute a set of shipping documents presented by the drawer to his bank for collection. An examination of the documents will establish that they appear to be in order. Points to note are:

i   The drawee will be able to obtain delivery of the goods.
ii   He may claim from the insurers in the case of loss.
iii   The invoice and bill amount agree.
iv   The bill of exchange is properly drawn.

v   Bills of lading are marked 'freight paid' (CIF invoices).

vi   The insurance cover is at least the amount of the invoice.

vii   According to the reference books, no additional documentary requirements are necessary to satisfy the importing authorities.

viii   The instructions on the collection order have been completed and are not contradictory.

Collection order

FOREIGN BILL AND/OR DOCUMENTS FOR COLLECTION

Drawer/Exporter	Drawer's/Exporter's Reference(s) (to be quoted by Bank in all correspondence)
Power Woollen Company Limited P O Box 799 Bradford West Yorkshire BD1 1AA	34/81 18-5-81 34/81

Consignee	Drawee (If not Consignee)
Tulla AS HC Andersens Boulevard 18 Copenhagen Denmark	

To (Bank)	For Bank use only

FORWARD DOCUMENTS ENUMERATED BELOW BY AIRMAIL. FOLLOW SPECIAL INSTRUCTIONS AND THOSE MARKED X

Bill of Exchange	Comm'l. Invoice	Cert'd./Cons. Inv.	Cert. of Origin	Ins'ce Pol./Cert.	Bill of Lading	Parcel Post Rec'pt.	Air Waybill
1	3			1	2/2		

Combined Transport Doc.	Other Documents and whereabouts of any missing Original Bill of Lading

	ACCEPTANCE	PAYMENT		Protest	Do Not Protest
RELEASE DOCUMENTS ON		X	If unaccepted ⟶		
If documents are not taken up on arrival of goods	Warehouse Goods	Do Not Warehouse	and advise reason by	Cable	Airmail
	Insure Against Fire	Do Not Insure	If unpaid ⟶	Protest	Do Not Protest X
Collect ALL Charges		X	and advise reason by	Cable X	Airmail
Collect Correspondent's Charges ONLY			Advise acceptance and due date by	Cable	Airmail
Return Accepted Bill by Airmail			Remit Proceeds by	Cable	Airmail X
In case of need refer to				For Guidance	Accept their Instructions

SPECIAL INSTRUCTIONS: 1. Represent on arrival of goods if not honoured on first presentation.

Date of Bill of Exchange	Bill of Exchange Value/Amount of Collection
18 May 1981	GBP 683.75

Tenor of Bill of Exchange
SIGHT

Bill of Exchange Claused:—	Please collect the above mentioned Bill and/or Documents subject to the Uniform Rules for Collections 1978 Revision ICC publication No 322 I/We agree that you shall not be liable for any loss, damage, or delay however caused which is not directly due to the negligence of your own officers or servants.
	Date and Signature
	Bradford 18 May 1981

Collection order and bill of exchange

INCORPORATING BILL OF EXCHANGE		ADDITIONAL COPY FOREIGN BILL AND/OR DOCUMENTS FOR COLLECTION

Drawer/Exporter

Power Woollen Company Limited
P O Box 799
Bradford
West Yorkshire   BD1 1AA

Drawer's/Exporter's Reference(s) (to be quoted by Bank in all correspondence)

34/81   18-5-81   34/81

Consignee

Tulla AS
HC Andersens Boulevard 18
Copenhagen
Denmark

Drawee (If not Consignee)

To (Bank)

English Banking Ltd
Mill Street
Bradford   BD1 1AA

For Bank use only

THIS FORM SHOULD ONLY BE USED IN CONJUNCTION WITH THE BRITISH BANKERS' ASSOCIATION APPROVED FORM "FOREIGN BILL AND/OR DOCUMENTS FOR COLLECTION" (SEE "Systematic Export Documentation", SITPRO 1978)

FORWARD DOCUMENTS ENUMERATED BELOW BY AIRMAIL. FOLLOW SPECIAL INSTRUCTIONS AND THOSE MARKED X

Bill of Exchange	Comm'l. Invoice	Cert'd./Cons. Inv.	Cert. of Origin	Ins'ce Pol./Cert.	Bill of Lading	Parcel Post Rec'pt.	Air Waybill
1	3			1	2/2		

Combined Transport Doc.	Other Documents and whereabouts of any missing Original Bill of Lading

	ACCEPTANCE	PAYMENT			Protest	Do Not Protest
RELEASE DOCUMENTS ON		X	If unaccepted ➤			
If documents are not taken up on arrival of goods	Warehouse Goods	Do Not Warehouse	and advise reason by		Cable	Airmail
	Insure Against Fire	Do Not Insure	If unpaid ➤		Protest	Do Not Protest
						X
Collect ALL Charges		X	and advise reason by		Cable	Airmail
					X	
Collect Correspondent's Charges ONLY			Advise acceptance and due date by		Cable	Airmail
						X
Return Accepted Bill by Airmail			Remit Proceeds by		Cable	Airmail
In case of need refer to					For Guidance	Accept their Instructions

SPECIAL INSTRUCTIONS   1. Represent on arrival of goods if not honoured on first presentation.

447/490
Tear

SITPRO OVERLAYS 1979

BILL of EXCHANGE for   GBP 683.75

At   Sight   Pay against this sole of exchange to our order the sum of: Six hundred and eighty three pounds 75.

Tulla AS
HC Andersens Boulevard 18
Copenhagen
Denmark

DRAWEE

Power Woollen Co Ltd
0274 4338

Richard King

FOR VALUE RECEIVED
Bradford 18 May 1981

Signature

First of three invoices

INVOICE FACTURE FACTURA RECHNUNG FACTUUR		C.C.C.N No. 6003
Seller (Name, Address, VAT Reg. No.) Power Woollen Company Limited P O Box 799 Bradford West Yorkshire BD1 1AA	**Invoice No. and Date (Tax Point)** 34/81 18-5-81	**Seller's Reference** 34/81
	Buyer's Reference 345	
Consignee Tulla AS HC Andersens Boulevard 18 Copenhagen Denmark	**Buyer (if not Consignee)**	
	Country of Origin of Goods United Kingdom	
	Terms of Delivery and Payment FOB UK port. Plus freight and insurance. Cash against documents through English Banking Ltd., Mill St.. Bradford.	

Vessel/Aircraft etc. Charlotte	**Port of Loading** London
Port of Discharge Copenhagen	

Marks and Numbers; Number and Kind of Packages; Description of Goods	Quantity	@ £	Amount (State Currency)
TUL 345 COPENHAGN 1/1	1 Carton - 1000 pairs woollen knee length stockings assorted colours Type 92	1000	.65 each	£650.00
	Freight		£30.00
	Insurance		£ 3.75

TOTAL GBP 683.75

Gross Weight (kg) 60kg	Cube (m.3) 1.25m3

Name of Signatory
Richard King

Place and Date of Issue
Bradford 18 May 1981

Signature

It is hereby certified that this invoice shows the actual price of the goods described, that no other invoice has been or will be issued, and that all particulars are true and correct.

Second of three invoices

		INVOICE	FACTURE FACTURA	RECHNUNG FACTUUR	

Seller (Name, Address, VAT Reg. No.)
Power Woollen Company Limited
P O Box 799
Bradford
West Yorkshire   BD1 1AA

C.C.C.N No. 6003

Invoice No. and Date (Tax Point) 34/81   18-5-81   **Seller's Reference** 34/81

Buyer's Reference 345

Consignee
Tulla AS
HC Andersens Boulevard 18
Copenhagen
Denmark

Buyer (if not Consignee)

Country of Origin of Goods
United Kingdom

Terms of Delivery and Payment
FOB UK port. Plus freight and
insurance. Cash against documents
through English Banking Ltd.,
Mill St.. Bradford.

Vessel/Aircraft etc. Charlotte   **Port of Loading** London

Port of Discharge Copenhagen

Marks and Numbers; Number and Kind of Packages; Description of Goods		Quantity	@ £	Amount (State Currency)
TUL 345 COPENHAGN 1/1	1 Carton - 1000 pairs woollen knee length stockings assorted colours Type 92	1000	.65 each	£650.00
	Freight			£30.00
	Insurance			£ 3.75

TOTAL GBP 683.75

Gross Weight(kg) 60kg   **Cube (m3)** 1.25m3

Name of Signatory Richard King

Place and Date of Issue Bradford 18 May 1981

Signature

It is hereby certified that this invoice shows the actual price of the goods described, that no other invoice has been or will be issued, and that all particulars are true and correct.

Third of three invoices

	INVOICE FACTURE RECHNUNG FACTURA FACTUUR		C.C.C.N No. 6003
Seller (Name, Address, VAT Reg. No.) Power Woollen Company Limited P O Box 799 Bradford West Yorkshire BD1 1AA	**Invoice No and Date (Tax Point)** 34/81 18-5-81	**Seller's Reference** 34/81	
	Buyer's Reference 345		
Consignee Tulla AS HC Andersens Boulevard 18 Copenhagen Denmark	**Buyer (if not Consignee)**		
	Country of Origin of Goods United Kingdom		
	Terms of Delivery and Payment FOB UK port. Plus freight and insurance. Cash against documents through English Banking Ltd., Mill St.. Bradford.		
Vessel/Aircraft etc. Charlotte	**Port of Loading** London		
Port of Discharge Copenhagen			

Marks and Numbers; Number and Kind of Packages; Description of Goods		Quantity	@ £	Amount (State Currency)
TUL 345 COPENHAGN 1/1	1 Carton - 1000 pairs woollen knee length stockings assorted colours Type 92	1000	.65 each	£650.00
		Freight		£30.00
		Insurance		£ 3.75

	TOTAL GBP 683.75
	Gross Weight(kg) 60kg **Cube (m³)** 1.25m3

Name of Signatory
Richard King

Place and Date of Issue
Bradford 18 May 1981

Signature

It is hereby certified that this invoice shows the actual price of the goods described, that no other invoice has been or will be issued, and that all particulars are true and correct.

Insurance certificate *(front)*

Exporter's Reference   34/81

Norwich Union Fire Insurance Society Ltd.
Maritime Insurance Company Ltd.

NORWICH HOUSE, WATER STREET, LIVERPOOL L2 8UP.

INSURANCE CERTIFICATE No. A.R. /   CODE No. 66/KK/

This is to Certify that
have been issued with an Open Policy and this certificate conveys all rights of the policy (for the purpose of collecting any loss or claim) as fully as if the property were covered by a special policy direct to the holder of this certificate but if the destination of the goods is outside of the United Kingdom this certificate may require to be stamped within a given period in order to comply with the Laws of the country of destination. Notwithstanding the description of the voyage stated herein, provided the goods are at the risk of the Assured this insurance shall attach from the time of leaving the warehouse, premises or place of storage in the interior.

Conveyance Charlotte	From London	
Via/To Copenhagen	To	Insured Value / Currency
		GBP 750 so valued

Marks and Numbers	Interest
TUL 345 COPENHAGN 1/1	1 Carton - 1000 pairs woollen knee length stockings assorted colours Type 92

CONDITIONS:- ALL RISKS as per current Institute Cargo Clauses. (All Risks)
Subject to Institute Replacement Clause. (as applicable)
Including War, Strikes, Riots and Civil Commotions as per current Institute Clauses.
Refer to Clauses as over.

SURVEY CLAUSE:- In the event of loss or damage which may give rise to a claim under this certificate, notice must be given immediately to the undernoted agent/s so that he/they may appoint a Surveyor if he/they so desire.
Agents at .... are ....
....

CLAIMS In the event of a claim arising under this Certificate it is agreed that it shall be settled in accordance with English Law and Custom and shall be so settled in Liverpool or at ....
by ....

G. W. Urmson

Liverpool Marine Underwriter

This Certificate Requires Endorsement.

Dated
Bradford 18 May 1981
Signed

The original Certificate must be produced when claim is made and must be surrendered on payment.

Insurance certificate *(back)*

IMPORTANT
PROCEDURE IN THE EVENT OF LOSS OR DAMAGE FOR WHICH UNDERWRITERS MAY BE LIABLE
LIABILITY OF CARRIERS, BAILEES OR OTHER THIRD PARTIES

It is the duty of the Assured and their Agents, in all cases, to take such measures as may be reasonable for the purpose of averting or minimising a loss and to ensure that all rights against Carriers, Bailees or other third parties are properly preserved and exercised. In particular, the Assured or their Agents are required:—

1. To claim immediately on the Carriers, Port Authorities or other Bailees for any missing packages.

2. In no circumstances, except under written protest, to give clean receipts where goods are in doubtful condition.

3. When delivery is made by Container, to ensure that the Container and its seals are examined immediately by their responsible official.

   If the Container is delivered damaged or with seals broken or missing or with seals other than as stated in the shipping documents, to clause the delivery receipt accordingly and retain all defective or irregular seals for subsequent identification.

4. To apply immediately for survey by Carriers' or other Bailees' Representatives if any loss or damage be apparent and claim on the Carriers or other Bailees for any actual loss or damage found at such survey.

5. To give notice in writing to the Carriers or other Bailees within three days of delivery if the loss or damage was not apparent at the time of taking delivery.

NOTE.—The Consignees or their Agents are recommended to make themselves familiar with the Regulations of the port Authorities at the port of discharge.

SURVEY AND CLAIM SETTLEMENT

In the event of loss or damage which may involve a claim under this insurance, immediate notice of such loss or damage should be given to and a Survey Report obtained from the Office or Agent nominated herein.

In the event of any claim arising under this insurance, request for settlement should be made to the Office or Agent nominated herein.

DOCUMENTATION OF CLAIMS

To enable claims to be dealt with promptly, the Assured or their Agents are advised to submit all available supporting documents without delay, including when applicable:—

1. Original policy or certificate of insurance.

2. Original or copy shipping invoices, together with shipping specification and/or weight notes.

3. Original Bill of Lading and/or other contract of carriage.

4. Survey report or other documentary evidence to show the extent of the loss or damage.

5. Landing account and weight notes at final destination.

6. Correspondence exchanged with the Carriers and other Parties regarding their liability for the loss or damage.

The Institute clauses stated herein are those current at the date of printing of this certificate but where such clauses are revised the Institute clauses current at the time of commencement of the risk hereunder are deemed to apply.

First of two bills of lading

© GCBS 1979	

Shipper
Power Woollen Company Limited

COMMON SHORT FORM BILL OF LADING

UK Customs Assigned No. 6003
B/L No. 67
Shipper's Reference 34/81
F/Agent's Reference

Consignee (if "Order" state Notify Party and Address)
Tulla AS

Name of Carrier
P. Bork Shipping Limited

Notify Party and Address (leave blank if stated above)

The contract evidenced by this Short Form Bill of Lading is subject to the exceptions, limitations, conditions and liberties (including those relating to pre-carriage and on-carriage) set out in the Carrier's Standard Conditions applicable to the voyage covered by this Short Form Bill of Lading and operative on its date of issue.
If the carriage is one where the provisions of the Hague Rules contained in the International Convention for unification of certain rules relating to Bills of Lading dated Brussels on 25th August, 1924 as amended by the Protocol signed at Brussels on 23rd February, 1968 (the Hague Visby Rules) are compulsorily applicable under Article X, the said Standard Conditions contain or shall be deemed to contain a Clause giving effect to the Hague Visby Rules. Otherwise, except as provided below, the said Standard Conditions contain or shall be deemed to contain a Clause giving effect to the provisions of the Hague Rules.
The Carrier hereby agrees that to the extent of any inconsistency the said Clause shall prevail over the exceptions, limitations, conditions and liberties set out in the Standard Conditions in respect of any period to which the Hague Rules or the Hague Visby Rules by their terms apply. Unless the Standard Conditions expressly provide otherwise, neither the Hague Rules nor the Hague Visby Rules shall apply to this contract where the goods carried hereunder consist of live animals or cargo which by this contract is stated as being carried on deck and is so carried.
Notwithstanding anything contained in the said Standard Conditions, the term Carrier in this Short Form Bill of Lading shall mean the Carrier named on the front thereof.
A copy of the Carrier's said Standard Conditions applicable hereto may be inspected or will be supplied on request at the office of the Carrier or the Carrier's Principal Agents.

Pre-Carriage by*

Place of Receipt by Pre-Carrier*
Bradford

Vessel
CHARLOTTE

Port of Loading
LONDON

Port of Discharge
COPENHAGEN

Place of Delivery by On-Carrier*
Copenhagen

Marks and Nos; Container No.	Number and kind of packages; Description of Goods	Gross Weight	Measurement
TUL 345 COPENHAGN 1/1	1 Carton stockings	60Kgs	1.25m3

*Applicable only when document used as a Through Bill of Lading

Particulars declared by Shipper

Freight Details; Charges etc.

RECEIVED FOR CARRIAGE as above in apparent good order and condition, unless otherwise stated hereon, the goods described in the above particulars.

IN WITNESS whereof the number of original Bills of Lading stated below have been signed, all of this tenor and date, one of which being accomplished the others to stand void.

GCBS CSF BL 1979 710		

Ocean Freight Payable at
Prepaid

Number of Original Bs/L
Two

Place and Date of Issue
London 16.5.1981

Signature for Carrier; Carrier's Principal Place of Business
P. Bork Shipping Ltd
London

Authorised and Licensed by the
General Council of British Shipping © 1979

Second of two bills of lading

© GCBS 1979

Shipper	COMMON	UK Customs	B/L No.
Power Woollen Company Limited	SHORT FORM BILL OF LADING	Assigned No. 6003	67

Shipper's Reference
34/81
F/Agent's Reference

Consignee (if "Order" state Notify Party and Address)

Tulla AS

Name of Carrier

P. Bork Shipping Limited

Notify Party and Address (leave blank if stated above)

*Applicable only when document used as a Through Bill of Lading

The contract evidenced by this Short Form Bill of Lading is subject to the exceptions, limitations, conditions and liberties (including those relating to pre-carriage and on-carriage) set out in the Carrier's Standard Conditions applicable to the voyage covered by this Short Form Bill of Lading and operative on its date of issue.
If the carriage is one where the provisions of the Hague Rules contained in the International Convention for unification of certain rules relating to Bills of Lading dated Brussels on 25th August, 1924, as amended by the Protocol signed at Brussels on 23rd February, 1968 (the Hague Visby Rules) are compulsorily applicable under Article X, the said Standard Conditions contain or shall be deemed to contain a Clause giving effect to the Hague Visby Rules. Otherwise except as provided below, the said Standard Conditions contain or shall be deemed to contain a Clause giving effect to the provisions of the Hague Rules.
The Carrier hereby agrees that to the extent of any inconsistency the said Clause shall prevail over the exceptions, limitations, conditions and liberties set out in the Standard Conditions in respect of any period to which the Hague Rules or the Hague Visby Rules by their terms apply. Unless the Standard Conditions expressly provide otherwise, neither the Hague Rules nor the Hague Visby Rules shall apply to this contract where the goods carried hereunder consist of live animals or cargo which by this contract is stated as being carried on deck and is so carried.
Notwithstanding anything contained in the said Standard Conditions, the term Carrier in this Short Form Bill of Lading shall mean the Carrier named on the front thereof.
A copy of the Carrier's said Standard Conditions applicable hereto may be inspected or will be supplied on request at the office of the Carrier or the Carrier's Principal Agents.

Pre-Carriage by*	Place of Receipt by Pre-Carrier*
	Bradford
Vessel CHARLOTTE	Port of Loading LONDON
Port of Discharge COPENHAGEN	Place of Delivery by On-Carrier* Copenhagen

Particulars declared by Shipper

Marks and Nos; Container No.	Number and kind of packages; Description of Goods	Gross Weight	Measurement
TUL 345 COPENHAGN 1/1	1 Carton stockings	60Kgs	1.25m3

Freight Details; Charges etc.

RECEIVED FOR CARRIAGE as above in apparent good order and condition, unless otherwise stated hereon, the goods described in the above particulars.

IN WITNESS whereof the number of original Bills of Lading stated below have been signed, all of this tenor and date, one of which being accomplished the others to stand void.

GCBS CSF BL 1979	
710	

Ocean Freight Payable at	Place and Date of Issue
Prepaid	London 16.5.1981
Number of Original Bs/L Two	Signature for Carrier; Carrier's Principal Place of Business

P. Bork Shipping Ltd
London

Authorised and Licensed by the
General Council of British Shipping © 1979

22. GLOSSARY OF TERMS USED IN THIS CHAPTER

Acceptance credit line a clean credit facility usually used to finance trade collections or open account business; involving the drawing of accommodation paper on a local bank, often in sums of £100,000 upwards, or foreign currency equivalent, generally for periods of up to six months.

Case of need the seller's agent in the buyer's country who may be contacted in case of problems arising in respect of the seller's goods.

Collecting bank usually the agent of the exporter's bank (which includes the presenting bank) and is involved in processing the collection order.

Collection a method of settlement whereby the seller initiates through the banking system the collection of money due to him from the buyer; this method of settlement tends to favour the buyer rather than the seller.

Collection order instructions given by the exporter to his bank for the handling of the collection; the remitting bank transmits these instructions to its collecting agent abroad.

D/A instruction for the commercial documents to be released to the drawee on acceptance of the bill of exchange.

Demurrage compensation payable to a ship owner, charterer or port authority for failure to load, discharge or remove goods within the time allowed.

Disclaimer under a collection the remitting bank 'disclaims' vicarious liability, and for actions other than the negligence of its own officers.

Dishonour non-payment or non-acceptance.

D/P instruction for documents to be released to the drawee only on payment.

Drawee party on whom a bill is drawn and the one to whom presentation is to be made according to the collection order.

Facsimile signature a reproduction signature in, for example, a stamped, printed or copied form.

Foreign bill bill drawn or payable abroad.

Maturity	due date of payment of a term bill or note.
Negotiation	purchase of an outward collection, thereby providing finance for the exporter.
Protest	formal re-presentation of a bill for payment or for acceptance after dishonour; the first step in taking legal action on a bill of exchange to recover the debt.
Rebate	a form of interest allowance for the payment of a term bill of exchange prior to maturity.
Recourse	the right to recover from a prior party to a bill of exchange which has been negotiated if such bill of exchange is not honoured.
Remitting bank	exporter's bank, which 'remits' the bill and/or documents for payment.

PAST EXAMINATION QUESTIONS

1 You have received from a bank in Germany documents for collection consisting of:

a sight draft £5,000 drawn on your customer, Imports Ltd
b invoice showing value of goods as £5,000 CIF London
c insurance certificate
d full set of bills of lading evidencing shipment of goods from Hamburg to London
The instructions from the German bank are to release the documents against payment of the sight draft. On presentation your customers offer £2,500 cash plus a postdated cheque for one month ahead for the balance when they have received the sales proceeds from the ultimate buyers in this country. What action should you take in response to this offer, and why?

(Institute of Bankers)

2 What do you understand by:
a commercial documents and financial documents
b a collection order
as defined in *Uniform Rules for Collections*?

(Institute of Freight Forwarders)

3 Some exporters give instructions that bills of exchange should be protested if unaccepted or unpaid. Why is this done? Do you consider that it is generally desirable?

(Institute of Export)

4 'In all cases, whether the bill is collected or negotiated, it is important that the bank should receive the clearest instructions from the customer.'
What major points would you expect such instructions to cover in the case of a documentary tenor bill of exchange drawn by a UK exporter on his overseas buyer and handed by the exporter to his bank for collection?

(Institute of Bankers)

CHAPTER FIVE

Documentary Credits

1. INTRODUCTION

The conflicting problems in a trading transaction between buyer and seller are:

a   That the buyer is anxious to receive, in good condition and before a stipulated date, the goods he has ordered; and he would prefer not to pay for them until he receives them.

b   That the seller wants to ensure the goods he is selling will be paid for and, particularly in the case of an international transaction, that he will receive payment before he parts with control of the goods. In certain circumstances he may even want an assurance of payment before he starts producing the goods.

    This conflict of interests calls for a compromise in the form of payment against documents representing the goods, and from the point of view of both parties the documentary credit is a satisfactory way of achieving this compromise. The simplest way of describing a documentary credit therefore may be that it is a conditional undertaking given by a bank at the request of a buyer to effect settlement to a seller against presentation of documents relating to goods as specified by the buyer. Credits in general tend to favour the exporter (see section 10 of this chapter), and as a result a seller may insist upon a buyer establishing in the former's favour a credit which will advise him of the documentary requirements and conditions he must fulfil before he gets paid. The exporter needs to have this information before shipment is made, or in some cases even before production is started. From the importer's point of view the credit he wants his bank to issue is an import credit (or outward credit), and it would normally be referred to as such by the importer and the issuing bank. An advising bank when it receives the credit is normally required to advise a beneficiary in his own country of the terms and conditions against which payment will be made, and therefore, from the advising bank's and beneficiary's point of view, this same credit is referred to as an export credit (or inward credit).

It is prudent commercial practice for intending buyers and sellers to take out status reports on each other through banking channels, should either party doubt the competence or ability of the other to fulfil the terms of the sales contract, even though the suggested basis of settlement is a documentary credit. Under documentary credits banks undertake to effect settlement against presentation of documents which appear to meet the stipulations of the credit and comply with all its other terms and conditions. It may at this stage be convenient to quote section (c) of the general provisions and definitions of the ICC *Uniform Customs and Practice for Documentary Credits* which govern the operation of documentary credits in 160 countries. 'Credits, by their nature, are separate transactions from the sales or other contracts on which they may be based and banks are in no way concerned with or bound by such contracts.' It has to be borne in mind however that in documentary credit operations the parties concerned are dealing in documents and not in goods. Therefore the protection available to the applicant depends upon the documents he calls for (see section 7 in this chapter).

2.   PARTIES CONCERNED WITH A CREDIT

A Correct documentary credit terminology	B Other names of parties
The applicant	Importer or buyer
Issuing bank	Importer's bank or buyer's bank
Advising bank	Correspondent or bank in the seller's country
Confirming bank	The bank is authorised by the issuing bank to add its confirmation; this may be the advising bank or it may be another bank nominated by the issuing bank and is usually, but not always, a bank in the country of the seller or exporter
Beneficiary	Seller or exporter

Column A shows the direction in which the credit moves, and the words used in this column describe the parties in the correct documentary credit terminology. The words listed in column B are synonymous with those in column A.

i   Buyer and seller enter into a contract of sale calling for settlement by documentary credit.

ii   The buyer (applicant) requests his bank (issuing bank) to issue a documentary credit in favour of the seller (beneficiary).

iii   The documentary credit is sent to a bank in the beneficiary's country (advising bank) which advises the beneficiary of the documents and other terms and conditions against which payment, negotiation or acceptance may be made.

iv   The seller should immediately check the documentary credit against the contract of sale to ensure he can comply with the credit requirements. If he feels he cannot comply he should at once seek to have the credit amended.

v   The seller ships the goods and presents his documents to any bank with which the credit is made available (frequently the advising bank).

vi   This bank examines the documents and decides whether to settle with the beneficiary in the terms of the credit – ie, by payment, negotiation or acceptance.

vii This bank, if it has effected settlement to the beneficiary, then forwards the documents to the issuing bank and obtains reimbursement as agreed between the two banks.

viii The issuing bank examines the documents and forwards them to its customer, the buyer, who pays for them in accordance with arrangements agreed between that bank and the customer.

3. REVOCABLE, IRREVOCABLE AND CONFIRMED CREDITS
(See also section 13 in this chapter.)

A credit may be issued in revocable or irrevocable form. If any bank authorised to do so has paid, negotiated or accepted in respect of documents presented in accordance with the terms of a revocable documentary credit, such actions will stand, provided they were made prior to that bank's receiving notice of amendment or revocation. The issuing bank may amend or revoke a revocable credit either upon the request of the applicant or when the issuing bank considers it will not be possible to obtain reimbursement from its customer. In the latter case it may be prudent for the issuing bank, in its own interest, to revoke the credit. On the other hand, irrevocable credits may not be amended or cancelled without the prior agreement of all parties.

If the credit is revocable any amendment advised may be rejected by the beneficiary. In practice the majority of amendments are requested by and therefore tend to favour the beneficiary, examples being the extension of shipment date or credit expiry date or an increase in the amount payable.

The documentary credit as a means of settlement tends to favour the exporter, since, under it, he obtains the ability and/or willingness of the issuing bank to pay; thus the exporter does not have to rely solely upon the buyer's undertaking to pay. A documentary credit is therefore normally established on the specific request of the seller in accordance with the agreement contained in the sales contract, although the authorities in certain countries insist on all or part of their external trade being settled and financed under documentary credits. Revocable credits tend to favour the exporter a little less than irrevocable and since they do not provide him with as much security of payment as irrevocable credits they are infrequently issued.

Revocable and irrevocable credits that are advised to the beneficiary are advised without engagement on the part of the advising bank. However, they do include an undertaking by the issuing bank to cover the negotiation of correct documents if they are presented before notice of revocation is received. Unless it is requested by the issuing bank to confirm (see below) its credit, the advising bank, in advising the beneficiary, will do so without any engagement on its part. If however such an advising bank is named in the credit as the bank where payment, negotiation or acceptance is to be effected, it implies that the necessary authority to do so has been given by the issuing bank. This does not mean that the advising bank will definitely take such action if correct documents are tendered to it, as any undertaking to the beneficiary is solely that of this issuing bank. It may be (for commercial, economic or political reasons current at the time the beneficiary tenders the documents) that the advising bank realises it would be unable to obtain reimbursement from the issuing bank for money paid to the beneficiary. Clearly in such circumstances no payment would be made, even if the documents were in order. The advising bank therefore advises credits 'without engagement'.

There are frequent occasions when the beneficiary will insist on a bank in his own country adding its undertaking to that of the issuing bank. When the bank which advises the credit does undertake to make payment against correctly tendered documents it is called the confirming bank, and the action of a second bank adding its undertaking is known as 'confirming'.

The total cost of confirming a credit is greater than simply advising one of the same amount and validity, as the undertakings of two banks are necessary when a credit is confirmed. Credits issued by the world's largest banks are not usually confirmed, as the undertaking of such a bank, even though in another country, is usually sufficient for the beneficiary's needs. It is however for consideration whether the head offices of certain major banks would necessarily support or pay the creditors of their own subsidiary in another country which, for political reasons perhaps, was prevented from honouring its obligations. It is believed that the leading UK banks would support their subsidiaries abroad.

4.   CREDITS AS A MEANS OF INTERNATIONAL SETTLEMENT

If settlement is to be made by means of a documentary credit the type of the documentary credit to be used is decided between the buyer and seller.

Importer's position	Type of credit	Exporter's position
This type of credit provides the importer with the greatest flexibility, since he may arrange for it to be amended or cancelled at any time up to the moment the bank with which the credit is available has paid, negotiated or accepted documents presented thereunder	**Revocable**	Least favourable type of credit, the danger being that goods may be shipped and the credit amended or revoked before documents are presented to the advising bank. He only has the undertaking of a bank abroad to pay since such a credit would not be confirmed
The credit may not be amended or cancelled without the consent of all parties; market prices of goods may fall and the importer is committed to pay an agreed price under the credit	**Irrevocable**	The issuing bank's undertaking is still subject to political, economic and commercial risks which may prohibit transfer of funds to the seller's country, but the terms cannot be amended or the credit itself be revoked without the beneficiary's consent
The importer's position is the same as with an irrevocable credit, as it is of no concern to an importer whether the credit bears the undertaking of a confirming bank or not, although if the confirming costs are for his account then it is the most expensive type of credit	**Confirmed**	Most favourable type of credit; guarantees payment to the beneficiary provided the credit terms are met and the standing of the confirming bank in the beneficiary's country is undoubted

5.   THE PROCEDURE OF ESTABLISHING A CREDIT

The applicant requests his own bank, the issuing bank, to issue the credit in favour of the beneficiary. To do this the applicant completes an application form that contains his instructions, including the terms and conditions under which the beneficiary is to receive settlement. An application form for the issue of a documentary credit currently used by a London bank is illustrated on the two pages overleaf. The instructions will cover:

- whether advice of the credit should be sent by mail, cable or telex
- whether the credit is to be issued as revocable or irrevocable and whether the advising bank is to be asked to add its confirmation
- the name and address of the beneficiary
- whether or not the beneficiary is to have the right to transfer the credit to a

- second beneficiary – ie, whether it is to be a transferable credit
- whether drafts are to be drawn and if so on whom, their tenor and whether the credit is available by payment, acceptance or negotiation
- details of the documents required in evidence of the transaction
- description of the goods, including details of quantity and unit price
- names of the places of shipment and destination
- the total amount and currency of the credit
- latest dates for shipment and expiry of the credit, and the period after date of issuance of the shipping documents during which they must be presented for settlement (Article 41 of *Uniform Customs and Practice*)
- shipping terms in the sales contracts – eg, FOB, CIF
- whether or not partial shipments are permitted
- whether or not transhipments are permitted

The form will be signed by the customer who, by doing so, agrees to various conditions usually included in the form, including the fact that the credit is issued subject to *Uniform Customs and Practice*. One condition may give the issuing bank a pledge over goods and documents relating to the credit. There may also be a statement to the effect that the issuing bank cannot be held responsible for negligence or default of the advising bank.

The issuing bank will check the following points before issuing the credit:

i   The financial standing, integrity, etc, of its customer (the applicant).

ii   That marine insurance for the transaction has or will be effected.

iii   *That the terms and conditions of the application form make sense* and are not contradictory or would prove to be detrimental to the applicant.

Note: in the event that the issuing bank is relying on the goods for security purposes, it must check that a valid import licence is held, if required, and that it will not expire prior to the arrival of the goods in the UK, assuming shipment will be made on the latest date permitted under the credit.

6.   BANK CONSIDERATIONS ON ISSUING A CREDIT

Before providing this facility the bank will have to consider its position *vis-à-vis* its customer. It is important that, when a customer approaches his bank to have a credit issued, his request should be vetted in the same way as it would be if he were seeking an advance. The usual canons of lending should be applied to the proposition. Having issued a credit, and having honoured its undertaking on production of the requisite documents, it may happen that the bank finds its customer does not have sufficient funds to reimburse it.

Most customers who request documentary credit facilities require a number of credits to be established in favour of their overseas suppliers over a period, rather than a single transaction. The issuing bank establishes a 'line of credit' with a maximum limit for this purpose, in much the same way as an overdraft or loan facility is arranged. If necessary one of the usual forms of bank security may be taken, and it may even be necessary to take cash or partial cover on a special account.

The customer should sign a certificate (letter) of pledge, usually incorporated in the application form to open a documentary credit (see pages 154-5), giving the bank rights over the documents of title and the underlying goods. Included in such a document would be a clause giving the bank power of sale over the goods, should the customer not meet his obligation to the bank. Other clauses make the customer

Request to open documentary credit *(front)*

TO **Midland Bank Limited**

Branch_____HAMPTON_____

Request to open Documentary Credit

Date_____7. 3. 1981_____

Please open for my/our account Documentary Credit, in accordance with the undermentioned particulars.
I/We agree that, except so far as otherwise expressly stated, this Credit will be subject to the Uniform Customs and Practice for Documentary Credits (1974 Revision), International Chamber of Commerce Publication No. 290. I/We undertake to execute (if not already executed) the Bank's usual Form of Indemnity.

Signed_____(R.J. Rankin)_____
p.p. T.J. Adamant & Co. Ltd.

Entries must not be made in this margin

When completing this form please follow carefully the general instructions overleaf.
Delete as appropriate

Type of credit	.Irrevocable i.e. cannot be cancelled without beneficiaries' agreement Revocable - - i.e. subject to cancellation - -
Method of advice	*airmail/ *cable .full rate .full advice cheapest rate brief details
Advising Bank Name and Address of beneficiary	FIRST BANK OF HONG KONG, HONG KONG *As far as possible this should be left to Midland Bank Limited* LI FUNG CHI & CO. APT:12, 1012 HIGH STREET, KOWLOON
Amount	£5,000...._____say_____FIVE THOUSAND POUNDS
Availability	Valid until ___6.6.81___ in ___HONG KONG___ for *negotiation/acceptance/payment *Enter date* *Enter place* This credit is available by drafts drawn at_____sight accompanied by the required documents
Documents required †	Invoice IN QUADRUPLICATE *Full set shipped Bills of Lading to order and blank endorsed, marked *Freight paid/freight payable at destination or *Air Consignment Note evidencing goods addressed to _____ or _____marked *Freight paid/freight payable *Combined Transport Document issued at destination by _____ *Insurance *Policy/Certificate for invoice amount plus _10_ % covering Marine and War Risks and including other conditions and risks as follows :_____ALL RISKS_____ _____ _____ _____ *Insurance effected by _____where no insurance is called for **Other Documents:** PACKING LIST IN DUPLICATE CERTIFICATE OF ORIGIN IN DUPLICATE
	T.J.Adamant & Co.Ltd. Adam Court, Hampton
Quantity & description of goods	ELECTRONIC COMPONENTS AS PER PRO-FORMA INVOICE NO. 9124/80 and 9160/80
Price per unit *if any*	£_____
Terms & relative port or place	*C.I.F., C&F, F.O.B., F.A.S., F.O.R., etc. _____LONDON_____ *This information is required in all cases*
Despatch/Shipment †Taking in Charge	From/xx ___HONG KONG___ to ___LONDON___ Part Shipments *allowed/not allowed Transhipment *allowed/not allowed
Documents to be presented	For *negotiation/acceptance/payment within ___21___ days of the date of issue of the Bills of Lading or other shipping documents but in any event within the credit validity
Special instructions *if any*	

†**Important**: Please see relevant paragraph overleaf.

962

Request to open documentary credit *(back)*

General instructions for opening Documentary Credit.

Responsibility of Bank

It should be clearly understood that the Bank is not directly concerned with the proper fulfilment of the contract between the seller and the buyer. Its duty is simply to receive documents on behalf of the customer which purport to comply with the conditions stated when opening the credit.

The Bank has the right to realise the goods or to take any steps, at its discretion, with a view to safeguarding its position.

Type of Credit

Irrevocable or Revocable : It is essential that definite instructions on this point are given on all occasions. An Irrevocable Credit becomes an engagement of the Bank itself, incapable of cancellation or of modification except by consent of the beneficiary. A Revocable Credit may be cancelled without the beneficiary's consent by the customer at any time, subject, however, to the customer remaining liable in respect of any negotiation, acceptance, or payment made by the Bank through which the Credit is advised, prior to receipt of notice of cancellation by that Bank.

Availability

Expiry Date : This must always be given. The expiry date can, of course, be extended on instructions from the customer. When credits are to be opened/advised through a bank abroad, expiry dates are understood to apply to the date of negotiation, or acceptance, or payment (as the case may be) in the place abroad at which the negotiation, or acceptance, or payment is to take place, and not to the date of arrival of documents or advices in London. Credits with a London expiry date can be opened in favour of beneficiaries abroad but it is not customary to advise such credits through a foreign bank.

"Negotiated" : This instruction should be used where drafts drawn by the beneficiary on Midland Bank Limited either in sterling or in the currency of a country other than that of the beneficiary are to be honoured if negotiated at the place and within the period of validity of the credit.

"Accepted"/"Paid" : These instructions are appropriate where the currency of the credit is that of the country of the beneficiary who is to draw drafts for acceptance on a bank abroad or claim payment from them. They are also appropriate where credits are to be opened in sterling with a London expiry date in favour of beneficiaries abroad or in favour of beneficiaries in the United Kingdom.

Documents Required

It is not sufficient to state "usual documents". The documents should be mentioned in detail. "On Board" (i.e. "shipped") Bills of Lading are normally required but if "Received for Shipment" Bills of Lading are acceptable, this should be indicated.

Short Form Bills of Lading and Bills of Lading evidencing shipment in containers will be accepted unless the credit specifically prohibits either or both of them.

If the credit terms provide for carriage by more than one method of transport or combined transport documents are called for without stating either the form of the documents and/or the party to issue them, the documents will be accepted as tendered, without regard to the content or to the name of the issuer. It is advisable always to allow transhipment when combined transport is intended.

General

Unless the credit provides otherwise, shipping documents bearing reference to extra charges in addition to the freight charges will be accepted. These charges include, for example, "Free **In/Out**" and other costs and charges incurred in container transport. Should additional charges not be acceptable the specific charges prohibited must be stated.

Unless instructions are given to the contrary, banks will take up documents presented to them up to 21 days from the date of the Bills of Lading or other shipping document, even for a short sea voyage. It is essential, therefore, for customers to calculate the maximum period they would wish to accept for presentation of documents to our correspondents abroad bearing in mind the normal airmail time required for the documents to reach us, and to stipulate the maximum number of days permitted between date of issue of the Bills of Lading or other Shipping Document and the date of presentation, even if a latest shipment date is stipulated.

responsible for warehousing and insuring the goods. A certificate of pledge may cover one transaction only or all documentary transactions made by a particular customer, whether the money is advanced against them or not.

Having agreed the amount of the 'line of credit' with its customer, the issuing bank will carefully vet each 'application to open a credit' form submitted, for the following points:

i   Has the customer signed the application form?

ii   Is the credit to be opened by mail or cable?

iii   Does the form show:
* the applicant's name?
* the beneficiary's name and address?
* the amount to be available in words and figures?
* the date and place of expiry?
* details of all documents required?
* description of the goods?
* details of goods shipped, latest date of shipment, latest date for presentation of documents, ports of shipment and discharge, part shipments, transhipment and shipping terms – FOB or CIF, etc?

In addition the form should draw attention to the fact that, when combined transport is involved, there will be places for taking in charge and delivering (to replace ports of shipment and discharge) and that transhipment has to be allowed – ie, that the documents called for must match other requirements of the credit and the other requirements of the credit must match the documents called for.

If the credit terms envisage a combined transport, the issuing bank must check that the required documentation is consistent with the credit requirements as a whole and that these requirements, in turn, match the documentation and the applicant's intentions.

The risks an issuing bank runs are:

a   Its customer may not be able to pay when the issuing bank is required to honour its undertaking under the credit and reimburse the advising bank for payments correctly made under the credit. Should this happen the issuing bank would have to rely on the security it has taken from the applicant, and this could mean reliance on a sale of the goods.

b   The goods may be damaged or lost in transit, so the issuing bank should see that the goods are insured. This is necessary as the bank will try to recover the appropriate sum from an insurance company if the customer is unable to pay. If the credit evidences an FOB or C & F contract of sale the insurance should be taken out by the importing customer. Under a CIF contract the responsibility is for the overseas beneficiary to produce an appropriate document covering risks as stated.

c   When they arrive the goods might not be landed if the required import licence has not been obtained or has expired before their arrival. This will be of consequence if the issuing bank has a financial interest in the goods.

d   It is possible, if the bank has a financial interest in the transaction and has to rely on the proceeds of the goods when they arrive, that they may prove to be unsaleable. The issuing bank must consider the customer's integrity, business acumen, past history of previous similar transactions, financial standing, connections and balance sheet considerations, and the conventional banking security that may be offered or obtained before establishing the credit.

7. CONSIDERATIONS AFFECTING THE APPLICANT

These may be summarised as follows:

a   In documentary credit operations all parties deal in documents, not goods. Therefore an underlying status report on the supplier should be obtained before entering into a contract, to ensure that the supplier appears to be a reputably constituted concern likely to produce what is required.

b   The order or contract should satisfactorily reflect the full intention of both parties regarding goods and settlement. Where capital goods are concerned the contract may require the supplier to provide a suitable performance bond. This document is an undertaking to pay the buyer up to a stated sum in the event of the seller not performing the contract as agreed. Banks are often requested to issue such bonds.

c   The contract may provide for settlement by a revocable credit. This gives the applicant the right to amend or cancel the credit. For example, a revocable credit calling for the beneficiary to make shipments in stages, perhaps at monthly intervals, would allow the applicant to determine whether the goods on each shipment were up to the required standard and, if not, to cancel the credit.

d   Many sales contracts are based on part-settlement to be made under an irrevocable credit and part by means of separate bills of exchange drawn on the buyer. These bills, which are not drawn under the credit, and are sent for payment or acceptance on a collection basis, usually accompany the shipping documents presented under the credit. The terms of the credit need to establish clearly whether or not the release of the shipping documents to the applicant is to be contingent upon his payment or acceptance of the accompanying bills.

e   Where the goods are being bought on FOB or C & F terms, the applicant is responsible for arranging insurance for the goods in case they are lost or damaged in transit. Further information on risks covered by insurance is given in Chapter 3.

f   The applicant will specify the documents that the beneficiary must tender before settlement will be made. Documents evidencing the movement of goods should enable the applicant to obtain delivery of the goods at destination. They may show shipment to the order of the shipper and be blank endorsed by him, or they may show the goods consigned to, or to the order of, the applicant or the issuing bank or a third party named in the credit. As a minimum requirement documents of movement should show that the goods have been taken in charge by a carrier or his agent. Such documents should not bear any clauses indicating a defective condition of the goods and/or the packaging – unless the applicant specifically authorises the acceptance of a particular clause, and this is shown in the credit. When the document of movement called for in the credit is a bill of lading the full set is normally required, in order to ensure that no unauthorised person can get delivery of the goods. If the contract requires the beneficiary to be responsible for insuring the goods, the applicant must specify in his credit instructions the type of document to be provided, the risks to be covered, and the amount for which the goods are to be insured.

g   The applicant will also call for a commercial invoice, which will evidence the goods, price and sum payable. The description of the goods in the invoice must exactly correspond with that given in the credit. The other documents called for may, however, describe the goods in more general terms, provided such general terms are not inconsistent with the description of the goods given in the credit.

h   Apart from these documents, the applicant may call for the beneficiary to present one or more third party documents. Certificates of inspection, quality, quantity, analysis, weight, packing, age, etc, may be required from the beneficiary, to be given by an independent third party named in the credit. These provide the applicant with *prima facie* assurance of the satisfactory condition, quality, etc, of the goods at the time of inspection. Further information on these documents can be found in Chapter 3. The applicant may sometimes call for the certificate of inspection to be signed by a specified individual. In this case the credit will be accompanied by a specimen of the signature of such individual. The applicant may also call for certain documents to meet the requirements of the authorities in the importing country, and sometimes in the exporting country also. Legalised or consular invoices, certificates of health or origin, etc, are required for certain goods and certain countries. Some documents, perhaps including commercial invoices, may on occasions have to be certified by chambers of commerce in the exporting country. Whenever the required document originates from the seller's country it must be specified in the credit.

i   Many documents are expressed in foreign currency. Applicants who are liable for payment under such credits may run an exchange risk between the time of issue and the date the credit is implemented. They may have a foreign currency account, or they may have resold in the same currency. In other cases the applicant may protect his position by arranging with his bank to cover the exchange risk by buying the required foreign currency spot and keeping it on an account, or by buying forward. Further details may be found in section 15 in this chapter.

j   The applicant is also concerned with dates. He will generally specify a latest date for shipment. He should specify a period after issuance of the shipping documents within which they must be presented for settlement under the credit. He must specify an expiry date – ie, the latest date by which documents must be presented under the credit.

k   The documentary credit may be used to provide finance for either the buyer or the seller. Ways in which this can be done are dealt with in greater detail in sections 10, 11, 21 and 22 in this chapter.

8.   CONSIDERATIONS AFFECTING THE BENEFICIARY

Apart from payment in advance before goods are exported the next most favourable system of settlement from an exporter's point of view is the documentary credit. In sections 3, 13 and 21 in this chapter the exporter's position in relation to a revocable, an irrevocable and a confirmed credit respectively are set out. Each of these types of credit affords a different degree of security of payment to the beneficiary, but in each there is a paramount requirement for compliance with the terms and conditions.

If the documents are not in order and cannot be amended and represented in time (see *Uniform Customs and Practice*, Article 41) it is the prerogative of the applicant to decide whether or not to authorise settlement. Beneficiaries must read the terms of a credit *carefully* as soon as they receive it to ascertain whether they can comply with the credit requirements. If they find that they cannot comply with the terms and conditions they must ask the applicant to authorise an amendment accordingly, so that when documents are submitted the beneficiary can rely on the undertaking of a bank to settle.

Under certain circumstances funds received by a beneficiary under a documentary credit would have to be repaid (for example, if the negotiating bank failed to take up the documents). In such circumstances settlement is made *with recourse* to the beneficiary. Otherwise settlement is made *without recourse*. The recourse position of a beneficiary under a documentary credit transaction may be illustrated as follows:

Type of settlement	Form of documentary credit		
	Revocable	**Irrevocable**	**Confirmed**
i By payment	Without recourse	Without recourse	Without recourse
ii By negotiation	With recourse	With recourse	Without recourse
iii By acceptance	Without recourse (except as drawer of the bill of exchange)*	Without recourse (except as drawer of the bill of exchange)*	Without recourse (except as drawer of the bill of exchange)*

*If the accepted bill was discounted with a third party, its right of recourse to the beneficiary would exist unless the bill had been claused 'without recourse'. However, the acceptance being that of a bank, it would create little likelihood of the beneficiary being called upon to repay.

(See also section 9 of this chapter.) If the credit amount is expressed in foreign currency the beneficiary may arrange to sell the proceeds forward to his own bank and thereby cover his exchange risk.

The advising bank may or may not be the beneficiary's bankers. As it is the issuing bank that chooses the advising bank, the issuing bank will use its own correspondents unless the applicant specifically requests that the credit be advised through the beneficiary's bank. The advising bank will act in accordance with instructions received from its principal, the issuing bank, and the exporter will not be allowed to avail himself of any contractual relationship between the issuing and advising banks, even if he is a customer of the advising bank. Nevertheless, if the beneficiary complies with the credit terms, he has the undertaking of the issuing bank to effect settlement under the terms and does not have to rely solely on the buyer's willingness and ability to settle. If the credit is confirmed the beneficiary will have the additional undertaking of another bank, the confirming bank, probably located in his own country.

9.   BANK POSITION ON ADVISING OR CONFIRMING A CREDIT

A bank may be requested to advise a credit without adding its confirmation. In this case it has no engagement to the beneficiary. Or it may be requested to advise the credit with the addition of its confirmation. If it agrees to do this then it accepts a commitment to the beneficiary in addition to that of the issuing bank.

It must be remembered that the method of settlement under the credit may be either by payment (against the documents themselves or against the documents supported by a sight draft) or by acceptance of a draft itself, drawn on a party stated in the credit, or by negotiation of a draft drawn at sight or term on some other party stipulated in the credit.

In the case of a credit available by payment at the advising bank, settlement is completed when the advising bank makes payment to the beneficiary, unless at that time it states that there are certain irregularities in the documents and that its payment is made under reserve.

In the case of a credit available by acceptance, if the draft is to be drawn on the advising bank itself then a similar comment applies – ie, the advising bank cannot go back on its commitment to the beneficiary unless at the time of giving its acceptance it has drawn attention to irregularities.

In the case of a credit available by negotiation, the position varies according to whether the advising bank has or has not added its confirmation. If it has not it negotiates with recourse to the beneficiary. If it has it negotiates without recourse to the beneficiary.

As stated above, when a bank confirms a documentary credit it gives its own undertaking to the beneficiary and assumes the risk of possibly not obtaining reimbursement in due course. If the confirming bank is resident in the beneficiary's country the act of confirming the credit provides the beneficiary with an undertaking from a local bank, thereby eliminating the possibility of default by the issuing bank or by restrictions imposed on the transfer of funds by the issuing bank's country. Many exporters require a confirmed credit to be established in their favour before they will consider manufacturing or shipping goods to buyers in certain countries abroad owing to current exchange restrictions imposed in the buyer's country. Therefore banks that are asked to confirm credits look at the following risks: (a) the financial standing of the issuing bank and (b) the economic and political state of the issuing bank's country. In cases where such risks exist, the confirming bank may sometimes require the issuing bank to make an advance payment in cover for amounts to be paid by the confirming bank subsequently. This cash cover will be held on a special suspense account and any sums not paid will be refunded to the issuing bank after expiry of the credit. Advising banks will also consider the nature of the credit itself; in particular the credit must be irrevocable, since no one would wish to confirm a revocable undertaking which may be cancelled or amended by the issuing bank.

10. REIMBURSEMENT UNDER A CREDIT

The issuing bank should inform the advising bank precisely how reimbursement will be made. The credit may authorise the bank or banks with which it is made available to pay, to negotiate or to accept drafts drawn by the beneficiary as follows:

Payment may be authorised on a sight basis against:
- sight bills drawn on such bank accompanied by specified documents
- documents without a sight draft attached

Certain credits may specify that drafts will only be payable against presentation of documents to the issuing bank. In such cases the documents can only be handled by an intermediary bank on a 'collection' basis. This, of course, tends to negate the value of the credit to the beneficiary.

Negotiation may be authorised against:
- sight bills drawn on the issuing bank
- sight bills drawn on another named bank
- sight bills drawn on the applicant
- term bills drawn on the issuing bank
- term bills drawn on another named bank
- term bills drawn on the applicant

Acceptance may be authorised against:
- term bills drawn on the advising bank

The paying, negotiating or accepting bank may reimburse itself by:
- debiting the account of the issuing bank in its own books
- instructing the issuing bank to credit a foreign currency account
- nominating a bank to which payment is to be made
- claiming on a bank which will be instructed by the issuing bank to honour such claim

Acceptance credits will specify when the discount charges are for the applicant's account, otherwise the beneficiary must pay them. If the credit states that the beneficiary may receive the face amount of the bill which is to be discounted by the advising bank, the discount costs will be charged to the issuing bank for the buyer's account. If the credit does not say anything about discounting, and the beneficiary wants immediate finance, the beneficiary will have to pay the cost of discounting the bill.

When beneficiaries do not require finance, and are prepared to provide trade credit to the importer, a deferred sight credit can be arranged under which the advising bank diarises to pass entries on an agreed future date. This means that, as the exporter will not be paid until this date, the advising bank will not require reimbursement until then; this gives the importer the benefit of deferred terms. The advising bank is not financing the transaction, the exporter is; and as there is no bill of exchange to be drawn on the advising bank there is no acceptance commission for the exporter to pay.

11. NEGOTIABLE CREDITS

In some cases negotiable credits may be restricted to a named bank, often the advising bank. In other cases such credits may be freely negotiable by any bank. Some negotiable credits may call for drafts to be drawn on the issuing bank or the applicant, at sight or term, but may also authorise the negotiating bank to purchase the bills on a sight basis. These are sometimes referred to as 'Far East negotiation credits' or 'authorities to purchase'.

There are two types of negotiable credit:

i   Credits that are treated as negotiable (for example, by the advising bank) are sight and term credits calling for drafts to be drawn on the applicant or issuing bank when the credit does not specifically authorise the advising bank to pay the beneficiary on a sight basis. As the bills of exchange are drawn to be payable in the importer's country, the advising bank can only negotiate. Because of the heavy stamp duty on drafts in various countries, a credit might state that it is negotiable although no draft is called for. Negotiation of drafts and/or documents is with recourse to the beneficiary unless the credit has been confirmed by the advising bank (see the preceding section and section 22 in this chapter).

ii When the advising bank is not the benficiary's own bank, the choice of correspondent is usually in the hands of the issuing bank, but the beneficiary, after receiving the credit, will often hand his documents to his own bank, and that bank may negotiate them, provided the credit is freely negotiable by any bank, and claim reimbursement directly from the issuing bank.

12. LIABILITY OF BANKS HANDLING CREDITS

In documentary credit operations all parties deal in documents and not in goods. Banks are, therefore, in no way concerned with the underlying sales or other contracts upon which the documentary credits may be based. Banks will determine on the basis of the documents alone whether to claim that payment, negotiation or acceptance was made in accordance with the credit terms. This means that the issuing bank cannot refuse reimbursement for correctly tendered documents just because the applicant cannot pay.

For these reasons banks must examine all documents with reasonable care to ascertain that they appear on their face to be in accordance with the terms and conditions of the credit (see *Uniform Customs and Practice*, Articles 7 and 8 in section 13 of this chapter).

Banks using the services of a correspondent do so for the account and at the risk of the applicant (see *Uniform Customs and Practice*, Article 12).

Uniform Customs and Practice for Documentary Credits lays down in fuller detail the liabilities and responsibilities of all parties.

13. 'UNIFORM CUSTOMS AND PRACTICE FOR DOCUMENTARY CREDITS'

International Chamber of Commerce Publication No. 290 (1974)

In 47 Articles and general provisions and definitions, this publication sets out the manner in which documentary credits will be handled for the mutual benefit and understanding of all parties involved. It is not legally binding unless the parties specify under the credit that they will be bound by such terms. However, the rules are applied in 160 countries and most banks make a statement on the application form for opening a credit that the rules will apply. The credit also states that it is issued subject to *Uniform Customs and Practice*, the full text of which is reproduced below.

General provisions and definitions

a   These provisions and definitions and the following Articles apply to all documentary credits and are binding upon all parties thereto unless otherwise expressly agreed.

b   For the purposes of such provisions, definitions and Articles, the expressions 'documentary credit(s)' and 'credit(s)' used therein mean any arrangement, however named or described, whereby a bank (the issuing bank), acting at the request and in accordance with the instructions of a customer (the applicant for the credit):

i   is to make payment to or to the order of a third party (the beneficiary), or is to pay, accept or negotiate bills of exchange (drafts) drawn by the beneficiary, *or*

ii   authorises such payments to be made or such drafts to be paid, accepted or negotiated by another bank, against stipulated documents, provided that the terms and conditions of the credit are complied with.

c   Credits, by their nature, are separate transactions from the sales or other contracts on which they may be based and banks are in no way concerned with or bound by such contracts.

d   Credit instructions and the credits themselves must be complete and precise.

In order to guard against confusion and misunderstanding, issuing banks should discourage any attempt by the applicant for the credit to include excessive detail.

e   A bank authorised to pay, accept or negotiate under a credit shall be the bank first entitled to exercise the option available under Article 32(b). The decision of such bank shall bind all parties concerned.

A bank is authorised to pay or accept under a credit by being specifically nominated in the credit.

A bank is authorised to negotiate under a credit either

i   by being specifically nominated in the credit, *or*

ii   by the credit being freely negotiable by any bank.

f   A beneficiary can in no case avail himself of the contractual relationships existing between banks or between the applicant for the credit and the issuing bank.

A Form and notification of credits

Article 1

a   Credits may be either
i   revocable, *or*
ii   irrevocable.

b   All credits, therefore, should clearly indicate whether they are revocable or irrevocable.

c   In the absence of such indication, the credit shall be deemed to be revocable.

Article 2

A revocable credit may be amended or cancelled at any moment without prior notice to the beneficiary. However, the issuing bank is bound to reimburse a branch or other bank to which such a credit has been transmitted and made available for payment, acceptance or negotiation, for any payment, acceptance or negotiation complying with the terms and conditions of the credit and any amendments received up to the time of payment, acceptance or negotiation made by such branch or other bank prior to receipt by it of notice of amendment or cancellation.

Article 3

a   An irrevocable credit constitutes a definite undertaking of the issuing bank, provided that the terms and conditions of the credit are complied with:
i   to pay, or that payment will be made if the credit provides for payment, whether against a draft or not
ii   to accept drafts if the credit provides for acceptance by the issuing bank or to be responsible for their acceptance and payment at maturity if the credit provides for the acceptance of drafts drawn on the applicant for the credit or any other drawee specified in the credit
iii   to purchase/negotiate, without recourse to drawers and/or *bona fide* holders, drafts drawn by the beneficiary, at sight or at a tenor, on the applicant for the credit or on any other drawee specified in the credit, or to provide for purchase/negotiation by another bank, if the credit provides for purchase/negotiation.

b   An irrevocable credit may be advised to a beneficiary through another bank (the advising bank) without engagement on the part of that bank, but when an issuing bank authorises or requests another bank to confirm its irrevocable credit and the latter does so, such confirmation constitutes a definite undertaking of the confirming bank in addition to the undertaking of the issuing bank, provided that the terms and conditions of the credit are complied with:
i   to pay, if the credit is payable at its own counters, whether against a draft or not, or that payment will be made if the credit provides for payment elsewhere
ii   to accept drafts if the credit provides for acceptance by the confirming bank, at its own counters, or to be responsible for their acceptance and payment at maturity if the credit provides for the acceptance of drafts drawn on the applicant for the credit or any other drawee specified in the credit
iii   to purchase/negotiate without recourse to drawers and/or *bona fide* holders, drafts drawn by the beneficiary, at sight or at a tenor, on the issuing bank, or on the applicant for the credit or on any other drawee specified in the credit, if the credit provides for purchase/negotiation.

c Such undertakings can neither be amended nor cancelled without the agreement of all parties thereto. Partial acceptance of amendments is not effective without the agreement of all parties thereto.

Article 4

a When an issuing bank instructs a bank by cable, telegram or telex to advise a credit, and intends the mail confirmation to be the operative credit instrument, the cable, telegram or telex must state that the credit will only be effective on receipt of such mail confirmation. In this event, the issuing bank must send the operative credit instrument (mail confirmation) and any subsequent amendments to the credit to the beneficiary through the advising bank.

b The issuing bank will be responsible for any consequences arising from its failure to follow the procedure set out in the preceding paragraph.

c Unless a cable, telegram or telex states 'details to follow' (or words of similar effect), or states that the mail confirmation is to be the operative credit instrument, the cable, telegram or telex will be deemed to be the operative credit instrument and the issuing bank need not send the mail confirmation to the advising bank.

Article 5

When a bank is instructed by cable, telegram or telex to issue, confirm or advise a credit similar in terms to one previously established and which has been the subject of amendments, it shall be understood that the details of the credit being issued, confirmed or advised will be transmitted to the beneficiary excluding the amendments, unless the instructions specify clearly any amendments which are to apply.

Article 6

If incomplete or unclear instructions are received to issue, confirm or advise a credit, the bank requested to act on such instructions may give preliminary notification of the credit to the beneficiary for information only and without responsibility; in this event the credit will be issued, confirmed or advised only when the necessary information has been received.

B Liabilities and responsibilities

Article 7

Banks must examine all documents with reasonable care to ascertain that they appear on their face to be in accordance with the terms and conditions of the credit. Documents which appear on their face to be inconsistent with one another will be considered as not appearing on their face to be in accordance with the terms and conditions of the credit.

Article 8

a In documentary credit operations all parties concerned deal in documents and not in goods.

b Payment, acceptance or negotiation against documents which appear on their face to be in accordance with the terms and conditions of a credit by a bank authorised to do so, binds the party giving the authorisation to take up the documents and reimburse the bank which has effected the payment, acceptance or negotiation.

c If, upon receipt of the documents, the issuing bank considers that they appear on their face not to be in accordance with the terms and conditions of the credit, that bank must determine, on the basis of the documents alone, whether to claim that payment, acceptance or negotiation was not effected in accordance with the terms and conditions of the credit.

d   The issuing bank shall have a reasonable time to examine the documents and to determine as above whether to make such a claim.

e   If such claim is to be made, notice to that effect, stating the reasons therefor, must, without delay, be given by cable or other expeditious means to the bank from which the documents have been received (the remitting bank) and such notice must state that the documents are being held at the disposal of such bank or are being returned thereto.

f   If the issuing bank fails to hold the documents at the disposal of the remitting bank, or fails to return the documents to such bank, the issuing bank shall be precluded from claiming that the relative payment, acceptance or negotiation was not effected in accordance with the terms and conditions of the credit.

g   If the remitting bank draws the attention of the issuing bank to any irregularities in the documents or advises such bank that it has paid, accepted or negotiated under reserve or against a guarantee in respect of such irregularities, the issuing bank shall not thereby be relieved from any of its obligations under this Article. Such guarantee or reserve concerns only the relations between the remitting bank and the beneficiary.

Article 9
Banks assume no liability or responsibility for the form, sufficiency, accuracy, genuineness, falsification or legal effect of any documents, or for the general and/or particular conditions stipulated in the documents or superimposed thereon; nor do they assume any liability or responsibility for the description, quantity, weight, quality, condition, packing, delivery, value or existence of the goods represented thereby, or for the good faith or acts and/or omissions, solvency, performance or standing of the consignor, the carriers or the insurers of the goods or any other person whomsoever.

Article 10
Banks assume no liability or responsibility for the consequences arising out of delay and/or loss in transit of any messages, letters or documents, or for delay, mutilation or other errors arising in the transmission of cables, telegrams or telex. Banks assume no liability or responsibility for errors in translation or interpretation of technical terms, and reserve the right to transmit credit terms without translating them.

Article 11
Banks assume no liability or responsibility for consequences arising out of the interruption of their business by acts of God, riots, civil commotions, insurrections, wars or any other causes beyond their control or by any strikes or lockouts. Unless specifically authorised, banks will not effect payment, acceptance or negotiation after expiration under credits expiring during such interruption of business.

Article 12
a   Banks utilising the services of another bank for the purpose of giving effect to the instructions of the applicant for the credit do so for the account and at the risk of the latter.

b   Banks assume no liability or responsibility should the instructions they transmit not be carried out, even if they have themselves taken the initiative in the choice of such other bank.

c   The applicant for the credit shall be bound by and liable to indemnify the banks against all obligations and responsibilities imposed by foreign laws and usages.

Article 13

A paying or negotiating bank which has been authorised to claim reimbursement from a third bank nominated by the issuing bank and which has effected such payment or negotiation shall not be required to confirm to the third bank that it has done so in accordance with the terms and conditions of the credit.

C Documents
Article 14

a   All instructions to issue, confirm or advise a credit must state precisely the documents against which payment, acceptance or negotiation is to be made.

b   Terms such as 'first class', 'well known', 'qualified' and the like shall not be used to describe the issuers of any documents called for under credits and if they are incorporated in the credit terms banks will accept documents as tendered.

C.1   Documents evidencing shipment or despatch or taking in charge (shipping documents)
Article 15

Except as stated in Article 20, the date of the bill of lading, or the date of any other document evidencing shipment or despatch or taking in charge, or the date indicated in the reception stamp or by notation on any such document, will be taken in each case to be the date of shipment or despatch or taking in charge of the goods.

Article 16

a   If words clearly indicating payment or prepayment of freight, however named or described, appear by stamp or otherwise on documents evidencing shipment or despatch they will be accepted as constituting evidence of payment of freight.

b   If the words 'freight pre-payable' or 'freight to be prepaid' or words of similar effect appear by stamp or otherwise on such documents they will not be accepted as constituting evidence of the payment of freight.

c   Unless otherwise specified in the credit or inconsistent with any of the documents presented under the credit, banks will accept documents stating that freight or transportation charges are payable on delivery.

d   Banks will accept shipping documents bearing reference by stamp or otherwise to costs additional to the freight charges, such as costs of, or disbursements incurred in connection with, loading, unloading or similar operations, unless the conditions of the credit specifically prohibit such reference.

Article 17

Shipping documents which bear a clause on the face thereof such as 'shipper's load and count' or 'said by shipper to contain' or words of similar effect, will be accepted unless otherwise specified in the credit.

Article 18

a   A clean shipping document is one which bears no superimposed clause or notation which expressly declares a defective condition of the goods and/or the packaging.

b   Banks will refuse shipping documents bearing such clauses or notations unless the credit expressly states the clauses or notations which may be accepted.

C.1.1 Marine bills of lading
Article 19

a   Unless specifically authorised in the credit, bills of lading of the following nature will be rejected:

    i   bills of lading issued by forwarding agents

    ii   bills of lading which are issued under and are subject to the conditions of a charter-party

    iii   bills of lading covering shipment by sailing vessels.

b   However, subject to the above and unless otherwise specified in the credit, bills of lading of the following nature will be accepted:

    i   'through' bills of lading issued by shipping companies or their agents even though they cover several modes of transport

    ii   short form bills of lading (ie, bills of lading issued by shipping companies or their agents which indicate some or all of the conditions of carriage by reference to a source or document other than the bill of lading)

    iii   bills of lading issued by shipping companies or their agents covering unitised cargoes, such as those on pallets or in containers.

Article 20

a   Unless otherwise specified in the credit, bills of lading must show that the goods are loaded on board a named vessel or shipped on a named vessel.

b   Loading on board a named vessel or shipment on a named vessel may be evidenced either by a bill of lading bearing wording indicating loading on board a named vessel or shipment on a named vessel, or by means of a notation to that effect on the bill of lading signed or initialled and dated by the carrier or his agent, and the date of this notation shall be regarded as the date of loading on board the named vessel or shipment on the named vessel.

Article 21

a   Unless transhipment is prohibited by the terms of the credit, bills of lading will be accepted which indicate that the goods will be transhipped en route, provided the entire voyage is covered by one and the same bill of lading.

b   Bills of lading incorporating printed clauses stating that the carriers have the right to tranship will be accepted notwithstanding the fact that the credit prohibits transhipment.

Article 22

a   Banks will refuse a bill of lading stating that the goods are loaded on deck, unless specifically authorised in the credit.

b   Banks will not refuse a bill of lading which contains a provision that the goods may be carried on deck, provided it does not specifically state that they are loaded on deck.

C.1.2   Combined transport documents

Article 23

a   If the credit calls for a combined transport document, ie, one which provides for a combined transport by at least two different modes of transport, from a place at which the goods are taken in charge to a place designated for delivery, or if the credit provides for a combined transport, but in either case does not specify the form of document required and/or the issuer of such document, banks will accept such documents as tendered.

b   If the combined transport includes transport by sea the document will be accepted although it does not indicate that the goods are on board a named vessel, and although it contains a provision that the goods, if packed in a container, may be carried on deck, provided it does not specifically state that they are loaded on deck.

C.1.3 Other shipping documents, etc
Article 24
Banks will consider a railway or inland waterway bill of lading or consignment note, counterfoil waybill, postal receipt, certificate of mailing, air mail receipt, air waybill, air consignment note or air receipt, trucking company bill of lading or any other similar document as regular when such document bears the reception stamp of the carrier or his agent, or when it bears a signature purporting to be that of the carrier or his agent.

Article 25
Where a credit calls for an attestation or certification of weight in the case of transport other than by sea, banks will accept a weight stamp or declaration of weight superimposed by the carrier on the shipping document unless the credit calls for a separate or independent certificate of weight.

C.2 Insurance documents
Article 26
a   Insurance documents must be as specified in the credit and must be issued and/or signed by insurance companies or their agents or by underwriters.
b   Cover notes issued by brokers will not be accepted, unless specifically authorised in the credit.

Article 27
Unless otherwise specified in the credit, or unless the insurance documents presented establish that the cover is effective at the latest from the date of shipment or despatch or, in the case of combined transport, the date of taking the goods in charge, banks will refuse insurance documents presented which bear a date later than the date of shipment or despatch or, in the case of combined transport, the date of taking the goods in charge, as evidenced by the shipping documents.

Article 28
a   Unless otherwise specified in the credit, the insurance document must be expressed in the same currency as the credit.
b   The minimum amount for which insurance must be effected is the CIF value of the goods concerned. However, when the CIF value of the goods cannot be determined from the documents on their face, banks will accept as such minimum amount the amount of the drawing under the credit or the amount of the relative commercial invoice, whichever is the greater.

Article 29
a   Credits should expressly state the type of insurance required and, if any, the additional risks which are to be covered. Imprecise terms such as 'usual risks' or 'customary risks' should not be used; however, if such imprecise terms are used, banks will accept insurance documents as tendered.
b   Failing specific instructions, banks will accept insurance cover as tendered.

Article 30
Where a credit stipulates 'insurance against all risks', banks will accept an insurance document which contains any 'all risks' notation or clause, and will assume no responsibility if any particular risk is not covered.

Article 31
Banks will accept an insurance document which indicates that the cover is subject to

a franchise or an excess (deductible) unless it is specifically stated in the credit that the insurance must be issued irrespective of percentage.

C.3 Commercial invoices
Article 32
a Unless otherwise specified in the credit, commercial invoices must be made out in the name of the applicant for the credit.
b Unless otherwise specified in the credit, banks may refuse commercial invoices issued for amounts in excess of the amount permitted by the credit.
c The description of the goods in the commercial invoice must correspond with the description in the credit. In all other documents the goods may be described in general terms not inconsistent with the description of the goods in the credit.

C.4 Other documents
Article 33
When other documents are required, such as warehouse receipts, delivery orders, consular invoices, certificates of origin, of weight, of quality or of analysis, etc, and when no further definition is given, banks will accept such documents as tendered.

D Miscellaneous provisions
Quantity and amount
Article 34
a The words 'about', 'circa' or similar expressions used in connection with the amount of the credit or the quantity or the unit price of the goods are to be construed as allowing a difference not to exceed 10 per cent more or 10 per cent less.
b Unless a credit stipulates that the quantity of the goods specified must not be exceeded or reduced a tolerance of 3 per cent more or 3 per cent less will be permissible, always provided that the total amount of the drawings does not exceed the amount of the credit. This tolerance does not apply when the credit specifies quantity in terms of a stated number of packing units or individual items.

Partial shipments
Article 35
a Partial shipments are allowed, unless the credit specifically states otherwise.
b Shipments made on the same ship and for the same voyage, even if the bills of lading evidencing shipment 'on board' bear different dates and/or indicate different ports of shipment, will not be regarded as partial shipments.

Article 36
If shipment by instalments within given periods is stipulated and any instalment is not shipped within the period allowed for that instalment, the credit ceases to be available for that or any subsequent instalments, unless otherwise specified in the credit.

Expiry date
Article 37
All credits, whether revocable or irrevocable, must stipulate an expiry date for presentation of documents for payment, acceptance or negotiation, notwithstanding the stipulation of a latest date for shipment.

Article 38
The words 'to', 'until', 'till', and words of similar import applying to the stipulated expiry date for presentation of documents for payment, acceptance or negotiation, or

to the stipulated latest date for shipment, will be understood to include the date mentioned.

Article 39
a   When the stipulated expiry date falls on a day on which banks are closed for reasons other than those mentioned in Article 11, the expiry date will be extended until the first following business day.

b   The latest date for shipment shall not be extended by reason of the extension of the expiry date in accordance with this Article. Where the credit stipulates a latest date for shipment, shipping documents dated later than such stipulated date will not be accepted. If no latest date for shipment is stipulated in the credit, shipping documents dated later than the expiry date stipulated in the credit or amendments thereto will not be accepted. Documents other than the shipping documents may, however, be dated up to and including the extended expiry date.

c   Banks paying, accepting or negotiating on such extended expiry date must add to the documents their certification in the following wording:

'presented for payment (or acceptance or negotiation as the case may be) within the expiry date extended in accordance with Article 39 of the *Uniform Customs*'.

Shipment, loading or despatch
Article 40
a   Unless the terms of the credit indicate otherwise, the words 'departure', 'despatch', 'loading' or 'sailing' used in stipulating the latest date for shipment of the goods will be understood to be synonymous with 'shipment'.

b   Expressions such as 'prompt', 'immediately', 'as soon as possible' and the like should not be used. If they are used, banks will interpret them as a request for shipment within thirty days from the date on the advice of the credit to the beneficiary by the issuing bank or by an advising bank, as the case may be.

c   The expression 'on or about' and similar expressions will be interpreted as a request for shipment during the period from five days before to five days after the specified date, both end days included.

Presentation
Article 41
Notwithstanding the requirement of Article 37 that every credit must stipulate an expiry date for presentation of documents, credits must also stipulate a specified period of time after the date of issuance of the bills of lading or other shipping documents during which presentation of documents for payment, acceptance or negotiation must be made. If no such period of time is stipulated in the credit, banks will refuse documents presented to them later than 21 days after the date of issuance of the bills of lading or other shipping documents.

Article 42
Banks are under no obligation to accept presentation of documents outside their banking hours.

Date terms
Article 43
The terms 'first half', 'second half' of a month shall be construed respectively as from the 1st to the 15th, and the 16th to the last day of each month, inclusive.

Article 44

The terms 'beginning', 'middle' or 'end' of a month shall be construed respectively as from the 1st to the 10th, the 11th to the 20th, and the 21st to the last day of each month, inclusive.

Article 45

When a bank issuing a credit instructs that the credit be confirmed or advised as available 'for one month', 'for six months', or the like, but does not specify the date from which the time is to run, the confirming or advising bank will confirm or advise the credit as expiring at the end of such indicated period from the date of its confirmation or advice.

E Transfer

Article 46

a   A transferable credit is a credit under which the beneficiary has the right to give instructions to the bank called upon to effect payment or acceptance or to any bank entitled to effect negotiation to make the credit available in whole or in part to one or more third parties (second beneficiaries).

b   The bank requested to effect the transfer, whether it has confirmed the credit or not, shall be under no obligation to effect such transfer except to the extent and in the manner expressly consented to by such bank, and until such bank's charges in respect of transfer are paid.

c   Bank charges in respect of transfers are payable by the first beneficiary unless otherwise specified.

d   A credit can be transferred only if it is expressly designated as 'transferable' by the issuing bank. Terms such as 'divisible', 'fractionable', 'assignable', and 'transmissible' add nothing to the meaning of the term 'transferable' and shall not be used.

e   A transferable credit can be transferred once only. Fractions of a transferable credit (not exceeding in the aggregate the amount of the credit) can be transferred separately, provided partial shipments are not prohibited, and the aggregate of such transfers will be considered as constituting only one transfer of the credit. The credit can be transferred only on the terms and conditions specified in the original credit, with the exception of the amount of the credit, of any unit prices stated therein, and of the period of validity or period for shipment, any or all of which may be reduced or curtailed. Additionally, the name of the first beneficiary can be substituted for that of the applicant for the credit, but if the name of the applicant for the credit is specifically required by the original credit to appear in any document other than the invoice, such requirement must be fulfilled.

f   The first beneficiary has the right to substitute his own invoices for those of the second beneficiary, for amounts not in excess of the original amount stipulated in the credit and for the original unit prices if stipulated in the credit, and upon such substitution of invoices the first beneficiary can draw under the credit for the difference, if any, between his invoices and the second beneficiary's invoices. When a credit has been transferred and the first beneficiary is to supply his own invoices in exchange for the second beneficiary's invoices but fails to do so on first demand, the paying, accepting or negotiating bank has the right to deliver to the issuing bank the documents received under the credit, including the second beneficiary's invoices, without further responsibility to the first beneficiary.

g   The first beneficiary of a transferable credit can transfer the credit to a second beneficiary in the same country or in another country unless the credit specifically states otherwise. The first beneficiary shall have the right to request that payment or negotiation be effected to the second beneficiary at the place to which the credit has been transferred, up to and including the expiry date of the original credit, and without prejudice to the first beneficiary's right subsequently to substitute his own invoices for those of the second beneficiary and to claim any difference due to him.

Article 47
The fact that a credit is not stated to be transferable shall not affect the beneficiary's rights to assign the proceeds of such credit in accordance with the provisions of the applicable law.

The copyright of Uniform Customs and Practice for Documentary Credits *Publication No. 290 (1974), is held by the International Chamber of Commerce and copies of the publication are available from the British National Committee of the ICC, Centre Point, 103 New Oxford Street, London WC1A 1QB and from the Publications Division, ICC Headquarters, 38 Cours Albert 1er – 75008 Paris, or from the ICC's national committees in over 50 countries.*

14. DISCREPANCIES, INDEMNITIES AND AMENDMENTS

The beneficiary of a credit is only entitled to receive settlement thereunder if he presents documents which appear on their face to be in accordance with the terms and conditions of the credit. Therefore any bank, required to pay, negotiate or accept under a credit, is entitled to reject documents that do not meet this requirement. The beneficiary thus loses the security of the bank undertaking given by the credit. In some cases, however, the beneficiary may be given what amounts to 'provisional settlement' against his providing an acceptable specific indemnity. This undertakes to indemnify the bank against any consequences arising from its making such 'settlement' despite the discrepancies. The measure of protection required by such paying, negotiating or accepting bank is, of course, entirely at the discretion of that bank, and it is under no obligation even to give 'provisional settlement' against an indemnity. Further, the indemnity of the beneficiary himself may be deemed insufficient: it may need to be issued or supported by his bank. In certain cases a credit may specifically state that no payment is to be made against an indemnity, in which case of course the paying, accepting or negotiating bank would not be able to effect provisional settlement against an indemnity.

It has to be remembered that during periods of economic trouble or falling prices buyers are much more likely to reject documents if any excuse presents itself.

It is of interest to note that approximately seven sets of documents out of ten presented by UK beneficiaries to UK advising banks during 1980 were not in order on first presentation. This suggests that beneficiaries are not taking the elementary precaution of satisfying themselves, when they receive a credit, that they can comply with its terms and conditions.

Should the advising bank, for example, have reservations about the creditworthiness of the beneficiary it might require the indemnity to be supported by the beneficiary's bankers as illustrated opposite. Indemnities should list the discrepancies in the presentation in detail and not be made out to cover all discrepancies. Otherwise a subsequent dispute could arise between the beneficiary and the advising bank whether a stated reason for non-payment constitutes a discrepancy, and is or is not therefore covered by the indemnity.

Example of an indemnity

To Joint Bank Limited,
Overseas Branch

In respect of credit 3872A issued by Foreign Bank
Inc, New York.

Dear Sir,
In consideration of your paying us the sum of US$16,469.06
under the above-mentioned credit, we hereby indemnify you from
all consequences which may arise notwithstanding the following
discrepancies:
1. Short shipment
2. Bills of lading evidence shipment to New York, whereas
the credit stipulates Baltimore.

UK Exporters Limited   British Bank Limited
Signed ....   Signed ....
        Director   Manager

Common discrepancies include:
- credit expired
- late shipment
- claused bills of lading
- presentation after permitted time from date of issue of shipping documents
- short shipment
- credit amount exceeded
- under-insured
- description of goods on invoice differs from that of the credit
- marks and numbers differ between documents
- goods shipped on deck
- bills of lading, insurance document or bill of exchange not endorsed correctly
- absence of documents called for under the credit

- insurance document of lower order presented than that required by the credit
- weights differ between documents
- class of bill of lading not acceptable – eg, charter-party, or house bills
- insurance cover expressed in a currency other than that of the credit
- absence of signatures, where required, on documents presented
- bills of exchange drawn on a wrong party
- bills of exchange drawn payable on an indeterminable date
- insurance risks covered not being those specified in the credit
- absence of 'freight paid' statement on bills of lading where the credit covers a C & F or CIF shipment
- no evidence of goods actually 'shipped on board'
- the amounts shown on the invoice and bill of exchange differ
- shipment made between ports other than those stated in the credit
- documents inconsistent with each other

If many discrepancies appear in a set of documents it is often inappropriate to take an indemnity and perhaps the documents might be forwarded to the issuing bank on a collection basis.

Alternative ways of handling documents presented out of order under a credit:
- return to the beneficiary to amend the documents; this is not always appropriate, because of the nature of the discrepancy or the timing of the presentation; representation must be made within the Article 41 period and within the validity of the credit
- take the beneficiary's indemnity, and pay
- take the indemnity of the beneficiary's banker, and settle
- pay under reserve; this means that if the issuing bank refuses to reimburse the paying, accepting or negotiating bank it will claim refund from the beneficiary of the sum paid under reserve; this method would normally be adopted only when the beneficiary was a customer of the paying, accepting or negotiating bank or was a company of undoubted standing
- cable for authority to settle; if so required by the beneficiary (and at his expense) cable to the issuing bank for authority to pay, accept or negotiate; the reply, if favourable, is likely to be worded 'you may pay (accept, negotiate) if otherwise in order'; this is usually suitable where only a few discrepancies exist
- send documents for collection; send documents to the issuing bank for that bank to decide whether or not to approve the discrepancies; this is commonly known as sending the documents on a collection basis; the issuing bank would, of course, need to secure the approval of the applicant before accepting the discrepancies
- pay despite the discrepancy, on the basis of specific knowledge of a negligible risk gained through practical experience; this is not a recommended procedure because by making payment outside the given mandate the advising bank becomes hostage to the whims of the applicant, and the commissions taken are insufficient premium for such risks
- return the documents to the beneficiary without making settlement

As previously stressed, credits should be closely inspected by the beneficiary immediately upon receipt. Should it be considered that the terms cannot be met completely the beneficiary should arrange for all necessary amendments to be received before he ships the goods, if he wishes to rely upon the credit as a secure means of settlement. The beneficiary must therefore contact the applicant immediately, telexing him if necessary and if time is short, asking the applicant to arrange for the issuing bank to telex the necessary amendment to the advising bank.

No irrevocable credit may be amended without the agreement of the beneficiary. However, in many cases the beneficiary may request or require the amendment because he cannot meet the credit terms as they stand. Revocable credits may be amended, or cancelled, at any time before payment, negotiation or acceptance has been made by the paying, negotiating or accepting bank, and without notice being given to the beneficiary.

Amendments to irrevocable credits are often not acknowledged by the beneficiary, and absence of acknowledgement of intention to reject an amendment (even if requested by the advising bank) will not bind the beneficiary to accept the amendment when he eventually submits the documents. Indeed the beneficiary is entitled to rely upon the original irrevocable undertaking and ignore any amendment he chooses. If more than one aspect of the credit is amended at the same time in a single letter of amendment, the beneficiary will have to accept or reject *all* the points contained in that letter of amendment. In practice beneficiaries will, if requested, indicate their intention to accept or reject an amendment, but, as mentioned above, failure to do so will not mean that the beneficiary is bound to accept the change, and he is still entitled to lodge documents conforming to the original terms of the credit and expect to be paid.

15. FOREIGN CURRENCY CREDITS

In every international trading transaction, with the possible exception of barter trade, one and sometimes both trading parties run an exchange risk. When the transaction is in sterling the UK party does not run the exchange risk; it is borne by the party abroad who has to buy or sell sterling.

This section relates to a situation in which the UK applicant or the UK beneficiary under an import or export credit runs the exchange risk of buying or selling foreign currency to meet his obligations under the credit. A UK applicant wishing to establish in favour of a foreign beneficiary a credit that is expressed in the beneficiary's currency will be liable for payment in that foreign currency when the correct documents are tendered or at the maturity of a term bill. In either event the date of payment will be in the future, and the value of sterling against the foreign currency may in the meantime rise or fall. The UK importer may wish to take a chance that the foreign currency will become weaker in terms of sterling, and that he will require less sterling than he had expected to buy the currency and settle his debt in due course. The UK beneficiary similarly may wish to take a chance that the foreign currency will become stronger in terms of sterling, so that when he comes to sell the foreign currency in due course he will receive more sterling than he had expected.

Importers can, if they wish, buy the foreign currency spot to be held on a currency account pending payment under the credit. The importer wishing to eliminate his exchange risk may also buy foreign currency forward, either fixed or option. Option forward contracts are more common under credits than fixed forwards because of the latitude given to the beneficiary under the credit to make shipment and present documents up to a specified date or dates. This will probably mean that at the time the credit is opened and the forward contract arranged the applicant will only be able to ascertain the dates between which he will require to take delivery of the foreign currency and not the actual date of delivery (see Chapter 8 for further details).

Beneficiaries of foreign currency credits may eliminate their exchange risks by covering forward with their own bank or with the advising bank at the time they (the beneficiaries) receive the credit from the advising bank. The beneficiaries may be able to calculate exactly when the foreign currency will become payable to them and therefore can arrange for a fixed forward sale of the foreign currency to the bank. However, if delivery dates are uncertain an option forward contract may be arranged. Beneficiaries can borrow the foreign currency pending receipt of funds under the credit to repay the foreign currency loan.

16. BACK TO BACK CREDITS AND COUNTER CREDITS

Diagram of a back to back credit transaction

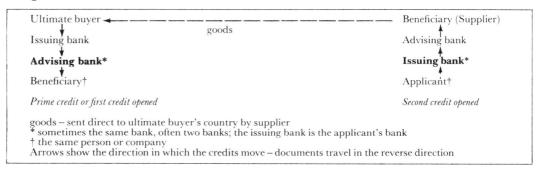

Such transactions involve two separate documentary credits. The first to be opened is established in favour of a beneficiary who may not himself wish or be able to supply the goods, but who asks his bank to issue a credit in favour of another beneficiary who is able and willing to supply the goods. The beneficiary of the first credit will therefore become the applicant for the second credit. *It is only to him and to his bank, the issuing bank of the second credit, that back to back and counter credits provide points worthy of attention and care, other than those usually encountered under a straightforward credit.* All other parties will be concerned with one credit only.

The issuing bank of the second credit will expect to receive reimbursement for payments it will have to make by presenting the documents, when tendered, under the first credit. The issuing bank of the second credit has to bear in mind that the advising bank under the first credit will not pay for the documents if they are not in order under the first credit. This emphasises the need for the terms and conditions of the second credit to match those of the first credit.

Points that should be noted by the issuing bank and the applicant under the second credit are as follows (the diagram at the beginning of this section may help when reading the following):

a Under a back to back credit the applicant of the second credit requires his bank to take the prime (first) credit as 'security' against which the second credit is to be opened. The issuing bank of the second credit must therefore be sure that reimbursement can be obtained from the advising bank of the prime credit, which is the expected source of funds for their customer.

b The prime credit should therefore be irrevocable, preferably confirmed and one which authorises the advising bank to pay rather than negotiate documents presented under it.

c Under a counter credit the bank issuing the second credit is granting a facility to its customer with the right to (and possibility of) debiting that customer for any payments made under the second credit. The bank then merely sees the first credit as a possible source of funds for its customer.

d As mentioned before the terms and conditions of the second credit must be identical to those of the prime credit but with the exception of the points listed below:

- The name of the applicant will be the same as that of the beneficiary of the prime credit, and the beneficiary of the second credit will be the supplier of the goods. In order to comply with Article 32 of *Uniform Customs and Practice*, when documents are submitted in due course under the prime credit the customer will have to substitute his own invoices, made out to the applicant of the prime credit, for the invoices from the supplier which are addressed to him. The issuing bank of the second credit must make sure that there will be no difficulty in obtaining the substituted invoices from their customer which may jeopardise reimbursement under the prime credit.

- If the customer (applicant of the second credit) wishes to make a profit on the transaction, the amount of the second credit which is made available to the supplier will be less than the amount of the prime credit. On presentation of documents, provided all is in order under each credit, the customer will expect to receive the difference between the two invoices referred to above.

- The second credit should have an earlier expiry date than the prime credit to provide sufficient time for the issuing bank of the second credit to examine the documents when they are received, for invoice substitution to take place and other matters mentioned below to be attended to, and to lodge correct documents with the advising bank of the prime credit before that credit expires.

- If the second credit is made payable and expires in the place of issue, the issuing bank of the second credit avoids the risk of documents being delayed in the post after payment and arriving too late for presentation under the prime credit, yet being received and paid under the second credit before expiry of the second credit. Both credits should therefore be available for payment or negotiation in the same centre.

- If the customer requires that the names of the supplier and ultimate buyer be not disclosed to each other, the second credit should call for documents to be issued under it in neutral names.

  Certain banks may, however, be prepared to help the customer by issuing a second credit on terms which do not exactly match those of the first credit. These are not pure back to back credits, although the banks concerned may sometimes so describe them. In these cases the following points need to be noted:

- If shipping terms under the prime credit are CIF and under the second credit FOB, the bills of lading coming from the supplier will be marked 'freight collect'; the bills of lading to be good tender under the prime credit must be marked 'freight paid'. At the time of issuing the second credit, the issuing bank might consider taking its customer's authority to debit his account for the freight to be paid and to diarise the lodgement of the bills of lading, when they arrive, with the shipping company's local agent. In due course the bills of lading accompanied by the payment for freight will be lodged to be marked 'freight paid' and returned as quickly as possible to the issuing bank of the second credit for presentation with the other documents under the prime credit.

- If the shipping terms under the prime credit are CIF and under the second credit FOB, the responsibility for insuring the goods under both contracts will be the customer's. The issuing bank of the second credit may consider taking and holding the insurance document required under the prime credit in the correct currency and for the correct amount as set out in that credit, in advance of documents being submitted under the second credit.

- If the terms of each credit are to be CIF then bills of lading will be marked 'freight paid' from the outset, as the supplier will be required to pay the freight through to final destination. The prime credit may also call for insurance cover for say, 10 per cent over the CIF value of the goods. If this be so, the issuing bank of the second credit will have to be careful not to copy this requirement when issuing the second credit. The result is likely to yield insurance cover in an amount insufficient for the prime credit, and the documents when presented under it to be rejected for the discrepancy 'under-insured'. The bank may allow its customer to substitute his insurance document in London when it arrives, or increase the amount of the insured value for the supplier to cover, and have this written into the second credit.

- If the ultimate buyer requires deferred terms by means of an acceptance documentary credit and the supplier is to receive cash against documents presented to a bank locally and therefore a sight credit, the prime credit will be an acceptance credit and the second credit a sight credit. This should pose no real difficulty to a customer who might wish to have immediate payment himself, provided that the prime acceptance credit authorises a first class advising bank to accept the term bills drawn on it by the beneficiary under the prime acceptance credit. Such a bill after acceptance can be readily discounted to provide cash to meet the reimbursement under the sight second credit and to pay the difference to the customer. The issuing bank of the second credit may consider it appropriate to take inchoate (uncompleted) term bills drawn by their customer on the advising bank of the prime credit, at the time the second credit is opened. It should also consider for whose account the discount charges under the prime credit are to be, and, if they are for its customer's account, whether the discounted proceeds will be enough to meet the sight credit disbursement.

- If one credit is drawn in one currency and the other is to be issued in another, the issuing bank of the second credit might consider it advisable for the customer to cover his exchange risk under a forward contract(s), not only to ensure maintenance of his profit margin but also to guarantee that sufficient proceeds will be received from the prime credit to meet reimbursement commitments under the second credit, irrespective of what may happen on the foreign exchange market.

A special problem can arise in any of the above types of transaction if incorrect documents are presented by the supplier as beneficiary of the second credit. Such documents would not meet the requirements of the first credit. The issuing bank of the second credit could, if so requested by his customer (the beneficiary of the first credit), contact the issuing bank of the first credit for approval of the irregularities. This would, of course, mean that the issuing bank of the second credit might be deemed not to have given its decision to take up or reject the documents under the second credit within the 'reasonable time' allowed to it by *Uniform Customs and Practice,*

Article 8 (d) and (e). The issuing bank of the second credit should consider requesting the advising bank of the prime credit to cable the issuing bank of the prime credit for authority to pay thereunder. Issuing banks shall have 'reasonable time to examine documents' presented, but must notify the advising bank as quickly as possible if the documents are not going to be taken up by the applicant. The issuing bank of the second credit can be exposed to excessive delay before being able to notify the advising bank under the second credit, and therefore runs the risk of the doctrine of ratification (see section 27 of this chapter, item *ii*, Bank Melli Iran v Barclays Bank (DCO)).

17. TRANSFERABLE CREDITS

Diagram of a transferable credit

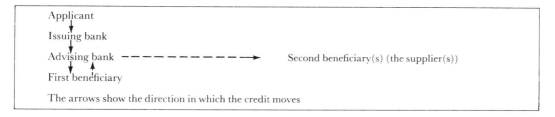

Article 46 of *Uniform Customs and Practice for Documentary Credits* sets out the conditions under which a transferable credit may be issued and transferred and the rights and responsibilities of the parties thereto. A credit is transferable only if it specifically indicates that it is. The transferable credit is usually established when the first beneficiary is not supplying the goods himself but wishes to transfer part or all of his rights and responsibilities under the credit to one or more second beneficiaries who will supply the goods. The first beneficiary will instruct the bank with which the credit is available to advise the second beneficiary of the amount to be transferred and the terms and conditions of the credit. The credit terms advised in the transferred portion must be identical with those of the principal credit, except that, if so requested by the beneficiary:

● the name and address of the first beneficiary may be substituted for that of the applicant on the second beneficiary's invoices
● the amount of the credit and any unit price stated may be reduced in the transferred portion so that the first beneficiary can draw the difference as his profit
● the period of validity and latest shipment date may be shortened

(*Note*: under *Uniform Customs and Practice*, Article 46(e), the second beneficiary has no right to transfer the portion of the credit advised to him.)

After receiving a transferred portion of the credit, the second beneficiary may present his shipping documents, in accordance with the credit terms, for payment, negotiation or acceptance. The concerned bank may pay, negotiate or accept, thereby settling directly with the second beneficiary, and will then inform the first beneficiary that it is holding the second beneficiary's documents. The first beneficiary has the right to substitute his own invoices for those of the second beneficiary; however, should the advising bank not receive the first beneficiary's invoices within a reasonable time after demand for them, it may forward all documents, including the second beneficiary's invoices, directly to the issuing bank and be entitled to reimbursement for payment made to the second beneficiary.

A transferable credit is often used when the first beneficiary is the agent of, or principal supplier to, the applicant, for goods stated in the credit. These credits are sometimes issued for very large amounts, and are occasionally known as 'shopping bag' credits. Under a shopping bag credit, the first beneficiary will be responsible for distributing the portions of the credit to various suppliers via the advising bank. Depending on the contractual relationship between the applicant and first beneficiary, the first beneficiary may be the commercial attaché of the applicant's country, or the principal supplier, or the applicant's representative agent or subsidiary company.

18. TRANSIT CREDITS

A London bank may be asked by banks overseas to advise and sometimes open a documentary credit in favour of a beneficiary in another overseas country. This is done through a correspondent bank in the beneficiary's country. This type of credit, when both beneficiary and applicant are resident abroad, is sometimes referred to as a transit credit, although some banks do not handle a sufficient volume of such business to warrant the distinction of describing them separately and other banks prefer to handle such transactions alongside credits advised and/or confirmed for UK beneficiaries.

Banks in the UK are requested to advise or open transit credits for various reasons, such as:

- settlement being effected in sterling, a major trading currency often acceptable to both buyer and seller, which can conveniently be arranged through the sterling (*vostro*) accounts maintained by UK banks for the hundreds of different banks abroad; transit credits need not be expressed in sterling since settlement may be arranged by UK banks in other currencies, particularly US dollars
- the standing of UK banks in the eyes of the world with respect to integrity, financial stability, experience/expertise in handling documentary credit transactions with absolute impartiality, and absence of exchange controls in the UK
- the UK government is most unlikely to declare a moratorium
- finance under a credit may be arranged in London for any period or currency, subject to market availability; where local finance in either of the other two countries is more expensive or not available, the London bank may discount term bills drawn on and accepted by them in foreign currencies
- when the opening bank is unknown in the seller's country (ie, its signatures cannot be verified)
- when direct communication between the buyer's and seller's countries is not possible for political reasons

Additionally, sellers sometimes require a credit to be confirmed by a bank in the UK, and passing the credit through such a bank (provided they have arranged a credit 'line') is a convenient way of providing such confirmation. This occurs more frequently when the buyer's country is considered by the seller to be politically unstable, or its currency to be unsound, or the buyer's bank to be other than first class. The London bank's confirmation, in such cases, makes the credit as good as that of the London bank.

Diagrams of transit credits

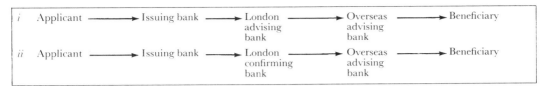

19. CLEAN REIMBURSEMENT CREDITS

When a bank is required to pay, accept or negotiate under a credit of an issuing bank with which it does not maintain an account in the currency of the credit, reimbursement is usually effected by the paying, accepting or negotiating bank being authorised by the issuing bank to claim reimbursement from a named third party bank. In certain cases the bank which may be required to pay, accept or negotiate may request the issuing bank to arrange for this third party bank to confirm to the paying, accepting or negotiating bank that it will honour such claims when made. In some cases the issuing bank may require the reimbursement claim of the paying, accepting or negotiating bank on the third party bank to be accompanied by a certificate that the documents sent directly to the issuing bank meet the requirements of the credit and that the terms and conditions of the credit have been fulfilled. This places a burden on the third party bank which has no interest in the documentary credit concerned. For this reason Article 13 of *Uniform Customs and Practice* states that banks should not call for such 'certificates of compliance'.

Clean reimbursement credits are transit credits the documents of which have been sent directly by the advising bank in the supplier's country to the importing applicant's bank. The reasons for establishing clean reimbursement credits through London banks are identical to those listed for transit credits; and in addition clean reimbursement credits have the advantage of speedier transmission of shipping documents.

The system of clean reimbursements may be illustrated as follows:

Issuing bank (abroad)	Reimbursing bank (in London)	Advising bank (abroad)
i Acts as principal to the reimbursing bank	*i* Acts as agent to the issuing bank	*i* Pays, accepts or negotiates documents correctly tendered by the beneficiary
ii Instructs reimbursing bank to honour claims of advising bank to issuing bank's debit	*ii* Honours claims of the advising bank	*ii* Forwards documents directly to issuing bank

'Hand-on' credits

These are documentary credits of the issuing bank addressed directly to the beneficiary; the advising bank merely hands them on to the beneficiary and confirms the authenticity of the signatures on the credits. If requested to do so the advising bank may also add its confirmation to the credit terms.

As the original credit is not addressed to the advising bank it is usual for the reimbursement instructions, in respect of credits which the advising bank is to pay or negotiate, to be sent to it by means of a separate covering letter or to be inserted on a file copy attached to the credit for that purpose. Some 90 per cent of all credits issued in the UK fall into this category since ICC standard forms and most other documentary credit forms are designed in this fashion.

20. REVOLVING CREDITS

The term 'revolving' is used to describe a credit which contains a condition that the credit amount is to be renewed or reinstated automatically in stated circumstances without the need for further specific amendment. The credit may be issued as revocable or irrevocable and may be confirmed by an advising bank, if so arranged. It is, however, essential that the credit as advised to the beneficiary should be absolutely clear and unambiguous about the manner in which renewal or reinstatement will be effected.

In theory, a credit may revolve around amount or around time. In practice, it is extremely rare for credits, particularly irrevocable (or confirmed) credits, to revolve in relation to amount. For example, a credit available for up to £5,000 at any one time, within an overall validity of six months, would allow reinstatement of each and every drawing immediately it was made and there would be no limit to the frequency of such drawings. The bank(s) and the buyer would, consequently, be involved in an incalculable and unacceptable liability. If an overall amount for the total of the drawings was specified there would be much more control, but the credit in question would then cease to be 'revolving' and become a conventional credit with a £5,000 limit, either on a single drawing or on the total of partial drawings. Again, the credit would be reinstated by the issuing bank after receipt of documents by them.

A credit which revolves in relation to time is a far more usual and practical instrument. For example, a credit could be made available for up to £5,000 per month with an overall validity of six months. The credit amount of £5,000 is automatically available each month irrespective of whether or not any sum was drawn during the previous month. Such a credit can be on either a 'cumulative' or 'non-cumulative' basis. The latter is more usual, but it is always necessary to specify which basis applies. If the credit in our example is 'cumulative', an amount unutilised from the £5,000 available during one month can be carried forward and added to the £5,000 available for the following or subsequent months. If on the other hand the credit is 'non-cumulative', any shortfall in drawings below the £5,000 available for a particular month is cancelled and it is not carried forward to the next or subsequent months.

As mentioned previously, it is necessary to differentiate clearly between a revolving credit and a credit with overall limits of value and validity, providing for part-shipment. For instance, a credit for the full value of goods, but requiring shipment of specific quantities of goods within nominated periods and allowing for part-shipments, is *not* a revolving credit. It is a credit available by instalments (see *Uniform Customs and Practice*, Article 36).

21. CREDITS AS A MEANS OF INTERNATIONAL FINANCE

The provision of finance to an exporter means that he gets paid as soon as possible, whereas the provision of finance to an importer means that he may be granted credit or allowed to defer payment. In addition to enabling settlement to be made between buyer and seller against provision of specified documents in compliance with its terms and conditions, a documentary credit may be used to provide finance, or a form of financial backing, for either the applicant for the credit (usually the buyer) or the beneficiary (usually the seller or supplier).

By agreement with the beneficiary and with the bank(s) concerned the applicant may use a documentary credit to defer providing his own funds by calling for the beneficiary to draw a term draft, either on the applicant or on a named third party, often the advising bank or the issuing bank.

In such cases the beneficiary may nevertheless be able to secure an immediate cash flow. If the draft has to be drawn on the issuing bank or on the applicant the credit will normally be a negotiation credit. This means that the beneficiary will be able to obtain funds from the bank with which the credit is available, although the beneficiary may have to bear the cost of such negotiation – ie, of obtaining his money before maturity of the term draft. From the viewpoint of the beneficiary this may have the further disadvantage that, excepting cases where the credit has been confirmed by the negotiating bank, a right of recourse will exist against him until documents have been taken up by the issuing bank.

If the term draft has to be drawn on the advising bank in the beneficiary's country the beneficiary will be entitled to have his draft accepted by such bank (subject to meeting the credit requirements) and will then have a bank draft. He may be able to discount this draft locally in order to secure immediate use of his funds. The beneficiary will, however, have to bear the costs involved, unless, as can happen, the credit authorises the accepting bank to settle with the beneficiary on the basis of the face value of such term drawing – ie, as if there had been a sight drawing. In this case all costs involved will be passed back to the applicant through the issuing bank.

If for any reason it is not agreed, or is deemed undesirable, to draw term drafts it may be possible for arrangements to be made for settlement under the credit to be made on a deferred basis. In such cases the beneficiary will present documents to the advising bank and such bank will settle at the later stipulated date. The documents will, however, be passed by the advising bank to the issuing bank immediately. If the credit is confirmed by the advising bank the beneficiary will receive an undertaking from that bank that it will effect settlement at the agreed future date. If on the other hand the credit has not been confirmed by the advising bank, the beneficiary will merely receive an acknowledgment for documents which conform to the credit terms and conditions, and an indication to the effect that the advising bank has been authorised to settle at the future date. This will not however be a commitment on the part of the advising bank to make such settlement. In both cases, of course, the beneficiary will have rights against the issuing bank if it has issued the credit in irrevocable form.

Attention is drawn in section 23 of this chapter to the manner in which the applicant can use a red clause credit to provide pre-shipment finance to the beneficiary. Section 17 also shows how the first beneficiary of a transferable credit obtains financial backing by means of such credit.

22. ACCEPTANCE CREDITS AND DISCOUNTING

Documentary acceptance credits are primarily designed to provide finance for the applicant, but if term bills are discounted they will provide working capital to finance the beneficiary too.

The reference above to negotiation under a credit and to discounting a draft drawn and accepted under a credit may be summarised as follows.

	Negotiation		Discounting
i	The credit may call for a bill of exchange to be drawn on a bank, or on the applicant, or may not call for a bill of exchange at all.	*i*	The bill of exchange is drawn on a bank in the country of the beneficiary of the credit.
ii	The bill of exchange, if one is called for, will not normally have been accepted at the time of negotiation.	*ii*	The bill of exchange must be accepted before the time of discounting.
iii	If no bill of exchange is called for the negotiating bank will 'negotiate' on the basis of the documents alone.	*iii*	There is a legal right of recourse against the drawer of the bill (beneficiary), but as the bill has been accepted by a bank this is usually only of academic interest since the bank is liable on its own acceptance.
iv	A bank which has not confirmed the credit negotiates with recourse to the beneficiary in the event of non-acceptance of the documents by the issuing bank; a confirming bank negotiates without such recourse.	*iv*	The accepted draft may be discounted by any bank willing to do so.
v	Negotiation is effected by the bank with which the credit is made available, often the advising bank. Many credits are, however, freely negotiable – ie, with any bank.		

The order of events relating to a documentary acceptance credit that calls for bills to be drawn on the advising bank is as follows:

- applicant applies for a documentary credit providing for acceptance of a bill in the country of the beneficiary
- issuing bank issues the credit
- advising bank advises the credit
- beneficiary presents (correct) documents, including a term bill on the advising bank
- advising bank accepts the bill and forwards documents to the issuing bank
- term bill is discounted
- beneficiary receives discount proceeds in full settlement
- issuing bank hands documents to applicant
- holder presents term bill at maturity to advising bank for settlement
- advising bank pays holder and obtains reimbursement from the issuing bank
- issuing bank debits the applicant (its customer)

23. PRE-SHIPMENT FINANCE

a   The red clause

The purpose of this clause in a documentary credit is to enable the beneficiary to obtain pre-shipment advances from the advising or confirming bank, at the expense of the beneficiary, but under the responsibility of the issuing bank, according to the conditions of the clause as set out in the credit.

The red clause is so named because it was, at one time, written in red ink by the issuing bank in order to draw attention to this special feature of the credit terms. It has been used, traditionally, in certain countries where goods, such as wood, cotton, meat, rubber, etc, need to be purchased and assembled prior to shipment by a beneficiary who requires advances in order to pay cash for the goods, either directly or at auction.

It is for the applicant (buyer) to decide whether, to what extent and under what conditions, he will authorise the issuing bank to allow this facility. The red clause will always specify the total value of advances that are authorised. This may be a given percentage or even the whole of the credit amount.

Depending upon his relationship with the beneficiary, the applicant will decide upon the degree of security which the advising or confirming bank is to take from the beneficiary in cover of the advances which it will make out of its own funds. This security will vary from the simplest form of acknowledgment to an undertaking of the beneficiary to provide full documents of title, by a specified date at the latest, effectively evidencing pledge to the bank making the advance.

Advances are usually made to the beneficiary in local currency. Should the credit be issued in another currency, there may be a difference in the rate of exchange between the date of the advance and the date of repayment. It is usual for any such difference to be for account of the beneficiary and to be deducted by the advising or confirming bank from the proceeds of the documents. If, however, the applicant agrees to be responsible for any exchange difference, the credit should mention this specifically.

It is always understood that the advising or confirming bank will recoup its advances, plus interest, out of the proceeds of the shipping documents eventually presented, and that it will have the right to claim such sums from the issuing bank should the beneficiary, for any reason, fail to present documents in accordance with the credit terms and conditions.

The actual wordings of the clauses used vary between bank and bank, but fall into two main categories:

i *Clean red clause:* advances are made against a simple written statement by the beneficiaries that the money will be used for the purpose specified.

ii *Documentary (or secured) red clause:* advances are made against the beneficiary's undertaking to provide warehouse receipts or other documents evidencing the right to possession of the goods and subsequently to deliver shipping documents in accordance with the credit terms. (The warehouse receipts are usually returned to the beneficiary in trust, so that he may obtain bills of lading.) In some cases the beneficiary is also required to produce evidence of insurance whilst the goods are in store.

It is not the responsibility of the advising or confirming bank actually to police the loan, but the statement shown in *i* above is usually required to protect the bank(s) from litigation, should the funds be misused by the beneficiaries.

In the event of any default by the beneficiary, resulting in a claim upon the issuing bank, the applicant is liable for repayment of the advance(s), plus interest, and all costs incurred both by the issuing bank and by the advising or confirming bank.

b Receipt and undertaking

In some cases the agreement or contract between an applicant and a beneficiary will require that the credit should provide for a pre-shipment advance to be made to the beneficiary. This is now quite usual, particularly when large value contracts are involved. Such advances are frequently made against the beneficiary's receipt supported by an undertaking to refund the advance if documents in conformity with the credit terms and conditions are not presented.

The credit may require the undertaking to be issued by the beneficiaries or by a bank, at the applicant's discretion. The wording of the undertaking should however be provided by the issuing bank to the advising or confirming bank.

This type of advance differs from the traditional 'red clause' advance. The advising or confirming bank does not make the advance out of its own funds. It reimburses itself immediately upon the issuing bank, which should also be responsible for initiating any subsequent claim against the undertaking.

24. REFINANCE ARRANGEMENTS

The advising or confirming bank is sometimes asked to make finance available to the issuing bank and/or the applicant (buyer) in relation to a credit. In such cases the beneficiary may not even be made aware of the background arrangements, since he will receive a sight payment credit.

Prior to the abolition of UK exchange controls, finance arrangements of this type, both in sterling and in foreign currency, were controlled by regulations issued from time to time by the Bank of England, but this is no longer the case.

The traditional method of sterling refinance is by the issue of inchoate (uncompleted) term bills of exchange drawn by the applicant on the advising or confirming bank. These bills are sent, together with the credit, to the advising or confirming bank by the issuing bank. The former bank is requested to advise a sight payment credit in favour of the beneficiary and retain the bills in safe custody. Upon presentation of documents in order, the advising bank (now the paying bank) pays the beneficiary at sight and debits the account of the issuing bank. Simultaneously, it completes the date and the amount on the term bills, accepts them and discounts them, crediting the proceeds to the account of the issuing bank. This account is, finally, debited with the amount of the term bill at its maturity. However, the issuing bank will have to bear payment commission and postages in respect of the sight credit and acceptance commission on the term bills as well as discount charges. This type of finance is unlikely to be required unless the market rates in the beneficiary's country are very much lower than those for similar funds for the same borrower available in the applicant's country.

The method which is now more usual is for the advising or confirming bank to advise a conventional sight payment credit in favour of the beneficiary, which is duly honoured upon presentation of documents in order. The issuing bank is debited on payment and this debit is offset by the proceeds of a matching currency loan arranged through the advising bank's deposit dealers. This loan is repayable, plus interest, at maturity. Alternatively, an amount paid under a credit may be debited to an advance account, opened in the name of the issuing bank, at an appropriate rate of interest. This method of finance can also be used to give an extended period of credit in the case of a credit requiring the beneficiary to draw a term bill of exchange on the advising or confirming bank. Any such arrangements depend upon the correspondent relationship which exists between the issuing bank and the advising or confirming bank and are the subject of special agreements between them.

There are also sources of third party funding by organisations such as the World Bank, etc, with the object of providing finance for essential imports into underdeveloped countries. This funding, on behalf of the buyer, is usually implemented by an 'agreement to reimburse', which takes the form of an undertaking issued by the organisation concerned to effect reimbursement on receipt of the bank's certificate of payment. Such arrangements are issued subject to the agreement of the advising or confirming bank; sometimes they are subject also to the approval by the organisation of the actual form of credit to be advised by that bank. The undertakings in these agreements take various forms: they may be entirely irrevocable or they may be revocable in certain defined circumstances. It is by no means unusual for an agreement to be limited to a specified amount in a foreign currency which is not the currency of the credit which it supports. There is, consequently, the possibility of an exchange risk which may not be covered by the terms of the agreement. In respect of this type of funding the advising or confirming bank may have to look to its correspondent relationship with the issuing bank, since it may have to arrange an agreed right of recourse to that bank in case of any failure of, or shortfall in, eventual reimbursement from the organisation issuing the agreement to reimburse.

25. THE USE OF CREDITS FOR OTHER THAN THE INTERNATIONAL MOVEMENT OF GOODS

Documentary credits are normally concerned, by means of undertakings to make payment against shipping documents, with settlements for goods that move from one country to another. They can however be adapted to create other conditional undertakings to pay, provided the conditions can be incorporated into suitable documents.

Examples

- US banks are prevented by law from giving guarantees covering, for example, overdrafts incurred by US residents in other countries. To overcome this restriction the borrower's US parent company sometimes issues credits which have the same effect, the document called for being a certificate from the lending bank to the effect that the lender has made formal demand for repayment of a stated sum due and has not been paid. The US parent company assumes liability for payments not made by their overseas subsidiary without actually issuing a guarantee.
- UK insurance companies' credits may be issued in their favour to obtain periodic reimbursement, against their certificate, of claims settled in the UK on behalf of overseas insurance companies.
- Change of ownership of ships is often settled by means of a documentary credit, the documents usually required being the clean bill of sale and possibly various registration and discharge certificates.
- Sometimes a documentary credit is opened to settle simple claims, contentious matters, or even refunds, the documents required being an invoice, a certificate of discharge, or a form of receipt. Such credits could cover, for example, the payment of royalties, school or medical fees, labour costs, wages, legal expenses, commissions, freight, insurance premiums, block bookings for hotels, and payments due under court order such as alimony.
- Some credits, known as 'stand-by' credits are based upon the concept of default by the applicant in performance of his commitment. The beneficiary should only draw under the credit in the event of such default.

Examples of stand-by credits are:

i   Banks may, in some areas, be prevented by local law from giving guarantees, or they may be requested by their principal to issue a credit instead of a guarantee. The credit may provide for settlement to be effected against the simple claim of the beneficiary, or it may require such claim to be accompanied by a fuller statement of the beneficiary and/or supporting documentation.

ii When a seller is making frequent periodic shipments to a buyer and settling by a straightforward mail transfer or similar means, the seller may call for a documentary credit in his favour to cover him should the buyer default at any time. The document called for would be a simple invoice without shipping documents, usually accompanied by a declaration that payment has not been received by any other means. It would therefore be used only if normal settlement were not received – ie, it is tantamount to a guarantee to the seller of the trading liabilities of the buyer up to the amount of the credit. A similar method is sometimes used to guarantee the settlement of margins by users of the London Metal Exchange or the other commodity markets in London or the US.

26. A SET OF DOCUMENTS PRESENTED UNDER A CREDIT

The examples which follow constitute a set of shipping documents presented by the UK beneficiary, Beecham Research International Limited, to the London advising bank for payment. Examination of the documents against the terms of the attached documentary credit reveals that the documents are in order. The credit is a classic Far East negotiation credit with drafts on the buyers but providing for immediate settlement of negotiations in London.

The credit has been amended on three separate occasions and these amendments feature on pages 191 to 193.

Two separate presentations of documents have been made. The first set – £4,500 in value – relate to goods despatched by air freight, and these feature on pages 194 to 201. The second set – £7,343 in value – relate to goods despatched by sea, and these are illustrated on pages 202 to 212.

In each of the above presentations all invoices were submitted in nine copies, although for illustrative purposes in this book only one copy of each invoice has been reproduced. Only one bill of lading, of the two issued in the second presentation, is reproduced – both original bills of lading were submitted when the documents were actually tendered to the advising bank.

Documentary credit *(front)*

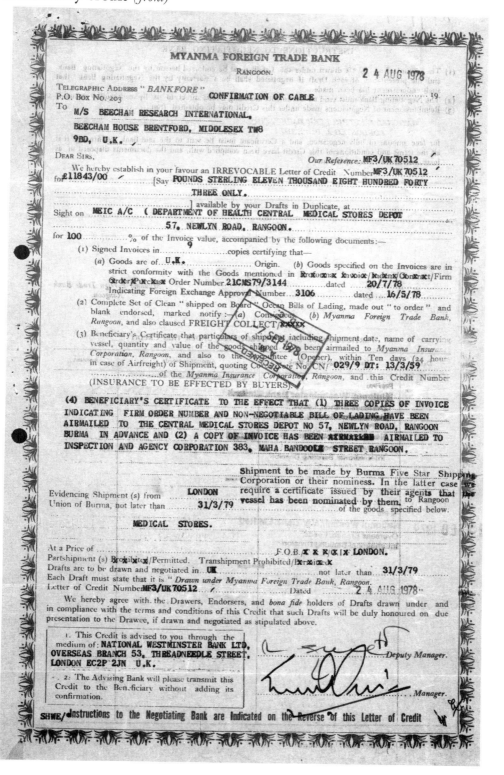

Documentary credit *(back)*

INSTRUCTIONS TO NEGOTIATING BANK

(1) The amount of any Draft drawn under this Credit must be endorsed hereon by the Negotiating Bank, and the presentation of each Draft if negotiated shall be a warranty by the Negotiating Bank that such endorsement has been made.

(2) The Negotiating Bank must send all documents including Drafts direct to us by consecutive airmails.

(3) Reimbursement of Negotiations made under this Credit may be obtained from..

NATIONAL WESTMINSTER BANK LTD.
LONDON EC 2, P, 2, JN.

for face amount of bills negotiated, and a Certificate must be sent to the said Bank, confirming that all the terms and conditions of this Credit have been complied with, and the documents disposed of as instructed in the Letter of Credit.

THE NEGOTIATING BANK IS AUTHORIZED TO REIMBURSE TELEGRAPHICALLY ON THE ABOVE BANK IF THE AMOUNT OF NEGOTIATION IS US$ 10,000/- (OR ITS EQUIVALENT) AND ABOVE. THE NEGOTIATING BANK IS ALSO REQUESTED TO CABLE ADVISE US OF AMOUNTS NEGOTIATED.

Myanma Foreign Trade Bank Rangoon.

PARTICULARS OF DRAFTS NEGOTIATED UNDER THIS CREDIT

Date	Name of Negotiating Bank	Amount in words	Amount
(1)	Per Pro National Westminster Bank Limited Overseas Branch, Leeds, International Banking Division Per Pro National Westminster Bank Limited Overseas Branch, Leeds, International Banking Division	Four thousand five hundred pounds	£4500—00
13 FEB 1979 (2)	Per Pro National Westminster Bank Limited Overseas Branch, Leeds, International Banking Division	Seven thousand three hundred & forty three pounds only.	£7343—00

National Westminster Bank Limited

Overseas Branch - Leeds
PO Box No 7
Priestley House
3 Park Row
Leeds LS1 5LA

Telephone Leeds 41961 (STD Code 0532)
Telex 557446 NWBLDS G
Telegrams Natwesover Leeds Telex

Please address your reply to the Manager

Your ref

Our ref **LDS 55981**

Date

ATTACHMENT TO MYANMA FOREIGN TRADE BANK, RANGOON, BURMA

LETTER OF CREDIT No. MF. **UK/70512**............

Your attention is drawn to the fact that this credit is subject to Uniform Customs and Practice for Documentary Credits (1974 revision) I.C.C. publication No. 290.

First of three amendments to the credit

National Westminster Bank Limited ↻

Overseas Branch - Leeds
PO Box No17
Priestley House
3 Park Row
Leeds LS1 5LA

Telephone Leeds 41861 (STD 0532) X 135
Telex 557446 NWBLDS G
Telegraphic Address Natwesover Leeds

Please address your reply to the Manager,
Documentary Credits Department

Our ref **LDSDC**   55981./SKB EXT. 146
EXPORTS

Date   10 November 1978

Beecham Research International
Beecham House
Brentford
Middlesex TW8 9BD.

B. R. I.

15 NOV 1973

ACCOUNTS DEP'

Dear Sirs

Amendment to Documentary Credit

A/c   Department of Health Central Medical Stores Depot. 57 Merlyn Rd
Rangoon

We have been requested to inform you that the terms and conditions of Credit No. MF7/UK7 512
issued by   Myanma Foreign Trade Bank, Rangoon

which we advised to you on 8.9.78   have been amended as follows:

1. Goods may also be despatched by air freight in which case
present Air consignment note marked Freight Collect and showing
Letter of Credit No. MF3/UK70512 evidencing despatch of relative
goods to Myanma Foreign Trade Bank, Rangoon Burma account of buyers
dated not later than 31/3/79

All other terms and conditions remain unchanged.

Yours faithfully,

Manager

countersigned

NWB10559 Rev Jun 77-1   Registered Number: 929027 England   Registered Office: 41 Lothbury, London EC2P 2BP

Second of three amendments to the credit

National Westminster Bank Limited ♻

Overseas Branch · Leeds
PO Box No17
Priestley House
3 Park Row
Leeds LS1 5LA

Telephone Leeds 41861 (STD 0532) X 135
Telex 557446 NWBLDS G
Telegraphic Address Natwesover Leeds

Please address your reply to the Manager,
Documentary Credits Department

Our ref LDSDC   55981   FP   12/78

Date   5 December 1978

Beecham REsearch International
Beecham House
Brentford
Middlesex TW8 9BD

Dear Sirs

Amendment to Documentary Credit

A/c Department of Health Central Medical Stores Depot

We have been requested to inform you that the terms and conditions of Credit No. MF3/UK70512
issued by Myanma Foreign Trade Bank

which we advised to you on 8 September 1978   have been amended as follows:

1. On Air Consignment Note to read 'FreightPaid' instead of Freight Collect.
    Air freight charges to be borne by suppliers.

All other terms and conditions remain unchanged.

Yours faithfully,   countersigned

Manager

NWB10559 Rev Jun 77-1   Registered Number: 929027 England   Registered Office: 41 Lothbury, London EC2P 2BP

Third of three amendments to the credit

National Westminster Bank Limited ♻

Overseas Branch - Leeds
PO Box No17
Priestley House
3 Park Row
Leeds LS1 5LA

Telephone Leeds 41861 (STD 0532)
Telex 557446 NWBLDS G
Telegraphic Address Natwesover Leeds

Please address your reply to the Manager.
Documentary Credits Department

Our ref **LDSDC**   55981   DAW

Date   19th January 1979

Beecham Research international
Beecham House
Brentford
MIDDLESEX TW8 9BD

Dear Sirs

Amendment to Documentary Credit

A/c   Department of Health Central Medical Stores

We have been requested to inform you that the terms and conditions of Credit No MF3/UK 70512
issued by   Myanma Foreign Trade Bank

which we advised to you on   8 September 78   have been amended as follows:

1. Transhipment now permitted.

All other terms and conditions remain unchanged.

Yours faithfully,   countersigned

                                                     P M. Nutbean.

Manager

NWB10559 Rev Jun 77-1   Registered Number: 929027 England   Registered Office: 41 Lothbury, London EC2P 2BP

First presentation: beneficiary's covering letter

Beecham Research International

Beecham House Brentford Middlesex TW8 9BD

Telegrams & Cables:
Beechover Brentford
Telex: 935986
Telephone: 01-560 5151
Ext.

A Branch of Beecham Group Limited   Registered in London: 227531   Registered Office: Beecham House Brentford Middlesex

PRESENTATION UNDER LETTER OF CREDIT, NEGOTIATING BANK REFERENCE. LDSDC. 55981......
ANY QUERIES PLEASE TO JOAN GRIFFITHS, 01-560 5151, EXTENSION 2201

Date: 30.1.79

National Westminster Bank Ltd.,
Priestley House,
3 Park Row,
Leeds LS1 5LA.

Dear Sirs,

We enclose the following documents:-

NON-NEGOTIABLE DOCUMENTS TO CUSTOMER

INVOICE No.(s) 51012/02..............
     MEIC
····A/C·Dept.·of·Health,·Central·Medical·
··Stores·Depot,·····················
·····57,·Newlyn·Road,·················
·· ···Rangoon, Burma.··················
···················5··············3····
INV(s)...........NN BL/AWB...........
Other................................

Comm. inv.	Cert. inv.	Consular inv.	Charges inv.	Packing list	Weight list	Cert of Origin	Insur. cert.	Insur. letter
9+1								1
B/L or AWB	Cert of shipment	Fwdrs./ Post rec	Boycott cert.	Shippers cert.	Benef'ys cert.	Health cert.	Cert of Analysis	Attest. cert.
1					2			
Clean report fdgs.	Original Credit & Amendments							
	1							

in connection with.......packages per........7...........air...................amounting to
....£4500.00...............Please remit the sterling proceeds by Banker's Payment
(at maturity in the case of Usance Credits), to our Account No.30201944 at the
Midland Bank's Branch at 69 Pall Mall, London SW1, under advice to us.

Yours faithfully,

(H.G. Sinclair)
Export Documentation Despatch Unit

0053/78

First bill of exchange *(front)*

(back)

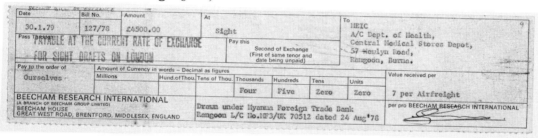

Second bill of exchange *(front)*

(back)

Invoice (assume eight other identical invoices were presented)

INVOICE FROM BEECHAM RESEARCH INTERNATIONAL
(A BRANCH OF BEECHAM GROUP LTD.)

TELEPHONE 01-560 5151
TELEGRAMS & CABLES BEECHOVER BRENTFORD
TELEX 935986

BEECHAM HOUSE   BRENTFORD   MIDDLESEX TW8 9BD

INV. 11

INVOICE TO:	CONSIGN TO:	YOUR ORDER NUMBER	INVOICE NUMBER
MEIC	MYANMA FOREIGN TRADE BANK	21CMS79/3144	51012/02

INVOICE TO:
MEIC
A/C DEPARTMENT OF HEALTH
CENTRAL MEDICAL STORES DEPOT
57 NEWLYN ROAD, RANGOON
BURMA

CONSIGN TO:
MYANMA FOREIGN TRADE BANK
RANGOON BURMA
A/EMM.E.I.C.
DEPARTMENT OF HEALTH
CENTRAL MEDICAL STORES DEPOT
57 NEWLYN ROAD, RANGOON, BURMA
(L/C No. MF3UK/70512)

YOUR ORDER NUMBER
21CMS79/3144

INVOICE NUMBER
51012/02

DATE
20/07/78

INVOICE/DESPATCH DATE
08/01/79

REGION 1   COUNTRY 0731   ORIGIN EEC/UK

SALES LEDGER
10049

ROUTING
AIRFREIGHT

PAYMENT
L/C

IMPORT LICENCE No.

MARK
RANGOON
O/NO. 21CMS79 ORIGIN:U.K.
L/C NO. MF3/UK 70512
DESCR. & QUAN.
NET/GR. WT.   MEAS.
51012/02-1UP

V.A.T.   ZERO RATED
V.A.T. No. 222 9121 95
CUSTOMER
TAX POINT 08/01/79

PRODUCT CODE	DESCRIPTION OF GOODS	QUANTITY	VALUE — CURRENT DOMESTIC OR FOR CUSTOMS	PRICE TO PURCHASER
	IRREVOCABLE LETTER OF CREDIT NO.MF3/UK70512 DATED 24 AUGUST 1978		EACH £15.00	£4500.00
	MEDICAL STORES / ITEM NO.8	300 PK		

GOODS SPECIFIED ON THE INVOICES ARE IN STRICT
CONFORMITY WITH THE GOODS MENTIONED IN FIRM ORDER
NUMBER 21CMS79/3144 DATED 20/07/78, INDICATING
FOREIGN EXCHANGE APPROVAL NO.3106 DATED 16/05/78

"2% I.A.C. COMMISSION ALREADY DEDUCTED AND TO
BE CLAIMED FROM THE BUYER"

WE CERTIFY THAT THE GOODS ARE OF U.K. ORIGIN

COVER NOTE NO. C/N 029/9 DATED 13/03/59

SALE C & F RANGOON

INSURANCE TO BE EFFECTED BY THE BUYERS

A.W.B. 07532910
FLIGHT TG.913
ON 12/01/79

ITEM	PACK NUMBERS	WEIGHT AND DIMENSIONS OF EACH PACK		
		Net Wt.	Gross Wt.	Dims.
	Nos. 1/6 cartons each	9.80kg	12.50kg	47x47x46cm.
	No. 7 carton	6.80kg	9.50kg	47x47x46cm.

Seven cartons in all
Cartons 1/6 each containing 45 packs
Carton 7 containing 30 packs

CERTIFIED TRUE AND CORRECT FOR BEECHAM RESEARCH INTERNATIONAL (BRANCH OF BEECHAM GROUP LTD.)

AUTHORISED CLERK

Air waybill *(front)*

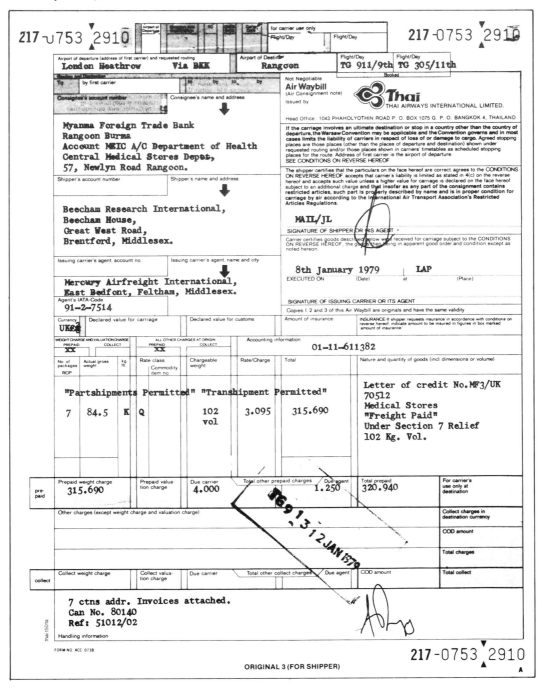

ORIGINAL 3 (FOR SHIPPER)

Air waybill *(back)*

Conditions of Contract

1.
As used in this contract. "Convention" means the Convention for the Unification of Certain Rules relating to International Carriage by Air, signed at Warsaw, 12th October, 1929, or that Convention as amended by the Hague Protocol, 1955 whichever may be applicable to carriage hereunder; "air waybill" is equivalent to "air consignment note", "shipper" is equivalent to "consignor", "carriage" is equivalent to "transportation" and "Carrier" includes the air carrier issuing this air waybill and all air carriers that carry the goods hereunder or perform any other services related to such air carriage. For the purposes of the exemption from and limitation of liability provisions set forth or referred to herein, "Carrier" includes agents, servants, or representatives of any such air carrier. Carriage to be performed hereunder by several successive carriers is regarded as a single operation

2.
a)
Carriage hereunder is subject to the rules relating to liability established by the Convention, unless such carriage is not "international carriage" as defined by the Convention. (See Carrier's tariffs and conditions of carriage for such definition.)
b)
To the extent not in conflict with the foregoing, carriage hereunder and other services performed by each Carrier are subject to (i) applicable laws (including national laws implementing the Convention), government regulations, orders and requirements, (ii) provisions herein set forth, and (iii) applicable tariffs, rules, conditions of carriage, regulations and timetables (but not the times of departure and arrival therein) of such carrier, which are made part hereof and which may be inspected at any of its offices and at airports from which it operates regular services.
c)
For the purpose of the Convention, the agreed stopping places (which may be altered by Carrier in case of necessity) are those places, except the place of departure and the place of destination, set forth on the face hereof or shown in Carrier's timetables as scheduled stopping places for the route.
d)
In the case of carriage subject to the Convention, the shipper acknowledges that he has been given an opportunity to make a special declaration of the value of the goods at delivery and that the sum entered on the face of the air waybill as "Shipper's Consignor's Declared Value — For Carriage", if in excess of 250 French gold francs (consisting of 65$^1/_2$ milligrams of gold with a fineness of 900 thousandths) or their equivalent per kilogram, constitutes such special declaration of value.

3.
Insofar as any provision contained or referred to in this air waybill may be contrary to mandatory law, government regulations, orders or requirements, such provision shall remain applicable to the extent that it is not overridden hereby. The invalidity of any provision shall not affect any other part hereof.

4.
Except as the Convention or other applicable law may otherwise require.
a)
Carrier is not liable to the shipper or to any other person for any damage, delay or loss of whatsoever nature (herein collectively referred to as "damage") arising out of or in connection with the carriage of the goods, unless such damage is proved to have been caused by the negligence or wilful fault of Carrier and there has been no contributory negligence of the shipper, consignee or other claimant;
b)
Carrier is not liable for any damage directly or indirectly arising out of compliance with laws, government regulations, orders or requirements or from any cause beyond Carrier's control;
c)
The charges for carriage having been based upon the value declared by the shipper, it is agreed that any liability shall in no event exceed the shipper's declared value for carriage stated on the face hereof, and in the absence of such declaration by shipper liability of Carrier shall not exceed 250 such French gold francs or their equivalent per kilogram of goods destroyed, lost, damaged or delayed, all claims shall be subject to proof of value;
d)
A carrier issuing an air waybill for carriage exclusively over the lines of others does so only as a sales agent.

5.
It is agreed that no time is fixed for the completion of carriage hereunder and that Carrier may without notice substitute alternate carriers or aircraft. Carrier assumes no obligation to carry the goods by any specified aircraft or over any particular route or routes or to make connection at any point according to any particular schedule, and Carrier is hereby authorized to select, or deviate from the route or routes of shipment, notwithstanding that the same may be stated on the face hereof. The shipper guarantees payment of all charges and advances.

6.
The goods, or packages said to contain the goods, described on the face hereof, are accepted for carriage from their receipt at Carrier's terminal or airport office at the place of departure to the airport at the place of destination. If so specifically agreed, the goods, or packages said to contain the goods, described on the face hereof, are also accepted for forwarding to the airport of departure and for reforwarding beyond the airport of destination. If such forwarding or reforwarding is by carriage operated by Carrier, such carriage shall be upon the same terms as to liability as set forth in Paragraphs 2 and 4 hereof. In any other event, the issuing carrier and last carrier, respectively, in forwarding or reforwarding the goods, shall do so only as agents of the shipper, owner, or consignee, as the case may be, and shall not be liable for any damage arising out of such additional carriage, unless proved to have been caused by its own negligence or wilful fault. The shipper, owner and consignee hereby authorize such carried to do all things deemed advisable to effect such forwarding or reforwarding, including, but without limitation, selection of the means of forwarding or reforwarding and the routes thereof (unless these have been herein specified by the shipper), execution and acceptance of documents of carriage (which may include provisions exempting or limiting liability) and consigning of goods with no declaration of value, notwithstanding any declaration of value in this air waybill

7.
Carrier is authorized (but shall be under no obligation) to advance any duties, taxes or charges and to make any disbursements with respect to the goods, and the shipper, owner and consignee shall be jointly and severally liable for the reimbursement thereof. No Carrier shall be under obligation to incur any expense or to make any advance in connection with the forwarding or reforwarding of the goods except against repayment by the shipper. If it is necessary to make customs entry of the goods at any place, the goods shall be deemed to be consigned at such place to the person named on the face hereof as customs consignee or, if no such person be named, to the carrier carrying the goods to such place or to such customs consignee, if any, as such carrier may designate.

8.
At the request of the shipper, and if the appropriate premium is paid and the fact recorded on the face hereof, the goods covered by this air waybill are insured on behalf of the shipper under an open policy for the amount requested by the shipper as set out on the face hereof (recovery being limited to the actual loss or damage not exceeding the insured value) against all risks of physical loss or damage from any external cause whatsoever, except those arising directly or indirectly from war risks, strikes, riots, hostilities, legal seizure or delay or inherent vice, and subject to the terms and conditions of such open policy which is available for inspection by the shipper. Claims under such policy must be reported immediately to an office of Carrier.

9.
Except as otherwise specifically provided in this contract, delivery of the goods will be made only to the consignee named on the face hereof, unless such consignee is one of the Carriers participating in the carriage, in which event delivery shall be made to the person indicated on the face hereof as the person to be notified. Notice of arrival of the goods will, in the absence of other instructions, be sent to the consignee, or the person to be notified, by ordinary methods. Carrier is not liable for non-receipt or delay in receipt of such notice.

10.
a)
No action shall be maintained in the case of damage to goods unless a written notice, sufficiently describing the goods concerned, the approximate date of the damage, and the details of the claim, is presented to an office of Carrier within 7 days from the date of receipt thereof, in the case of delay, unless presented within 14 days from the date the goods are placed at the disposal of the person entitled to delivery, and in the case of loss (including nondelivery) unless presented within 120 days from the date of issue of the air waybill;
b)
Any rights to damages against Carrier shall be extinguished unless an action is brought within two years after the occurrence of the events giving rise to the claim.

11.
The shipper shall comply with all the applicable laws, customs and other government regulations of any country to, from, through or over which the goods may be carried, including those relating to the packing, carriage or delivery of the goods, and shall furnish such information and attach such documents to this air waybill as may be necessary to comply with such laws and regulations. Carrier is not liable to the shipper or any other person for loss or expense due to shipper's failure to comply with this provision.

12.
No agent, servant or representative of Carrier has authority to alter, modify or waive any provision of this contract

Beneficiary's certificate (credit item three)

Beecham Research International

Beecham House Brentford Middlesex TW8 9BD

Telegrams & Cables:
Beechover Brentford
Telex: 935986
Telephone: 01-560 5151
Ext:

A Branch of Beecham Group Limited   Registered in London: 227531   Registered Office: Beecham House Brentford Middlesex

TO WHOM IT MAY CONCERN:

LETTER OF CREDIT MF3/UK70512
ORDER NUMBER 21CMS 79/3144
INVOICE NUMBER 51012/02

We hereby certify that particulars of shipment including
flight details, quantity and the value of the goods flown,
have been airmailed to Myanma Insurance Corporation, Rangoon,
and also to MEIC A/C (Department of Health Central Medical
Stores Depot, 57 Newlyn Road, Rangoon) within 24 hours of shipment, quoting cover note no:- CN/029/9 DT: 13/3/59 of the
Myanma Insurance Corporation, Rangoon and Letter of Credit No:-
MF3/UK70512.

Yours faithfully,
BEECHAM RESEARCH INTERNATIONAL

R.L. DARKE
Shipping Dept.

Beneficiary's copy letters

Beecham Research International

Beecham House Brentford Middlesex TW8 9BD

Telegrams & Cables:
Beechover Brentford
Telex: 935986
Telephone: 01-560 5151
Ext:

A Branch of Beecham Group Limited   Registered in London: 227531   Registered Office: Beecham House Brentford Middlesex

1356

To.. Myanma Insurance Corporation ....

.... Rangoon, ...

.... Burma. ....

Date... 12/1/79 ....

Our Invoice ref.. 51012/02 ....

Dear Sirs,

<u>Letter of Credit no</u> .... MF3/UK70512 ....

<u>For the Account of</u> .... MEIC A/C DEPT. OF HEALTH
MEDICAL STORES DEPOT.

In accordance with the requirements of the above quoted Letter of Credit, we give the following details:-

Description of Goods..... MEDICAL STORES ....

VIZ 300 PK. OF ITEM NO. 8 (PART SHIPMENT)
....

Vessel/Flight.. TC913/12-1-79 ......Date of Export/A.W.B. 0753 2910
HEATHROW, LONDON
Port/Airport of shipments...................................

Insurance Cover Note/Open Policy no.. CN/029/9 DATED: 13/3/59
FOREIGN EXCHANGE APPROVAL NO.3106 16/5/78
Import Licence no. - ....Bank Regn.no..................

Value of Goods..

Freight and charges...................................

Total value.. C&F RANGOON   £4500.00 ....

A copy of this letter has been sent to:-

(a) MEIC A/C DEPARTMENT OF HEALTH, CENTRAL MEDICAL STORES DEPOT, 57 NEWLYN RD.,
.... RANGOON, BURMA.

(b) ....

(c) ....

We trust that the above information will enable you to make the necessary insurance arrangements, and certify that this letter was airmailed to you within 24 hours of shipment.

Yours faithfully,
BEECHAM RESEARCH INTERNATIONAL.

R. L. DARKE
SHIPPING DEPT.

Beneficiary's certificate (credit item four)

Beecham Research International

Beecham House Brentford Middlesex TW8 9BD

Telegrams & Cables :
Beechover Brentford
Telex : 935986
Telephone : 01-560 5151
Ext :

A Branch of Beecham Group Limited Registered in London : 227531 Registered Office : Beecham House Brentford Middlesex

London, January 15, 1979

TO WHOM IT MAY CONCERN:

          LETTER OF CREDIT MF3/UK70512
          ORDER NUMBER 21CMS 79/3144
          INVOICE NUMBER 51012/02
          ==================================

    We hereby certify that three copies of invoice 51012/02
indicating O/No. 21 CMS79/3144 and Airwaybill Number have
been airmailed to The Central Medical Stores Depot, No.57,
Newlyn Road, Rangoon, Burma, in advance and that a copy invoice
has been airmailed to The Inspection and Agency Corporation,
383, Maha Bandoola St., Rangoon, Burma.

                    Yours faithfully,
            BEECHAM RESEARCH INTERNATIONAL

                    R.L. DARKE
              Shipping Department

Second presentation: beneficiary's covering letter

Beecham Research International

Beecham House Brentford Middlesex TW8 9BD

Telegrams & Cables:
Beechover Brentford
Telex: 935986
Telephone: 01-560 5151
Ext.

A Branch of Beecham Group Limited   Registered in London: 227531   Registered Office: Beecham House Brentford Middlesex

PRESENTATION UNDER LETTER OF CREDIT, NEGOTIATING BANK REFERENCE....**LDS 55981**........
ANY QUERIES PLEASE TO JOAN GRIFFITHS, 01-560 5151, EXTENSION 2201

Date: 8.2.79

National Westminster Bank Ltd.,
Priestley House,
3 - 5 Park Row,
Leeds LS1 5LA

Dear Sirs,

We enclose the following documents:-

> NON-NEGOTIABLE DOCUMENTS TO CUSTOMER
>
> INVOICE No.(s)**51012/01 51013 51014 51019**
> MEIC A/C Department of Health,
> Central Medical Stores Depot,
> 57 Newlyn Road,
> Rangoon
> INV(s)...**7of4**.....NN BL/AWB..**2N/N**.....
> Other......**Packing Lists: 5of4**........

Comm. inv.	Cert. inv.	Consular inv.	Charges inv.	Packing list	Weight list	Cert of Origin	Insur. cert.	Insur. letter
10of4								1
B/L or AWB	Cert of shipment	Fwdrs./ Post rec	Boycott cert.	Shippers cert.	Benef'ys cert.	Health cert.	Cert of Analysis	Attest. cert.
2					2			
Clean report fdgs.	Original Credit							
	Still with you from previous documents							

in connection with..**79**.....packages per...........**Pinya**.................amounting to

......**£7343.00**.........Please remit the sterling proceeds by Banker's Payment (at maturity in the case of Usance Credits), to our Account No.**30201944** at the Midland Bank's Branch at 69 Pall Mall, London SW1, under advice to us.

Yours faithfully,

(H.G. Sinclair)
Export Documentation Despatch Unit

0053/78

First bill of exchange *(front)*

(back)

Second bill of exchange *(front)*

(back)

First invoice (assume eight other identical invoices were presented)

INVOICE FROM BEECHAM RESEARCH INTERNATIONAL	

TELEPHONE 01-560 5151
TELEGRAMS & CABLES BEECHOVER BRENTFORD
TELEX 935986

(A BRANCH OF BEECHAM GROUP LTD.)

BEECHAM HOUSE   BRENTFORD   MIDDLESEX TW8 9BD

INV. 11

INVOICE TO:	CONSIGN TO:	YOUR ORDER NUMBER	INVOICE NUMBER
MEIC A/C DEPARTMENT OF HEALTH CENTRAL MEDICAL STORES DEPOT 57 NEWLYN ROAD, RANGOON BURMA	CENTRAL MEDICAL STORES DEPOT RANGOON BURMA	21CMS79/3144	51012/01

MARK		DATE	INVOICE/DESPATCH DATE
C M S D RANGOON		20/07/78	15/01/79

	REGION	COUNTRY	ORIGIN
	1	0731	EEC/UK

O/NO.21CMS79 ORIGIN:U.K.
L/C NO. MF3/UK70512
DESCR. & QUAN.
NET/GR. WT.   MEAS.
51012/1UP

V.A.T. ZERO RATED	SALES LEDGER	ROUTING
V.A.T. No. 222 9121 95	10049	"PINYA"
CUSTOMER	PAYMENT	IMPORT LICENCE No.
TAX POINT 15/01/79	L/C	

PRODUCT CODE	DESCRIPTION OF GOODS	QUANTITY	VALUE – CURRENT DOMESTIC OR FOR CUSTOMS	PRICE TO PURCHASER
	IRREVOCABLE LETTER OF CREDIT NO.MF3/UK70512 DATED 24 AUGUST 1978			EACH
	MEDICAL STORES / ITEM NO.1	200 PK	£3.75	750.00
	MEDICAL STORES / ITEM NO.2	200 PK	£7.50	1500.00
	MEDICAL STORES / ITEM NO.3	2000 SGL	£0.85	1700.00
	MEDICAL STORES / ITEM NO.4	500 PK	£2.85	1425.00
	GOODS SPECIFIED ON THE INVOICES ARE IN STRICT CONFORMITY WITH THE GOODS MENTIONED IN FIRM ORDER NUMBER 21CMS79/3144 DATED 20/07/78, INDICATING FOREIGN EXCHANGE APPROVAL NO.3106 DATED 16/05/78		SALE FOB LONDON	£5375.00
	"2% I.A.C. COMMISSION ALREADY DEDUCTED AND TO BE CLAIMED FROM THE BUYER"			
	WE CERTIFY THAT THE GOODS ARE OF U.K. ORIGIN			
	COVER NOTE NO. C/N 029/9 DATED 13/03/59			

ITEM	PACK NUMBERS	WEIGHT AND DIMENSIONS OF EACH PACK		
		Net Wt.	Gross Wt.	Dims.
Nos.	1/9 cartons each	36.00kg	37.50kg	56x29x56cm.
Nos.	10/13 cartons each	8.80kg	11.50kg	47x47x46cm.
No.	14 carton	37.30kg	40.00kg	47x47x46cm.

Fourteen cartons in all

Cartons 1/9 each containing 216 SGL item 3
Cartons 10/13 each containing 50 packs
  item 2 & 72 packs item 4
Carton 14 containing 56 SGL item 3, 200
  packs item 1 & 212 packs item 4

CERTIFIED TRUE AND CORRECT FOR BEECHAM RESEARCH INTERNATIONAL (BRANCH OF BEECHAM GROUP LTD.)

AUTHORISED CLERK

Second invoice (assume eight other identical invoices were presented)

INVOICE FROM **BEECHAM RESEARCH INTERNATIONAL**
(A BRANCH OF BEECHAM GROUP LTD.)

TELEPHONE 01-560 5151
TELEGRAMS & CABLES BEECHOVER BRENTFORD
TELEX 935986

BEECHAM HOUSE   BRENTFORD   MIDDLESEX TW8 9BD

INV. 11

INVOICE TO:	CONSIGN TO:	YOUR ORDER NUMBER	INVOICE NUMBER
MEIC A/C DEPARTMENT OF HEALTH CENTRAL MEDICAL STORES DEPOT 57 NEWLYN ROAD, RANGOON BURMA	CENTRAL MEDICAL STORES DEPOT RANGOON BURMA	21CMS79/3144	51013

DATE 20/07/78

INVOICE/DESPATCH DATE 12/01/79

REGION	COUNTRY	ORIGIN
1	0731	EEC/UK

MARK

C M
S D
RANGOON

O/No. 21CMS79 ORIGIN: U.K.
L/C No. MF3/UK70512
DESCR. & QUAN.
NET/GR. WT.   MEAS.
51013/1UP

V.A.T.   ZERO RATED
V.A.T. No.   222 9121 95
CUSTOMER
TAX POINT 12/01/79

SALES LEDGER 10049

ROUTING "PINYA"

PAYMENT L/C

IMPORT LICENCE No.

PRODUCT CODE	DESCRIPTION OF GOODS	QUANTITY	VALUE – CURRENT DOMESTIC OR FOR CUSTOMS	PRICE TO PURCHASER
	IRREVOCABLE LETTER OF CREDIT NO. MF3/UK70512 DATED 24 AUGUST 1978			
	MEDICAL STORES / ITEM NO.6	500 PK		EACH £2.50 £1250.00
				SALE FOB LONDON
	GOODS SPECIFIED ON THE INVOICES ARE IN STRICT CONFORMITY WITH THE GOODS MENTIONED IN FIRM ORDER NUMBER 21CMS79/3144 DATED 20/07/78, INDICATING FOREIGN EXCHANGE APPROVAL NO.3106 DATED 16/05/78			
	"2% I.A.C. COMMISSION ALREADY DEDUCTED AND TO BE CLAIMED FROM THE BUYER"			
	WE CERTIFY THAT THE GOODS ARE OF U.K. ORIGIN			
	COVER NOTE NO. C/N 029/9 DATED 13/03/59			

ITEM	PACK NUMBERS	WEIGHT AND DIMENSIONS OF EACH PACK
Nos.	B1/B4 cartons each	Net wt. Gross wt. Dims. 37.00 40.00 61x42x58cm. Four cartons in all Each containing 125 packs

CERTIFIED TRUE AND CORRECT FOR BEECHAM RESEARCH INTERNATIONAL (BRANCH OF BEECHAM GROUP LTD.)

AUTHORISED CLARK

Third invoice (assume eight other identical invoices were presented)

INVOICE FROM **BEECHAM RESEARCH INTERNATIONAL**
(A BRANCH OF BEECHAM GROUP LTD.)

TELEPHONE 01-560 5151
TELEGRAMS & CABLES BEECHOVER BRENTFORD
TELEX 935986

BEECHAM HOUSE   BRENTFORD   MIDDLESEX TW8 9BD

INV. 11

INVOICE TO:	CONSIGN TO:	YOUR ORDER NUMBER	INVOICE NUMBER
MEIC A/C DEPARTMENT OF HEALTH CENTRAL MEDICAL STORES DEPOT 57 NEWLYN ROAD, RANGOON BURMA	CENTRAL MEDICAL STORES DEPOT RANGOON BURMA	21CMS79/3144	51014

DATE 20/07/78

INVOICE/DESPATCH DATE 12/01/79

REGION	COUNTRY	ORIGIN
1	0731	EEC/UK

MARK

C M S D

RANGOON
L/C NO. MF3/UK70512
DESCR. & QUAN.
NET/GR. WT.   MEAS.
51014/1UP

V.A.T.   ZERO RATED
V.A.T. No.   222 9121 95
CUSTOMER
TAX POINT 12/01/79

SALES LEDGER	ROUTING
10049	"PINYA"

PAYMENT	IMPORT LICENCE No.
L/C	

PRODUCT CODE	DESCRIPTION OF GOODS	QUANTITY	VALUE – CURRENT DOMESTIC OR FOR CUSTOMS	PRICE TO PURCHASER
	IRREVOCABLE LETTER OF CREDIT NO. MF3/UK70512 DATED 24 AUGUST 1978		PER DOZE	
		DOZENS		
	MEDICAL STORES / ITEM NO.7	120	£3.85	£462.00
			SALE FOB	LONDON
	GOODS SPECIFIED ON THE INVOICES ARE IN STRICT CONFORMITY WITH THE GOODS MENTIONED IN FIRM ORDER NUMBER 21CMS79/3144 DATED 20/07/78, INDICATING FOREIGN EXCHANGE APPROVAL NO.3106 DATED 16/05/78			
	"2% I.A.C. COMMISSION ALREADY DEDUCTED AND TO BE CLAIMED FROM THE BUYER"			
	WE CERTIFY THAT THE GOODS ARE OF U.K. ORIGIN			
	COVER NOTE NO. C/N 029/9 DATED 13/03/59			

ITEM	PACK NUMBERS	WEIGHT AND DIMENSIONS OF EACH PACK		
		Net.Wt.	Gross Wt.	Dims.
Nos.	1/15 cartons each	10.30kg	11.70kg	33x27x21cm.
Nos.	16/30 cartons each	10.30kg	11.70kg	33x27x27cm.
Nos.	31/45 cartons each	10.30kg	11.70kg	33x27x27cm.
Nos.	45/60 cartons each	10.30kg	11.70kg	33x27x27cm.
	Sixty cartons in all			
	Each containing two dozens			

CERTIFIED TRUE AND CORRECT FOR BEECHAM RESEARCH INTERNATIONAL (BRANCH OF BEECHAM GROUP LTD.)

AUTHORISED CLERK

Fourth invoice (assume eight other identical invoices were presented)

INVOICE FROM **BEECHAM RESEARCH INTERNATIONAL**

(A BRANCH OF BEECHAM GROUP LTD.)

TELEPHONE 01-560 5151
TELEGRAMS & CABLES BEECHOVER BRENTFORD
TELEX 935986

BEECHAM HOUSE   BRENTFORD   MIDDLESEX TW8 9BD

INV. 11

INVOICE TO:	CONSIGN TO:	YOUR ORDER NUMBER	INVOICE NUMBER
MEIC A/C DEPARTMENT OF HEALTH CENTRAL MEDICAL STORES DEPOT 57 NEWLYN ROAD, RANGOON BURMA	CENTRAL MEDICAL STORES DEPOT RANGOON BURMA	21CMS79/3144	51019

MARK

C   M
S   D
RANGOON

O/NO. 21CMS79   ORIGIN:U.K.
L/C NO.MF3/UK70512
DESCR. & QUAN.
NET/GR. WT.   MEAS.
51019/1UP

DATE 20/07/78	INVOICE/DESPATCH DATE 15/01/79

REGION	COUNTRY	ORIGIN
1	0731	EEC/UK

V.A.T.   ZERO RATED
V.A.T. No.   222 9121 95
CUSTOMER
TAX POINT 15/01/79

SALES LEDGER	ROUTING
10049	"PINYA"

PAYMENT	IMPORT LICENCE No.
L/C	

PRODUCT CODE	DESCRIPTION OF GOODS	QUANTITY	VALUE – CURRENT DOMESTIC OR FOR CUSTOMS	PRICE TO PURCHASER
	IRREVOCABLE LETTER OF CREDIT NO.MF3/UK70512 DATED 24 AUGUST 1978			
	MEDICAL STORES / ITEM NO.5	200 PK		EACH £1.28 £256.00
				SALE FOB LONDON

GOODS SPECIFIED ON THE INVOICES ARE IN STRICT
CONFORMITY WITH THE GOODS MENTIONED IN FIRM ORDER
NUMBER 21CMS79/3144 DATED 20/07/78, INDICATING
FOREIGN EXCHANGE APPROVAL NO.3106 DATED 16/05/78
"2% I.A.C. COMMISSION ALREADY DEDUCTED AND TO
  BE CLAIMED FROM THE BUYER"
WE CERTIFY THAT THE GOODS ARE OF U.K. ORIGIN
COVER NOTE NO. C/N 029/9 DATED 13/03/59

ITEM	PACK NUMBERS	WEIGHT AND DIMENSIONS OF EACH PACK
No.	1 carton	12.90kg Net-15.40kg Gross-60x41x32cm. One carton in all

CERTIFIED TRUE AND CORRECT FOR BEECHAM RESEARCH INTERNATIONAL (BRANCH OF BEECHAM GROUP LTD.)

AUTHORISED CLERK

Bill of lading (*front*) (assume another identical document was presented)

Bill of lading *(back)*

1. Wherever the term "Merchant" is used in this Bill of Lading, it shall be deemed to include the Shipper, the Receiver, the Consignee, the Holder of the Bill of Lading and the Owner of the cargo.
CLAUSE PARAMOUNT.

2. The Hague Rules contained in the International Convention for the Unification of certain rules relating to Bills of Lading dated Brussels the 25th August 1924, as enacted in the country of Shipment shall apply to this contract, provided that unless the contrary is proved, the Rules as enacted in the country of shipment shall be deemed to be identical with the rules as enacted in Burma. When no such enactment is in force in the country of shipment, the Burma Carriage of Goods by Sea Ordinance and the Rules contained in the Schedule thereto shall apply, as, if the goods were being carried from a port in Burma to any port, whether in or outside Burma.

3. This Bill of Lading and all rights and liabilities thereunder, shall be governed by and interpreted and construed in accordance with the laws of Burma for the time being in force, and insofar as these laws do not extend or apply, by the laws of England for the time being in force.

It is agreed that all questions and disputes arising under this Bill of Lading shall be brought before and decided by the Burma Courts in Rangoon, and all parties elect Rangoon as their domicile for the purpose of local jurisdiction. The Carrier shall, however, be at liberty, in any case, should he so desire to have all or any of his claims brought for adjudication before any non-Burma Courts, tribunals or authorities, or submitted to the arbitration of a single arbitrator, wherever in Burma or elsewhere.

4. The Carrier shall not be liable for loss or damage to the goods during the period before loading and after discharge from the vessel, provided that in any case, in which tally is not made ex ship, it shall be on the merchant to show that the loss or damage, if any, occurred whilst the goods were in the actual custody of the Carrier.

Without prejudice to the foregoing, vessel shall not be responsible for cargo delivery and expenses incurred at port of discharge consequent upon insufficient securing or marking will be payable by consignee unless:

(a) Every piece is distinctly and permanently marked with oil paint.
(b) Every bundle is securely fastened, distinctly and permanently marked with oil paint and metal tagged, so that each piece or bundle can be distinguished at port of discharge.

5. The voyage agreed by the contract of carriage recorded in this Bill of Lading includes sailing without pilots; proceeding via any route; proceeding to and staying at any port or ports, place or places whatsoever in any order, whether in or out of the usual, customary or scheduled route or in a contrary direction to or beyond the port of discharge named herein, once or oftener for any purpose whatsoever, whether in connection with the present or any prior or subsequent voyage; omitting to call at any one or more of the usual, customary or scheduled port or ports; carrying the said cargo past the said port of destination or within, and then beyond, and then back to the said port of destination; towing whether to save life or property or otherwise howsoever, or being towed; undergoing trials or making trial trips with or without notice; adjusting compasses; repairing or drydocking with or without the said goods on board, and delaying or reducing speed upon the said voyage for any purpose whatsoever.

6. Whether expressly arranged beforehand or otherwise, the Carrier shall be at liberty to carry the goods to their port of destination by the said or other vessel or vessels either belonging to the carrier or others, or by other means of transport by land and / or water and / or air proceeding either directly or indirectly to such port and to carry the goods or part of them beyond their port of destination, and to tranship, and store the goods either on shore or afloat and reship and forward the same at carrier's expense — but at merchant's risk. When the ultimate destination at which the Carrier may have engaged to deliver the goods is other than the vessel's port of discharge, the Carrier acts as forwarding agent only.

7. In the event of the carriage defined in this Bill of Lading forming part of a through transit of the said goods beginning prior to, the loading of the same in the said or a substituted vessel at the port of loading named herein and terminating subsequent to the discharge of the said goods at the port of discharge named herein, the Carrier shall still be under no responsibility for any loss or damage or delay to the said goods whatsoever or howsoever arising which occurs prior to the loading on or after the discharge from the said vessel or substituted vessel, even though such through transit has been arranged by or through the Carriers and/or the Carrier for the whole of such transit has been collected by them. Further if the ultimate destination of the said goods as expressed in this Bill of Lading or otherwise arranged by the Carriers be other than the port of discharge named herein, the Carriers, in effecting the carriage of the said goods from the said port of discharge to the said ultimate destination, act as forwarding agents only at the expense of the Shippers and/or Consignees.

Freight and charges, whether prepayable or payable at destination (collect freight), and whether paid or not, shall be considered as fully earned upon shipment or loading and non-returnable in any event.

8. Loading, discharge, landing, storing and delivery, including stevedoring, lighterage and porterage, in or off ports of loading or ports of discharge shall be for the Merchant's account and shall, if required by the Carrier, be arranged by the Carrier's agents, provided that the person(s) and/or body, as the case may be, who would carry out any of the above mentioned operations on any part of them, while is carried out after the goods leave the vessel's tackle, shall be deemed to be the Merchant's agent(s). Loading and discharge may commence and proceed without previous notice, if goods contracted for shipment are not tendered when the vessel is ready to load, the Carrier is relieved of any obligation to load such cargo and vessel may leave port without further notice and deadfreight is to be paid. The Merchant in his absolute discretion may load and confirm to load the goods, and to take delivery of and continue to receive the goods thereunder by day and night, including Saturdays, Sundays and Holidays, notwithstanding any custom of the port. Otherwise the Carrier, Master or Agents shall be at liberty without further notice to their customary wharf or warehouse or discharge the goods and any such discharge to be deemed a final fulfilment of the contract hereunder.

If the goods are not applied for within a reasonable time they may be sold at the owner private or by public auction.

The Merchant shall accept his reasonable proportion of unidentified loose cargo.

9. Live animals, plants and deck cargo are carried only on the stipulation that the Merchant accepts and shall bear every risk and liability in connection with same, including mortality, disease, accident, jettison, injury, damage and loss howsoever caused, and whether or not resulting from any neglect or default of the servants of the Carrier in the management of such animals, plants or deck cargo, or from unseaworthiness, unfitness or insufficiency of the vessel or any of her fittings, equipment or stores or insufficiency or effectiveness of water or fodder. No injury, damage or loss to or of such animals, plants or deck cargo, whether arising from jettison or otherwise shall be recoverable in general average. If any animals, plants or deck cargo become injured or damaged or develop disease or be likely in the judgment of the Master to be injurious or dangerous to other live animals or plants or to any cargo or to any person on board, such injured, damaged or diseased animals or plants or deck cargo may upon the Master's instructions be destroyed without liability to the Carrier.

10. The port of discharge for optional cargo must be declared to the vessel's agents at the first of the optional ports not later than 48 hours before the vessel's arrival there. In the absence of such declaration the Carrier may elect to discharge at the first or any optional port and the contract of carriage shall then be considered as having been fulfilled. Any option can be exercised for the total quantity under this Bill of Lading only.

11. (a) Freight, whether prepayable or payable at destination (collect freight) and whether paid or not, shall be considered as fully earned upon shipment and non-returnable in any event. The Carrier's claim for any charges under this contract shall be considered definitely established in like manner as soon as the charges have been incurred. Prepayable freight shall fall due upon shipment and collect freight and charges when the contract is determined by fulfilment or otherwise howsoever. Interest at the prevailing rate shall run from the date when freight and charges are due.

(b) The Merchant shall be liable for expenses of fumigation and of gathering and assorting of loose cargo and expenses incurred in repairing damage to and replacing of packing.

(c) All dues, duties, taxes, stamps and charges, including those which under any denomination may be levied on any basis such as amount of freight, weight or volume of cargo or tonnage of the vessel, shall be paid by the Merchant.

(d) The Merchant shall be liable for all fines, damages, losses, expenses which the Carrier, vessel or cargo may incur or suffer through non-observance of, or non-compliance with, or non-fulfilment of, formalities required by any regulations, including import, export or transit regulations of any Government or authority, including customs or port authorities.

(e) The Carrier is entitled in case of incorrect declaration of contents, weights, measurements or value of the goods to claim double the amount of freight which would have been due if such declaration had been correctly given. For the purpose of ascertaining the actual facts, the Carrier reserves the right to obtain from the Merchant the original invoice and to have the contents inspected and the weight, measurement or value verified.

12. The Carrier shall have a lien for any amount due under or in connection with this contract, including freight, deadfreight, primage, forwarding charges, charges for carriage to port of shipment, demurrage, damage for detention, average, fines, damage losses; and expenses and any other amounts paid or to be paid for the Merchant's account, whether same are indicated on this Bill of Lading or not, as well as for the costs and expenses of maintaining and/or enforcing such lien and the Carrier shall be entitled to sell the goods privately or by auction to cover any claims.

13. General Average to be adjusted at any port or place at Carrier's option and to be settled according to the York-Antwerp Rules, 1974. For this purpose the Merchant is bound to declare, if required, the value of the goods. Such deposit as the Carrier or his Agent, without prejudice, may deem sufficient to cover the estimated contribution of the goods and any special charges thereon shall if required, be paid to the Carrier or his Agent, prior to the delivery and will be placed on trust-account in bank in joint name of the Carrier and of a trustee designated by the Average Adjustors nominated by the Carrier.

14. In the event of accident, danger, damage or disaster before or after commencement of the voyage resulting from any cause whatsoever, whether due to negligence or not, for which or for the consequence of which the Carrier is not responsible by statute, contract or otherwise, the Merchant shall contribute with the Carrier in General Average to the payment of any sacrifice, losses or expenses of a General Average nature that may be made or incurred, and shall pay salvage and special charges incurred in respect of the cargo. If the salving vessel or vessels is owned or operated by the Carrier, salvage shall be paid for as fully as if the salving vessel or vessels belonged to strangers. Such deposit as the Carrier or his Agents may deem sufficient to cover the estimated contribution of the goods and any salvage and special charges thereon shall, if required, be made by the Merchant to the Carrier before delivery.

15. If the ship comes into collision with another ship as a result of the negligence of the other ship and any act, neglect or default of the master, mariner, pilot or the servants of the Carrier in the navigation or in the management of the ship, the owner of the goods carried hereunder will indemnify the Carrier against all loss or liability to the other non-carrying ship or her Owners in so far as such loss or liability represents loss of, or damage to, or any claim whatsoever of the owners of said goods, paid or payable by the other non-carrying ship or her owners to the Owners of said goods and set off, required or recovered by the other or non-carrying ship or her owners as part of their claim against the carrying ship or Carrier. The foregoing provisions shall also apply where the Owners, Operators or those in charge of any ship or ships or objects other than, or in addition to, the colliding ship or objects are at fault in respect to a collision or contract.

16. (a) The Master and the Carrier shall have liberty to comply with any order or directions or recommendations in connection with the transport under this contract given by any Government or Authority, or anybody acting or purporting to act on behalf of such Government or Authority, or having under the terms of the insurance on the vessel the right to give such orders or directions or recommendations.

(b) Should it appear that the performance of the transport would expose the vessel or any goods onboard to the risk of seizure or damage or delay, resulting from war, warlike operations, blockade, riots, civil commotions or piracy or any person onboard to the risk of loss of life or freedom, or that any such risk has increased, the Master may discharge the cargo at port of loading or any other safe and convenient port.

(c) Should it appear that for any reason, including insufficient depth of waters, conditions of tide, weather conditions, epidemic, quarantine, ice, labour troubles, labour obstructions, strikes, lockout, any of which on board or on shore, difficulties exist or may be likely to arise which may prevent the vessel from leaving the port of loading or reaching or entering the port of discharge or there discharging in the usual manner and leaving again, all of which safely and without delay, the Master may discharge the cargo at port of loading or any other safe and convenient port.

(d) The same shall apply if it appears or may be anticipated that for any such reasons as referred to in this clause difficulties exist or may be likely to arise which may prevent the vessel from reaching or entering the port of loading or there loading in the usual manner and leaving again, all of which safely and without delay.

(e) The discharge of any cargo under the provisions of this clause shall be deemed due fulfilment of the contract. If in connection with the exercise of any liberty under this clause any extra expenses are incurred, they shall be paid by the Merchant in addition to the freight, together with return freight if any and a reasonable compensation for any extra services rendered to the goods.

(f) The Merchant shall be informed if possible.

17. If the vessel is not owned by or chartered by demise to the Company or Line by whom this Bill of Lading is issued (as may be the case notwithstanding anything that appears to the contrary) this Bill of Lading shall take effect only as a contract with the owner or demise charterer as the case may be as principal made through the agency of the said Company or Line who act as agents only and shall be under no personal liability whatsoever in respect thereof.

18. All qualifying words in the Mate's Receipt describing the conditions of the goods or otherwise relating to the goods at the time of shipment shall be deemed to be incorporated in this Bill of Lading.

19. Cargo landed without marks or with wrong marks may be apportioned by the Carrier, the Master or their agent(s) in his (their) absolute discretion among the various consignees of the cargo whose lots may be short, and such apportionment to be accepted by said consignees as found.

20. The vessel will not be accountable for gold, silver, bullion, specie, jewellery, documents, plated goods, genuine works of art or other precious articles, precious stones or precious metals unless the Bill of Lading is signed for such goods and the value declared herein and extra freight agreed upon is paid. Such cargo will only be delivered upon presentation of Bill of Lading on board vessel, upon which all liability of the vessel shall cease and if delivery be not taken during the vessel's stay in port, such cargo shall as from the date of the arrival of the vessel at or off the port be at sole risk of the Merchant.

21. The Carrier undertakes that the vessel is classed 100 A1 at Lloyd's or highest class in the American Bureau of Shipping or any other recognised classification society, and shall hold Lloyd's RM Certificate or the customary [...] Certificate from the Society in which the refrigerating machinery and insulation are classed and the ship is loaded. Cargo in any insulated space or spaces a survey has been held and a certificate issued that the Classification Society's surveyor or other competent surveyor at such insulated space or spaces, refrigerating machinery, appliances and dunnage battens are, in the opinion of the surveyor, fit for the carriage of refrigerated cargo, and the existence of the aforesaid class and the production of the aforesaid certificate shall be conclusive evidence against the shippers, consignees and endorsees of the Bill of Lading that the Carrier has exercised due diligence before and at the beginning of the voyage to make such insulated space or spaces, refrigerating machinery, appliances and dunnage battens fit and safe for the reception, carriage and preservation of the goods, and has exercised due diligence to make the vessel in the said respects seaworthy, properly equipped and supplied but the said class certificate shall not be conclusive evidence in respect of a defect which came into existence after the time of such survey.

22. In the event of accident, danger, damage or disaster before or after commencement of the voyage, resulting from any cause whatsoever, whether due to negligence or not, for which or for the consequence of which the Carrier is not responsible by Statute, contract or otherwise the Merchant shall be bound by the measures and arrangements of the Carrier and/or the Master and/or Agent(s).

23. The vessel is free to carry cargo of an inflammable, explosive or dangerous nature, ammunition or warlike stores, and contraband, and may sail armed or unarmed.

24. In case the Master in his absolute discretion considers it impossible, unsafe or inconvenient to discharge the cargo, the subject matter of this Bill of Lading, or any part thereof at port of destination, for any reason whatsoever, including any of the reasons above mentioned and including congestion in the port or at quays or berths or impractability of lighters, actual or threatened blockade, interdict, impracticability of entering into the said port, war, civil war, rebellion, riots, civil commotion, strikes or lockouts, quarantine, unfavourable state of weather, including surf or ice, and unfavourable conditions at the said port, prior to or upon or subsequent to the vessel's arrival, the Master shall be entitled to wait at or near the said port for such time as the Master, in his absolute discretion, may deem reasonable until the discharge of the said cargo can be effected there, or discharge the cargo at port of loading or any other safe and convenient port.

25. If through any cause whatsoever, including any of the causes above mentioned, all the vessel's cargo (hereinafter called "the total cargo") having the same port of destination as the cargo forming the subject matter of this Bill of Lading or any part of the total cargo is not discharged at the port of destination within 48 hours of the arrival of the vessel at or off the said port, the Carrier and/or the Master and/or their Agents shall jointly and severally be entitled to claim and recover from the Merchant demurrage in respect of the time the vessel waits at or off the said port beyond the said 48 hours; the demurrage payable under this Bill of Lading shall be such percentage of the total demurrage payable as the freight under this Bill of Lading bears to the total freight for the total cargo, the total demurrage payable being at the rate of four shillings per dead weight ton of ship per day.

26. Wherever the vessel and/or the Carrier are (is) expressly or impliedly exonerated, exempted, excluded, released or immune from liability hereunder or in connection herewith towards the Merchant and/or third parties, the vessel, the Carrier, the Master, their Agents and Representatives shall all be and be deemed to be so exonerated, exempted, excluded, released and immune from liability, and in particular, without prejudice to the generality of the foregoing, it is further understood and agreed that as the Line Company or Agent who has executed this Bill of Lading for and on behalf of the Carrier or Master is not a principal in the transaction, said Line Company or Agent shall not be under any liability arising out of the contract of carriage not as Carrier nor bailee of the goods.

Provided that nothing in this Clause contained shall affect any liability of the Master and/or the Agents and/or the Representatives towards the Carrier.

All rights given to the vessel and/or the Carrier and/or the Master and/or their Agents and/or Representatives hereunder or in connection herewith can be exercised and enforced, and all proceedings hereunder or in connection herewith can be instituted and prosecuted, by any one of the Carrier, the Master, the Agents and the Representatives, or by all or any of them jointly and severally.

27. It is agreed and understood that the production of a certificate duly signed by the Master stating that the goods or part thereof fell overboard from lighters after having been discharged from the vessel shall serve as prima facie proof of such loss and of the due discharge of the goods from the vessel without any necessity of producing the Master in person.

28. The shipper, the receiver, the consignee, the holder of the Bill of Lading and the owner of the cargo are jointly and severally liable towards the Carrier for all the various undertakings, responsibilities and liabilities of the Merchant hereunder or in connection herewith.

29. The necessity for service of notarial or other official notices under or in connection with these presents is hereby waived and dispensed with.

Beneficiary's certificate (credit item three)

Beecham Research International

Beecham House Brentford Middlesex TW8 9BD

Telegrams & Cables:
Beechover Brentford
Telex: 935986
Telephone: 01-560 5151
Ext:

A Branch of Beecham Group Limited   Registered in London: 227531   Registered Office: Beecham House Brentford Middlesex

TO WHOM IT MAY CONCERN

LETTER OF CREDIT NUMBER: MF3/UK 70512

We hereby certify that particulars of shipment including shipment date,
name of carrying vessel, quantity and value of the goods shipped have been
Airmailed to, Myanma Corporation, Rangoon and also to MEIC A/C (Department
of Health Central Medical Stores Depot, 57 Newlyn Road, Rangoon) within
10 days of shipment, quoting Cover Note no: CN/029/9 DT: 13.3.59 of the
Myanma Insurance Corporation, Rangoon, and this Credit number.

Yours faithfully,
BEECHAM RESEARCH INTERNATIONAL

B. Worthy

Shipping Department

Beneficiary's copy letters

Beecham Research International

Beecham House Brentford Middlesex TW8 9BD

Telegrams & Cables:
Beechover Brentford
Telex: 935986
Telephone: 01-560 5151
Ext:

A Branch of Beecham Group Limited   Registered in London: 227531   Registered Office: Beecham House Brentford Middlesex

To...... Myanma Insurance Corporation ......

...... Rangoon. ......

Date. February. 5,. 1979 ....

Our Invoice ref. 51012/01, 51013,
51014, 51019

Dear Sirs,

Letter of Credit no MF3/UK 70512

For the Account of MEIC A/C (Department of Health, Central
Medical Stores Depot, 57 Newlyn Road, Rangoon.

In accordance with the requirements of the above quoted Letter of
Credit, we give the following details:-

Description of Goods...... Medical Stores (part shipment) ......

Vessel/Flight. PINYA ...... Date of B/Ladg/A.W.B. 30.1.79 B/L.37 ......

Port/airport of shipments...... London

Insurance Cover Note/~~Open Policy~~ no. CN/029/9 DT: 23/3/59

Import Licence no...... - ...... Bank Regn.no...... - ......

Value of Goods.. £7343.00 F.O.B.

Freight and charges.... -

Total value..... £7343.00 F.O.B.

A copy of this letter has been sent to:-

(a). MEIC A/C (Department of Health, Central Medical Stores Depot, 57 Newlyn Road,
Rangoon.

(b)......

(c)......

We trust that the above information will enable you to make the
necessary insurance arrangements.

Yours faithfully,
BEECHAM RESEARCH INTERNATIONAL.

B Worthy

SHIPPING DEPT.

Beneficiary's certificate (credit item four)

Beecham Research International

Beecham House Brentford Middlesex TW8 9BD

Telegrams & Cables:
Beechover Brentford
Telex: 935986
Telephone: 01-560 5151
Ext:

A Branch of Beecham Group Limited   Registered in London: 227531   Registered Office: Beecham House Brentford Middlesex

London, February 5, 1979

To whom it may Concern

Letter of Credit number: MF3/UK 70512

We hereby Certify that three copies of invoice indicating firm Order number, and a non-negotiable Bill of Lading have been Airmailed to the Central Medical Stores Depot No.57, Newlyn Road, Rangoon, Burma, in advance.

A copy of the invoice has also been Airmailed to, Inspection and Agency Corporation, 383 Maha Bandoola Street, Rangoon.

Yours faithfully,
BEECHAM RESEARCH INTERNATIONAL

Shipping Department

27. KEY LEGAL CASES

The purely legal aspects of documentary credits are outside the scope of this book but the advanced student or experienced practitioner should be aware of some of the leading cases and judgments which have a direct bearing on the subject. Among the works in English which deal in detail with the law relating to documentary credits, the following are recommended:

The Law of Bankers' Commercial Credits
H. C. Gutteridge and Maurice Megrah
Sixth edition, 1979, London

Bank Credits and Acceptances
Henry Harfield
Fifth edition, 1974, New York

An outline of ten key legal cases is included for general interest.

i   *J. H. Rayner v Hambros Bank Ltd, 1942*
Groundnuts: the case concerned a dispute over the description of the goods which did not comply with the wording on the credit. The credit called for Coromandel groundnuts. The bill of lading showed 'machine shelled ground nut kernels'. The oil seed business recognised both descriptions as being the same. The trial judge found for the plaintiff, but the Court of Appeal reversed the judgment as it maintained that the bank was right and the description did not comply with the terms of the credit. It could not be assumed that the bank would have knowledge of trade custom.

ii *Bank Melli Iran v Barclays Bank (DCO), 1951*
New Chevrolet trucks: held that whilst Barclays (DCO) had paid against incorrect documents, the Bank Melli Iran had failed to notify the defendants within a reasonable length of time. The plaintiffs were estopped from denying the documents' validity. Failure by the issuing bank to inform the advising bank of rejection within a reasonable period of time amounts to ratification of the acceptability of the documents. This case occurred before the UK banks subscribed to *Uniform Customs and Practice*, where, in the 1974 revision, Article 8(e), it is stipulated that rejection must be notified 'without delay'.

iii *Cape Asbestos Co Ltd v Lloyds Bank Ltd, 1921*
Asbestos: a revocable credit was established which Lloyds Bank advised. One draft was paid and Lloyds Bank did not advise plaintiffs of cancellation, believing it still to be operative. Further shipment was made, an invoice was issued for more than the balance of the credit, and bill of lading was made out in favour of the buyers instead of the bank. The buyers obtained possession of the goods and collecting payment was impossible. The plaintiffs claimed from the defendant bank the balance of the credit. The bank normally advised of cancellation of a credit, but this time forgot. Held: the bank was not liable as they had no liability to advise revocation to beneficiary. This decision is reinforced by Article 2 of *Uniform Customs and Practice*, which states that a revocable credit may be amended or cancelled at any time without prior notice to the beneficiary.

iv   *Trendex Trading Corporation v Central Bank of Nigeria, 1976*
Cement: following its government's instructions, the bank refused to honour payment, claiming sovereign immunity which, had it been substantiated, would have prevented Trendex from taking an action against a sovereign state. The Court of Appeal held in favour of Trendex since the bank had not proved its entitlement to sovereign immunity, and that international law was normally part of English law, under which there were no grounds to support the bank's refusal of payment.

v   *Hamzeh Malas and Sons v British Imex Industries Ltd, 1958*
Steel rods: two instalments and payments were made under two confirmed credits with Midland Bank. After the first instalment the buyers applied for an injunction restraining the sellers from recovering any money under the second credit. The injunction was refused because the bank was under an absolute obligation to pay (see also Chapter 7, section 7, 'The Harbottle case', on the important question of an absolute obligation to pay. If this were not so there would be little value to be attached to a bank's documentary credit, or a confirmation thereof, or any other guarantee or undertaking by a bank or third party).

vi   *Equitable Trust Co of New York v Dawson Partners Ltd, 1926*
Vanilla beans: a credit was issued through the Equitable Trust in favour of a seller in Jakarta, with instructions to provide finance on presentation of certain documents, including a 'certificate of experts'. The Equitable Trust paid on the tender of a certificate issued by *one* expert. The seller was fraudulent, shipping rubbish which the single expert did not notice. Held: Equitable Trust had paid contrary to Dawson Partners' instructions and could not debit them.

vii   *Soprama SpA v Marine and Animal By-products Corporation Ltd, 1966*
Chilean fish full-meal: documents tendered to the bank were not correct; the bill of lading was not marked 'freight paid' and the CIF description was wrong. After expiry, the second presentation directly to the buyers was also rejected. Held: both presentations were correctly treated.

viii   *Midland Bank Ltd v Seymour, 1955*
Feathers from Hong Kong: Seymour entered into contracts with a Chinese firm (Taiyo); payment by irrevocable documentary credit opened through the plaintiff bank. Taiyo turned out to be a worthless firm; the first shipment when it arrived turned out to be rubbish. The firm disappeared after collecting substantial sums under the documentary credit in exchange for documents which appeared to be in order. Seymour claimed: *i* that the bank did not act in accordance with the terms of the credit, and therefore had no authority for debiting to his account the payments it made; *ii* the bank was guilty of negligence in withholding information about Taiyo that could have been beneficial to Mr Seymour. Held: description of the invoice was not in accordance with the credit terms. Documents could correctly be rejected. The bank had no duty to disclose any information about Taiyo to Seymour and therefore negligence could not be proved, so the second point above failed. The first point above has been reinforced by Article 32 of *Uniform Customs and Practice*.

ix   *Commercial Banking Co of Sydney Ltd v Jalsard Pty Ltd, 1973*
Battery-operated Christmas lights: documents were issued by two firms of

surveyors who checked the quantity and condition of the goods. The buyer stated that the documents did not satisfy the description of a certificate of inspection as they did not state that the goods were in accordance with the sales contract. The Judicial Committee of the Privy Council were of the opinion that as the documents stated that the goods and packages had been inspected and were in apparent good order and condition the terms of the credit had been complied with.

x   *The Creditanstalt case*

Drugs: After six years of litigation, the Bank of England in 1981 mediated and the dispute was settled out of court with the two sides agreeing to share liability and bear their own legal costs. This in many ways was unsatisfactory since it settled none of the underlying issues. However, the issues at stake are so important that no work on documentary credits would be complete without some mention of the factors which involve a dispute about the fundamental concept of honouring obligations entered into under a documentary credit. The amount in dispute was US$20.7 million under three credits. Creditanstalt issued the credits in 1974 and later was served with an injunction, issued by a subsidiary company, to withhold payment. Creditanstalt maintained: (*a*) the goods were worthless; (*b*) that they were the victims of fraud and issued the credit in ignorance of the background; and (*c*) because of the fraud the credits were invalid. A consortium of banks led by Singer & Friedlander, who raised the finance for the transaction and to whom the rights under the credits were assigned, maintained that: (*a*) Creditanstalt had previously confirmed in writing that the documents would be accepted; (*b*) the goods were in fact as described; and (*c*) that banks pay against documents not against goods anyway, and that they are in no way concerned with the sales of other contracts upon which the credits may be based. *Uniform Customs and Practice* general provisions and definitions (c), Articles 7, 8a and b, and 9, appeared to support this view. A further complication arose as to whether the consortium had a valid claim as assignees.

28. GLOSSARY OF TERMS USED IN THIS CHAPTER

Acceptance	the act of giving a written undertaking on the face of a term bill of exchange to pay a stated sum on the maturity date indicated.
Acceptance credit	a documentary credit which *inter alia* requires the beneficiary to draw a term bill for subsequent acceptance by either the issuing bank or the advising bank as the credit stipulates; such credits are used as a vehicle to finance the importer.
Advising	act of conveying the terms and conditions of a credit to the beneficiary; the advising bank is the issuing bank's agent, usually located in the beneficiary's country.
Amendment	alteration to the terms of a credit; amendments must stem from the applicant, be issued and

Amendment *(continued)*	advised to the beneficiary; the beneficiary has the right to refuse an amendment if the credit is irrevocable.
Anticipatory credit	more commonly known as a red clause credit *(qv)* under which an advance payment may be made by the advising bank in anticipation of documents being subsequently presented by the beneficiary under the credit.
Applicant	one who applies to his bank to issue a documentary credit; in the majority of credits issued the applicant is an importer of goods.
Back to back credit	two documentary credits, the second being issued on the understanding that reimbursement will stem from documents eventually presented under the first credit issued.
Beneficiary	party in whose favour a credit is established; in the majority of credits issued the beneficiary is an exporter of goods.
Confirming	act of an advising bank assuming the liability for payment, acceptance or negotiation of correctly presented documents under a credit.
Credit (1)	documentary credit, a conditional undertaking by a bank to make payment.
Credit (2)	granting of deferred terms of payment to an importer.
Credit (3)	to place to the account of.
Credit rating	an assessment of the degree of creditworthiness of an organisation; used to determine whether a beneficiary credit status is sufficient for the advising bank to accept the beneficiary's own indemnity for discrepancies on documents presented under a credit.
Discounting	act of purchasing an accepted term bill of exchange; bills discounted under credits in London may be in respect of import, export or merchanting transactions.
Discrepancy	any deviation from the terms and conditions of a credit, or the documents presented thereunder, or any inconsistency between the documents themselves.

Documentary credit — conditional undertaking by a bank to make payment; often abbreviated to the word 'credit'.

Draft — bill of exchange presented with documents submitted under a credit; not to be confused with a 'banker's draft', which is not a bill of exchange but is sometimes used as a vehicle for reimbursement.

Import licence — if the goods are subject to import licensing restrictions a valid import licence should be obtained by the importer, usually from the Import Licensing Branch, Department of Trade and Industry, 1 Victoria Street, London SW1.

Inchoate bill — a bill of exchange on which certain details have been omitted; such bills may accompany refinance credits when issued and are held by the advising bank pending presentation of shipping documents by the beneficiary, after which the advising bank completes the bill which may then be used to provide finance for the applicant.

Indemnity — undertaking given in respect of discrepancies on documents presented under a credit; the beneficiary who issues the indemnity is primarily liable to repay funds received from the advising bank in settlement under the credit, if the advising bank cannot obtain reimbursement from the issuing bank as a result of documents being rejected by the applicant.

Irrevocable credit — constitutes a definite undertaking of the issuing bank to pay, accept or negotiate provided the terms of the credit are observed; it may be advised to the beneficiary without engagement by the advising bank, and cannot be amended or cancelled unless all parties to the credit agree.

Negotiation (1) — 'doing a deal', 'treating', 'bargaining', 'settling terms'.

Negotiation (2) — see this entry in the glossary of Chapter 4; the system for purchasing items payable abroad which are then sent to the foreign centre for collection and payment.

Negotiation (3) — purchase under a confirmed credit (without recourse to the beneficiary) or under an unconfirmed credit (with recourse to the beneficiary) of drafts which under the credit terms the issuing bank has undertaken to pay.

Negotiation (4) — a form of 'payment' of a credit by a bank other than the advising bank; this may be the beneficiary's bank which would claim reimbursement from the issuing bank directly, after crediting the beneficiary.

Open general licence (OGL) — goods that are not subject to a specific import licence may be imported, as à rule, under OGL.

Packing house credit — another name for a red clause credit (*qv*); the wool credits of this type often being issued in favour of an Australian wool packing house or shipper.

Pledge — taken from the applicant on the application form to open a credit; this protects the issuing bank from any liquidator appointed having the right to distribute to the applicant's creditors generally the proceeds of the goods sold under the credit.

Pre-shipment finance — one form of pre-shipment finance is the red clause credit; an advance payment is another.

Recourse — the right, expressly taken by a bank, to recover principal and interest from the borrower; it is inherent in most 'lending' facilities and certain documentary credit transactions.

Red clause credit — credit with a clause, printed in red, which authorises the advising bank to make an advance payment to the beneficiary.

Re-discounting — sale on the London bill market of bills of exchange previously discounted by a bank; most of the commercial paperwork arising from documentary credit transactions is bank bills.

Revocable credit — one which may be amended or cancelled without notice to the beneficiary.

Revolving credit — credit automatically reinstated after each drawing, with limits as to the duration of the facility and as to the (cumulative or non-cumulative) amount involved for each drawing.

Settlement — under a credit may be by payment, negotiation or acceptance.

Shipment date — the date inserted on the bills of lading evidencing goods received on board is regarded for credit purposes as being the date of shipment.

Shopping-bag credit	certain transferable and revolving credits are established in favour of beneficiaries who are agents of the applicant; the agent thereunder 'farms-out' portions of the credit to various suppliers.
Stand-by credit	may be established as security for an advance when guarantees are appropriate but cannot be obtained.
Transferable credit	permits the beneficiary to transfer all or some of the rights and obligations under the credit to a second beneficiary or beneficiaries.

PAST EXAMINATION QUESTIONS

1   A London banker advises you of the issue of a documentary credit in your favour by its New York correspondent. The credit is irrevocable on their part and the relative drafts can be negotiated through the office of the London banker. The credit (in US dollars), covering shipment from Liverpool to New York, expired on Sunday, 20th May 1979. It calls for 100 cases of muffins and crumpets (half and half in each case) at $56 per case CIF. The documents required are invoices, a complete set of clean 'on board' bills of lading to order and blank endorsed, together with a policy of insurance for the CIF value plus 10 per cent. You present your documents on Monday, 21st May 1979. The invoice you submit shows 103 cases of muffins and pikelets (the customary term for crumpets in your district) but the amount claimed is for only 100 cases at the specified price. The insurance certificate dated 18th May 1979 covers all 103 cases for £2,266 (being the sterling value plus 10 per cent). The forwarding agent's bill of lading dated 17th May 1979, however, describes the goods as muffins and pikelets without mentioning the proportions of each.

a   Could the London banker refuse to negotiate?

b   If you think he should negotiate, state the reasons for his action.

c   If you think he should refuse to negotiate, state your reasons for believing him to be justified.

(Institute of Export)

2   A bank issues its documentary credit in terms which permit the overseas beneficiary to draw term bills of exchange on it. How can the bank get security from the commercial transaction to which the credit relates?

(Institute of Bankers)

3   'The object of a documentary credit is to provide a guarantee of payment to the seller. It is not and cannot be a guarantee to the buyer that he will receive the goods he has ordered.'

Comment on this dictum and describe some of the methods by which buyers try to obtain protection from a documentary credit.

(Institute of Bankers)

4   What is a transferable credit? Under what circumstances is it used?

(Institute of Export)

There are many other aspects of documentary credit facilities, and a knowledge of the subject is essential to answer the many questions on finance and methods of settlement properly and to the customer's and to the examiner's satisfaction.

CHAPTER SIX

Credit Insurance and Preferential Export Finance

1. INTRODUCTION – THE BENEFITS AND PROBLEMS OF GRANTING CREDIT

In order to sell their goods abroad in competitive markets exporters must be able to *(a)* produce goods of a high quality; *(b)* meet strict delivery dates; *(c)* quote a firm, reasonable and competitive price; and *(d)* if requested provide buyers with time in which to pay (grant credit).

Foreign competitors will often be able to match *(a)*, *(b)* and *(c)* above, and if that happened the contract would probably go to the supplier who could provide the buyer with the longest deferred terms of payment. The granting of credit can therefore be a powerful tool in obtaining sales.

To the seller the benefit of granting credit is that he may increase his sales. To the buyer the benefit of being granted credit is that he may spread the payment period, and perhaps afford to pay for the goods out of current earnings. The problems of granting credit may be identified by the following questions and observations:

- is the seller running the risk of over-trading by over-extending credit to his debtors?
- can the exporter provide the finance himself? If so, is the exporter maximising the use of his own resources?
- can the exporter obtain finance from elsewhere? If so, can he pass the cost on to the buyer and still quote a competitive price?
- is the interest payable on borrowings subject to fluctuation which may involve the exporter in a loss or reduction of profit if it is included in the sale price?
- the longer the credit period granted the greater is the risk of something happening which will result in the seller not being paid, unless the transaction is arranged under a documentary credit; the major risks are default by the buyer, and economic or political risks prohibiting the transfer of funds to the UK
- from a national viewpoint the longer the period of credit granted the longer the

UK is denied reflection in its balance of payments of the results of the exports
How much credit should be granted? This will depend upon:

- what funds are available, for how long, and at what price
- the nature of the goods: consumer goods will have a shorter life and therefore a shorter credit period than goods of a capital or permanent nature; in any event the period of credit granted should not exceed the life of the asset purchased
- the creditworthiness of the buyer and of the buyer's country

2. ECGD

a ECGD facilities at a glance

(This chart is reproduced by courtesy of Export Credits Guarantee Department)

☐ Insurance guarantees   ◯ Bank guarantees   △ Facilities combining insurance and finance

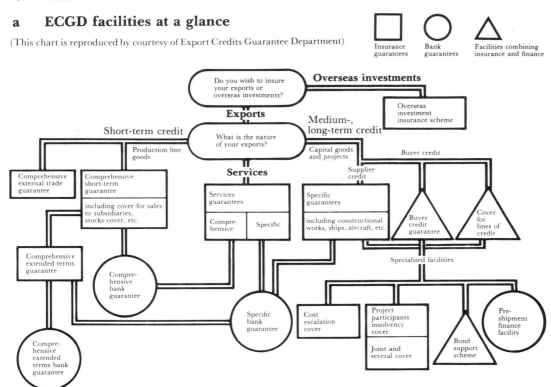

b ECGD services

☐ *1 Comprehensive short-term guarantee*

Intended for exporters of consumer or consumer durable goods sold on terms of payment not exceeding 180 days.

☐ *2 Comprehensive external trade guarantee*

Protects UK merchants or confirmers trading in goods dispatched from one overseas country to another against risk of non-payment. Goods must be sold on credit not exceeding 180 days.

◯ *3 Comprehensive bank guarantee*

Holders of 1, trading on credit terms of less than two years, can supplement their policy by a 100 per cent ECGD guarantee direct to financing banks. Finance is provided from date of shipment at ⅝ per cent above base rate.

☐ *4 Comprehensive extended terms guarantee*
Holders of 1 trading in goods sold on longer than six months credit but less than five years can obtain cover, through this guarantee.

◯ *5 Comprehensive extended terms bank guarantee*
For holders of 4 this guarantee helps provide finance in the same way as 3.

☐ *6 Services guarantees*
For firms who carry out services for principals overseas, the comprehensive option is suitable for a recurrent pattern of business whereas the specific option is for where only one service is to be carried out.

☐ *7 Specific guarantees*
Provide insurance for exporters whose goods are unsuitable for ECGD's comprehensive policies – this could be major capital goods projects, or business which involves substantial work on site or a long manufacturing period.

△ *8 Buyer credit guarantee*
ECGD guarantees UK bank loan direct to an overseas buyer – this enables the UK exporter to be paid on cash terms and can also facilitate progress payments during manufacture. Minimum eligible contract value is £1 million.

△ *9 Cover for lines of credit*
Credit made available to an overseas bank by a UK bank, guaranteed by ECGD. Amount of credit, period for which it is available, terms and interest rates, minimum size of contract, specified for each line.

◯ *10 Specific bank guarantee*
For exporters (holding 7 or 4) with contract on credit of longer than two years ECGD gives a guarantee to financing bank, which provides finance at preferential export interest rate which varies according to buyer's country and length of credit.

☐ *11 Cost escalation cover*
This provides partial protection against certain UK cost increases for firms with capital goods contracts worth over £2 million with a manufacturing period of at least two years.

☐ *12 Project participants insolvency and Joint and several cover*
Covers UK consortium members against fellow members' insolvency (minimum contract £20 million) and other contingencies (minimum contract £50 million).

△ *13 Bond support scheme*
ECGD can support the issue of performance and other bonds for contracts worth £250,000 or more.

◯ *14 Pre-shipment finance*
Guarantees pre-shipment finance for banks for overseas contracts insured with ECGD with a contract value of £1 million or more. This finance is not at a preferential interest rate.

☐ *15 Overseas investment insurance scheme*
Provides UK investors with insurance for up to 15 years against political risks in respect of new investment overseas. Investor must be a company carrying on business in the UK or a subsidiary of such a company.

c   **The purpose of the Export Credits Guarantee Department (ECGD)**

The purpose of ECGD is to encourage exports from the UK by providing export credit insurance at a reasonable price without involving expense to the taxpayer. ECGD operates under the Export Guarantees and Overseas Investment Act and for 'commercial' business follows the recommendations of an advisory council, a body which includes representatives from industry, commerce and finance. In respect of business which cannot be justified on a purely commercial basis ECGD may, nevertheless, consider giving insurance cover in 'the national interest', but even in these circumstances the normal underwriting criteria are applied. This means that ECGD must conduct its business on commercial principles and retain the freedom to decline business likely to result in loss, whether because of a buyer's limited creditworthiness, the economic risk in a market or the form of cover requested.

ECGD describes its business as being 'based on a normal commercial relationship between buyer and seller: this requires that neither the details nor the existence of an ECGD policy shall be disclosed (except to the exporter's bankers or brokers in confidence). In return the department binds itself and its agents not to disclose that any particular transaction or exporter is covered by a policy. ECGD's business lies only with the exporter and ECGD is not, in its normal commercial business, an instrument of the general political or commercial policy of HM Government. It follows that neither the department nor its agents are at liberty to discuss with buyers, the buyers' banks or their governments the terms on which it will insure business or the terms which exporters may offer their buyers'.

d   **The Berne Union**

The Berne Union is an international association of credit insurers established in 1934. There are about 35 members representing credit insurance institutions in some 26 countries. Its main function is international co-operation through regular meetings to study export credit and overseas investment insurance techniques. In recent years it has concentrated on working towards a common policy in credit insurance with a view to avoiding a 'credit race' between exporters in different countries. Credit insurers wish to discourage abnormally long credit or competition in credit giving, and to this end the Berne Union has a 'five-year understanding' under which members agree not to insure transactions involving over five years' post-shipment supplier credit or where the credit terms requested are inconsistent with the accepted pattern for the goods in question.

There are a number of detailed differences between the insurance coverage available to UK exporters and the facilities in other countries, but the broad pattern is similar. The financing facilities are usually provided in other countries by the primary commercial banks in the first instance, although lending in excess of one year is usually re-discounted through a separate institution. The Canadian Export Finance Corporation and the Italian Medio Credito are two such institutions.

Apart from its representation in the Berne Union, the ECGD also takes part in international co-operation and discussions on credit insurance and other matters within the EEC and OECD (Organisation for Economic Co-operation and Development).

3.   THE LONDON CREDIT INSURANCE MARKET

In addition to the Export Credits Guarantee Department (ECGD) there are a few export credit insurance companies in the private sector in the United Kingdom. To assist exporters there are also a number of specialist insurance brokers who bring business both to ECGD and the private insurers.

	ECGD	Other institutions
Type of institution	Department of government	Limited company
Financial objectives	To operate at no net cost to public funds by maintaining a sufficient reserve to meet current and expected future liabilities. Any surpluses may be ploughed back in the form of lower premiums in later years whenever possible	To make profits for the shareholders
Nature of risks	*Del credere*, political and economic	*Del credere*
Nature of business insured	*UK exports and re-exports only*	Primarily home sales, but also a significant volume of exports
Support security for the lending banker	Direct guarantee. Assignment of policies	Assignment of policies only

Selling abroad invariably involves a greater credit risk and a longer period of credit than home sales. Over the years there has been a broadening of the range of cover available; additionally, ECGD now provides, in certain circumstances, guarantees to banks which enable them to provide finance:

● to UK exporters for exports (supplier credit)
● to overseas buyers of UK goods/services (buyer credit)

ECGD and the private sector insurers do not, however, themselves provide finance directly to commercial borrowers.

4.   ECGD COMPREHENSIVE SHORT-TERM GUARANTEES (insurance policies)

a   The nature of comprehensive cover

The word 'comprehensive' (ie, all-embracing) relates to the business which ECGD requires the exporter to offer for cover: in other words, all the exporter's business should be insured. This type of cover relates to goods where the business is of a continuous and repetitive nature (ie, mainly but not exclusively consumer goods) where many buyers are concerned, and perhaps many different export markets. The policies are issued by ECGD for the whole export turnover for a period of not less than 12 months and allow the exporter to grant up to six months' credit to the overseas buyers. Should a longer period be required a supplemental extended terms guarantee may be issued to holders of the comprehensive short-term guarantee. The supplemental guarantee allows the exporter to grant up to five years' credit for capital goods, subject to prior approval by ECGD of each individual contract; the exporter must *a* declare his shipments monthly for the purpose of paying the premiums; *b* not ship to a buyer who has already defaulted on payment; *c* not reveal to the buyer that the transaction is credit insured. If the exporter wants to offer ECGD less than all his export turnover the department may accept the business for an increased premium, provided it is offered an acceptable spread of risk.

b   Additional pre-credit cover

The basic guarantee will cover the exporter from the date of shipment. The additional pre-credit cover runs from the date of the contract. As ECGD is on risk for a shorter period with a basic guarantee, there being no pre-credit cover, the premiums are lower than with the pre-credit cover. In the event of ECGD making a claims payment the exporter would be expected to remit to the department the proceeds of any subsequent re-sale of the goods involved. If there is a ready alternative market for the goods, the seller will obtain little or no benefit from having the more expensive pre-credit cover. On the other hand, goods made specially for one buyer, that would perhaps yield only scrap value if the buyer defaulted, should be covered for the pre-credit period.

c   Foreign currency cover

Contracts expressed in foreign currency, under which the exporter has either sold the foreign currency forward or borrowed the foreign currency, may involve the exporter in an exchange loss in the event of delayed or non-forthcoming payment. This possible loss may be reduced by an ECGD endorsement to the comprehensive short-term guarantee, the supplemental extended terms guarantee, or to the specific guarantee (which is referred to in the next section) but only for such foreign currencies as ECGD may specify. Under the endorsement to the comprehensive short-term guarantee ECGD will, in the event of default by the buyer, pay up to 10 per cent more sterling than would otherwise be payable, and for this extra cover no additional premium is payable. For business covered under the endorsement to the supplemental extended-terms guarantee or the specific guarantee the exporter can select any margin of cover he desires but will pay an additional premium related to the extra amount of cover he is seeking.

d   How premiums are assessed

A fundamental principle of insurance is spread of risk. Political and economic risks cannot be determined accurately, for such is the nature of world affairs that no one can determine with any great accuracy what actions a nation may take. There are very many thousands of individual buyers throughout the world who provide a wide spread of risks, but these buyers come from what is, after all, only a limited number of countries. If the monetary authorities of any particular country impose regulations prohibiting the transfer of funds from that country, all payments due will be subject to claims from the exporters under the ECGD comprehensive policies. The premiums charged on the comprehensive short-term guarantees are based on the principle of spread of risk arising from the comprehensive nature of the facility. In 1978 the average premium for this cover was 32p per £100 insured.

The premiums are payable in two parts:
- a fixed amount (non-refundable) payable at the beginning of each year of the insurance
- a flat rate payable monthly on all exports declared that month, at a rate agreed at the beginning of each year of insurance

The amounts payable will depend upon the size of the export turnover and also on the extent to which ECGD has been required to vet applications under the credit limit service. Exporters do not have to submit all small or repeat orders to ECGD for individual approval of credit terms; they are given 'discretionary limits' under the comprehensive short-term guarantee facility, usually up to £5,000 provided a satisfactory status report is obtained on the buyer.

e   The risks involved

Risks covered by ECGD are:	Risks specifically not covered are:
1 Insolvency of the buyer	1 The exporter's failure to comply with the provisions of the policy
2 The buyer's failure to pay within six months of due date for goods he has accepted	2 Non-acceptance or non-payment due to causes within the exporter's control
3 The buyer's failure to take up goods that have been despatched to him (where not caused or excused by the exporter's action, and where ECGD decides that legal action would serve no useful purpose)	3 Exchange risks normally covered by banks under forward exchange contracts
4 Government action which blocks or delays transfer of payment to the exporter	4 Any loss arising from breach of exchange control regulations in force in the buyer's country or the country in whose currency payment is to be made, etc
5 Any other action by the government in the buyer's country which prevents performance of the contract such as goods shipped in unacceptable vessels	5 The buyer's failure to obtain the appropriate authority to import and make payment
6 Cancellation or non-renewal of the UK export licence, or imposition of a new export licensing or exchange restriction or restrictions	6 An event which normal commercial insurance covers – eg, marine risk, fire, theft, damage, pilferage, etc
7 Exchange shortfall resulting from UK sellers having to accept payment in a local currency in settlement of a sterling debt	7 Losses within the UK other than export licensing
8 War, revolution, or similar disturbance outside the UK	8 Insolvency, or any act or default on the part of the collecting bank or exporter's agent
9 Political events, economic difficulties, etc	9 Losses arising from breach of contract by the exporter
10 Repudiation of the contract in cases where ECGD agrees that the buyer has 'government' status	10 Losses arising from the breaking of laws in either the UK or the buyer's country
	11 Cancellation of the contract by the buyer (non-government) before goods are despatched

Under the first two of the above risks ECGD covers 90 per cent of loss; under the third the exporter bears a 'first loss' of 20 per cent of the full original price, and ECGD bears 90 per cent of the balance; under the remainder ECGD bears 90 per cent of the loss if the cause arises before shipment, 95 per cent if it arises subsequently.

f   When claims are payable
Claims are payable in the event of the following and at the following times:
- for insolvency of the buyer; immediately on proof of insolvency
- for protracted default on goods accepted; six months after the due date of payment
- for failure to take up goods; one month after resale
- for any other cause of loss; four months after due date of payment, or date of the event causing the loss, whichever is later

5.   SPECIFIC GUARANTEES AND SPECIAL POLICIES

Individual contracts involving capital goods or projects not suitable for the comprehensive cover may be separately insured, the premium charged being up to approximately ten times more than for a similar value comprehensive cover, because of the lack of spread of risk. Up to five years may be granted under a specific policy (but for very large projects terms in excess of five years may be agreed) and the risks covered are similar to the comprehensive cover except that the private buyer's failure to take up goods exported is not covered. Many of the contracts covered by this type of insurance involve government buyers. A maximum of 90 per cent cover is provided, except where a contract of three years' credit or more, which has run trouble-free for one year during which time part repayments have been made, is involved, and then the cover extended by ECGD may become 100 per cent. This 100 per cent facility may also apply against a supplemental extended terms guarantee which is only available to holders of a comprehensive short-term guarantee. Exporters invoicing in foreign currency and covering their risks by forward contracts on currency borrowing (see Chapter 8, sections 4 – 6) may protect themselves from loss on close-outs by means of the foreign currency contracts endorsement. Cost escalation cover for goods that take at least two years to produce, and contracts of £2 million minimum, is available unless the contract involves the EEC. For cash payments and buyer credit the extent of the cover is 75 per cent and for credit sales 70 per cent cover. Cover for performance bonds is discussed in Chapter 7.

In addition to the comprehensive and specific policies, there are special types of policy for purposes which range from aircraft to external trade, from shipbuilding to overseas stocks, from earnings from invisible exports to overseas surveys and business promotion, from dealings with UK merchants and confirming houses to overseas construction work, from stocks of UK goods sent abroad on trial or demonstration to sales to overseas subsidiaries.

6.   ASSIGNMENT OF ECGD POLICIES

In many cases the exporter's only objective is to obtain insurance cover. However, the existence of cover can facilitate the obtaining of finance for exports, although it must be pointed out that banks may be willing to provide finance without the existence of such cover. As collateral security banks may take an assignment over an exporter's specific or comprehensive guarantee when providing finance by loan, overdraft, negotiation or bill advance.

It should be noted that an assignment may relate to the benefits of the whole policy, or be restricted to the cover provided for a specific country or buyer, or simply be an assignment of the rights connected with a particular transaction. ECGD provides suitable forms for such purposes. Such an assignment does not constitute a book debt and therefore does not require registration at Companies House in accordance with Section 95 (2) of the Companies Act 1948.

On the other hand an exporter can assign his rights under his ECGD policy to his bank, which may influence the bank to provide finance in a marginal case when otherwise it would decline to do so. Any such assignment of an ECGD policy is not to be regarded as first class security and there should be no confusion over the fact that ECGD calls its insurance policies 'guarantees'. They are not guarantees as far as the banker and exporter are concerned and can only be looked upon as *insurance policies*. An offer of any assignment of the rights under a policy to a bank should, therefore, be approached with some caution, for when a bank is asked to finance an exporter's activities against an assignment the bank's rights and benefits become no more than the rights and benefits of the exporter himself. This is because only the exporter will know whether or not the cover with ECGD has been prejudiced by false or undisclosed information or failure to carry out the contract satisfactorily. The bank will, therefore, exercise conventional banking judgment regarding the exporter's integrity and ability, and limit the risk to his resources. The normal rates of bank lending usually apply to advances against an assignment.

7.   SHORT-TERM DIRECT ECGD BANK GUARANTEES

There are two schemes, which are dealt with below:
● comprehensive open account guarantee
● comprehensive bill guarantee
Under both schemes banks have agreed to provide finance at an interest rate of base

rate + ⅝ per cent per annum, minimum 4½ per cent per annum, ECGD charging a premium of 15p per £100 per annum for issuing its guarantees.

a   Comprehensive open account guarantee

This guarantee was introduced in July 1967 and covers 'cash against documents' business and open account business on up to six months' credit where the business is covered by an ECGD comprehensive short-term guarantee. Although it is no longer a qualification for consideration by ECGD for a direct guarantee to be issued in favour of an exporter's bank the exporter is usually expected to have held a current comprehensive short-term guarantee beforehand. All being well, ECGD agrees a limit for the guarantee, the bank agrees to provide finance in a like amount, and the facility then works on a revolving basis (similar to an ordinary overdraft limit) during the life of the guarantee. ECGD's guarantee also covers the interest due to the bank under the facility.

The bank will normally advance 100 per cent of the net invoice value, and the monies are advanced *with recourse* to the exporter. To operate the facility the customer has to present to his bank a warranty in a form specified to him by ECGD in which the exporter warrants that the business is fully covered within the terms of his basic insurance cover. A copy invoice and evidence of export are also required. The bank makes its advance against the exporter's promissory note issued for 100 per cent of the net invoice and maturing at the end of the month in which the relevant payment is due from the buyer, the advances being fully covered under ECGD's guarantee. A charge per promissory note is made, although any number of transactions for which payment falls due in the same month can normally be covered by one note. The guarantee covers the bank in case the exporter does not pay on the due date. In order to provide evidence of a commercial debt the exporter under this scheme gives a promissory note in favour of the lending bank, and this is held by the bank until payment is received. This arrangement is necessary since under this scheme there are usually no bills of exchange drawn by the exporter on the overseas buyer, trade being on open account terms. Thus, under this facility the bank is making a simple loan to the exporter against his promissory note, and the exporter is under obligation to repay the bank, which does not have to rely on the exporter receiving payment from his buyer on the due date. The exporter will be able to claim under the comprehensive short-term guarantee from ECGD in the event of non-payment by the buyer. In section 4 f of this chapter, the timing of payment of claims is laid out, and depending on the circumstances of the claim it follows that the exporter may be out of funds for a time despite the fact that the exporter has credit insurance and that his bank has provided finance under the open account guarantee scheme.

b   Comprehensive bill guarantee

This guarantee was introduced in July 1965, since when revisions have taken place, and it covers exports when bills of exchange or promissory notes are issued with a tenor of less than two years and when the business is covered by an ECGD comprehensive short-term or supplemental extended terms guarantee. ECGD, all being well, agrees a limit for the guarantee, the bank agrees to provide finance in a like amount, and the facility than works on a revolving basis, as with an ordinary overdraft limit, during the life of the guarantee.

How does the facility work?

When the exporter requires a bill or note to be financed under the guarantee he must present it together with:

- a warranty in a form specified to him by ECGD in which the exporter warrants that the business is fully covered within the terms of his basic insurance cover
- a copy of the invoice(s)
- acceptable evidence of exportation as laid down by ECGD

An advance with recourse is made for 100 per cent of the face value of unaccepted bills or sight drafts; this sum is credited to the customer's account to the debit of the bank's special export loan account. Accepted bills or signed promissory notes are purchased without recourse to the exporter. Near its maturity date the bill or note is sent for the collection of the proceeds, and the proceeds are credited to the loan account to repay the bank's lending. The lending bank makes a handling charge for every bill or note.

The bank has *no recourse* to its customer for the purchase of an accepted bill or note; if it is unpaid at maturity the bank claims on ECGD. If, however, an unaccepted bill or sight draft is financed the bank retains recourse to the customer until the time of acceptance, or the time of payment in the case of a sight draft. The exporter is required to complete a recourse agreement with ECGD; this will enable ECGD to recover from him sums claimed by the lending bank in advance of or in excess of claims payable under the exporter's own standard ECGD policy.

8. MEDIUM- AND LONG-TERM DIRECT GUARANTEES

Exports to EEC countries are excluded from the following facilities, and UK exporters to those countries are therefore denied access to the preferential financing arrangements outlined in this section.

a Specific bank guarantee

This type of ECGD guarantee is available in respect of specific contracts for capital goods, production goods, and constructional works, or services. A contract for almost any amount will qualify, provided the deferred terms of payment are for two years or more up to a maximum of five years (or up to seven years, in some cases, to match competition from other countries).

The guarantee issued by ECGD relates to one contract only and obviously is not revolving as with the open account and bills guarantees. The amount of finance provided by the bank would be up to 100 per cent of the principal value of the exporter's bills of exchange ('bills') or buyer's promissory notes ('notes') and would be by way of an advance if the bills had not been accepted by the buyer, with the bank having the right of recourse to the exporter. On acceptance of the bills the advance would be transformed into a purchase or, in the case of bills already accepted and of signed notes, these would be purchased by the bank; the finance thus being provided being without recourse by the bank to the exporter. The bank can finance these bills or notes only after the goods have been shipped or the work, in the case of construction or services, has been accepted by the overseas buyer. The terms of the finance to be provided are written into a 'facility letter' prepared and signed by the bank and accepted by the customer before the facility becomes operative. Against such a guarantee the banks have agreed to provide finance at an unchanging (fixed) rate of interest which is fixed at the time the guarantee is issued. This, it will be appreciated, is important to the exporter because it enables him to quote a fixed rate of interest to his buyer which he knows is not going to vary with fluctuations in his bank's base rate. ECGD will determine the rate of interest to be charged by the banks, case by case, depending upon the buyer's country and credit terms granted; it will usually fall within the range 7½ to 8 per cent fixed for credit of two to five years (the position as at 31st December 1980).

Once again, as with the bills guarantee, the exporter must sign a recourse agreement with ECGD so as to cover ECGD in case it has to pay the bank sums which would not have been paid under the exporter's policy. Contracts valued at £1 million or more may be covered for pre-shipment finance, but not at preferential interest rates. The bank takes a commitment fee from the exporter because the bank's money is committed for a relatively long period; a negotiation fee may also be charged to cover the cost to the bank of the considerable documentation involved. A management fee may also be charged. ECGD will, if required, cover the bank's facility interest on the basis that the department will pay in the event of the bank's being unable to obtain first any such sums from the exporter.

b Comprehensive extended terms banker's guarantee

This facility is designed for the exporter whose business involves the granting of credit of two to five years' duration on frequent occasions under his comprehensive policy. The facility terms for each contract financed in this way are identical to those applicable to the specific bank guarantee in **a** above, and merely enable exporters to obtain an advance agreement for the financing of a whole year's expected medium-term export turnover. Contracts are then approved by the bank individually and the finance drawn as goods are shipped. A fixed interest rate of 7½, 8 or 8½ per cent per annum is charged depending on the buyer's country (the position as at 31st December 1980).

c Foreign currency specific bank guarantee

In the past the finance made available under a specific bank guarantee (and also under a comprehensive extended terms banker's guarantee) has been in sterling only, but contracts expressed in certain foreign currencies have been eligible for financing; in such cases the foreign currency is converted into sterling, at a rate of exchange agreed by the bank, for the purpose of calculating the amount of finance to be provided. Foreign currency specific bank guarantees which allow finance to be made available in certain specified currencies are now available. This guarantee would apply to one-off foreign currency contracts of £1 million equivalent minimum, with credit terms of two years or more. The system, so far as the financing arrangements are concerned, has been designed to operate along similar lines to the buyer credit foreign currency contracts scheme, explained below, except of course that the above captioned facility is supplier credit.

d Buyer credit guarantees

Under the open account, bills, and specific bank guarantees, the banks normally make finance available direct to the UK supplier, these guarantees being referred to as 'supplier credit guarantees'. Under a buyer credit guarantee from ECGD, the loan is made directly to the overseas borrower, and in recent years has usually been in foreign currency. As the UK supplier under the contract completes certain parts of the contract, he is paid cash by the bank, and hence the loan to the overseas borrower is created or increased by the bank. If the loan is in foreign currency the exporter will usually estimate the dates on which he expects to make drawings under the loan and then enter into forward foreign exchange contracts with his bank in order to cover the exchange risk.

In due course the UK supplier has been paid in full in sterling; what remains is the loan in foreign currency by the bank to the borrower. The bank has no recourse to the UK exporter, and charges the borrower a fixed interest rate determined by ECGD. To qualify for a buyer credit guarantee, the contract should be for not less than the equivalent of £1 million. Additionally, ECGD requires that between 15 and 20 per cent of the contract price must be paid to the supplier by the buyer out of his own resources. UK suppliers should contact both ECGD and their bank as soon as possible to find out whether the negotiations with their buyers should proceed on a supplier or buyer credit basis. Under a buyer credit foreign currency facility there are four separate legal agreements which have to be negotiated side by side and concluded before any finance can be provided:

i   The sale/supply contract between the UK supplier and the overseas buyer, covering the goods or services to be provided.

ii   The loan agreement between the lending bank(s) (usually in a consortium), ECGD and the overseas borrower for between 80 and 85 per cent of the contract value.

iii The support agreement between ECGD and the lending banks, which includes a guarantee from ECGD covering non-payment of both principal and interest and also contains an 'interest make-up' arrangement between ECGD and the lending banks.

iv   The premium agreement between ECGD and the exporter under which the latter undertakes to pay the premium on the guarantee for the loan financing his contract.

The support agreement will set out the funding terms of the foreign currency buyer credit scheme. Medium- and longer-term fixtures are often difficult or impossible to obtain on the Euro-currency markets, whereas under normal market circumstances US dollars come on offer for periods of up to one year. It would be extremely difficult in practice to match the longer-term loans required for this type of finance by borrowing funds for the same period.

In order to get round this problem the lending banks will agree to take in Euro-currency deposits of the currency required for a period of between three and twelve months, usually six months. This deposit is to be renewed at the end of each (six-monthly) period until the portion of the medium-term loan to the buyer, which it is funding, matures. The cost of, say, six months, covering finance plus an agreed mark-up for the lending bank of, say, 1 per cent per annum, will come to a figure which may be more or less than that charged for the longer-term finance to the buyer. If the cost of funds for one period of, say, six months plus the mark-up, exceeds the interest earned by the lending banks, ECGD will reimburse the difference. On the other hand if the receipts from the buyer exceed the agreed return to the banks, the latter must pay the difference to ECGD. The lending banks are therefore guaranteed their income and are not exposed to the rising short-term interest rates on the funding deposits costing them more than the return from lending for a much longer period at a fixed rate. ECGD are a party to the loan agreement, and as such become lenders in last resort in the event of the lending banks being unable to obtain renewal of the covering finance. Chapter 10 describes Euro-currency operations. Sterling financing may be considered by ECGD under buyer credit schemes when contract values are less than £5 million, or special circumstances exist.

e   Cover for lines of credit

An ECGD line of credit facility is a buyer credit type of finance with *loan proportions* and interest rates identical to other ECGD buyer credit facilities. Some lines of credit relate solely to particular projects, in which case the borrower is often a government or government agency which determines what contracts are to be financed. Other lines are 'general purpose', in which case the borrower is usually a bank which has to approve the buyer and contract to be financed under the line. Both types can be used for the purpose of financing the purchase of UK goods and/or services, with individual contract values as small as £10,000 being acceptable for financing. Sale contracts for financing must be signed before the credit expires. The UK exporter will receive cash on shipment and the loan being buyer credit by nature is between the UK bank and the overseas borrower.

9.   REFINANCE AND INTEREST MAKE-UP SCHEME

In order to facilitate the provision of finance for exports at preferential fixed interest rates various refinance and interest make-up schemes have been provided by the government. Prior to April 1978, all such finance was provided by the English and Scottish clearing banks and the total sterling finance outstanding in March 1978 was £4,073 million. Although the interest charged to borrowers was mainly in the range $5\frac{1}{2}$ to 8 per cent per annum, the banks received on finance provided from their own resources an agreed rate of interest roughly in line with current commercial interest rates. In addition a proportion of the finance was refinanced – ie, taken over by ECGD. In April 1978 any authorised bank registered in the UK became eligible to provide fixed rate sterling finance for exports and to receive an agreed rate of interest roughly in line with commercial rates.

The refinancing scheme, however, no longer applies to new business entered into on and after 1st April 1980, although the banks are continuing to receive interest make-up support from ECGD for both sterling and foreign currency export lending, enabling them to receive an agreed rate of interest roughly in line with commercial rates. Furthermore, since 1st April 1980 all acceptable banks recognised under the 1979 Banking Act are eligible to act as sole lenders or leaders of syndicates. Additionally, acceptable deposit taking and non-deposit taking institutions as well as recognised banks are eligible to participate as members of lending syndicates.

10.   DIRECT INVESTMENT COVER

The ECGD overseas investment insurance scheme offers protection for UK investors against three major types of political risk – expropriation or nationalisation, war damage, and currency inconvertibility – where the UK investor is unable to convert and transfer overseas profits, earnings or the return from original investment. The standard percentage of loss payable by the insurer is 90 per cent.

To qualify for cover the investment must be new. The scheme does not cover existing projects, although it could be applied to major additions to an existing investment. It is therefore most important that investors apply for cover before committing themselves to the investment. The scheme does not exclude ordinary portfolio investment in a new project catering for those specialist institutions which invest in developing countries; accordingly portfolio investment is permitted subject to an initial minimum of £50,000.

The cover is provided for a minimum of three years and a maximum of 15. It covers both the original investment and, in the case of an equity investment, up to another 100 per cent of the original investment for earnings retained in the business and the remittance of earnings not retained. For loans it covers the principal plus interest up to 100 per cent of the principal. The premium is a flat annual 1 per cent on the current insured amount for all countries, covering all the risks insured. A further one-half per cent commitment premium is charged on the difference between the current insured amount and the maximum insured amount.

PAST EXAMINATION QUESTIONS

1   In the comprehensive guarantee, the Export Credits Guarantee Department specifies the 'risks covered' but also states the losses for which it is not liable. Enumerate the latter.

(Institute of Export)

2   Describe the following guarantees issued by the Export Credits Guarantee Department:
a   comprehensive short-term guarantee
b   comprehensive bill guarantee
c   comprehensive open account guarantee

(Institute of Bankers)

3   Explain the basic function of the Export Credits Guarantee Department, and detail the several ways in which the department helps to make finance available for exporters.

(Institute of Freight Forwarders)

4   If an exporter takes full advantage of the services offered by ECGD, he can not only facilitate bank advances but also save on interest charges. What are these services and what savings can be made? Confine your answer to the export of consumer goods sold on short-term credit.

(Institute of Freight Forwarders)

CHAPTER SEVEN

Trade Finance and Guarantees

1. INTRODUCTION AND GLOSSARY OF TERMS USED IN THIS CHAPTER

The bridging of a cash shortage experienced by an exporter who awaits payment for goods he has shipped may be described as 'export finance'.

The bridging of a cash shortage experienced by an importer who is required to make payment for goods he has bought, achieved by deferring the payment or by staggering payments over a period, may be described as 'import finance'.

'Merchant finance' provides a merchant with credit or cash to fund the period between paying his supplier and receiving payment from the ultimate buyer.

This chapter describes the financing methods adopted by such traders, excluding the ECGD-backed facilities described in the previous chapter, and then discusses the variety of contractual guarantees banks and others can provide to satisfy a wide range of different needs.

A short glossary of terms follows, and this is supplemented in section 5a by a more detailed list of the types of guarantees given by banks.

Aval	undertaking of payment usually given by banks on bills of exchange or promissory notes; the avaliser incurs primary liability for payment at maturity, although he is not a party to the bill prior to avalisation; such 'guarantees' of trade debts are common on the continent and are gaining usage in the UK, particularly in connection with forfaiting business.
Conditional bonds	usually issued by surety companies, although banks will normally provide them when required, but on

Conditional bonds
(continued)

the basis of payment against specific documents only; in certain cases these may be called by the beneficiary only when the principal's default is declared by a previously agreed independent judgment or arbitration.

Counter indemnity

undertaking given by the principal to support the issue of a guarantee by a bank on his behalf.

Discount (bills)

purchase of an accepted term bill of exchange for less than its face value, and its retention until maturity and payment of the face amount, or previous rediscounting.

Eligible paper

bank bills payable in the United Kingdom and accepted by those British and Commonwealth banks the names of which appear on a list published by the Bank of England; the list includes the London and Scottish clearing banks, members of the Accepting Houses Committee, the larger British overseas banks and those Commonwealth banks that have had branches in the City of London for many years, together with certain other banks and some Bank of England customers of long standing; the bills are eligible for rediscount at the Bank of England, and qualify as reserve assets for UK banks up to a maximum of 2 per cent of total eligible liabilities.

Forfaiting

fixed interest finance provided by without recourse negotiation of a series of debts represented by guaranteed obligations maturing at varying dates.

Merchanting

trade involving the purchase of goods or services often from a non-resident of the merchant's country of domicile and the sale of the same often to another non-resident.

On-demand bonds

bonds which give the beneficiary an absolute right of call on first demand without any reason having to be given; beneficiaries have been known to make unfair calls and they are sometimes known as 'suicide bonds'.

Tender

an offer to supply goods and/or services at a quoted price and on stated terms made by one party to another party with a view to a commercial contract being awarded.

2.   FINANCIAL FACILITIES FOR UK EXPORTERS

Exporters may be sole traders, export houses and entrepôt houses, or very large industrial concerns engaged in the manufacture of heavy plant and machinery or the construction of dams, power stations, etc. Their needs obviously differ according to their capital resources; their requirements can range from short-term finance, cash against documents up to two years, through to medium-term credit facilities of up to five years, and long-term facilities of five years or more.

The needs of the smaller concerns can arise in a number of ways. The buyer abroad may require credit terms from the time of arrival of the goods for a period longer than is usually granted to a buyer in the home market. Also the actual period of shipment may take a number of weeks, and either the buyer or the seller will have to finance or pay for the finance of goods in transit. Payment by overseas buyers, therefore, might be on receipt of the goods or at one, two, three or more months after the date of arrival of the carrying vessel at the port of destination. In certain cases the UK exporter may be successful in persuading his buyer to open a sight documentary credit in the exporter's favour which can facilitate a much earlier payment.

The various ways in which an exporter in this short-term context can obtain finance, or virtually immediate payment, while allowing credit to the overseas buyer are as follows:

a   By an application to his bankers for an **overdraft or loan** in the ordinary way, either against normal acceptable security or on an unsecured basis on the strength of his balance sheet. In this latter category the application can be enhanced if it is demonstrated that the overseas debtors in the balance sheet are backed by an ECGD comprehensive policy (see Chapter 6). The deferred terms, or credit, granted to the overseas importer may therefore be arranged by settlement on open account terms, or by drawing a term bill on the buyer forwarded on a D/A collection basis through his bank.

b   By applying to his banker for a **negotiation facility**, a documentary loan or overdraft facility – eg, advances against collections (see Chapter 4). It is emphasised that with a facility of this nature the bankers may rely first on the right of recourse to the drawer as security and secondly on the goods and perhaps the reputation of the drawee established through status enquiries. It is important to understand the difference in the terminology between D/P (documents against payment) and D/A (documents against acceptance). In the first case the bank's cover is constructive control over the goods until payment is made; in the second case the goods are released against the drawee's acceptance of the bill and the risk then rests on the standing of the acceptor, hence the need to know that standing. In this latter context it is of additional benefit to the banker if the risk is diminished through the backing of ECGD cover.

c   An exporter may have a **documentary credit** advised in London in his favour issued by the overseas buyer's banker abroad. If the documentary credit is transferable the credit facility needed by the exporter can be obtained by his transferring the benefit of the credit to the supplier of the goods. Chapter 5, section 17, deals with the mechanics of this operation. A sight credit will enable the exporter to draw cash after shipment and on presentation of the correct shipping documents. Under a documentary acceptance credit the exporter can have the accepted bill of exchange discounted and the proceeds paid over to him. It may be a condition of the underlying sales contract that, in order to be granted the necessary period of credit, the importer is required to meet the discount charges; if this is the case, the exporter is virtually receiving payment on a sight basis (see Chapter 5).

d   An exporter can obtain finance by means of bills of exchange accepted by a clearing bank or merchant bank and sometimes called a **London acceptance credit**. The bank will indicate the limit it is willing to make available to the exporter in this line of credit, and then the exporter can draw clean bills of exchange on the bank to the extent of the facility for a term of 30, 60, 90, 180 days, or longer. By virtue of the name (ie, the standing) of the acceptor, such bills of exchange are readily rediscountable in London to provide immediate funds for the exporter, and to provide liquidity for the accepting bank should it be required. One of the conditions set by the bank for sanctioning such a facility will be that as bills are forwarded to it for acceptance they must be covered by the underlying documentary trade bills drawn on overseas buyers for amounts equal to, or more than, the clean (accommodation) bill of exchange put forward for acceptance, and with their payment dates earlier than the maturity of the accommodation bill (see Chapter 4). This facility should not be confused with a documentary acceptance credit, which is a documentary credit available by a term bill of exchange drawn by the beneficiary on the issuing or advising bank (see (c) above).

e   In order to promote exports the **Export Credits Guarantee Department sponsors two short-term credit schemes**. The first covers export finance for a period from 'cash against documents up to two years' for the overseas buyer, and can be obtained by exporters through their bankers. By this scheme, once his application has been approved by his bank and ECGD, the exporter can have bills or promissory notes purchased by his bank, if of a tenor of up to two years, the bank having as cover an ECGD comprehensive bill guarantee. The second scheme covers export finance for a period from 'cash against documents up to six months', and is known as the comprehensive open account guarantee. A fuller description of both schemes may be found in Chapter 6. Bank advances under both may be covered up to 100 per cent by the ECGD guarantees.

f   Section 15 of Chapter 1 outlines how the exporter can turn to **factoring** organisations for their various services, which include the provision of immediate cash without recourse, against documentary bills covering goods sold on credit terms. Criticism has been levelled in the past against the factor's insistence upon his interest being revealed to the overseas buyer. To meet this criticism another form of finance has been developed known as 'undisclosed non-recourse finance'. In this instance, instead of selling the goods directly to the overseas buyer on credit terms, the exporter sells them for cash to the financing organisation concerned. The exporter is then appointed as agent for the delivery of the goods to the overseas buyer and for the collection of proceeds in due course. The part played by the financing organisation remains undisclosed, and the exporter's direct relationship with the buyer is undisturbed. In the main, factoring companies offer their services only to customers with a minimum export turnover of £50,000.

g   Manufacturers who are required to provide deferred credit terms, with payments spread over up to, say, eight years, and who wish to obtain finance for the buyer without recourse to themselves, might consider **forfaiting**. This involves the non-recourse negotiation of a series of promissory notes, or occasionally avalised bills of exchange and sometimes guaranteed book debt obligations, at an all-in fixed rate. It may also include the bank's commitment to provide in advance an agreed/fixed rate for financing obligations to be presented in due course by the manufacturer, in effect a forward quotation of a negotiation rate, for which an additional commitment fee is sometimes taken. The forfaiting bank in making an outright purchase assumes complete responsibility; the political and economic risks are included. Indeed so does a bank confirming a documentary credit assume complete responsibility. The period of credit over which the bank will provide finance will depend largely upon its view of the political/economic scene in the buyer's country. It is normal practice to insist upon receipt of the buyer's promissory notes duly avalised by an acceptable bank, or other guaranteed obligations, before purchasing them. A warranty may sometimes be taken from the manufacturer that the contract of sale has been completed to the buyer's satisfaction and that payment is due and will be made at maturity in transferable funds. Forfaiting provides the following advantages for the exporter:

- unburdening the balance sheet of the exporter from receivables and/or contingent liabilities position, which, with medium-term trade credit extensions, can involve considerable and sharply increasing amounts
- improvement of liquidity (each of these two advantages results in an increased credit capacity for the exporter)
- no effect on overdraft and other credit limits granted by banks
- avoidance of losses which can arise out of the retained risk position under government or private insurance coverage schemes and of impediments to liquidity during the customary period for study of the exporter's claim
- avoidance of the risks of higher financing costs arising from increasing interest rates
- shifting of the exchange rate fluctuation risks
- removal of all administrative and collection problems and related risks

Exporters, confronted with the increasing demand for favourable credit terms for their sales, will find a valuable and flexible instrument in the possibilities of forfaiting, particularly as discount rates can be agreed in advance of final contractual terms concluded with buyers. Forfaiting can provide a fast, flexible financing and payment vehicle, particularly appropriate for contracts with EEC buyers where ECGD-backed finance is not available. It has developed on the continent with the financing of off-shore obligations rather than in the UK, partly as a result of the question of the tax liability the bank might incur on the unrealised profits on long-date obligations held in portfolio. The settlement of the point in 1978 by the House of Lords in the International Commercial Bank case ([1978] 1 All ER 754), and the abolition of UK exchange controls in 1979, has made forfaiting a more viable form of financing for UK banks to undertake.

h Faced with a request for credit terms, an exporter could turn to the UK member of a **hire purchase** credit union (see Chapter 1, section 15). Assuming there is a member in the importer's country, such an organisation could lighten the exporter's burden by providing the importer with a required credit and paying cash to the exporter. The arrangement in effect converts an import on credit terms into a domestic hire purchase agreement.

i On the question of export finance for larger contracts on a medium- or long-term basis, reference should be made to ECGD facilities in Chapter 6. Euro-currency loans can also be arranged, and further details are given in Chapter 10.

j Trade credit. If the importer pays in advance, he is, of course, financing the exporter and probably requires a discount for doing so (see Chapter 2, section 3).

3. FINANCIAL FACILITIES FOR UK IMPORTERS

Finance for UK importers may be provided through the following facilities (dealt

with at (a) to (f) below):
- loan or overdraft
- loan against goods (produce loan)
- clean acceptance credit facility
- documentary acceptance credit
- hire purchase
- trade credit (provided by the supplier) settlement by means of open account, clean collection, or documentary collection D/A

a   Loan or overdraft

Unsecured lendings on a fluctuating overdraft or specific loan basis are common when the importer is of undoubted standing. The limits agreed upon will enable the customer to include payments made to foreign exporters in respect of goods entering the UK. Proceeds from the sale of these goods, when paid into the account, will reduce the loan or overdraft. Even when the customer is 'undoubted' control should be exercised to ensure that the proceeds of each transaction are credited to the account; the current account should fluctuate from debit to credit regularly.

b   Loan against goods (produce loan)

Importers and merchants dealing in basic commodities such as wool, foodstuffs, non-ferrous metals and other raw materials, who require finance for transactions which may tend to be large in proportion to their resources, may be granted a produce loan. This may be arranged as a single loan or on a revolving limit for a number of smaller transactions over an agreed period. The points the lending bank will consider before agreeing to such an advance are as follows:

i   Knowledge of the borrowing customer. His integrity must be undoubted, his ability in business must be sound, and his past record of trading and conducting his account fully satisfactory.

ii   Knowledge of the proposition. How much is required? As a rule the overall amount to be lent should not exceed the proprietor's stake in his business, though the proportion advanced is often higher than for other propositions. The bank may lend a proportion of whichever is the lower of the cost or market value of the goods, retaining a margin for each transaction. The amount of the margin retained will depend primarily upon whether or not the goods have been pre-sold to an undoubted buyer on whom a good status report is held. Advances against goods that have not been pre-sold will tend to attract a higher margin than when repayment of the advance is assured.

For how long is the lending required? As a generalisation, banks do not wish to lend against stock that does not turn over regularly, and a produce advance should be self-liquidating within between seven days and three months from the sale of the goods. The source of repayment will be the sale of the security (goods), and, as mentioned previously, if the ultimate buyer is known and considered certain to pay for the goods as agreed, repayment is virtually guaranteed. Where the goods have not been pre-sold the lending bank must rely upon the business ability of the customer to find a satisfactory buyer to take them up.

iii   Knowledge of the goods. In the event of the borrower being unable to pay and the ultimate buyer (if there is one) defaulting, the lending bank will look to the sale of the goods to obtain reimbursement. The following questions must be answered:

* are the goods perishable or durable? If perishable, a buyer must be found quickly and the risk of total loss may be considered
* do the prices of the goods locally and internationally fluctuate widely? If so, assuming the worst, the forced sale value of the goods will probably be at their lowest
* do the goods require any special handling or storage facilities if they are not taken up immediately upon arrival? If so, it is necessary to ensure that adequate facilities exist
* are there special market conditions relating to the method by which the goods are bought and sold? If there are, the bank should know of the market constraints and the way in which the goods may be disposed of should it become necessary

iv   Whilst any conventional security may be offered and accepted, it is usual for the security for a produce advance initially to take the form of the shipping documents while the goods are in transit to the UK. As soon as the vessel arrives, if the loan is not repaid at that time, the goods themselves will probably become the bank's security. If a freight forwarder, acting for the bank, is handed the documents required for clearing the goods with instructions to warehouse them in the bank's name, the goods themselves will remain the bank's security. Finally, the goods may be released to the customer for delivery to the ultimate buyer. The bank would then authorise the warehouse, using a delivery order, to release the goods to the borrowing customer, probably against the latter's trust receipt in favour of the bank.

v   The following steps should be taken to ensure that the bank's position is covered:
* status enquiries should be taken up on all parties concerned with the transaction: the seller, the ultimate buyer (if known), any forwarding agent or warehouse used to move or store the goods
* sighting of sale invoices on the ultimate buyer, if pre-sold
* the latest balance sheet and accounts should be obtained from the borrower
* sighting of an import licence, unless the transaction is under open general licence
* a general letter of hypothecation or letter of pledge should be taken from the customer. Both these documents should give the bank the right to sell the goods in the event of default – ie, specific mention should be made in these documents of the right of sale in the event of default. A *pledge* offers direct security for one or more transactions lodged by the customer from time to time. The bank is entitled to exclusive possession of the property until the debt is discharged; ownership under a pledge remains with the customer, but the bank may sell the goods after repayment of the loan has been demanded and refused. A *general letter of hypothecation* gives the bank the right to dispose of the goods immediately without first making demand on the customer for repayment of the loan. These documents provide security so long as the bank holds the goods or documents relating to them.
* shipping documents should be lodged and should include a full set of endorsed bills of lading or a document of movement showing the goods consigned to the bank's order, and an insurance policy or certificate indicating that the goods are adequately insured
* these will be held by the bank informally pending arrival of the vessel, and a diary note will be made to ensure that instructions are given to the customer

or forwarding agent to take delivery of the goods immediately they arrive and warehouse them in the bank's name

* the advance is made by loan and is therefore simple to control
* when the vessel arrives the shipping documents may either be handed to a freight forwarder or to the customer for the purpose of warehousing the goods in the bank's name. If the customer is to be handed the bank's security it will be against a trust receipt in which the customer undertakes to warehouse the goods in the bank's name and deliver to the bank the warehouse receipt or warrants obtained. The customer's integrity is of great importance in this type of transaction as the agreement of the borrower to comply with the bank's instructions is the only security held at this time (see also Chapter 3, section 6 f)
* the goods must be adequately insured whilst in the warehouse, and the customer must agree to pay the premiums and all warehouse charges
* control over the warehoused goods is necessary to ensure that one particular consignment does not remain unsold, and that charges are, indeed, paid up
* goods will have to be released from the warehouse for delivery to the ultimate buyer, and a trust receipt should again be taken if a delivery order on the warehouse is given to the customer. This time the trust receipt will stipulate that payment of gross receipts from the sale of the goods must be handed to the bank within a stated number of days

c   Clean acceptance credit facility

Such accommodation bill finance for the importer can be provided when settlement is on an inward bill for collection or open account facility. The importer may be required to pay for his shipping documents on a sight basis and will not receive payment for the goods sold until some time afterwards, say 80 days. The importer will draw an accommodation bill on his bank at 90 days' sight and obtain the bank's acceptance. The bill is then discounted and the discount proceeds are used to pay for the sight inward collection. At maturity the holder of the bill will present it to the bank for payment, but by then the bank should have received the proceeds of the sale of the goods from the importer. Normally a letter of pledge would be taken from the customer by the bank; later a trust receipt, if documents and/or goods are to be held by the customer, might be considered appropriate additional security.

d   Documentary acceptance credit

A documentary credit may be used to provide credit for importers. Such acceptance documentary credits are dealt with in greater detail in Chapter 5.

e   Hire purchase

An importer may obtain finance in the form of a hire purchase agreement arranged through an international credit union or branch network of the finance house in the UK. In settlement for the goods imported he will pay the instalments due directly to the UK hire purchase company. Hire purchase credit restrictions imposed from time to time tend to limit the extent of this type of finance.

f   Trade credit

Trade credit may be provided by the exporter in the form of 'open account' settlement, or by means of any term bill drawn on the buyer, provided documents are sent directly or are released on a D/A basis.

4. FINANCIAL FACILITIES FOR MERCHANTING TRADE

Merchanting or third party trade, so far as a UK resident is concerned, comprises those transactions where goods, though bought and sold by a UK resident, are not actually imported into and exported from the UK. The alternative methods of financing are dealt with below.

i   *Trade credit:* the merchant's ideal situation is for the ultimate buyer to pay him before he has to pay the supplier, when no bank assistance would be required. But merchanting finance is normally needed in order to bridge the gap when the merchant pays the supplier first, and gets his money later from the ultimate buyer.

ii   *Overdraft:* merchants should take great care before borrowing weak currencies which often are available at relatively high interest rates (see Chapter 8, section 7 b). Overdrafts provide the merchant with what he often thinks is the greatest flexibility so far as repayment is concerned. This is an important matter for the borrower, who would not wish to pay more interest than he must. There is no doubt that an overdraft may be repaid by simply crediting the current account as soon as proceeds from the ultimate buyer are received. Repayment to an equal or lesser extent may be provided under the other financing techniques mentioned (see the table at the end of this section). Merchants who have a sizeable turnover may be able to operate an invoicing policy to minimise the cost of a foreign currency overdraft, by making payment in weaker currencies bought forward at a discount and by invoicing in strong currencies sold forward at a premium, depending, of course, on what they can negotiate in these respects with the supplier and with the ultimate buyer (see Chapter 8, section 7, on invoicing policy).

iii   *Fixed term loan:* this may be provided, subject to market availability and market practice, for periods ranging from overnight to five years, depending upon the choice of currency and amount required. The loans may be arranged on a fixed interest basis for the entire period of the loan, or on a floating rate basis whereby the rate is changed at predetermined intervals to accord with current market interest rate levels. Loans may be for any amount, but the larger borrowings may normally be funded directly from Euro-currency market sources and thereby obtain the benefit of finer 'wholesale' rates (see Chapter 10). It is a condition of this type of lending that early repayment requests be resisted. However, it may be possible to break such a loan on payment of a penalty commensurate with the return on the lending which may be denied to the bank. This is quite likely to occur if interest rates have fallen in the meantime, or there exists a positive yield curve in the currency borrowed (lower interest rates for the short periods, rising in steps towards the longer interest periods; the funds could only then be re-employed at a lower return for the period of the original loan remaining).

iv   *Trade bill finance:* the supplier might draw a term trade bill of exchange on the merchant. The merchant then accepts the bill and his bank discounts it as a good trade bill, enabling the merchant to remit the proceeds to the supplier straightaway in settlement. The payment from the ultimate buyer, it is to be hoped, will be received before this trade bill matures. The disadvantage here is that the supplier might not wish to incur the contingent liability on the paper he is asked to draw. The bill is discounted as a trade bill, at a higher discount cost than that for a fine bank bill.

v   *Negotiation:* at the time the supplier requires to be paid, a merchant acting as a middleman may draw his trade bill on the ultimate buyer and give it to his bank for negotiation. The negotiated proceeds in foreign currency may be used to pay the supplier in settlement, and the bank will forward the bill to its agent in the buyer's country for collection. The merchant will be charged for the period the negotiating bank is out of funds (see Chapter 4, section 19).

vi   *Bank accommodation acceptance facility:* in order to fund a merchant's cash flow between settlement with his suppliers and eventual receipt of funds from his buyers, the merchant may draw bills of exchange on his bank under a clean bank accommodation acceptance facility. After the bank has accepted the bill it may be discounted for cash, and at maturity the merchant may draw another bill on the bank under the same facility which may also be discounted to provide funds to meet the payment due on the maturing bill drawn earlier.

vii   *Documentary acceptance credit:* this is generally recognised as a more expensive method of financing, since the credit will provide the supplier with a bank's undertaking to pay for documents presented in order. It should be stressed that as soon as the issuing bank opens a credit it is on risk until any drafts drawn on it have reached maturity and are paid; it will make no difference to the bank's position whether discounting takes place or not (see Chapter 5, sections 6 and 17).

Because of the considerable variety of merchanting business, it is necessary sometimes to structure a facility to meet the individual requirements of a merchanting customer. It is possible to provide merchants with combinations of, or developments on, the financing techniques listed above.

Summary table

Facility	Is early repayment allowed?	Is acceptance commission charged?	Usual pricing basis	Recommended currency
Trade bill	Yes, by rebate	No	Trade bill discount rate	The major trading currencies
Overdraft	Yes, credit currency account	No	Foreign currency overdraft rate	The major trading currencies
Fixed term loan	No, except as agreed under penalty	No	London Euro-currency market rates	As required
Bank accommodation acceptance line	Yes, by rebate	Yes	Fine bank bill rate	The major trading currencies
Negotiation	Yes, without penalty	No	Foreign bill negotiation rate	As required
Documentary acceptance credit	Yes, by rebate	Yes	Fine bank bill rate	The major trading currencies
Forfaiting	Not applicable	No, but with avalisation or guarantee charge	Straight discount or yield to maturity, interest being compounded annually, semi-annually or quarterly	US$ Dm Sw. Fc H. Fl Sterling F. Fc

5. GUARANTEES GIVEN BY BANKS

a Summary of the types of guarantees given by banks

i *Tender*
Exhibits 1 and 2, pages
255-6 and see (b) below

Given in support of a customer's tender, as assurance of the intention of the customer to sign the contract if his tender is accepted. Usually a request to a bank abroad to issue against the UK bank's indemnity. Counter indemnity held from customer.

ii *Performance*
Exhibits 3 and 4, pages 1
257-8 and see (c) below

Given in support of a customer's obligation to fulfil a contractual commitment. Normally issued before the cancellation of the tender guarantee, although tender guarantees are sometimes extended and amended to become performance bonds.

iii *Overdraft/loan*
Exhibit 5, page 259; and
see (d) below

Given in support of loans or overdrafts, granted by overseas banks, usually to overseas subsidiary companies of the principal. May be in sterling or foreign currency for various periods, usually for shorter rather than for long-term transactions.

iv *Guarantees for the refund of advance payments and progress payments*
Exhibits 6 and 7, pages
260-61 and see (e) below

Given in support of advance payments; a variety of performance guarantee. This is a safeguard whereby the seller arranges for his bank to give the beneficiary its undertaking to refund the amount advanced if goods are not shipped or the contract not complied with. Such guarantees may provide for the liability of the bank to be reduced (usually *pro rata*) with past performance of the contract in respect of which the guarantee is given.

v *Retention money guarantees*

Given in support of contracts which call for, say, 10 per cent of each payment to be withheld until the project is completed and accepted by the contracting buyer, sometimes a year after completion. The guarantee enables the contractor to receive the total amount of each payment whilst assuring the buyer that the funds will be callable if the contractor is unable to fulfil his obligations.

vi *Customs guarantees relating to the temporary import of goods without payment of duty*

Given to customs authorities in lieu of cash deposits in respect of import duty on goods temporarily imported. When the goods are returned the guarantees are released, but if the goods remain in that country the guarantees will be implemented.

vii	*Travel carnets*	Given in respect of travellers who wish to import their cars, permitting them to enter that country without payment of import duty.
viii	*Salvage*	Given to tug owners, for example, who have a lien over a vessel towed into port pending Lloyd's Committee's arbitration findings and the making of final payment. It will remain in force until payment is effected.
ix	*Bail bonds*	Given to the court in order to secure the release of a vessel under arrest. The warrant of arrest 'nailed to a vessel's mast', is usually issued to obtain redress for, for example, damage to port facilities by a vessel. The bond is released after the money is paid.
x	*General average* See Chapter 3, section 4 **e** *v*	Every shipper runs the risk of an act of general average being declared over a vessel and its contents in which he has goods. Although covered by insurance, the shipper has to contribute, either by means of a cash deposit or by his bank giving an average bond, before his goods will be released. The bond will be released after settlement under the insurance policy for the contributions payable by the shipper for loss suffered by the vessel and/or cargo.
xi	*Indemnities* Exhibit 8, page 262	* Given to shipping companies in respect of absence of bills of lading, to enable importers to take delivery of the goods and avoid demurrage charges.
	See Chapter 5, section 14	* Given to banks under documentary credits for discrepancies in documents presented.
xii	*Stand-by credits* See Chapter 5, section 25	Payment may be under a documentary credit calling for a simple receipt or for a draft or claim to be supported by a statement that the seller has not fulfilled a contract or that a loan, etc, has not been repaid. This facility is often used as a substitute for performance type guarantees.
xiii	*Avalisation*	Given by banks on bills of exchange or promissory notes which have the effect of guaranteeing a trade debt. The bank is normally not a party to the bill or note prior to avalisation by which it makes itself primarily liable for payment thereon at maturity.

xiii Avalisation (continued)   Common on the continent and slowly gaining usage in this country, although not as yet recognised in English law.

b   Tender guarantees *(Exhibits 1 and 2, pages 255-6)*

A tender guarantee is an undertaking, usually given by a bank or surety company at the request of the tenderer (supplier/contractor) or his bank on behalf of the supplier/contractor. In the event of default (failing to accept the contract if awarded to the tenderer) the guarantor provides within the limits of the guarantee to make payment of a stated sum of money to the beneficiary (the party inviting the tender). The object of the tender guarantee is to assure the buyer inviting tenders that he will not be wasting his efforts and money in evaluating tenders from various countries and in placing the contract; he also wants to protect himself from any damage that may possibly result if he loses offers from other companies by offering a contract to party who does not keep his word.

The tender guarantee is issued by the supplier/contractor's bank sometimes directly to the buyer/employer or indirectly through a bank in the buyer/employer's country. It stipulates that the bank is liable up to the stated amount on the guarantee submitted and that it will pay the total amount of the guarantee 'on first demand' should the beneficiary of the guarantee inform it that the supplier/contractor has failed to accept the contract if awarded to him. A counter indemnity is invariably taken by the supplier's/contractor's bank issuing the guarantee. The bank's liability depends upon the precise wording of the guarantee. (This applies not only to tender guarantees but also to support any of the other guarantees listed from *i* to *x* in (a) above.)

In 1977 ECGD introduced cover against foreign exchange risks encountered when an exporter of capital goods places a tender for a contract in a foreign currency. This is of particular relevance to exporters undertaking major projects overseas who may find that several months may elapse between the time they tender and the time a contract is signed (if indeed it ever is awarded to them). Cover is provided to guarantee the sterling receipts even if the value of the quoted foreign currency falls during this critical period. This is an area of contingent risk since the contract might never be awarded to the exporter. As such, prior to October 1979, the banks in the UK could not provide forward exchange cover as there existed no firm underlying commercial commitment. Now, however, this restriction has been lifted, and UK banks may provide forward exchange cover for this or any other reason.

The system operates as follows: the exporter pays ECGD a flat fee of £5,000 at the time he tenders for the contract. If the contract is signed subsequently a further premium is payable according to the duration of ECGD's exposure to risk and the sterling amount guaranteed. The minimum cover is for a three month period and the maximum is for nine months. ECGD's cover is limited to a maximum depreciation of foreign currency of 25 per cent, and the exporter has to bear the risk of a three per cent fall himself; in addition ECGD will retain any gains that may be made. After the contract is signed the exporter obtains forward exchange cover from his bank (although this may now be arranged before the contract is signed if the exporter desires; of course he might not get the commercial contract and then be left with a forward contract to close-out).

c   Performance bonds *(Exhibits 3 and 4, pages 257-8)*

If a buyer/employer requires confirmation, in the event of the supplier/contractor failing to meet his commitments within the period he has undertaken in the contract, that money will be forthcoming from a third party source, the buyer/employer might request the issue of a performance bond. Everything said above about the tender guarantee, in form and contents, also applies to the performance bond; only the risks are different. The bank guarantees that the buyer/employer will be paid for any claims he may have for non-completion or faulty completion by the supplier/contractor up to the total amount guaranteed, if claims are made within the validity and terms of the guarantee.

d   Overdraft or loan guarantees *(Exhibit 5, page 259)*

This guarantee is issued to support local lending by a bank in the borrower's country. The lending bank is asked to advance a specific sum of money by loan or overdraft, the repayment of which, and sometimes interest, is covered in the guarantee. Such guarantees are accompanied by a request to the lending bank to ensure that any borrowing by a corporate beneficiary is *intra vires* the powers of the borrower. It is a normal requirement that a certified copy of the borrower's board resolution, suitably worded, be sighted by the lending bank.

e   Guarantees for the refund of advance payments and progress payments *(Exhibits 6 and 7, pages 260-61)*

Advance payments are quite usual in foreign trade when the export is goods of a capital nature specially produced for the buyer and/or the provision of services – examples being power stations, steelworks, bridges, ships, etc. They are also a feature of transactions involving consumer products from time to time. The normal advance payment is 10 per cent of the contract amount, but may be more, and is usually due on receipt of the guarantee. Further payments may follow at predetermined times, either in equal periodic payments or at specified stages of production. If the buyer/employer wishes to have security for his advance payments he asks the supplier/contractor for a guarantee issued by a bank in the supplier/contractor's country or in his own country. The bank guarantees that the buyer/employer will be paid for any claims he may have for non-repayment by the supplier/contractor up to the total amount guaranteed if claims are made within the validity and terms of the guarantee. The guarantee may, of course, provide for *pro rata* reduction in the amount of the guarantee with part performance of the contract.

It is preferable that the validity of the advance payment guarantee should be after the delivery date agreed between buyer and seller, so that the buyer can declare his claim under the guarantee after the contractual delivery date, but before the guarantee expires. To avoid misunderstandings the bank issuing the guarantee should ensure that the validity date (the latest date on which the guarantee may be called) is precisely defined in the guarantee.

f   ECGD performance bond cover

The great size of many export contracts, requiring performance bonds to be issued for between 10 and 20 per cent of the contract value, has had an impact upon the creditworthiness of some of the largest companies, and their bankers have tended to 'contain' lending limits accordingly, causing some exporters to have serious liquidity problems.

The immense contingent liabilities that have to be written into their balance sheets as footnotes resulting from outstanding guarantees is the principal factor contributing to reduction of creditworthiness. ECGD's scheme to ease this problem involves those contracts which are worth £250,000 or more and are sold on a cash or very short-term credit basis. It is recommended that the exporters contact their bank and ECGD at the earliest possible time in negotiations, and certainly before entering into any commitments, since ECGD will be prepared to consider applications to indemnify the bank for issuing tender guarantees and advance payment guarantees as well as performance bonds. Under its indemnity ECGD will reimburse the guarantor bank for the full amount of any call on the guarantee. Accordingly ECGD take a right of recourse against the exporter in a recourse agreement. The exporter, in the event of a call, will be expected to reimburse ECGD immediately, and can expect to be refunded only if he can prove that the default was outside his control or that he was not in default under the terms of the contract.

Under the majority of ECGD guarantees (see Chapter 6) it is possible for an exporter to obtain insurance against the unfair calling of performance bonds. This is done by a rider to the insurance policy and payment of an additional premium. The cover is for 100 per cent of any loss, provided that the exporter can show afterwards that he was not in default of the contract or that his failure to perform the contract was due to specified events outside his control.

6.   'UNIFORM RULES FOR CONTRACT GUARANTEES'

International Chamber of Commerce Publication No. 325 (1978)

This code was written with a view to securing uniformity of practice between the parties involved, and endeavours to find a fair balance between their respective interests without losing sight of the commercial purpose of the guarantee. The full text of the 11 Articles is reproduced here.

Scope

Article 1

1   These rules apply to any guarantee, bond, indemnity, surety or similar undertaking, however named or described ('guarantee'), which states that it is subject to the Uniform Rules for Tender, Performance and Repayment Guarantees ('contract guarantees') of the International Chamber of Commerce (Publication No. 325) and are binding upon all parties thereto unless otherwise expressly stated in the guarantee or any amendment thereto.

2   Where any of these rules is contrary to a provision of the law applicable to the guarantee from which the parties cannot derogate that provision prevails.

Definition

Article 2

For the purposes of these rules:

(a)   'tender guarantee' means an undertaking given by a bank, insurance company or other party ('the guarantor') at the request of a tenderer ('the principal') or given on the instructions of a bank, insurance company, or other party so requested by the principal ('the instructing party') to a party inviting tenders ('the beneficiary') whereby the guarantor undertakes – in the event of default by the principal in the obligations resulting from the submission of the tender – to make payment to the beneficiary within the limits of a stated sum of money;

(b)   'performance guarantee' means an undertaking given by a bank, insurance company or other party ('the guarantor') at the request of a supplier of goods or services or other contractor ('the principal') or given on the instructions of a bank, insurance company, or other party so requested by the principal ('the instructing party') to a buyer or to an employer ('the beneficiary') whereby the guarantor undertakes – in the event of default by the principal in due performance of the terms of a contract between the principal and the beneficiary ('the contract') – to make payment to the beneficiary within the limits of a stated sum of money or, if the guarantee so provides, at the guarantor's option, to arrange for performance of the contract;

(c)   'repayment guarantee' means an undertaking given by a bank, insurance company or other party ('the guarantor') at the request of a supplier of goods or services or other contractor ('the principal') or given on the instructions of a bank, insurance company or other party so requested by the principal ('the instructing party') to a buyer or to an employer ('the beneficiary') whereby the guarantor undertakes – in the event of default by the principal to repay in accordance with the terms and conditions of a contract between the principal and the beneficiary ('the contract') any sum or sums advanced or paid by the beneficiary to the principal and not otherwise repaid – to make payment to the beneficiary within the limits of a stated sum of money.

Liability of the guarantor to the beneficiary
Article 3

1   The guarantor is liable to the beneficiary only in accordance with the terms and conditions specified in the guarantee and these rules and up to an amount not exceeding that stated in the guarantee.
2   The amount of liability stated in the guarantee shall not be reduced by reason of any partial performance of the contract, unless so specified in the guarantee.
3   The guarantor may rely only on those defences which are based on the terms and conditions specified in the guarantee or are allowed under these rules.

Last date for claim
Article 4

If a guarantee does not specify a last date by which a claim must have been received by the guarantor, such last date ('expiry date') is deemed to be:
(a)   in the case of a tender guarantee, six months from the date of the guarantee;
(b)   in the case of a performance guarantee, six months from the date specified in the contract for delivery or completion or any extension thereof, or one month after the expiry of any maintenance period (guarantee period) provided for in the contract if such maintenance period is expressly covered by the performance guarantee;
(c)   in the case of a repayment guarantee, six months from the date specified in the contract for delivery or completion or any extension thereof.

If the expiry date falls on a non-business day, the expiry date is extended until the first following business day.

Expiry of guarantee
Article 5

1   If no claim has been received by the guarantor on or before the expiry date or if any claim arising under the guarantee has been settled in full satisfaction of all the rights of the beneficiary thereunder, the guarantee ceases to be valid.

2   Notwithstanding the provisions of Article 4, in the case of tender guarantees:
   (a)   upon acceptance by the beneficiary of the tender and the award of the contract to the principal or, if so provided for in the written contract, or if no contract has been signed and it is so provided for in the tender, the production by the principal of a performance guarantee or, if no such guarantee is required, the signature by the principal of the contract, the tender guarantee issued on his behalf ceases to be valid;
   (b)   a tender guarantee also ceases to be valid if and when the contract to which it relates is awarded to another tenderer, whether or not that tenderer meets the requirements referred to in paragraph 2 (a) of this Article;
   (c)   a tender guarantee also ceases to be valid in the event of the beneficiary expressly declaring that he does not intend to place a contract.

Return of guarantee
Article 6
When a guarantee has ceased to be valid in accordance with its own terms and conditions or with these rules, retention of the documents embodying the guarantee does not in itself confer any rights upon the beneficiary, and the document should be returned to the guarantor without delay.

Amendments to contracts and guarantees
Article 7
1   A tender guarantee is valid only in respect of the original tender submitted by the principal and does not apply in the case of any amendment thereto, nor is it valid beyond the expiry date specified in the guarantee or provided for by these rules, unless the guarantor has given notice in writing or by cable or telegram or telex to the beneficiary that the guarantee so applies or that the expiry date has been extended.
2   A performance guarantee or a repayment guarantee may stipulate that it shall not be valid in respect of any amendment to the contract, or that the guarantor be notified of any such amendment for his approval. Failing such a stipulation, the guarantee is valid in respect of the obligations of the principal as expressed in the contract and any amendment thereto. However, the guarantee shall not be valid in excess of the amount or beyond the expiry date specified in the guarantee or provided for by these rules, unless the guarantor has given notice in writing or by cable or telegram or telex to the beneficiary that the amount has been increased to a stated figure or that the expiry date has been extended.
3   Any amendment made by the guarantor in the terms and conditions of the guarantee shall be effective in respect of the beneficiary only if agreed to by the beneficiary and in respect of the principal or the instructing party, as the case may be, only if agreed to by the principal or the instructing party, as the case may be.

Submission of claim
Article 8
1   A claim under a guarantee shall be made in writing or by cable or telegram or telex to be received by the guarantor not later than on the expiry date specified in the guarantee or provided for by these rules.
2   On receipt of a claim the guarantor shall notify the principal or the instructing

party, as the case may be, without delay, of such claim and of any documentation received.

3 A claim shall not be honoured unless:
  (a) it has been made and received as required by paragraph 1 of this Article; and
  (b) it is supported by such documentation as is specified in the guarantee or in these rules;
  (c) such documentation is presented within the period of time after the receipt of a claim specified in the guarantee, or, failing such a specification, as soon as practicable, or, in the case of documentation of the beneficiary himself, at the latest within six months from the receipt of a claim.

In any event, a claim shall not be honoured if the guarantee has ceased to be valid in accordance with its own terms or with these rules.

Documentation to support claim
Article 9
If a guarantee does not specify the documentation to be produced in support of a claim or merely specifies only a statement of claim by the beneficiary, the beneficiary must submit:
  (a) in the case of a tender guarantee, his declaration that the principal's tender has been accepted and that the principal has then either failed to sign the contract or has failed to submit a performance guarantee as provided for in the tender, and his declaration of agreement, addressed to the principal, to have any dispute on any claim by the principal for payment to him by the beneficiary of all or part of the amount paid under the guarantee settled by a judicial or arbitral tribunal as specified in the tender documents or, if not so specified or otherwise agreed upon, by arbitration in accordance with the Rules of the ICC Court of Arbitration or with the UNCITRAL Arbitration Rules, at the option of the principal;
  (b) in the case of a performance guarantee or of a repayment guarantee, either a court decision or an arbitral award justifying the claim, or the approval of the principal in writing to the claim and the amount to be paid.

Applicable law
Article 10
If a guarantee does not indicate the law by which it is to be governed, the applicable law is that of the guarantor's place of business. If the guarantor has more than one place of business, the applicable law is that of the branch which issued the guarantee.

Settlement of disputes
Article 11
1 Any dispute arising in connection with the guarantee may be referred to arbitration by agreement between the guarantor and the beneficiary, either in accordance with the Rules of the ICC Court of Arbitration, the UNCITRAL Arbitration Rules or such other rules of arbitration as may be agreed between the guarantor and the beneficiary.
2 If a dispute between the guarantor and the beneficiary which touches upon the rights and obligations of the principal or the instructing party is referred to arbitration, the principal or the instructing party shall have the right to intervene in such arbitral proceedings.

3   If the guarantor and the beneficiary have not agreed to arbitration or to the jurisdiction of any specific court, any dispute between them relating to the guarantee shall be settled exclusively by the competent court of the country of the guarantor's place of business or, if the guarantor has more than one place of business, by the competent court of the country of his main place of business or, at the option of the beneficiary, by the competent court of the country of the branch which issued the guarantee.

The copyright of Uniform Rules for Contract Guarantees, *Publication No. 325 (1978), is held by the International Chamber of Commerce, and copies of the publication are available from the British National Committee of the ICC, Centre Point, 103 New Oxford Street, London WC1A 1QB, and from the Publications Division, ICC Headquarters, 38 Cours Albert 1er – 75008 Paris, or from the ICC's national committees in over 50 countries.*

7.   THE HARBOTTLE CASE

In R. D. Harbottle (Mercantile) Limited v National Westminster Bank Ltd and Others, 1977, the exporter, Harbottle, contested that payment by Natwest of a claim made on a performance bond was not a justifiable payment since Harbottle alleged that the basis of the claim was false. Natwest had issued the performance bond to the extent of five per cent of the contract amount, in accordance with the express consent and wishes of the exporter. Payment was to be made on first demand, and Natwest was given Harbottle's counter indemnity and authority to debit their account on first demand. Following a dispute between Harbottle and their Egyptian buyers, demand was made. It was held that despite any differences between the exporter and the overseas buyer, which no doubt would have to be settled by litigation or arbitration, the bank's obligations stood separate. Harbottle had taken the risk of this with the unconditional wording of the performance bond and indemnity. The court held that as the bank had pledged its word, and in the absence of any evidence of fraud, there was no reason why the bank should not pay.

This case and another, Edward Owen Engineering Limited v Barclays Bank International Limited, 1977, which again involved the calling of an on-demand bond, highlighted the absolute obligation of the guarantor to pay such a bond on first demand. The majority of contractual guarantees issued are of the on-demand variety, which buyers naturally prefer to have. The alternative, a conditional bond, is not unlike a documentary credit, inasmuch as the beneficiary of the guarantee (in this case the buyer) may only obtain monetary redress from the guarantor (bank or surety company) against documentary evidence that payment is due.

Guarantees issued by banks abroad, especially in the Middle East, usually incorporate an automatic extension at the request of the beneficiary – a 'pay or extend' clause is therefore customary in such cases. Most buyers today who seek such guarantees insist on the on-demand type, which has given rise to some concern by banks and manufacturers alike. The unqualified terms normally demanded must of course be carefully considered by the manufacturer and not 'automatically agreed'. The guarantor banks closeley monitor these contingent liabilities particularly in view of the growth of such requests during the 1970s, and have been concerned about the impact upon the creditworthiness of some major manufacturers.

SPECIMEN DOCUMENTS

The exhibits listed above and illustrated on pages 255 to 263 are not necessarily representative of forms used in all banks in the UK or overseas.

Exhibit 1 **Indirect tender guarantee**

To
. . . . Bank   Date . . . .
Tender Guarantee No.. . . . .
Our customers, Messrs . . . .
have submitted to . . . . (issuing office)
an offer for delivery of . . . .
acceptance of which takes place on . . . .
(request for issue of tender No. . . . . . .)
We are requesting you hereby   )
We are requesting you by cable   )   (cable confirmation attached)
to issue the requested Tender Guarantee up to an amount of . . . .
in favour of. . . . . valid until . . . .
and to inform. . . . .   )   e.g. address of the
and to deliver the original to. . . .)   principal's foreign
in accordance with instructions. . . .)   representative

We, the X-Bank, hereby irrevocably undertake to indemnify you for all losses,
costs and damages for which you may be liable under your guarantee, and to
pay to you on your first written demand an amount of up to

. . . .
(in words) . . . .

for which a claim is being made against you for which you are liable under
your guarantee.

It is further agreed that you make a payment on the demand of the beneficiary
under your guarantee without an obligation on your part to check whether he
has a claim to it.

Our liability under this guarantee expires at the latest on . . . .
Claims must be made by registered letter or cable to reach us by that date,
otherwise our liability becomes invalid. The original of this document must be
returned to us after expiry or on settlement of claims under the guarantee.

X-BANK

Exhibit 2 **Direct tender guarantee**

To

. . . .   Date   . . . .

(issuing office)

Tender Guarantee No. . . . .

re: Your request to issue Tender No. . . . .

Our customers, Messrs . . . .
have submitted to you a tender for delivery of . . . .
which closes on   . . . .

We, the X-Bank, hereby irrevocably undertake to make a payment at once of
an amount up to a total of

. . . .
(in words) . . . .

on your first written demand against return of the original of this document
and your written declaration that the above-mentioned tender has been taken
up completely or partly, but Messrs . . . . . have not signed the contract in due
time.

Our obligation under the guarantee expires on . . . . at the latest. Claims
must be made by registered letter or cable to reach us by that date, otherwise
our liability becomes invalid. The original of this document must be returned
to us after expiry or on settlement of claims under the guarantee.

X-BANK

Exhibit 3 **Indirect performance bond**

To
. . . . .Bank   Date . . . .

Performance Bond No. . . . . . .

Our customers, Messrs . . . .
have concluded on. . . . . under No. . . . .
with . . . .
a contract for the delivery of . . . .
at a total price of. . . . . cif/fob. . . . .

We hereby request you   )
We hereby request you by cable) . . . . (cable confirmation attached)
to issue the requested performance bond up to an amount of. . . . . . (. . . .% of
the contract price). . . . .
in favour of. . . . . valid to. . . . .
and to inform. . . . .)   eg address of the
and to deliver the original to. . . . .)   principal's foreign
in accordance with the instructions of. . . . .)   representative

We, the X-Bank, hereby irrevocably undertake to indemnify you for all losses,
costs and damages for which you may be liable under your guarantee and to
pay to you on your first written demand an amount of up to

. . . .
        (in words) . . . .

for which a claim is being made against you under the guarantee. It is further
agreed that you make payment on the demand of the beneficiary under your
guarantee without an obligation on your part to check whether he has a claim
to it.

Our liability under this guarantee expires at the latest on . . . . . . Claims must
be made by registered letter or cable to reach us by that date, otherwise our
liability becomes invalid. The original of this document must be returned to us
after expiry or on settlement of claims under the guarantee.

In case of a claim under the guarantee, we shall make payments according to
the regulations in force concerning payment transactions between the UK
and your country.

                              X-BANK

Exhibit 4 **Direct performance bond**

To
. . . . (Foreign buyer)   Date . . . .

Performance Bond No. . . . .

re: Contract No. . . . .   of   . . . .

Between you and Messrs . . . .
hereafter referred to as the vendor, a contract for delivery of
. . . . under No. . . . . was entered into on . . . . at a total
price of . . . .   cif/fob . . . .

We, the X–Bank, hereby irrevocably guarantee the correct fulfilment of the
above-mentioned contract by the vendor and undertake hereby irrevocably to
make a payment at once of an amount up to a total of

. . . .
(in words) . . . .

on your first written demand against return of the original of this document
and your written declaration that the vendor has not complied with the
contract.

Our liability under this guarantee expires at the latest on . . . . . . Claims must
be made by registered letter or cable to reach us by that date, otherwise our
liability becomes invalid. The original of this document must be returned to us
after expiry or on settlement of claims under the guarantee.

In case of a claim under the guarantee, we shall make payments according to
the regulations in force concerning payment transactions between the UK
and your country.

X–BANK

Exhibit 5   **Overdraft guarantee**

To Banco de Z

Sirs,

In consideration of you advancing by way of fluctuating overdraft on the account of Z. B. Carsona SA we hereby guarantee repayment of such advances upon receipt of written demand, provided that our total liability under this guarantee shall not exceed the sum of £4,000.00 (pounds four thousand) inclusive of interest and bank charges. This guarantee shall remain in force until such time as you advise us in writing that we are released from all liability towards you hereunder, or until we determine our liability by giving 15 days notice in writing. Upon receipt of such notice by you no further advances are to be made with recourse to us.

X-BANK

Exhibit 6 **Indirect advance payment guarantee**

To
. . . . .Bank   Date . . . .

Advance Payment Guarantee No. . . . .

Our customers, Messrs . . . .
hereafter called the vendor, have concluded on . . . .
under No. with. . . . .
hereafter called the buyer, a contract for the delivery of. . . . .   at a total price
of . . . . cif/fob . . . .
The contract provides that the buyer will make an advance payment to the
vendor of . . . .% of the total price agreed in the contract on the condition that
repayment is guaranteed on request through your bank/a bank in your
country.
We hereby request you   )
We hereby request you by cable) . . . . Cable confirmation attached
to issue the requested advance payment guarantee amounting to . . . . . . in
favour of the buyer, valid until. . . . .
This guarantee becomes valid on receipt of the advance payment by the
buyer (possibly replaced by: on his account with our bank) and is reduced
automatically by . . . . . .% of the amount of each part shipment agreed in the
contract on presentation of shipping documents to us.

We, the X-Bank, hereby irrevocably undertake to indemnify you for all losses,
costs and damages for which you may be liable under your guarantee and to
pay to you on your first written demand an amount of up to

. . . .
(in words) . . . .

for which a claim is being made against you under the guarantee.

It is further agreed that you make a payment on the demand of the beneficiary
under your guarantee without an obligation on your part to check whether he
has a claim to it.

Our liability under this guarantee expires at the latest on . . . . . .Claims must
be made by registered letter or cable to reach us by that date, otherwise our
liability becomes invalid. The original of this document must be returned to us
after expiry or on settlement of claims under the guarantee.

In case of a claim under the guarantee, we shall make payments according to
the regulations in force concerning payment transactions between the UK
and your country.

X-BANK

Exhibit 7 **Direct advance payment guarantee**

To
. . . . (foreign buyer)   Date . . . .

Advance Payment Guarantee No. . . . .

re: Contract No. . . . .   of . . . .

Between you and Messrs . . . .
called vendor hereunder, a contract for delivery of . . . .
under No. . . . .   was entered into on . . . .
at a total price of . . . .   cif/fob . . . .

You have undertaken to pay to the vendor an advance of . . . .
that is . . . . . . % of the total price.

We, the X-Bank, hereby irrevocably guarantee repayment at once of the
advance made to the vendor up to a total of

. . . .
(in words) . . . .

on your first written demand against return of the original of this document
and your written declaration that the vendor has not completed the contract.

This guarantee becomes valid on receipt of the advance payment on the
account of the vendor with our Bank, but expires at the latest on
. . . .
expires on presentation to us of the shipping documents, at the latest on
. . . .

Claims must be made by registered letter or cable to reach us by that date,
otherwise our liability becomes invalid. The original of this document must be
returned to us after expiry or on settlement of claims under the guarantee.

In case of a claim under the guarantee, we shall make payments according to
the regulations in force concerning payment transactions between the UK
and your country.

X-BANK

Exhibit 8 **Indemnity for missing bill of lading**

Date . . . .

To
Shippers   . . . .
re: Letter of indemnity . . . .
for   . . . .
shipped on ss/ms . . . .
from . . . . to . . . .

I/We am/are the consignee/s of the above-mentioned shipment, for which I/we have not yet received the Bill of Lading. I/We hereby undertake to deliver to the owner and/or shipper and/or charterer and/or captain of the above-mentioned ship the Bill of Lading, correctly endorsed, promptly after receipt and to indemnify him/them for all damages and claims which may arise from the release of the goods without a Bill of Lading, as well as for freight and costs. The conditions of the Bill of Lading are hereby expressly acknowledged.

. . . .
(legally binding signature)

We hereby guarantee the performance of the above transaction up to an amount of . . . . (in words) . . . .
In case of a claim being made under the guarantee, payment will be made in accordance with the regulations in force concerning payment transactions between the United Kingdom and . . . .

X-BANK

Exhibit 9 **Counter indemnity**

To X- Bank,
 London.
 We confirm having requested you to give the tender guarantee
 for £750,000.00 to the beneficiary, E.B. Yung in respect of
 tender number 19 for the supply contract number 3 covering
 refrigeration plant, in accordance with the terms endorsed
 hereon.
 We hereby indemnify you from all actions, claims and demands
 which may be brought against you, and against all losses costs
 or damages and any expenses incurred by reason of having directly
 or indirectly undertaken such obligation.
 You are hereby authorised to pay on any demand made by the
 beneficiary or on their behalf sums as demanded up to the limit
 of the liability as defined by yourselves, without reference or
 confirmation from ourselves.
 In addition you are authorised to debit any account of the undersigned in respect of any payments made hereunder.

 Dated ....19..

 Signed by
 in the presence of:
 Signature
 Address

 Occupation

PAST EXAMINATION QUESTIONS

1   A UK exporter of consumer goods may be financed by his bank or from other sources. List the various methods of finance he might receive, and against each facility indicate:

a   the recourse position of the exporter, and

b   how the buyer might be granted deferred terms thereunder

(Foundation Course in Overseas Trade)

2   How could a UK bank:

a   assist a British importer to pay his overseas supplier against documentary evidence of the shipment of the goods

b   provide the importer with three months' credit against the security of the goods?

(Institute of Bankers)

3   Name the four main types of guarantees or bonds which banks are requested to issue on behalf of contractors for large overseas projects. Describe the purpose of each.

(Institute of Bankers)

4   Describe the main types of bonds for which ECGD guarantees may be available as supporting operations.

(Institute of Bankers)

CHAPTER EIGHT

Foreign Exchange

1. INTRODUCTION AND GLOSSARY OF TERMS USED IN THIS CHAPTER

a Introduction

Commercial foreign exchange business arises primarily from trading and trade-related transactions, although investment monies, dividends, and royalty payments, as well as gifts, legacies, loans and interest payments, give rise to very substantial flows of funds moving from one currency to another. For each international trading transaction either the importer or the exporter, and sometimes, both, will be involved in a foreign exchange operation, unless one or both maintains a foreign currency account.

The currency used for the settlement of international trade may be the currency of one of the countries involved. For instance, trade between France and Spain would normally be settled in French francs or Spanish pesetas. For a variety of reasons there are a large number of countries the currencies of which are seldom used, and many countries' currencies are never used for the settlement of international trade. Trade between a South American country and elsewhere will normally be settled in US dollars. Indeed the US dollar is the most widely used currency for international settlement purposes. Sterling, most West European currencies, the Canadian dollar and the Japanese yen are the so-called major 'trading currencies' along with US dollars. This term implies that the currencies are used for the purpose of settling international indebtedness and are 'traded' in the foreign exchange market. While there are about 15 major trading currencies, some banks in the London foreign exchange market will deal in over 40 different currencies from time to time. The less common currencies dealt in are sometimes referred to as 'exotics'.

On the infrastructure of these commercial transactions the banks' foreign exchange dealers conduct their professional dealing operations directly with other banks abroad, or indirectly via foreign exchange brokers with other banks in London.

The foreign exchange market is an international money market; deals are concluded by telephone and telex, with written confirmations of the transactions following later. This market differs from the various money markets described in Chapters 1 and 10, since 'foreign exchange', as the phrase implies, concerns transactions in which a dealer will buy one currency and sell another.

b   Glossary of terms

One is tempted to insert in this glossary the word 'xenophobia' – fear of things 'foreign'. Businessmen in general have often sought to avoid foreign business, foreign currency transactions, or anything 'foreign', and have consequently remained uninformed on these matters. So the word foreign has too easily acquired the sinister connotation of 'alien', and the subject, though really simple and logical, has come to be regarded as complex. It is the intention in this chapter to dispel the mistaken concept that foreign exchange is too difficult to learn and consequently something to avoid.

Basis point	(see 'pip, or point' below).
Bear	speculator who expects a currency to become weaker and sells that currency forward expecting to make a profit on exchange.
Broker	one who brings together dealers who are buyers and dealers who are sellers of foreign currency, charging a brokerage for the service.
Bull	speculator who expects a currency to become firmer (see 'firm' below) and buys that currency forward expecting to make a profit on exchange.
Close-out	action taken by dealers to complete a forward contract in the event of the counterparty being unable or unwilling to fulfil his obligations under it.
Cross rate	the direct relationship between two non-indigenous currencies of the centre concerned with the transaction; for example, all non-sterling exchange rates for deals done in the UK are cross rates – eg $/Dm and US$/Can$
Dealer	one authorised by his bank to deal on the foreign exchange market.
Discount	the forward margin of a currency that is less expensive forward than the spot rate; the discount is added to the spot rate to which it relates.
Firm	a currency which is becoming more expensive in terms of other currencies.

Forward   deal where the exchange is to be made more than two working days from the date of the deal (see 'spot').

Forward forward   forward sale against further forward purchase, or forward purchase against further forward sale.

Jobbing   another term for 'arbitrage' as carried out by dealers in the professional interbank foreign exchange market; local factors which influence rates in one centre may give rise to jobbing opportunities.

Long   excess of purchases over sales (see 'short').

Margin   difference between the spot and forward prices of a currency; if the forward price of the currency is greater than the spot price the margin is said to be 'at a premium'; if the forward value of the currency is less than the spot price the margin is described as a 'discount'; where there is no margin the forward value is referred to as 'par'.

Open position   the long (above) or short (below) position at any time on which an exchange risk is run.

Option   the customer's right to deliver or to take delivery of a specified sum in foreign currency at any time or times during an agreed period.

Par   when the forward rate of exchange is the same as the spot rate.

Pip, or point   one-tenthousandth part of a US$ (the unit varies according to the currency).

Premium   the forward margin of a currency that is more expensive forward than the spot rate; the premium is deducted from the spot rate to which it relates.

Rate of exchange   the price or value of a unit of one currency in terms of another.

Short   excess of sales over purchases (see 'long').

Spot   the exchange rate is fixed immediately for delivery of the currency two working days from the date of the deal (see 'forward').

Spot against forward position	extent to which spot currency holdings are married against forward sales; found by subtracting forward purchases from forward sales.
Spot against forward transaction	a transaction in which a purchase or sale of spot currency is made against a corresponding sale or purchase of the same currency forward.
Spot next	simultaneous selling of currency for delivery at spot and buying it back for delivery the day after, and *vice versa.*
Spread	difference between the dealer's buying and selling, or borrowing and lending, rates.
Swap	a spot purchase against a forward sale, or a spot sale against a forward purchase.
Tom-next	simultaneous selling of a currency for delivery tomorrow and repurchase on the spot delivery date (the following day), or *vice versa.*
Turn	profit or loss derived from the purchase or sale, or borrowing or lending, of a currency.
Value date	date on which funds are actually available for use by the bank in its *nostro* account abroad, being the date agreed for settlement of a foreign currency transaction.
Weak	a currency may be described as weak when it is potentially cheaper in terms of other currencies.

2.   SPOT RATES OF EXCHANGE AND HOW THEY ARE DETERMINED

When a dealer is buying a currency he will want as much of it as he can possibly get for each currency unit he offers; but when he is selling he will only give away as little of it as he is forced to. The dealer will quote a rate at which he will sell and a rate at which he will buy. Therefore if anyone wishes to do business with that dealer he must do so on the terms laid down by the dealer. In other words, the dealer is the master of the situation. So when a customer approaches a bank and wishes to do business with it, he can do so only on the terms laid down by the bank. If a customer wishes to sell, he can do so only at the bank's buying rate; and if a customer wishes to buy, he can do so only at the bank's selling rate. There is nothing to prevent a customer from approaching a number of banks for quotations, although the rates could move against him in the meantime.

There are always two sides to a transaction. If the customer buys US dollars, the bank is selling US dollars. If the customer sells deutschemarks, the bank is buying deutschemarks. In everyday life, if we buy a newspaper from a shop, we are selling currency in the form of coin to the shop. When two banks deal with each other, one bank quotes the rates (ie, market rates) and the other is the 'customer'.

Currency rates are rates which are quoted as so much foreign currency per one pound sterling. The pound is the reference currency in this example. Therefore when a dealer is buying a currency in exchange for his pound he wants as many foreign currency units as he can possibly obtain in exchange for that one pound. Similarly, when he is selling a currency he is going to give away as little foreign currency as possible in exchange for the pound he will receive from the customer. Let us look at it in terms of US dollars.

Let us assume that the spread is 2.00–2.01. The bank will sell dollars at 2.00; in other words, the bank will give the customer two dollars for each pound it receives. It has sold low; but when the bank buys dollars from the customer it will want the customer to give it as many dollars and cents as it can possibly get. Therefore it might say to the customer, 'I want 2.01 dollars from you for each pound that I give you'.

The bank is *selling* dollars low: it is selling as few units of currency at $2.00 for £1 as it can. The bank is *buying* dollars high: it is buying more units of currency at $2.01 for £1.

You will notice that the bank's selling rate is the first rate (on the left) and the bank's buying rate is the second rate (on the right) and, without exception, all quoted currency rates have the bank's selling rate on the left (or stated first) and the bank's buying rate on the right (or stated second). This applies whether we are talking about spot or forward rates. There are no exceptions whatsoever.

A list of rates may be seen in the daily financial press. These are merely indications of the dealing prices that applied on the previous working day in the interbank market for large amounts.

3. RATES OF EXCHANGE FOR DIFFERENT TRANSACTIONS

A rate of exchange is the price of one currency in terms of another. All principal rates of exchange against sterling are quoted as 'currency rates' – ie, so many units of foreign currency to one pound sterling. All the 'rules' mentioned in other sections of this chapter relate to currency rates. An exchange rate is merely the expression of the amount of one currency (the referred currency) equal to one unit of another currency (the reference currency). Theoretically, either of the currencies could act as the reference currency – ie, the statement US$ $1.9633 = £1$ is equivalent to the statement £0.50935 = US$1 $(1/1.9633 = 0.50935)$. Market practice however is to use the US dollar as the reference currency with only a few exceptions; notably the US$/£ rate, where the pound is the reference currency; and the US$/Can$ rate where the Canadian dollar is the reference currency.

Below are listed some spot and forward exchange rates as quoted by dealers in London on 2nd December 1980. The currency headings denote the referred currency and by the side of each the appropriate reference currency is noted. The column headed Canada is, however, an exception as the referred currency in this column is the US dollar and the Canadian dollar is the reference currency. The forward rates are explained in section 4 of this chapter.

The anomalous behaviour of the US$/£ rate and the US$/Can$ rate has its roots in the history of modern foreign exchange dealing. Before the second world war sterling was the predominant international currency, used in trade and as a reserve currency, in spite of the fact that the balance of economic power had long since passed across the Atlantic. In Europe therefore it was dealer practice to use sterling as the reference currency – ie, the European countries would be predominantly dealing in exchanging their own currency for sterling and *vice versa*. In practical terms the European dealers were in the business of buying and selling sterling, this being the accepted currency of international trade. They thus put a price on sterling in terms of their own currency, which is the same as saying they used exchange rates with the pound as the reference currency.

With the post-war decline of sterling's role the foreign exchange business largely became a question of buying and selling dollars, and the established manner of quoting exchange rates was to use the dollar as the reference currency. The US$/£ rate remained the same, however, partly because of its common usage as the link between the major trading currencies, and partly because the manner of quoting the rate was the same in London and New York.

The manner of quoting the US$/Can$ rate derives from the practice in New York, which is the largest centre for dealing in Canadian dollars. Historically, dealing in New York was dominated by the buying or selling of Canadian dollars and sterling, and the dealers quoted US dollar prices for these currencies – ie, they would quote the US$ value of £1 or Can$1. Thus, in both cases, the US dollar was the referred currency. This way of quoting the Canadian dollar has subsequently been adopted by all European centres.

It should now be clear that the quotation of the US$/£ rate and the US$/Can$ rate is the same in New York as in Europe. For all other currencies, however, New York uses the inverse of European rates – ie, whereas Europe always uses the dollar as the reference currency, New York always uses the dollar as the referred currency.

SPOT AND FORWARD EXCHANGE RATES QUOTED IN LONDON ON 2nd DECEMBER 1980

Currency	US$ = £1		Dm = $1		Swiss Fc = $1		Lira = $1	
Spot	2.3555 :	2.3565	1.9350 :	1.9358	1.7435 :	1.7450	918.75 :	919.50
1 month	90 :	100	155 :	145	194 :	186	1.50 :	.50
2 months	150 :	160	288 :	278	363 :	355	1.50 :	.50
3 months	210 :	220	398 :	388	530 :	522	−1.00 :	+.25
6 months	300 :	310	663 :	648	935 :	920	7.25 :	9.25
12 months	330 :	350	1040 :	1010	1465 :	1430	25.00 :	35.00

Currency	French Fc = $1		Guilder = $1		Can$ = US$1		Yen = $1	
Spot	4.4840 :	4.4860	2.0962 :	2.0972	8390 :	8396	215.20 :	215.40
1 month	330 :	310	173 :	169	35 :	40	1.60 :	1.50
2 months	535 :	515	308 :	303	60 :	65	2.95 :	2.85
3 months	730 :	705	431 :	426	80 :	85	4.00 :	3.85
6 months	940 :	890	683 :	673	120 :	130	6.75 :	6.55
12 months	975 :	875	1000 :	970				

The rates quoted in the above example, and elsewhere in this book, are illustrations only, and are unlikely to be accurate reflections of the prices of one currency in terms of another at the time of reading.

The above are typical of the spot and forward quotes as given in London and anywhere in Europe. The first thing you will note is that each quote involves two rates: this is because dealers always make a two-way price, because they stand ready either to buy or to sell. Thus, in response to an enquiry from another dealer or a broker, they must give a rate at which they will sell (offer) the currency, and a price at which they will buy (bid) the currency. Now the reader will understand that a bid to buy the referred currency is at the same time an offer to sell the reference currency, and therefore it is essential to know which currency is being offered or bid. Dealer practice is necessarily firm on this point: the first of the two quotes is always an offer to sell the referred currency and the second is always a bid to buy the referred currency. Thus the first quote as you read it is always lower than the second, because for the same amount of the reference currency a dealer wishes to offer less of the referred currency than he is bidding to buy. It is essential that this basic point be fully understood, and the reader should make sure he is clear on this.

Most of the spot rates shown above are quoted to four decimal places; in other words, to one-tenthousandth of the basic unit of the referred currency. However, the Italian lira and Japanese yen are given to only two decimal places – ie, one-hundredth of the basic unit. This is because the lira and yen are low value units, in fact of the order of one hundred times smaller than most currencies. This smallest division of a currency is given a special name by dealers; it is called a 'point' or a 'basis point'. A point therefore could be one-tenthousandth of a dollar, mark, franc or guilder, etc, or one hundredth of a lira or yen.

Market rates are the rates quoted for buying and selling currency on the foreign exchange market. These rates (or prices) are quoted by one bank to another, often through the intermediary of a foreign exchange broker. They apply only to marketable amounts which vary according to the activity of the market at any time, and according to the currency dealt in. Market rates are basically wholesale rates – ie, for large transactions only. Details of these rates are shown in the financial press. The spread (that is, the difference between the buying and the selling rates) in the market rates tends to be relatively small, particularly if the market is active with plenty of buying and/or selling of one currency for another.

In the UK, cross rate is the price of any currency other than sterling in terms of any other currency other than sterling, examples being $/Dm, H.Fl/S.Fc, and B.Fc/N.Kr. Apart from US$/£ (which is not a cross rate), the exchange rates for all other currencies against the dollar are cross rates. Most of these cross rates are called 'currency rates', being so many units of foreign currency to one US dollar.

A large bank will have many thousands of transactions daily in foreign currencies, many of them being for relatively small amounts.

A clearing bank's foreign exchange dealers will receive orders from the following sources on behalf of customers and UK beneficiaries *who wish to sell foreign currency*:

- direct from the bank's branches and large exporting customers
- inland payments department's currency section, being funds received from abroad by mail or cable for account of a UK beneficiary
- bills department, being the foreign currency proceeds of bills sent for collection from non-resident drawers, and the bills against which the bank has advanced or negotiated
- documentary credits, being payments made to UK beneficiaries
- securities, being the dividends of foreign quoted securities received from abroad

The bank's dealers will buy the foreign currency offered under the above-mentioned transactions and which has been or will be credited to the bank's *nostro* account abroad, and credit its customers' accounts with the sterling proceeds.

Foreign exchange dealers receive orders from the following parts of the bank on behalf of the customers *who wish to buy foreign currency*:

● direct from branches and large importing customers
● payments abroad department, in respect of MTs, TTs, and drafts
● bills department inwards, being foreign currency settlements due to overseas residents in respect of imports into the UK
● documentary credits department, in respect of payments by way of reimbursement due to advising banks abroad

The bank's dealer will sell the foreign currency required under the above-mentioned transactions in respect of funds which will be or have been debited to the bank's *nostro* account abroad and its customers' accounts will be debited with the sterling equivalent.

It is not possible for the foreign exchange dealer to quote individual rates for each transaction unless, of course, the amount is large. For small amounts therefore the dealers will issue a daily quotation to the branches and departments handling the underlying transactions. Some major UK banks employ an Ansaphone service internally; others use their computer terminals to assist in obtaining rates for their customers with the minimum of delay. An illustration of the relative spread of rates banks quote for different transactions is as follows:

	Bank sells			Bank buys
i	Market rate	US$2.3555	US$2.3565	Market rate
ii	Payments abroad (MT, TT) Inward bills Credits (imports)	US$2.3550	US$2.3570	Inland payments Outward bills Credits (exports)
iii	Foreign notes	US$2.3545	US$2.4075	Foreign notes

The spread of rates for transactions listed at *ii* above is wider than, and outside, the market rates at *i*. The market rates can and will fluctuate throughout the day, and the bank's dealers wish to ensure that the very small transactions, which in total may add up to a sizeable sum, are exchanged at a rate at which the bank will not lose. Modern communication systems for transmitting payment instructions are such that the difference in time between either cable or airmail transfers being sent and acted upon is minimal. For the smaller transactions, therefore, banks do not usually load the rate of exchange, as was once the case, to compensate for an interest charge for the time they are short of funds. The rates for foreign notes are outside those quoted for the other transactions listed above. This is to compensate for the freight and insurance costs of importation or repatriation and the cost of holding non-interest earning cash in the form of foreign notes. Coin rates are wider still, because the heavier weight of coin means that considerable freight costs must be applied to a relatively small value in the event of possible repatriation.

It should be stressed that dealers must be notified of all transactions over a figure specified in the bank's books of instruction. For these they will quote a specific rate, which may or may not coincide with the day's rates for small transactions. Without such information the dealers will not be able to establish what their foreign exchange position is.

4. FORWARD RATES AND HOW THEY ARE DETERMINED

A forward exchange contract is an immediately firm and binding contract between customer and banker for the purchase or sale of a specified quantity of a stated foreign currency, at a rate of exchange fixed at the time of making the contract, and for performance by delivery and payment at a future time agreed upon when making the contract. The contract is binding: performance must therefore take place, with any unused portion cancelled by 'closing out' (see section 5 of this chapter).

Forward contracts may be 'fixed' or 'option' forwards. A fixed forward is a forward contract for which one specific date is agreed upon for performance to take place – eg, 27th July.

A forward option is one for which a specific period of time is agreed upon and performance must take place during such period – eg, 15th January to 15th March. The actual date within the option period when it is exercised is chosen by the customer.

The word 'option' does not mean the customer has a choice whether or not he deals, he actually has dealt; it means that an option is given to him as to when he takes or gives the currency concerned, but the contract must be completed by the customer either taking or giving the currency eventually or 'closing the contract out'.

The essential thing about option dealing is that the bank always takes the worst view of what the customer may do to them. Therefore there are some logical, but apparently strange, results when option and fixed contracts are at a premium or a discount. This may be better explained by means of examples.

Spot dollars are 2.00½ – 2.00¾, the one month dollars are ½–¼ cents premium.
The bank sells one month dollars fixed at 2.00.
The bank sells one month dollars option during the month at 2.00.
The bank buys one month dollars fixed at 2.00½.
The bank buys one month dollars option during the month at 2.00¾.

When the bank is selling a currency which is at a premium it will always deduct the premium irrespective of whether the contract is fixed or option, because if it is an option the customer might not take it up until the last day for which the contract is running. Therefore the bank is entitled to charge the full premium. Similarly, when buying for a fixed date the bank must give the customer the benefit of whatever premium may be ruling, but when the bank is buying option at any time during the month the customer has the choice of delivering the currency spot and therefore the bank will only pay him the spot price.

Now we will take an example of a currency which is at a discount.

Belgian francs spot 60.25–60.30, one month 10c–15c discount.
The bank sells one month Belgian francs fixed at 60.35.
The bank sells one month Belgian francs option during the month at 60.25.
The bank buys one month Belgian francs fixed at 60.45.
The bank buys one month Belgian francs option during the month at 60.45.

When the bank sells francs at one month fixed the customer is entitled to whatever discount may be available, but when the bank sells francs option one month the customer may decide to take delivery at spot, thus he is not entitled to the benefit of discount and therefore the bank pays him the spot price. When the bank buys francs one month fixed there can be no argument, the full discount is payable and therefore the bank takes it. When the bank buys francs option for one month, the customer has the choice of delivering right up to the end of the period, therefore the bank is again entitled to the full discount for that period.

When the bank is buying a currency forward which is quoted at a premium it will give the benefit of any premium to the customer if he can fix a date before which he will not deliver. Similarly, when the bank is selling a forward currency which is quoted at a discount it will give the benefit of the discount to the customer, provided he will fix a date before which he will not take delivery.

The following example (based upon fact) may make the position clearer:

Spot Canadian dollars	1.96¼		–1.96½	
1 month	½	–	¼	premium
2 months	¾	–	½	premium
3 months	1	–	¾	premium
4 months	¹⁄₁₆ premium–		¹⁄₁₆	discount
5 months	¼	–	½	discount
6 months	½	–	¾	discount

It will be seen that the first three months are at a premium, the four months at par-middle, and the five and six months are quoted at a discount. The problem is:

How does the bank sell dollars option six months?

How does the bank buy dollars option six months?

The solutions are:

i   The bank sells dollars option six months at 1.95¼; in other words, three months' premium off the spot rate.

ii   The bank buys dollars option six months at 1.97¼; this is ¾ discount added to 1.96½.

The reasoning follows the previous examples. When the bank is selling dollars, the customer has the opportunity of taking them up after only three months; therefore he should pay the three months' premium. Similarly, when the bank is buying dollars, the customer might not deliver them until the last date, he has that option, therefore the bank is entitled to the discount.

Some customers will require their banker's assistance in this matter; others, who understand it, will try to obtain forward rates beneficial to themselves. Let us take, for example, a British exporter who signs a contract to supply $100,000 worth of goods to an American buyer. The order is signed today, but the British seller knows that he has to import raw materials, manufacture the goods, pack them, ship them to the US, and then give his buyer up to three months' credit from the date of arrival of the goods in an American port. Assume that the exporter is experienced in these matters, and wants to get his sterling as soon as possible and at the best possible rate. Knowing that the forward dollar at that particular time is quoted at a premium, he will endeavour to arrange a forward option from the earliest date at which he expects to receive his dollars – although he will want sterling as soon as he gets the dollars.

Looking at this particular example, he can say it will be at least three months before the goods arrive in the US, for the reasons outlined above, and he may therefore receive payment at any time from three to six months from now (the date when he is selling forward). The customer will therefore ask the bank to buy forward dollars from him for delivery between three and six months, or, in market jargon, option between three and six months. In other words, the customer has fixed a date before which he will not deliver the dollars to the bank – ie, three months from the date of fixing the option – and a latest date at which he must deliver – ie, six months from that date. The customer will be entitled to the benefit of the three months' premium being deducted from the spot price. Using the following rates:

Spot US dollars	2.00⅜	– 2.00⅝	
1 month	1 cent –	½ cent premium	
2 months	1¼ cents –	¾ cent premium	
3 months	1¾ cents –	1¼ cents premium	
4 months	2 cents –	1½ cents premium	
5 months	2¼ cents –	1¾ cents premium	
6 months	2½ cents –	2 cents premium	

Then, on the basis of the above example, the customer will sell dollars to the bank at his option three to six months and the bank will deduct 1¼ cents (the bank's three months' buying price) from $2.00⅝ (the bank's spot buying price), which gives a three months' price of $1.99⅜. This represents an increased and quite legitimate profit to the customer.

When a currency is being quoted at a discount on the forward rates and a customer wishes to buy that currency forward, he will, if at all possible, try to fix a date before which he will not require delivery of the currency concerned. Assume that the customer is importing goods from Belgium, and that the Belgian supplier will give him credit for two months after the date of receipt of the goods in this country: the customer knows that it will be four months before the goods are delivered to him, and that he then has the choice of paying up to the end of another two months after that. The customer will approach the bank and ask it to sell him Belgian francs for delivery at his option between four and six months. The customer therefore, having fixed the first date before which he will not take delivery of these francs, is entitled to the benefit of the discount being added to the spot selling price of the bank for four months. Using the following rates:

Spot Belgian francs	60.12 – 60.15	
1 month	4c–	7c discount
2 months	6c–	9c discount
3 months	8c–	10c discount
4 months	11c–	14c discount
5 months	13c–	15c discount
6 months	16c–	19c discount

The bank will sell francs to the customer on the basis of 11 cents discount – that is, the bank's selling price for four months' francs added to the spot rate of 60.12, which makes an outright price for four months of 60.23.

You will notice in the table overleaf (which has been repeated for ease of reference) that the forward rates are not quoted in the same way as the spot rates, although two rates are still given – ie, an offer and a bid. What is in fact quoted is the number of points by which the forward rate differs from the spot rate; thus, to calculate the outright forward rate it is necessary to add or subtract the number of points from the relevant spot rate. Unfortunately the forward quotes do not indicate whether they should be subtracted or added to the spot rate. It is however quite simple to decide whether they should be added or subtracted, and dealers are so used to handling forward quotes that they do not bother to indicate it.

SPOT AND FORWARD EXCHANGE RATES QUOTED IN LONDON ON 2nd DECEMBER 1980

Currency	US$ = £1		Dm = $1		Swiss Fc = $1		Lira = $1	
Spot	2.3555 :	2.3565	1.9350 :	1.9358	1.7435 :	1.7450	918.75 :	919.50
1 month	90 :	100	155 :	145	194 :	186	1.50 :	.50
2 months	150 :	160	288 :	278	363 :	355	1.50 :	.50
3 months	210 :	220	398 :	388	530 :	522	−1.00 :	+.25
6 months	300 :	310	663 :	648	935 :	920	7.25 :	9.25
12 months	330 :	350	1040 :	1010	1465 :	1430	25.00 :	35.00
Currency	French Fc = $1		Guilder = $1		Can$ = US$1		Yen = $1	
Spot	4.4840 :	4.4860	2.0962 :	2.0972	8390 :	8396	215.20 :	215.40
1 month	330 :	310	173 :	169	35 :	40	1.60 :	1.50
2 months	535 :	515	308 :	303	60 :	65	2.95 :	2.85
3 months	730 :	705	431 :	426	80 :	85	4.00 :	3.85
6 months	940 :	890	683 :	673	120 :	130	6.75 :	6.55
12 months	975 :	875	1000 :	970				

A moment's reflection should convince the reader that if one subtracts from the spot rate to get the outright forward rate then the referred currency is more valuable at the forward date than at the spot date, because the forward rate gives less for the same amount of the reference currency. Similarly if one adds, then the referred currency is cheaper at the forward date. When a currency is dearer at the forward date we say it is at a premium to the spot. If cheaper, we say it is at a discount to the spot rate. Thus we derive the basic rule: 'premiums are subtracted and discounts are added'.

We have still however not worked out which of the above forward quotes should be subtracted (ie, are premiums) and which should be added (ie, are discounts). As stated above, the solution is simple. We first take the middle spot rate and consider what outright rates would result from, first, adding the forward quotes to and, second, subtracting them from, the middle spot; and we choose the action which results in the offer side being lower than the bid side.

Example:

	Offer	Bid
The spot Dm/US$ rates above are	1.9350	1.9358
The 1 month forward Dm/US$	155	145

Taking a middle spot rate of 1.9354, if we add the forward quotes we will get outright forward rates of 1.9505 – 1.9503. This cannot be correct, as the offer side must always be lower than the bid side; thus we conclude that the forward quotes must be subtracted and are therefore premiums.

Care is required when considering the Canadian column because, as mentioned previously, the referred currency here is US dollars not Canadian dollars, which are in fact the reference currency. Thus, although the same reasoning can be applied, the resulting premiums or discounts would be for the US dollar and not the Canadian dollar, and you will appreciate that saying the US dollar is at a premium to the

Canadian dollar is the same as saying the Canadian dollar is at a discount to the US dollar. You will see that in the three month forward lira the offer side is to be subtracted and the bid side added. In such cases of course our normal rule would not work and therefore the − and + signs must be included in the quote.

5. CLOSE-OUT OF FORWARD CONTRACTS

What should happen when a customer does not require to take up all the foreign currency he has bought under a forward contract? Assume that the bank contracts to sell to the customer $50,000 for delivery over three months: at the end of three months the customer has taken up only $40,000, and the bank is required to calculate what must happen to the remaining $10,000. The customer is deemed to have taken up the whole contract but to have sold back to the bank, at the bank's spot buying price, the unutilised balance of the forward contract.

The detailed procedure is as follows. The bank sells at the forward price the remaining balance of $10,000, and the customer is debited with that amount. Simultaneously, the bank buys back the $10,000 at its spot buying price, and the customer is credited with that equivalent in sterling. In actual fact, of course, banks do not go through the long-winded procedure of delivering dollars to the customer and buying them back from him; they merely do two calculations: $10,000 at the forward selling price and $10,000 bought back by the bank at its spot buying price. The sterling difference between the two is then either debited to the customer's account or credited to the customer's account, depending on which way the exchange rates have moved.

For example: the above $10,000 remains after $50,000 has been sold by the bank to an importer under a forward option contract over three months at $2.0020. If the spot rates on the close-out day happened to be:

a   2.0040–2.0060, or
b   1.9980–2.0000, then:

	Contract amount	Contract rate	£ equivalent	Close out rate	£ equivalent	Balance over customer's account
a	$10,000	2.0020	£4,995.00	2.0060	£4,985.04	debit £9.96
b	$10,000	2.0020	£4,995.00	2.0000	£5,000.00	credit £5.00

In other words, the close-out rates in example *(a)* have not moved in the customer's favour as they have in example *(b)*.

6. EXTENSION OF FORWARD CONTRACTS

It can happen, however, that a customer who is unable to deliver, or does not wish to receive, currency under his forward contract may want to do so at some time in the near future, and consequently requests the bank to continue the forward deal without interruption. The forward exchange dealer does this by deducting the applicable premium from or adding the applicable discount to the closing-out (spot) price. Thus, for example, under an extended fixed forward contract to purchase currency from the customer the bank will deduct the premium (on the buying side) from the close-out spot price (on the selling side).

Commission on foreign exchange transactions

The detailed procedures of taking commission vary between banks. As a generalisation, if any commission is taken at all it is normally taken on foreign exchange transactions with UK residents other than interbank or market deals. The most usual rate is 1‰ (1 per mille): minimum 25p, maximum £10.

7.   PROTECTION AGAINST EXCHANGE RISKS, AND INVOICING POLICY

a   Invoicing in sterling

Despite the unprecedented devaluation of sterling during 1976 the UK balance of payments did not benefit as one might have expected from the resulting relative cheapness of UK goods and services.

The reasons can be summarised as follows:

i   Settlement for UK imports, consisting largely of food, consumer goods and raw materials, was almost all on a cash against documents or very short-term credit basis, with 90 per cent of the total payments being made in foreign currency and only 10 per cent in sterling. Whereas proceeds of UK exports, which contain a high proportion of manufactured and capital goods frequently sold on medium- or long-term credit, were being invoiced in the ratio of 80 per cent in sterling to 20 per cent in foreign currency.

ii   Reluctance of foreign buyers to be invoiced in a currency other than sterling, which in their recent experience had cost them less of their own currency to settle in due course than it would have cost at the date of the contract or tender. It is obviously better for an importer to make payment in a currency which in time will become worth less in terms of his own. The UK exporters of capital goods were frequently being told by potential buyers, particularly from Eastern Europe, that as matter of policy payment could only be made in the currency of the supplier (sterling).

iii   Most exporters were unable to increase the price of their goods fast enough to keep pace with sterling's devaluation during 1976; nor indeed were they able to increase output and marketing efficiency to sell a sufficiently greater number of units at the devalued return and so take full advantage of the situation.

iv   Conservatism in invoicing policies. The UK has for many years been the banker to the world, and the role of sterling as a principal currency of settlement logically followed. During the latter part of 1976 the UK authorities introduced a number of measures designed to reduce the use of sterling as a trading currency. (These measures were completely withdrawn in 1979.) Nevertheless, as many UK traders over the years had been using sterling they had no desire to change a lifetime's habit. Foreign currencies can present complications the trader can do without. His accounting procedures, exchange-risk exposures, computer system compatibility with foreign currency transactions, etc, posed and still pose problems traders tend to resist. It is part of the banker's role to help minimise or eliminate these difficulties. Apart from anything else there was no guarantee during 1976 that sterling would not recover, to harden against the US dollar, as happened during 1977–80 when to invoice in sterling made sound commercial sense. Whenever possible exporters should be encouraged to maintain a flexible invoicing policy designed to equate with prevailing economic circumstances in order to maximise trading profits and minimise costs, but frequent changes back and forth are not acceptable to buyers as a rule.

The areas which require careful assessment prior to a decision as to which currency to select for settlement are:

- the expected future relative strengths of alternative settlement currencies, (including sterling, where appropriate, for preference), currencies that are relatively stable and have long-term strength
- comparative interest rates for the same period in different currencies; this should equate with the precise period for which the finance is required, if known
- the degree of exchange-risk exposure, if any, which may be considered acceptable, and the methods of limiting or eliminating such exposure

b   Invoicing in foreign currency

Advantages derived by exporters and merchants who invoice in foreign currency may be obtained:

- when the receivable foreign currency is quoted at a premium and the exporter or merchant is selling the currency forward fixed; a smaller benefit may be derived under an option forward contract, particularly if the option period is wide; exporters and merchants are advised to consider limiting the period of any option contract wherein they are selling foreign currency quoted at a premium on the forward, in order to obtain the greatest benefit
- when the cost of granting credit may be reduced by the function of the premium received, and improved credit terms may lead to increased sales
- when the foreign importer receives an invoice in his home currency; this sometimes leads to payment being made promptly, as the importer has no foreign exchange formalities with which to contend; the importer's buying decisions are simplified, as he can translate costs immediately (being expressed in his own currency)
- when the receivable currency is appreciating in value; stable price lists may lead to higher sales when the lists are compared with competitor's prices that may be increased on a regular basis to keep pace with inflation in the form of rising costs and falling currency values; receivables will yield more domestic currency for the exporter or merchant when converted into the home currency (sterling)
- when the receivable currency is stable; interest rates for any borrowing by the exporter or merchant, pending the receipt of funds, tend to be low when compared with weaker currencies which are usually associated with volatile and high interest rate structures
- when the foreign importer is required to make a payment in a stronger currency than his own; the importer is likely to make prompt payment (he leads – see 'Leads and lags' below), perhaps making early payment or rebating bills which are not yet due, since any delay might involve him in having to find more of his own currency to settle the invoice later on
- when the exporter or merchant maintains a foreign currency account; the receipts and payments may be hedged, thereby reducing the exchange-risk exposure

Disadvantages may be experienced by UK exporters and merchants who invoice in foreign currency:

- when sterling appreciates against the receivable currency (unless of course the currency has been sold forward or is otherwise hedged)
- when the funds are not received; any forward contract entered into will have to be closed-out, possibly involving an exchange loss; any foreign currency loan outstanding will have to be repaid and the foreign currency to do so will have to

be purchased at the spot rates then ruling, which may also involve the exporter or merchant in an exchange loss

- when new procedures are introduced; staff must be trained, new accounting procedures established, computer programmes written or amended – all this will take both time and money; the increase in administration costs may also be accompanied by an increase in bank charges such as exchange commission
- when planning and forecasting profits; fluctuating exchange rates make accurate forecasting even more difficult (see *ii* below)
- when invoicing in a potentially strong currency; sales volume might be reduced, particularly if the currency of the invoice is not the buyer's home currency (ie, US dollar invoice on a Brazilian buyer)

i   *Foreign currency account*
It is possible for UK residents to buy foreign currency and to hold it on a current or an interest-bearing account pending the making of future payments abroad. It is also possible for exporters to retain the proceeds of exports in foreign currency on such accounts. A currency account may provide the trader with the chance to net payments and receipts in the same currency, without losing on the exchange rates on each transaction.

ii   *Borrowing foreign currency*
If a foreign currency is borrowed by a UK exporter, the currency may be sold immediately for sterling. In due course the foreign currency proceeds will arrive from the buyer and will be credited to the foreign currency loan account in repayment. The exporter crystallises his exchange position at the outset with the spot sale of foreign currency and therefore does not risk an exchange exposure. If the proceeds are not received for any reason an exchange risk will be run as the loan is expressed in foreign currency, which in the meantime could have hardened against sterling and the difference would be borne by the exporter.

A trader who is selling goods expressed in foreign currency and advertises them in catalogue format will not wish to alter his prices too frequently to keep pace with exchange rate fluctuations as this would reflect adversely on his sales turnover and cause him a considerable administrative burden and cost. The trader might wish to cover his exchange exposures on potential sales by means of forward exchange contracts. Another useful solution to this problem is derived by the trader identifying the anticipated flow of foreign currency income over a six or 12 month period ahead. As an alternative he may borrow the foreign currency from the bank. The 'borrowed' foreign currency is sold for spot sterling thereby covering the trader's risk on currency fluctuations and helping him to maintain a stable price list which should be conducive to sales. Should the exporter have an ECGD credit insurance policy it is possible for a foreign currency contracts endorsement to be obtained on it. For consumer goods the cover is up to 10 per cent of the exporter's basic entitlement in the event of a valid claim being made, and any further loss as a result of borrowing in foreign currency or the closing-out of a forward contract falling within this figure will be covered.

Comparative interest rates in different currencies for like periods should be checked and costs and benefits calculated. If, for example, the choice of currencies was sterling and US dollars, the financing period three months, the cost of borrowing sterling 14½ per cent per annum, and the cost of borrowing dollars 13½ per cent per annum; the exporter would appear to gain 1 per cent per annum by reducing his sterling borrowing or by investing the sterling at a higher yield by taking a loan in US dollars which would be sold spot for sterling.

If there exists a widespread belief that a particular currency will become cheaper in terms of other currencies, it is likely that there will be an increased loan demand from foreign borrowers who may anticipate that they will be able to repay in due course with less of their own currency, thereby reducing the total liability. An increase in loan demand is one factor which contributes towards the relatively higher interest rates usually associated with the potentially weaker currencies. Another reason is often the desire by the authorities to attract foreign investment to bolster up the reserves, and domestic interest rates in the past have been largely influenced by direct as well as by indirect central bank involvement (see sections 9 and 13 in this chapter).

iii Forward contracts

Bankers are often asked by customers with firm or potential commercial commitments for advice whether they should buy, or sell, forward. The answer is invariably the same: the customer should cover his exchange risk. Normally the customer has sufficient trouble to obtain his legitimate profit on his trading; he should not endeavour to increase that profit by speculating in exchange. From the moment a customer enters into a forward contract, for example, he knows immediately how much he will have to pay or receive in due course. He has no further risk and can go home and sleep at night regardless of what may be happening on the foreign exchange market (see also sections 4, 5 and 6 of this chapter). Advice on forward contracts, sought by those with no commercial contracts in mind, should be given by experienced dealers only who are in direct touch with the market.

Exporters invoicing in currencies potentially stronger than their own may normally be able to sell their foreign currency receivables forward at a premium. This is to say that the forward currency, being in demand, commands a higher price than the spot value, so the exporter can perhaps obtain a better yield on his overseas sales and at the same time enjoy protection against exchange fluctuations.

iv Fixed exchange rates

The UK exporter who calculates his invoice prices in foreign currency, and against the total inserts an exchange rate against sterling, is in effect turning what appears to be a foreign currency invoice into a sterling one. This has the effect of passing the exchange risk to the foreign buyer.

v Barter agreements

There are four basic forms of barter trade:
* *straight barter* or compensation trade; this is often difficult to arrange; no payment takes place between contracting countries; bi-lateral trading countries operate a similar system, clearing settlements by paying buyer and seller each in his own currency
* *unbalanced barter*; the value of the goods exchanged is different and is made up in local currency
* *balanced barter*; the value of the goods is the same
* *triangular barter*; the settlement of compensation trade by a sale or purchase to or from a third country through the medium of a clearing account

These forms of trade are specialised processes and have relevance to Comecon countries' business with the West, as well as LDCs (lesser developed countries) of Asia, Africa and South America. The combined effect of volatile exchange rates and freedom from exchange control limitations on these arrangements will probably stimulate an increase in barter operations transacted in London during the 1980s.

c   A practical case study, and summary

A comparative return to a UK exporter who contracted to sell £50,000 worth of goods for settlement six months later, using different invoicing techniques, on the basis of 1976 actual rates.

i	*Invoicing in sterling:*	the exporter received £50,000, six months later, but was borrowing sterling at 16 per cent pa over the period; his net return was £46,000.
	Comment:	by hindsight not recommended with the then prevailing state of sterling. A year later sterling interest rate levels for six month money had fallen by almost 10 per cent.
ii	*Invoicing in US$ without forward cover:*	the exporter invoiced for $90,000 when the rate was $1.80; when the dollars arrived the rate had fallen to $1.64, and he therefore received £54,878; the cost of borrowing sterling for six months was £4,000, so his net return was £50,878.
	Comment:	although this will appear to be the most attractive method, it is not recommended as the rates *may* have gone the other way. A year later the rate for sterling improved to US$1.99, and in 1980 reached $2.45.
iii	*Invoicing in US$ covering the risk forward:*	the exporter received the premium of 6.92 cents on $1.80 spot, making the forward rate $1.7308; this gave £52,000 which, less the cost of sterling, gave him a net return of £48,000.
	Comment:	profit was taken at the outset, and the exporter had the security of knowing exactly how much would be received. A year later the US$ went to a discount against six months' forward sterling for a short period.
iv	*Invoicing in US$ then borrowing dollars which are immediately sold for spot sterling, dollar borrowing being repaid in six months from proceeds:*	the spot dollars sold at $1.80 yield £50,000; this was applied against the sterling overdraft costing 16 per cent pa; the dollar loan cost 8 per cent pa, and the dollar interest due after six months was $3,600 which, when converted at maturity at $1.64, cost £2,195; the net return was £47,805.
	Comment:	care should be taken to cover the exchange risk on interest payments when the sums are material; in

Comment (continued):   this case the loss was £115 which he could have saved if he had covered the interest forward at 1.7308.

To summarise, the exporter has a number of ways of reducing or eliminating his exchange risk. They are:

i   By invoicing his buyer in the home currency – eg, a UK exporter invoicing in sterling. This means that the importer abroad has to buy sufficient sterling to cover the invoice and pay in his own foreign currency. The buyer therefore runs the exchange risk.

ii   By maintaining a foreign currency account which may be credited with the export proceeds thereby avoiding the necessity of exchanging currencies and suffering the attendant risk of loss. However, great care should be exercised because on balance sheet date such accounts may give rise to 'translation losses' on unrealised but taxable profits. It is a Companies Act requirement for UK companies to issue sterling balance sheets.

iii   By borrowing the foreign currency from his bank and selling it straightaway for sterling. When the proceeds in foreign currency are received they repay the loan made in that currency by the bank.

iv   By fixing the rate at the outset with his bank, invoicing in foreign currency and selling the proceeds under a forward contract.

v   By invoicing in foreign currency and fixing the exchange rate on the invoice. The effect of this is to turn what may seem to the overseas buyer to be an invoice payable in his own currency into an invoice in sterling.

vi   By barter trade whereby goods and/or services are received in settlement for goods and/or services exported.

vii   By ECGD cover up to 10 per cent over and above the maximum sterling liability in respect of losses on the close-out of forward contracts or refinancing a foreign currency loan.

8.   SUPPLY AND DEMAND

'Supply and demand' is an economic concept related to market situations. The foreign exchange market is essentially a free market. The price of the commodity, money, is expressed in terms of a similar commodity (one currency in terms of another) and is called the rate of exchange. The exchange rate may fluctuate according to the dictates of supply and demand. If a particular currency is plentiful, and is being offered by many dealers on the market, it will tend to become cheaper in terms of other currencies that are being purchased in exchange – the price of the currency being readily supplied and offered for sale will fall. Conversely, if a currency is in demand, and few people are offering it for sale, the price of that currency will rise.

The factors which create a demand, or lack of demand, for a particular currency are very often difficult to identify or isolate. However, the following factors (dealt with in greater detail in sections 9 to 13 in this chapter) are known to affect rates of exchange:

- international interest rate differentials
- confidence – economic, political and commercial actions, and speculation
- national balance of payments situation
- limiting factors such as central bank intervention and exchange control
- rates of internal inflation and the relative purchasing power of currencies

9. INTERNATIONAL INTEREST RATES

The normal method of short-term portfolio investment in any centre, either here or abroad, is by means of treasury bills. It is also possible to invest abroad in deposit accounts, through discount houses, hire purchase companies, stocks, bonds, CDs, or commercial paper, but for the sake of simplicity the following example is based upon treasury bills. References to interest rates are generally in the context of what an investor might expect to receive gross, not the rate of discount which would be applied in practice.

Let us assume that London is on a rate of 15 per cent and New York has an equivalent rate of 13 per cent; there is therefore a 2 per cent interest differential in favour of London, which means that there is an incentive for people abroad to move funds from New York to London. If an American wishes to buy a UK treasury bill he cannot do so with dollars – treasury bills in London can only be bought with sterling – consequently the American must sell dollars and buy sterling. With the sterling he buys a treasury bill, and at the end of the duration of the bill he receives a certain amount of sterling back, greater than he started with, which he will then convert into dollars. He has made a greater profit than he would had he left his money in American treasury bills. There is, however, one snag to this transaction: if in the intervening three months of the treasury bill the pound were to depreciate in value, the American would receive fewer dollars than he started with when he sold his sterling at the end of three months. However, forward exchange provides a means of covering against a possible loss resulting from a devaluation: the method is for the customer to do a 'swap'. This means he sells his dollars spot and buys them forward. The two deals are done at the same time, and by selling the spot dollars he receives spot sterling; and when he sells his forward sterling he receives forward dollars. So for the duration of the 'swap', which is normally for the period of the investment, in this case a three-month treasury bill, he is completely covered against any change in the rate of exchange.

There is of course not just one person wishing to do this type of transaction, but many. Accordingly, we find there is a large demand for forward dollars, and when there is a large demand for anything it becomes expensive. So a substantial demand for forward dollars means that forward dollars will get more expensive than spot dollars. Therefore, forward dollars go to a premium.

It must be borne in mind that if forward dollars go to a premium, forward sterling goes to a discount, it is the same thing. It is possible to calculate the cost of covering forward, and this cost, represented as a percentage per annum, increases as more people wish to do this type of transaction (see section 15 in this chapter).

The percentage per annum cost of covering forward gradually approaches the interest differential between London and New York; in our example it is 2 per cent. In theory it never quite reaches 2 per cent because people will cease to do this type of transaction when it becomes less profitable to do so. So we would expect the cost of covering forward to go up to about $1\frac{15}{16}$ per cent and no further, because after that the customer is obtaining the benefit of only $\frac{1}{16}$ per cent by coming to London, and the $\frac{1}{16}$

per cent (or less) is not really worthwhile, taking into account the work and cost of making the transaction.

The interest rate theory involved in such a transaction is also subject to some modifications. For instance, residents of countries with exchange control limitations may have a large amount of their currency to invest and find they can obtain a higher rate in New York than they can locally. If, for example, New York were on 15 per cent and locally it was 13 per cent, this would be the case. If they wished to invest money in New York and cover the transaction by means of a 'swap', the exchange control in their country would prohibit it. So straightaway there is one modification to the rule.

There are many people, however, who are prepared to take a calculated risk on a currency revaluing. So a non-resident in order to invest in London, say, might sell spot dollars or some other currency. With the spot sterling he acquires he buys treasury bills and keeps them for three months. This means that the investor maintains an open position in sterling on his books, hoping of course that sterling will strengthen against his home currency in the meantime.

The effect of this is that the forward rates are not influenced at all; there is no covering forward, but there is an offering of dollars or francs spot which may be taken in by the Bank of England on behalf of the Exchange Equalisation Account and, therefore, the UK's gold and convertible currency reserves will rise. Much of the 'hot' money which came to London in 1979 was the result of non-residents of the UK buying sterling spot for purposes of investment (see section 14 in this chapter).

10. CONFIDENCE

If investors and those with assets denominated in the currency of a particular foreign country are concerned about the political situation in that country there is a tendency for them to sell that currency forward. We can take the example of the UK, when in 1975 there were fears that the government would be unable to cope with militant trade unions and effectively curb exorbitant wage demands responsible for the highest inflation rate in the UK's history. We saw then that forward pounds were sold, which meant, of course, that they went to a bigger discount. These were sales of sterling by non-resident banks and investors.

An example of a political factor was the assassination of President Kennedy, when people outside the US as well as people in that country thought his successor would be even more against big business than he. As a result people sold forward dollars, which, of course, reduced the premium forward dollars had over forward sterling. Economic factors, or potential economic factors, will affect the forward market in the same way.

If investors think interest rates are going to rise in a certain country, they will sell the currency forward in anticipation of interest rates rising. In anticipation of a rise in the UK interest rates from, say, 15 per cent to 15½ or 16 per cent, forward sterling will be sold while it is still relatively cheap to do so; but the fact that people sell forward sterling leads to a bigger discount on forward sterling, so that, if and when the interest rate rises, the forward rates will remain unchanged, because they have moved sufficiently far to anticipate the rise. If interest rates do not rise, forward sterling will get stronger as people anticipate conditions in various countries and try to buy or sell their currencies forward in order to be first on the 'bandwagon'. In other words, there is a speculative element in this business.

Speculation

If people think a currency is going to devalue, they obviously wish to protect themselves by making sure they have none of that currency on their books. So they sell all their spot holdings, but they may still require some currency with which to run their accounts in that country. They obtain these balances by buying the currency spot and selling it forward, doing so in a sufficient amount to give them the capital necessary to run their accounts. Then, when speculation really gets under way, we find that people are not content with just selling their spot balances and covering themselves by buying spot and selling forward to run their accounts, they go further. They sell that particular currency outright on the forward market.

In 1975–6, when the pound came under suspicion, non-residents of the UK were selling pounds three months outright, six months outright, and even further forward – ie, they did not buy any spot pounds to balance their books. That meant they stayed permanently short on their books of these pounds. They did not have to deliver them until the forward matured. When the pound devalued they met their forward maturity by buying spot sterling and made a profit.

The pressure of the selling forward causes the forward to go to a substantial discount. Calculated as a percentage per annum, it may go up to 10, 15 or 20 per cent. Interest rates no longer have any influence on the matter. The cost of covering French francs forward in March 1976, when the franc left the EEC common float, ran overnight to 700 per cent per annum (see section 15 in this chapter).

In the same way as one can speculate against a currency, so one can speculate in favour of a currency – that is, to be a 'bull' of a certain currency. In other words, one buys a currency in the hope that it will considerably appreciate in value. If, for example, the opinion in the foreign exchange world is that a particular currency is going to revalue (increase in value) against other currencies, then, obviously, those who wish to make a profit out of such an eventuality will want to buy some of this currency and hold on to it. If the currency is bought spot the buyer takes delivery of it in two days' time. But he then has to pay for it. This is the snag. He may not have the money to pay, or, if he has, he will not wish to tie up his liquid assets by leaving the currency lying idle on an account abroad or in the UK where it earns no interest. So the obvious thing to do is for the speculator to buy the currency forward without, of course, making his books square by selling any spot. In other words, he buys forward currency outright. He hopes that before he takes delivery the currency will have revalued and he can sell out at a profit.

Such action, in this example, by many investors, institutions and international commercial corporations leads to an excessive demand for such forward currency, and this demand causes a rise in price; so, of course, the forward value of the currency goes to a premium. As in the case of speculation against the currency, discussed in the previous paragraphs, the demand for this forward currency completely swamps the earlier stated theory of interest rates. In other words, speculation is now in control of the forward market for that particular currency. In the 1979-80 dollar crisis many holders of dollars sold them for Swiss francs, deutschemarks, and sterling. The result of the tremendous demand for Swiss francs and marks in the 1971 dollar crisis led to the authorities of those countries imposing negative interest rates on non-resident accounts. This charge for leaving money on deposit or current accounts is an effective way of ensuring that the home currency of such countries is not bought and that unwanted foreign currency does not accrue to that country's reserves. Negative interest in Germany was however in effect for only a very short period, and it was abolished in Switzerland in 1980.

11. LEADS AND LAGS

Foreign currency pending:	A UK exporter (receiving foreign currency) might:	A UK importer (paying foreign currency) might:
1 Devaluation	*a* Lead (shorten credit)	*b* Lag (take even longer to pay)
2 Revaluation	*c* Lag (grant longer credit)	*d* Lead (pay early-rebate bills)

Sterling pending:	A foreign importer (paying in sterling) might:	A foreign exporter (receiving sterling) might:
1 Revaluation	*a* Lead (pay early)	*b* Lag (give longer credit)
2 Devaluation	*c* Lag (delay payment)	*d* Lead (reduce credit)

The two items numbered 1 in the table are the same thing (devaluation of a foreign currency = revaluation of sterling). Similarly, the items numbered 2 above are the same: if sterling becomes worth less in terms of a foreign currency it is the same as saying that the foreign currency becomes worth more in terms of sterling.

The table notes the probable actions of businessmen when they consider that the currency of the transaction may become worth much more, or much less, than at present in terms of the home currency, assuming they have not covered their foreign exchange risk with a forward contract.

a UK exporters receiving payment in foreign currency that might become worth less later (devalue) will press harder than usual for payment (lead). Since foreign currency received after devaluation will not yield so much sterling as it would have before devaluation, the exporter runs a potential risk if he has not covered his exchange risk forward. If the foreign currency is pending devaluation, sterling must be pending revaluation in terms of that currency. If a UK exporter invoices in sterling he runs no foreign exchange risk; it would be borne by the foreign importer. When sterling is pending revaluation the foreign importer will wish to buy sterling immediately to settle his debt in that currency before it becomes worth more (revalues) in terms of his own. He will settle his debts perhaps well in advance of their due dates, and by paying early 'leads'.

b UK importers having to make payment in foreign currency that could become cheaper later in terms of sterling will defer payment (lag), in the hope that they might be able to purchase the same amount of foreign currency for less sterling. Similarly, foreign exporters expecting sterling to appreciate in terms of their own currency will endeavour to delay receipt of sterling proceeds (lag), so that, if revaluation of sterling intervenes, the proceeds will yield more units of their own currency when sold.

The effects of (a) and (b) will be felt, for example, whenever there is a lack of confidence in a foreign currency in terms of sterling, as shown in the following illustration:

	Before US$2.10 = £1	
Devaluation of, say, US$	=	Revaluation of, say, sterling
The value of $ falls (more $ = £1)	After US$2.45 = £1	The value of sterling rises (more $ = £1)

As the probability of a devaluation of a currency becomes more apparent, more and more businessmen will lead or lag. The overall effect is to bring about:

i   A considerable change in the timing of payments.

ii   A change in the balance of payments figures. Where goods are invoiced in sterling foreign importers are paying early, and where UK exporters are invoicing in currency they are demanding early settlement. So there will be an acceleration in the demand for sterling. The foreign exporters selling in sterling may endeavour to delay receipt of sterling and the UK exporters invoiced in currency would probably delay paying for a while longer. This would result in the current demand for foreign currencies being minimised.

iii   A rate of exchange is the price of one currency in terms of another, and the effect of leads and lags on the value of the foreign currency pending devaluation is to exaggerate the situation. By their actions, a surplus of the foreign currency is placed on the market and sterling is in shorter supply. The price of sterling will rise in terms of the foreign currency, and the value of the foreign currency will fall in terms of sterling.

12. BALANCE OF PAYMENTS

All other things being equal – ie, parity between interest rates, there being no political or economic factors to affect the forward rates, and no speculation against the particular currency concerned – any country which has an overall surplus in its balance of payments will have its currency quoted at a premium on the forward. For, by virtue of the fact that more money is coming into the country than is going out, more people abroad will buy the currency forward in order to settle their debts than there will be others selling it forward. Hence the demand for forward currency will cause that currency to go to a premium.

A relaxation of exchange control regulations can give rise to an increase in demand for a particular currency, and an imposition of new exchange control regulations can reduce the level of demand.

13. CENTRAL BANK OPERATIONS IN THE FOREIGN EXCHANGE MARKET

a   Fixed and floating rates of exchange

Rates are said to be 'fixed' when the monetary authorities of the countries concerned agree to limit the degree to which the spot rates of their currencies may fluctuate against other currencies. The Bank of England manages the UK Exchange Equalisation Account, which contains the official UK foreign currency reserves.

'Floating' exchange rates mean that the monetary authorities of the countries concerned have no obligation to ensure that the exchange values of their currencies are kept within clearly defined limits. In other words, the market price of one currency in terms of another will be allowed to rise and fall in accordance with the factors that dictate the supply of, or demand for, a particular currency. If UK traders enter into commitments to pay foreign currency in the future, the rate of exchange applicable at the time of payment may have changed considerably. It becomes increasingly difficult for banks to quote reasonable forward exchange rates to their customers when exchange fluctuations are frequent and substantial. The amount of foreign currency to be paid or received by a trader when converted into sterling could be more or less than expected, either increasing the anticipated profit or reducing it, or even resulting in a loss.

During the 1971 US dollar crisis currencies were allowed to float freely, and fixed rates of sterling against other currencies were re-established in December 1971. In June 1972 sterling was floated again as a massive lack of confidence against sterling was rapidly draining the UK foreign currency reserves.

The European common float, sometimes known as the 'snake', comprised the following currencies prior to the formation of the European Monetary System (EMS): deutschemark, Dutch guilder, Belgian and Luxemburg francs, Danish krone, Swedish krona and Norwegian krone. The snake was designed to provide currency stability between members (and to an extent achieve a short-term stability) by the member central banks maintaining the value of their own currencies within 2¼ per cent of an agreed parity with the other members. There was no obligation with regard to other currencies, against which members of the snake floated freely. Every so often there was an internal realignment of parities, usually as a result of the strength of the deutschemark and the relative weakness of other currencies.

The European Currency Unit (ECU), briefly described in the final section of this chapter, is central to the European Monetary System (EMS) which came into existence in March 1979. Of the nine EEC countries at that time (Greece joined the EEC later but not the EMS) only the UK remained outside the EMS. Seven of the remaining eight countries agreed to maintain the value of their currencies within plus or minus 2¼ per cent of a fixed central rate against the ECU as determined by the central banks. Italy maintained a wider band arrangement of plus or minus 6 per cent. This system gives rise to a need for a parity grid to calculate the upper and lower intervention point limits for each currency against the ECU, and, in turn, from this against each of the other national currencies in the EMS. It is important to realise that, as the ECU is not a currency which can be bought and sold on the foreign exchange markets, intervention must be through national currencies. As each of the EMS currencies plus sterling is part of the ECU, a change in the value of one of the currencies changes the ECU. This has the effect of reducing the degree of change in that currency's ECU value. However, each country has a different weighting for its currency within the ECU, so the extent of impact on the ECU value created by a change of deutschemark values is much greater than that of the Danish krone. It therefore follows that a given percentage change in the value of the deutschemark will have a smaller effect within the EMS parity grid than a similar percentage change in the value of, say, the Danish krone.

b   Operations in spot transactions when rates were fixed

The British government at the Smithsonian Agreement in Washington in 1972 agreed with the IMF to maintain the spot value of the pound to within 2¼ per cent either side of the US$2.6057, allowing for a total possible market fluctuation for spot transactions of 4½ per cent. Other leading currencies were also fixed against the US dollar, so there were maximum limits to which spot sterling could fluctuate against other currencies. When the spot value of sterling fell to near the lower limit of US$2.5471 the Bank of England entered the market to buy sterling and sell dollars. This had the effect of absorbing surplus sterling and releasing a further supply of dollars and thereby maintained or improved the price (rate of exchange) of sterling. On the other hand, had the spot value of sterling reached the upper limit of US$2.6643, the Bank of England would have bought surplus dollars for the UK reserves, thereby absorbing some of the surplus offered and preventing the value of sterling from rising still further.

c   Operations in the forward market

Central banks can, if they so desire, intervene in the forward market. Forward rates have never been fixed and may therefore freely fluctuate in accordance with supply and demand. If the discount on forward sterling is increasing because of speculation and bad balance of payments the Bank of England may intervene in the forward market by buying forward sterling and selling forward dollars. This buying of forward sterling reduces the discount on forward sterling and the Bank, if it pressed the business strongly enough by buying sufficient spot dollars and selling forward dollars, could force the discount on forward sterling until it reached almost par. The important thing in this complicated subject is to remember that the central banks can influence forward rates one way or the other if they wish. Other central banks have intervened in their own currencies in different ways, although not necessarily in the same way as the Bank of England which has on occasions intervened extensively in the forward market.

d   Two-tiered exchange rates

From time to time certain countries operate a two-tiered exchange rate system. At present, 1981, only Belgium of the countries the currencies of which are regularly traded on the foreign exchange market has a two-tiered system: the Belgian convertible and financial francs. The reason for the system is to segregate the purpose for payments into two categories to enable the Belgian authorities to control their economy by endeavouring to regulate non-commercial transactions. Several East European countries have a two-tiered system to segregate the commercial from the tourist rate.

14.   'HOT' MONEY

'Hot' money is a vast sum of international money which is available for investment or for speculative purposes. When it is used for investment the money moves from one country to another in order to obtain the benefit of higher interest rates. When it is speculative it is money which will flow from a weak currency into a stronger in the hope that the stronger currency will increase its value and enable a capital profit to be made.

An example is money which went into Switzerland and Germany in 1971 from the US and other countries, because people thought the currencies of those two countries would increase their value. The deutschemark had already increased its value, but speculators thought it would be revalued. Hot money also went into Germany in 1970 because it was thought that there would be another change in the parity of the mark. Hot money has come to this country on many occasions because our interest rates have been higher than those in other countries. An example of hot money coming in occurred in the early part of 1971 when, as our interest rates were higher than those of other countries, there was an inflow; as a result our gold and convertible currency reserves increased to such an extent that exchange control restrictions (EC Notice 82) were imposed temporarily, prohibiting interest payments to non-residents, to discourage hot money entering.

It must therefore be borne in mind that although hot money is not necessarily speculative it is always dangerous; it can flow out of a country as quickly as it comes in. An example is the outflow of money from the UK in June 1972 and in 1975–6.

Hot money is useful in bolstering the reserves when they are running low, and that is one reason why interest rates are increased when a country is encountering a balance of payments crisis. But increasing interest rates is a false move because the inflow into the reserves helps to disguise the basic monetary situation and leads politicians to look at the reserves rather than the country's economy and the capacity of its industries to be profitable.

Hot money may come into a country and remain uncovered on the forward, but if the money comes in for investment purposes there is a good chance that it will be covered forward and thus have an effect upon forward rates.

15. THE COST OF FORWARD COVER, AND THE RELATIONSHIP BETWEEN THE DOMESTIC AND EURO INTEREST RATES

Investors need to know what the additional cost or profit on a foreign exchange 'swap' transaction will be in order to assess the true net return on their investment. Banks also assess the cost of forward cover in market deals where, for example, they are required to pay interest on a foreign currency deposit for which there is no demand for lending purposes. How is the cost calculated?

As a first example, take US dollars which are at a premium: the spot price 2.00½, one month, ½ cent premium; therefore the outright one month price becomes 2.00. The one month margin is raised to one year by multiplying by 12; the resultant figure is then divided by the forward price, *viz*: 12 × ½ equals 6, 6 divided by 2.00=3 per cent pa.

For another example, working on a three months' dollar price: spot dollars 2.00½ three months' dollars, 1 cent premium; therefore the actual three months' price becomes 1.99½. The three months' premium is raised to a year by multiplying by 4, and this is divided by the forward price of 1.99½; therefore 4 divided by 1.99½=2.005 per cent pa.

For the next example, let us take a currency at a discount. Belgian francs spot 60.40, the one month margin 15 cents discount; therefore the actual one month price outright becomes 60.55. Then, 15 multiplied by 12, divided by 60.55 = 2.973 per cent pa. In like manner, the three months' of 25 cents discount, the spot 60.40, the actual three months' price becomes 60.65. And, 25 multiplied by 4 = 100, which divided by 60.65 = 1.649 per cent pa.

The formula to remember is:
'Discount or premium × number required to raise the period to one year × 100 divided by the forward rate.'

Is the result which is calculated a profit or a cost? One person's profit may be said to be the other's cost, so assuming an investor sells US$ spot for sterling and at the same time buys back US$ forward fixed at a premium, the investor is selling his dollars at one price and buying them back later at a more expensive price. Clearly this is a cost to the investor. Had the currency been at a discount on the forward the investor in the example would have made a profit on the swap, since his repurchase of dollars would have been at a price cheaper than his selling price.

Does the bank lose money on transactions in which the customer is making a profit on foreign exchange swap transactions? The statement in the previous paragraph that 'one person's profit may be said to be the other's cost' implies that if the customer makes a profit on a swap the bank may make a loss. This is not necessarily so. The bank as a dealer may buy forward currency from one source and sell forward currency to another, and if the overall level of demand for delivery of a currency on a particular day is high the premium on the forward currency given to one party by the bank is paid by another in the rates quoted by the bank to sellers of the forward currency on the one hand, and to buyers of the forward currency on the other.

The bank will quote forward prices which are indicative of the level of demand now for the currency to be delivered on a stated day in the future (option contracts attracting rates which presume delivery to be given or taken by the customer at the worst time for the bank over the option period). These prices are made in the light of the present level of demand, and in anticipation of a dealing profit in forward currency. The investor, on the other hand, is merely comparing the cost or profit of forward cover with the spot price at the time he does the swap deal. As an alternative the investor may choose not to cover his exchange risk forward and just buy the currency he needs spot. Naturally he will run the risk of the currency he buys spot weakening by the time he wishes to sell it; indeed anyone who buys or sells a currency outright is running an exchange risk.

One important point to note is that forward margins are not indicative of what the banks in the foreign exchange market consider to be the likely future spot price of the currency. The forward margins are only a function of the present level of demand for a particular currency to be delivered at a fixed time in the future. Traders should not be tempted to use forward prices as a guide to the future spot value of a currency; the two are not related in any way.

The relationship between domestic interest rates and Euro interest rates may be illustrated in the following example.

Exchange control regulations or statutory reserve requirements which banks in certain countries have to maintain can restrict the extent to which a domestic currency may be available for non-residents. Banks in London, for example, that wish to lend US dollars to their customers may borrow the dollars from US-based banks which must meet the reserve costs which may be added to the interest charged for lending the US dollars to non-resident banks. Alternatively, the dollars may be borrowed from banks outside the USA (without this constraint). Sterling may of course be freely bought and sold by non-residents of the UK on the foreign exchange market, and banks in, say, Paris may borrow US dollars which may then be sold spot for sterling. This creates sterling out of US dollars, and the sterling may then be lent to customers of the Paris bank. Such banks will measure the cost of creating this Euro sterling by adding to the cost of borrowing the US dollars the cost of the $/£ swap, including the interest which will be paid in dollars and received in sterling.

In this example, the Paris lending bank will need to repay the dollars in due course to the depositor, plus interest, and as they have swapped the dollars for sterling, they must buy back dollars forward, plus interest, to cover exchange exposure. US dollars are normally quoted at a premium on the forward against sterling, so this represents an additional cost to the Paris bank and will be added to the cost of the dollars borrowed initially.

Assume the following rates:

Spot $1.9430.

Six months' forward premium, 2.6 cents.

Forward $ (six months' fixed), 1.9170.

Therefore, applying the formula for the cost of forward cover:

$$\frac{0.026 \times 2 \times 100}{1.9170} = 2.71 \text{ per cent pa cost of swap}$$

Cost of borrowing US dollars for six months in the interbank market was 9.25 per cent pa. The cost of covering the interest receivable in sterling and payable in US dollars is approximately 2.71 per cent of 9.25 – ie, 0.25 per cent pa.

The total cost of creating sterling from US dollars for six months is:

$$
\begin{array}{l}
9.25 \text{ per cent} \\
2.71 \text{ per cent} \\
\underline{0.25 \text{ per cent}} \\
12.21 \text{ per cent pa}
\end{array}
$$

Having calculated the cost of this Euro-sterling the Paris bank will have the price on which to base its sterling lending. It is of course possible for domestic sterling to be deposited by non-banking institutions directly with banks abroad. The domestic rate for six months' sterling ruling at the time happened to be 9.6875 per cent pa – a difference of 2.5225 per cent. The Euro-sterling rate is not a direct function of the domestic sterling rate for reasons illustrated above; the rate difference is a function of the impact of interest arbitrage (or the creation of sterling out of US dollars). Whenever sterling is under pressure and there is a large demand from those who wish to acquire a diminishing liability (a borrowing which can be repaid more cheaply later with the home currency), then the Euro-sterling rates will widen against the domestic rates for similar periods, as borrowers create Euro-sterling out of US dollars and force up the premium on the forward dollar as the demand for the swaps builds up.

16. PRESS REPORTS

In order to keep abreast of current affairs in the foreign exchange market it is necessary to understand the foreign exchange market comment for the previous day quoted in the leading newspapers. Moreover, customers of the bank may from time to time enquire about the figures and about information that has been reported in relation to some transaction carried out by the bank. Frequently incorporated in these reports are the terms 'weaker', 'firmer', 'stronger' and 'hardened'. Remember that if the pound is weaker it is buying fewer foreign currency units per pound. For example, if yesterday the pound was worth $2.09½ and today it is weaker by ⅛ of a cent, then today the pound buys $2.09⅜. Similarly, if the pound is firmer today it is worth more foreign currency units. For example, if yesterday the pound against the American dollar was 2.10½ and today it is firmer by ¼ of a cent, then today's rate for the pound against dollars is 2.10¾. Again, if the deutschemark hardened against the pound it means there are fewer deutschemarks per pound today than there were yesterday. If the Swiss franc has weakened against the pound it means there are more Swiss francs on offer per pound today than there were yesterday.

Let us look at the following press extract:

'The Bank of England spent $30–40 million from the official reserves yesterday. It bought spot sterling persistently and also intervened in the market for three, six and twelve months forward. In spite of intervention the spot rate lurched down to 1.9350, a new low since November when the Bank sold tens of millions of dollars a week to hold the market rate of 2.0000. Expectations that the July trade figures, due early next week, will be bad also helped to cloud the scene.'

This indicates that the Bank of England intervened to stop the slide against sterling developing. Intervention meant using reserves (gold and foreign exchange) to buy sterling – ie, loss of UK reserves – which, in this case, meant selling between $30 and $40 million in one day. Bank of England intervention was both in the spot market to try to hold the rate and also in the forward market up to one year to keep the discount from widening too greatly and to show long-term confidence in the pound.

The pressure to sell sterling was so great (loss of confidence in the pound plus normal trading in the market) that the rate 'lurched' – ie, fell suddenly, and by a comparatively large amount – despite heavy Bank of England intervention – to the lowest level since November when our reserves were heavily used to stabilise the rate at 2.0000. The size of the intervention, and the use of the word 'lurched', suggest a large-scale loss of confidence in the pound. The monthly trade figures show the visible trade balance. July figures were due in a few days and were expected to show a larger adverse balance, likely to have a depressing effect on the value of the pound, still further adversely affecting the rate.

17. COMPOSITE CURRENCY UNITS

Composite currency units have been created for two different purposes. Initially they were designed to provide a form of protection against longer-term exchange risks run by borrowers and/or investors in the international capital market. Later on one of the units, the European Unit of Account (EUA), was used to provide a single medium of accounting and financial transactions of international organisations connected with the European Economic Community.

Since 1961 some 70 Euro-currency issues have been arranged in EUAs. The EUA comprises fixed amounts of the following currencies: Dutch guilder (0.286), Belgian franc (3.66) Luxemburg franc (0.14), German marks (0.828), Danish krone (0.217), sterling (0.0885), French franc (1.15), Italian lira (109), and Irish £ (0.00759). At midday each day the middle spot rate on the Brussels foreign exchange market is communicated by the Belgian central bank to the EEC which arranges for the publication of the day's value of the EUA.

The value of the EUA in terms of the Belgian franc is calculated by multiplying the exchange rate as determined above by the fixed amounts given in brackets above, then totalled.

The Special Drawing Right (SDR) unit of account is the only composite unit to include a currency outside its own geographical group. The US$ is the predominant currency in what was a 'basket' of 16, each being weighted according to its importance in international transactions. As from 1st January 1981 the SDR comprises five major currencies as indicated below.

US dollars	42%
Deutschemarks	19%
Yen	13%
French francs	13%
Sterling	13%

The Eurco is a weighted basket of nine European currencies.

The Arab Currency Unit (ARCRU) is based upon 12 Arab currencies.

The European Currency Unit (ECU) is based on six European currencies. The ECU is a renamed EUA, and as at 12th March 1979 was made up as follows:

Danish ore	22
Irish pence	0.75
Luxemburg cents	14

Belgian francs   3.5
French francs   1.2
Dutch cents   28.5
Italian lire   109
W. German pfennigs 83
English pence   9

At that time this one ECU was equal to US\$1.35 and to SDR 1.05. This is a basket of EEC currencies of countries (apart from the UK) in the European Monetary System (EMS); the share of each in the ECU reflects the importance of the economy it represents. (Section 13 of this chapter describes the EMS in the context of fixed and floating exchange rates.)

PAST EXAMINATION QUESTIONS

1   On 1st April a UK exporter sold goods to a West German buyer to a value of Dm225,000, payment terms providing for remittance of:
Dm75,000 on 1st May
Dm75,000 on 1st June
Dm75,000 between 1st June and 1st July.
The exporter at once covered all his exchange forward. The 1st May and 1st June instalments were received in full on their respective dates, but a credit note in respect of an earlier transaction was offset against the final instalment and the exporter agreed that he had been paid in full when he received Dm67,500 on 16th June.
It was later discovered that the credit note should have been for Dm2,500 only, and the exporter received an adjusting remittance of Dm5,000 on 18th July. Using the rates given below, calculate the total sterling amount received by the UK exporter.

1st April spot	4.09	– 4.10	
1 month forward	2¼	–	2 pfennigs premium
2 months' forward	4½	–	4 pfennigs premium
3 months' forward	7½	–	7 pfennigs premium
16th June: spot	4.08	– 4.09	
18th July: spot	4.05	– 4.06	

No exchange commission is to be charged.

(Institute of Bankers)

2   'Floating exchange rates mean uncertainty of the sterling profit on a transaction.'

a   Explain the meaning of this quotation from *The Economist*. What is a forward exchange contract, and how is it used to avoid uncertainties in rates of exchange?

b   Define the terms: 'fixed', 'option', 'premium', 'discount', in connection with forward exchange contracts.

(Institute of Bankers)

3   Explain fully what you understand by the term Forward Exchange Market. What are the factors which influence this market and how do they operate?

(Institute of Freight Forwarders)

4   You have sold goods invoice value Dm10,000 to a German buyer, payment to be made in 60 days. As you wish to protect yourself against exchange fluctuations you have asked your bank to cover this in the forward market. The bank's quotations are as follows:

Spot Dm	4.10	–	4.15	
1 month forward premium	7	–	6	pfennigs
2 months' forward premium	7½	–	6½	pfennigs
3 months' forward premium	8	–	7	pfennigs

What rate will the bank quote? Could the exchange risk have been covered in any other way?

(Institute of Freight Forwarders)

CHAPTER NINE

Exchange Control

1. INTRODUCTION

Since the first edition of this book in 1976 there have been very considerable changes in UK exchange control. At the end of 1976 the further measures that were then introduced to limit the use of sterling for non-resident purposes brought to a peak the exchange regulations that had obtained over the 40 years of exchange control (1939–79). Within three years all exchange controls had been removed.

The present position regarding UK exchange control is that HM Treasury has made a number of Orders exempting persons in or resident in the UK, the Channel Islands and the Isle of Man from their obligations under the Exchange Control Act 1947.

The Exchange Control Act 1947 is, therefore, still on the statute book, and new exchange control regulations could be introduced at any time and with immediate effect. For the moment, then, there is just one valid notice, dated 24th October 1979: EC 84, Removal of Exchange Controls.

The 1981 Spring Budget heralded a possible selective re-introduction of exchange controls. This would be to limit or to prevent capital inflows into the United Kingdom, thereby taking some external demand pressure off sterling in order to stabilise the exchange rates at an acceptable level. Similar measures were adopted in 1976 by West Germany and Switzerland and only recently (1981) removed. If introduced, the controls would prohibit or restrict payment of interest on non-resident bank and/or other deposit accounts maintained by banks in the UK. Indeed, if the measures to exclude capital inflows needed to be tightened even further, the imposition of negative interest on such deposits is a possibility.

2. AN OUTLINE OF EXCHANGE CONTROLS IN FORCE IN THE UK TO OCTOBER 1979

The United Kingdom is a major manufacturing and trading nation, and successive governments over the years have been aware of the importance of ensuring that any regulations introduced do not impact adversely upon our trading relationships. The general policy in the past was to limit the outflow of capital and to regulate any other factors which could have a direct or indirect impact upon the foreign exchange reserves of the UK or the value of sterling in terms of other currencies. From June 1979 the regulations were relaxed to permit outward direct investments to be funded with sterling at official exchange rates, and from October 1979 the regulations were abolished.

Exchange control was used for the fine tuning of the economy. It is swift to implement to meet the needs of changing circumstances, and its effect may be immediate or may be deferred, as required. For very many years London has been banker to the world, with sterling used widely as a reserve currency and a major trading currency. London being the principal commercial and financial centre of the world, it followed that sterling was vulnerable to the influences of traders (see Chapter 8, section 11) and to the actions of foreign holders of sterling (investors and speculators) The authorities have in the past sought ways to minimise the effects of large movements of sterling, and the consequent volatile exchange rate, without damaging the role of London and its benefits to UK invisible earnings, a task which has not been easy.

In order to assist with the administration of the Exchange Control Act (ECA), the Bank of England granted certain delegated powers to various financial institutions. Authorised banks could deal in gold and foreign exchange, open and run accounts in foreign currencies, approve certain specified applications for exchange control permission, and act as authorised depositories. Authorised depositories were permitted to handle transactions involving foreign securities; they included authorised banks, authorised solicitors, stockbrokers and accountants. For exchange control purposes the world was divided into three geographical areas which equated with the various trading relationships with which the UK was concerned. The areas were:

i   The scheduled territories (UK, Channel Islands, Isle of Man, the Republic of Ireland, and Gibraltar). The area was virtually free from controls for transactions taking place within it, which involved residents of the area and the use of sterling. In 1979, when the Republic of Ireland joined the EMS and the UK did not, the Irish punt and UK sterling parted company on the foreign exchange markets. Accordingly the appropriate exchange control regulations were established by the Republic of Ireland to accord with this situation.

ii   The EEC except the UK and the Republic of Ireland (Belgium, Denmark, France, Germany, Italy, Luxemburg and the Netherlands).

iii The rest of the non-scheduled territories (RNST), excluding Rhodesia (to which special regulations pertained at that time). This area included almost all the Americas, most of Asia, Eastern Europe and more than half the countries of Western Europe, Africa and the Middle East.

The successful administration of UK exchange control was dependent upon the correct designation of accounts.

Notices which were cancelled on 24th October 1979 are listed below. They illustrate the nature of the controls exercised over the 1939–79 period (see also the past examination questions at the end of this chapter).

Notice	Concerned
EC 1	Authorised banks, authorised depositaries, definition of scheduled territories, overseas sterling area
EC 2	Import and export of notes, assurance policies, bills of exchange, etc
EC 3	Administration
EC 4	Sterling finance to bodies corporate resident in the scheduled territories and controlled by non-residents
EC 6	Certificates of deposit and government bills, including treasury bills
EC 7	Foreign currency securities, investment currency, treasury bills and certificates of deposit payable in foreign currency
EC 8	Sterling securities, treasury bills payable in sterling and sterling acceptances
EC 9	Estates and intestacies of deceased residents of the UK and settlements *inter vivos* by residents of the UK
EC 10	Issue of securities and entries in registers
EC 11	Interest, dividends and capital payments on securities
EC 12	Travel
EC 18	Direct investment
EC 25	Education outside the scheduled territories
EC 27	Exemption
EC 28	Determination of residence
EC 29	Emigration to countries outside the scheduled territories
EC 30	External accounts and foreign currency accounts, and the marking of cheques and payments and other instruments of payment received for the credit of external accounts
EC 31	HM diplomatic service officers, other HM civil servants, members of HM forces and employees of the British Council serving outside the scheduled territories
EC 41	Foreign currency and foreign currency accounts maintained by residents
EC 45	Exports from the UK
EC 47	Dealings in notes and coin denominated in the currencies of countries outside the scheduled territories
EC 53	Payments to non-residents for imports into the UK
EC 54	Dealings in foreign currencies
EC 60	Scheduled territory payments
EC 62	Dealings in gold
EC 66	Borrowing by residents of the UK
EC 67	Credits and guarantees and sterling loans and overdrafts to non-residents
EC 68	Merchanting trade by residents of the UK
EC 73	Sterling payments in the UK by order of non-residents
EC 74	Insurance
EC 75	Shipping and air transport payments
EC 76	Cash gifts, personal loans and payments to dependants
EC 78	Sundry payments
EC 79	Rhodesia
EC 80	Solicitors' clients' accounts
EC 81	Property for private use outside the scheduled territories
EC 82	Inflows
EC Commodities Notices	Cover metals; sugar; oils; seeds and fats; cocoa; coffee; grain and feed; rubber; cotton; and wool

3. THE EFFECT OF EXCHANGE CONTROL ABOLITION IN THE UK

For a working lifetime UK residents, bankers and others have lived with the stern discipline of exchange control regulations. This statutory code was taught and practised as a way of everyday life for those involved in international business. In Plato's *Republic* the slaves, when their chains were cut from them, were able to see the real things of life for the first time, and it took a while before they could understand and believe in their new experience and freedom. One question put to the Bank of England shortly after the relaxations had been announced perhaps illustrates the immediate effect. 'Is it really legal,' the enquirer asked, 'to take out of the country thousands of pounds in notes? How much can I honestly take?' Back came the swift reply: 'As many suitcases full as you can carry, so long as you don't exceed the airline's weight limitation on your baggage.'

Companies carrying on business in the UK and individuals previously designated as 'UK residents' may now *inter alia*:

i   Maintain foreign currency accounts with banks in the UK or abroad.

ii   Settle debts with anyone, anywhere, in any currency.

iii   Buy and sell foreign currency, for any reason whatever, spot or forward.

iv   Keep foreign notes, coin and travellers' cheques for as long as they like.

v   Take as much sterling or foreign currency abroad as they want for holidays, house purchase, investment, emigration, or any other purpose.

vi   Buy gold bullion and keep it anywhere they want.

vii   Buy any foreign stocks, bonds, shares, certificates of deposit or other investments, using any currency they want to pay for them.

viii   Cover exchange exposure by buying foreign currency spot and holding it.

ix   Remit unlimited sums abroad for gifts.

x   Import goods and pay for them irrespective of amount.

xi   Cover contingent liabilities forward.

xii   Establish businesses abroad by way of branches, subsidiaries, affiliates or trade investments, and finance them in any way, including by share transfer.

xiii   Grant credit for unlimited periods to anyone, anywhere.

xiv   Lend money to anyone, anywhere, without limitation.

xv   Issue bonds or debentures in foreign currency or sterling for sale to anyone, anywhere.

xvi   Borrow foreign currency for any purpose.

xvii   Deposit sterling with banks outside the UK.

xviii Speculate in commodities or foreign exchange.

xix   Make advance payments and arrange for banks to issue red clause credits, and derive appropriate cash discounts from overseas suppliers.

xx   Engage in barter trade.

4. EXCHANGE CONTROL ABROAD

The management of most national economies involves a mix of fiscal controls such as taxation and import tariffs, and monetary controls like exchange control and official intervention in money supply operations (credit squeezes, MLR changes, tap stock issues, etc).

Most countries have some form of exchange control which is subject to change as the respective authority considers it necessary. While it is beyond the scope of this book to examine these regulations in depth, it is appropriate that bankers and traders in particular should be aware of their existence. Limitations on payments abroad or on the importation of the home currency are common enough, and for practical purposes a knowledge of relevant current regulations is essential. Up to date information on other countries' exchange control regulations is available from the international divisions of banks in London. The UK, USA, Canada, West Germany and Switzerland are free of exchange controls at the time of writing (April 1981).

PAST EXAMINATION QUESTIONS

1   'There are two recognised foreign currency markets in the United Kingdom, the official market . . . and the investment currency market . . .'(*Bank of England Quarterly Bulletin*, September 1976) Describe what is meant by the official market and the investment currency market, indicating why transactions in investment currency take place at a premium over the exchange rate in the official foreign exchange market.

(Institute of Bankers)

2   'Exchange control is not intended to impede trade'. Discuss this statement in the context of exports sold in foreign currency on deferred credit terms to continental buyers.

(Foundation Course in Overseas Trade)

3   Write brief notes on TWO of the following:
    a travel allowances for residents of the UK;
    b the purchase of property abroad for private use by a UK resident;
    c receipts of foreign currency and external sterling resulting from the sale of goods exported from the United Kingdom.

(Institute of Bankers)

4   Outline how exchange control is used to regulate the United Kingdom economy.
(Institute of Freight Forwarders)

The questions above would not now be applicable in the absence of UK exchange controls. They are reproduced in order to provide the reader with illustrations of the extent of the controls in force prior to October 1979.

CHAPTER TEN

International Funding and Financing

1. INTRODUCTION AND GLOSSARY OF TERMS USED IN THIS CHAPTER

A distinction may be drawn between the finance of working capital for trading purposes, described in previous chapters, and the longer-term finance required by companies for major projects or for 'capital' purposes. The permanent equity or issued shares, or the long-term loan stock of a company's liabilities, are required as a funding base for fixed assets such as long-term investments and major projects undertaken by the company.

With the exception of the ECGD-backed facilities described in Chapter 6, this chapter covers various aspects of Euro-currency finance provided for a variety of purposes by UK-based banks; it also illustrates how such assets may be funded.

The following glossary should be glanced through before the chapter is read so that the reader may be generally aware of its contents.

Amortisation	the writing-off of a debt in staged payments.
Arbitrage	the switching of funds from one financial market to another to take advantage of higher yield or capital gain opportunities as a result of interest or exchange rate differentials prevailing between two or more centres.
Average life	the total of the amounts outstanding at the end of each year of the loan for its entire life, divided by the total principal sum borrowed to give the average life of the loan in years.
Back to back loan	companies with surplus liquidity in one currency may wish to obtain funds in another, for investment

Back to back loan
(continued)

or expansion, by employing their own surplus resources without conversion or incurring exchange exposure, or without incurring increased interest costs by borrowing unmatched funds; this may be arranged by means of a parallel, or back to back, loan.

Balloon repayment

when interest payments are rolled up and not paid until the end of the loan period, at which time the loan plus interest is repaid in one lump sum.

Bearer bond

security of which ownership by the holder is presumed.

Bid rate

the lower side of interest rate quotations; it is the rate of interest a bank is prepared to pay for deposits or to acquire securities.

Bond

interest bearing security, usually with coupons attached and in bearer form.

Bullet

loan or placing for which no 'managed' sinking fund is established, and repayment of the loan is made at maturity in a lump sum.

Call (1)

right to demand repayment of a debt.

Call (2)

right to repay a debt and redeem outstanding loan stock.

Call (3)

option to purchase securities at a determined price and during a specified period.

Call account

deposit account, usually interest bearing, from which funds may be withdrawn 'at call' (on notice being given).

Capital (1)

equity or shares (authorised and/or issued).

Capital (2)

equity plus reserves plus profit retained plus loan and debenture stock.

CEDEL

clearing system for Eurobonds based in Luxemburg, where Eurobonds are physically exchanged and stored.

Certificate of deposit

interest bearing negotiable bearer certificate which evidences a time deposit with the bank.

Co-manager

the manager of an issue may invite other financial institutions to join the management team as co-managers.

Confirmation — written acknowledgment of a firm deal involving a placing or deposit or sale or purchase of funds or securities; for reasons of bank security, no dealer should be permitted access to confirmations.

Convertible bond — loan stock that carries the right for the holder to exchange for other securities, usually the ordinary share stock of the borrower, at a predetermined conversion price.

Cost of funds — term sometimes used as the basis for a loan pricing, particularly when the source of funding is uncertain or includes reserve assets costs; a precise definition of what is meant by this term should be established if it is to be of any practical value; it should be noted that the normal funding cost of a commercial loan is the offered rate, being the rate which the bank has to pay to another bank in the market for the funds obtained for the purpose.

Coupon — part of a bond giving the holder the right to be paid predetermined interest; the coupon may be physically cut off the bond and sent to the stated paying agent when due for payment.

Debenture — formal acknowledgment of a debt, usually incorporating a charge over the unencumbered assets of the company issuing it; the rights of debenture holders rank before those of shareholders and unsecured creditors in the event of the issuer's liquidation.

Debt-equity ratio — ratio of a company's ordinary share capital to its fixed interest capital, including debentures, loan stock, and preference shares; calculations are often simply based on the ratio of ordinary shares plus retained reserves to prior charge capital.

Deposits — current liabilities of a bank in the form of current account funds or monies at call, notice or fixed term, in sterling or foreign currency.

Discount (accounting) — calculation of the present value of a cash flow of future payments.

Discount (bills) — purchase of an accepted term bill of exchange for less than its face value.

Discount (bonds) — under-par value of securities.

Discount (forex) — forward margin of a currency that is less expensive than the spot rate.

Domestic issue   loan stock or equity raised in the indigenous capital market and currency of the country of issue: Dutch florins raised in Holland, US dollars raised in the USA, etc.

Drawn bond   redeemable bearer bond that has been selected for repayment (drawn) and should be returned by the holder to a specified paying agent, or to the issuer, for payment.

Eurobond   bearer security normally issued in a currency other than that of the country of issue, and sold internationally.

Euroclear   clearing system for Eurobonds, based in Brussels where Eurobonds are physically exchanged and stored.

Euro commercial paper   'managed' issues of promissory notes made, or bills of exchange drawn, by the borrower; usually guaranteed by the borrower's parent company.

Euro-currency   bank deposits recorded in the name of a non-resident of the country of the currency lodged.

Federal funds rate   the nearest US equivalent to the UK domestic sterling overnight interbank rate; the market is a very important money market, providing a main source of banks' short-term funds; federal funds lent or sold in the market are deposits in excess of the US banks' reserve requirements.

Fixed rate loan   term loan for which the interest rate for the whole period is determined at the outset.

Float (1)   to issue a security (equity or loan stock).

Float (2)   freedom from mandatory intervention by the authorities in the foreign exchange market.

Float (3)   outstanding amounts of money in transmission that can be identified and employed.

Floating rate note   capital loan stock bearing interest that will be determined at regular intervals by a formula based upon prevailing short-term money market rates.

Front end costs   commision, fees or other payments that are taken at the outset of a 'loan', as, for example, discounting; the front end charges for capital issues are very considerable and, in calculating the total cost, a

Front end costs
(continued)

borrower should be aware of the additional cost of being short of such disbursements at the outset when compared with the cost of interest payments that are payable after the loan period and not before.

Front end finance

loan finance provided for the buyer; under ECGD-backed medium-term credit facilities between 15 and 20 per cent of the contract amount must come from the buyer's own resources; the financing of this element, usually by means of a Euro-currency loan, is called 'front end finance'.

Funding

acquisition of liabilities to match, cover or balance the particular asset or assets for which they are required.

Gearing

there are several formulae used, so the basis of a gearing ratio should always be established to be meaningful by ensuring comparisons of like with like; a commonly used formula is:

$$\frac{\textit{Total liabilities (footings) less Capital base}}{\textit{Capital base}}$$

... where the capital base is 'capital plus reserves plus loan stock minus goodwill, if any'.

Hedge

action taken to reduce liability to market price fluctuations of an asset.

Intra vires

as permitted by the Memorandum and Articles of Association of a company, or by appropriate board resolution.

Kassenobligation

listed bearer stock issued by the German government agencies or Girobanks which differs from most Euro market paper in that its interest is subject to withholding tax.

Leverage

degree of exposure of securities to market risks; the capital structure of a company may be increased by issues of loan stock as well as equity, and the risk relationship between the two may be described as the leverage.

LIBOR

London interbank offered rate; the rates upon which loans are frequently determined; LIBOR will vary according to market conditions and will of course depend upon the loan period as well as the currency in question; it may be found that at the same time, for the same currency and for the same

LIBOR *(continued)*   period, the quotation of a LIBOR figure by one bank in London and another in London will differ slightly; this would be expected if one bank were already long of the currency for that period, having just taken in a matched deposit, and the other bank's position were different.

Liquidity   ability to service debt and redeem or re-schedule liabilities when they mature, and the ability to exchange other assets for cash.

Listing   obtaining a quotation on a stock market for loan stock or equity which may then be traded on the stock exchanges.

Marketability   degree of investment demand for a particular asset offered at a given price.

Mark-up   margin taken by the lender over the cost of funds.

Maturity   date on which a loan, bill or other debt instrument falls due for repayment.

Mis-matched maturity   when the maturities of the funding cover and the loan or other asset do not coincide.

Names   a control of the interbank money markets is exercised by the individual banks limiting the total volume of business they will be prepared to conduct with every other bank on a name by name basis.

New York prime loan rate   the US banks' equivalent of the UK base rate; it is not a market rate as such but forms the rating basis for some short-term commercial loans; the rates are not altered on a daily basis for practical loan administration reasons; however, when the trend of the cost of the underlying funds changes, NYPLR will be moved into line; loans may be based on fixed or on floating prime rates; the majority are based on the latter so that the loan will fluctuate broadly in line with market conditions; loans that are based on fixed prime will run to maturity on the basis of the prime rate ruling at the time funds are drawn down, and as such must be considered as any other fixed interest lending.

Note   promise or obligation to pay; promissory notes, bank notes, and floating rate notes all contain the issuer's primary responsibility for payment.

Offer	price over which a loan may be based, or a security purchased from the market, or a bill discounted.
Off-shore	outside the jurisdiction of a particular country.
Paper	usually means commercial paper such as bills of exchange or promissory notes, but may refer to any securities.
Par (1)	nominal value of a security.
Par (2)	issue price of a security if floated at its full face value.
Par (3)	when the spot and forward prices of a currency are the same.
Placing	an interbank deposit which may be a straight market placing, or a private placing of short-, medium- or long-term funds.
Portfolio	bank's or investor's loan and investment assets.
Private placing	sometimes a quicker method of raising unlisted medium- or long-term funds than a listed public issue, since only one or a limited number of investors will be involved.
Prospectus	offering circular containing information about the borrower and the terms and conditions of the proposed loan issue.
Rating	assessment of the quality of an issue by an established rating agency.
Redemption	cancellation of a security by payment; redemption may be mandatory on a certain date, optional by the borrower after a certain date or conditional upon certain described and defined events having taken place (such as a change in tax laws which might jeopardise the borrower's position).
Roll over	revisal of interest rates at agreed intervals, based on a formula agreed at the time the loan was made.
Schuldscheine	an instrument which represents a participation in a German loan, on which interest is paid in full to foreign investors without deduction of withholding tax.

Secondary market market in which securities are traded after issue when the initial distribution has finished.

Securities notes, equity, loan stocks, bonds or other debt instruments.

Selling group the banks and other financial institutions that have been brought together by a lead-manager to take up the securities being issued for sale to their customers.

Sinking fund monies set aside by a borrower, usually at regular intervals and normally from revenue, for the purpose of establishing a reserve to repay a loan at maturity.

Stand-by credit arrangement to lend money in case of need, usually at market rates and sometimes with a commitment fee; overdraft facilities are sometimes used as stand-bys by corporate borrowers.

Straight debt fixed interest rate Eurobond without the option to convert to equity.

Subordination clause sometimes inserted in the terms of a capital loan stock issue whereby the rights of the stockholders rank after the rights of some or all unsecured creditors of the borrower in the event of his liquidation.

Tap security such as a certificate of deposit issued on an 'as required' basis by the borrower; it is not a 'managed issue' (see 'tranche').

Tombstone advertisement which lists the managers and underwriters and sometimes the providers of a recently floated issue.

Tranche 'managed' issue of securities, often in relatively small denominations.

Trustee institution in which the rights of the bond or note holders may be vested.

Underwriter financial institution that agrees to purchase the unsubscribed securities of a new issue.

Units of account composite currency units designed to reduce exchange exposures of both borrower and investor.

Warrant

attachment to a fixed interest security that gives the holder certain rights, such as the right to purchase a given security at a stated price; the warrant can normally be detached from the bond and traded separately.

Withholding tax

deducted in certain countries from interest payable to non-residents; depending on whether a double taxation agreement exists between the investor's country and that of the investment, the investment may or may not prove profitable.

Yankee bond

US domestic issue for a foreign borrower.

Yield, current

ratio of the coupon (interest) to the market price expressed as a percentage; the maturity and frequency of interest payments are not considered.

Yield curve

relationship between the maturity dates of an instrument and the yield; a positive yield curve is one where the shortest maturity bears the least interest and the longest the most.

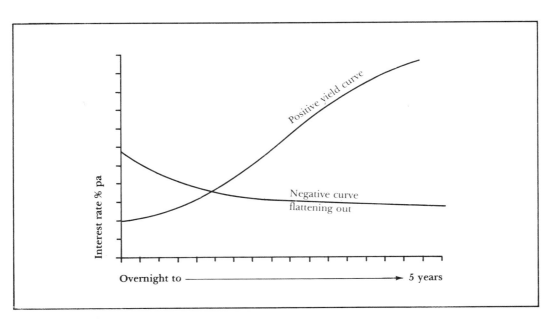

Many investors run 'risk positions' by borrowing short (at low interest rates) and investing in long date obligations riding a profitable positive yield curve; if there is an overall increase in the level of interest rates, or the curve flattens or goes negative, the investor will lose money because his funding costs will exceed his interest income.

Yield, direct   the discount to yield based on the total life of the asset at simple interest.

Yield, effective   calculated on the annual, semi-annual or quarterly compounded interest basis over the period of the actual investment.

Yield to maturity   return on a security held to maturity at a given price; a variety of this is the 'yield to average life' when the average life (*qv*) is substituted for final maturity in the formula.

2. SUMMARY OF A BANK'S FOREIGN CURRENCY FUNDING SOURCES

Methods of raising funds (liabilities)	Balance sheet classification	Is a sinking fund usually established?	Is a credit rating for the issue usual?	Usual maximum period (in years)
Foreign currency current account	Deposit	No	No	Less than 1
Foreign currency short-term 'notice' accounts	Deposit	No	No	Less than 1
Foreign currency short-term 'fixed' accounts	Deposit	No	No	Less than 1
Euro-currency market deposit	Deposit	No	No	2
Medium-term non-bank Euro-currency deposit	Deposit	No	No	5
'Tap' London US$ certificates of deposit	Deposit	No	No	5
'Tranche' London US$ certificates of deposit (fixed or floating rate)	Deposit	No	No	5
Back to back loan	Deposit	No	No	10
US commercial paper issue	Deposit	No	Yes	Less than 1
Private placement	Capital or deposit	No	No	15
Floating rate capital notes issue	Capital	No	No	15
Straight Eurobond issue	Capital	Yes	No	15
Convertible Eurobond issue	Capital	Yes	No	15
Domestic public bond issue (if US$ 'yankee bond')	Capital	Yes	Yes (if US$)	30
Domestic public debenture with warrants	Capital	Yes	Yes	—

Foreign currency may also be created through the foreign exchange market by outright purchase, using sterling (see Chapter 8). It should be stressed that the 'open' position each bank holds is determined by the bank's own management and is closely monitored.

The maximum period for lending fixed-term funds varies greatly according to the currency, the state of the market and the size of demand for particular forms of investment. If interest rates for long-term issues appear to trough the investors might switch their preference for new issues to floating rate paper until an upward trend in rates is truly established. The figures indicated above reflect the maximum periods for transactions that took place in the first quarter of 1977.

A credit rating as referred to above is an evaluation of the investment quality and creditworthiness of a security. A rating agency, such as Moody's Investors' Service, Standard and Poor's Corporation or Fitch Investors' Service, researches into the affairs of the potential borrower and gives a classification accordingly. To ensure the success of certain issues, namely that the paper being issued will attract investors, it is sometimes necessary to obtain a high credit rating.

In order to ensure the orderly amortisation (writing-off) of long-term debts, a sinking fund may be created whereby the borrower sets aside funds out of earnings for the repurchase of the securities during their life. This has the effect of reducing the average life of the issue.

The liabilities side of a balance sheet may be composed of *i* equity, long term debt and loan stocks, which together form the capital items with any retained profits in the form of reserves, and *ii* current short-term liabilities which include deposits. The relationship between *i* and *ii* gives rise to the capital gearing ratio, a figure of great importance to a corporate treasurer, particularly during periods of high inflation or of rapid expansion when the current liabilities (deposits) have grown much faster than the capital. In these circumstances rights and loan stock issues are two ways of maintaining capital adequacy.

A well-managed company or bank would not normally want all or even most of its debt payable in the immediate future, but have the maturities of its debt (all its liabilities) spread over a period, to match as closely as possible the expected life of the assets being funded. While it is not the normal policy of a bank to identify the funding cover for a specific asset (a 'book' is run), it would seem appropriate to fund fixed assets such as property and subsidiary companies with long-term rather than to borrow short for such purposes. The company's liquidity ratio (its barometer which establishes whether it can pay its way and stay in business) often depends upon a good funding strategy. There are many major factors to consider in debt management, some of which include:

- the overall corporate strategy: acquisitions, disinvestments, the rate and manner of expansion, and the percentage mix of assets in the business
- the timing, availability and cost of funds for periods required, and the risks of mismatching
- the currency of the funds required and the risks of mismatching
- foreign exchange control regulations
- UK and foreign taxation and other statutory controls

The above list is by no means comprehensive as there are many specialised money markets abroad which a branch or subsidiary may be able to tap locally, even if they may not be directly available to a foreign borrower. For example, in Germany funds may be raised locally by a German-based operation, in a 'schuldscheine' issue or by way of 'kassenobligations'.

It is beyond the scope of this book to cover in detail all the sources of finance listed above. Accordingly sections 4, 5 and 6 of this chapter provide a background to the more important sources of foreign currency funds for a UK-based bank.

3.   HOW A BANK MAY EMPLOY ITS FOREIGN CURRENCY FUNDS

Types of loans and other assets. Lending by:	Liquidity	Normal maximum period
Loans:		
i Foreign currency overdraft	Repayable on demand	Reviewed annually
ii Negotiation	Recourse agreement	6 months
iii Discount	Rediscountable	6 months
iv ECGD-backed supplier and buyer-credit loans	Refinanceable with ECGD	7 years
v Forfaiting	Sometimes resaleable	8 years
vi Commercial Euro-currency floating rate roll over loan	At maturity	1 – 10 years
vii Commercial Euro-currency fixed rate loan	At maturity	2 years
viii Market placing	—	2 years
ix Back to back loan	Matched liability	10 years
Other assets:		
x Foreign notes and coin	Cash held	—
xi *Nostro* accounts	Cash at banks abroad	—
xii Other banks' certificates of deposit	Readily meltable but subject to market fluctuations	5 years
xiii Investments in Eurobonds issued by other borrowers	Negotiable bearer bonds but subject to wider market fluctuations than CDs	15 years
xiv Participations in foreign affiliates and subsidiaries	Trade investment	—
xv Working capital for branches abroad	—	—

4.   EURO-CURRENCY

a   Introduction

The Euro-dollar market is by far the best known of the markets in foreign currency deposits that have grown up over the last 25 years in Europe and elsewhere and has developed into the largest international money market. The proceeds are widely used in financing international trade and also, converted into other currencies, for domestic financing. Such a market has been in existence on a substantial scale only since about 1957, and London was its first, and has remained its largest, centre. Singapore and Hong Kong compete for the rôle of the leading Far East financial centre, and there are also markets in Paris, Brussels, Luxemburg, Frankfurt, Amsterdam, Zurich, Milan, the Gulf States and Japan, with increasing activity in the Caribbean and Bahamas.

Because the most traded currency is the US dollar (possibly accounting for 80 per cent of the market) the term 'Euro-dollar' is most frequently used to describe the market. Terms such as 'Euro-sterling' or 'Euro-deutschemark' are, however, used when non-dollar currencies are involved.

When Euro-sterling is involved the off-shore account holding banks give instructions to UK banks to move amounts from one sterling *vostro* account to another *vostro* account as the funds in question are borrowed by one overseas bank and are lent to another. The borrowing and lending between banks is carried out principally in Paris and Brussels. The principal market in all other currencies is London – notably US dollar, deutschemark, Swiss franc, Italian lira, Dutch guilder, French and Belgian francs, Scandinavian currencies, Japanese yen and Canadian dollar.

b   Description

A Euro-currency is a freely convertible currency that is held outside the control of the monetary authorities of the country of origin of the currency. The currency itself never leaves the country of origin and the only aspect of, say, a Euro-dollar which differs from any other dollar is the question of ownership. A Euro-currency is owned by a non-resident of the country of the currency and represents external (to that country) bank balances. The *vostro* accounts and other external accounts in London in sterling are the basis for the Euro-sterling market in Paris. Euro-dollars are, in fact, dollars that have been placed in banks in America at the disposal of banks outside the US, mainly (though not exclusively) in Europe. In other words, the Euro-dollar market is a market in which European and other foreign banks accept (borrow) and place (lend), for varying periods of time, deposits in banks in the USA.

c   Mechanics

Normally one might expect that an owner of a dollar deposit (whether an individual, a corporation or a bank) would keep it with a bank in America in his own name. In Euro-dollar operations there may be a departure from this practice in that there is an intermediary between the owner of the deposit and the US bank (possibly a chain of intermediaries) through which the title to the deposit has been transferred.

A typical example would involve the use of Euro-dollars to pay for imports. Let us assume that an owner (non-resident of the US) of funds has an account with bank A in New York and is being offered $15\frac{1}{2}$ per cent on a six-month deposit. Seeking a higher rate of return, the owner ascertains that a UK bank is prepared to pay, say, $15\frac{3}{4}$ per cent for a six-month dollar deposit and he agrees to place (lend) the deposit with the UK bank.

Instructions are given for the deposit to be transferred to the UK bank's account held with one of the bank's American correspondents (say, bank B). The dollars have now entered the Euro-dollar market.

The UK bank may then place the deposit with an Italian bank at, say, 16 per cent, and the Italian bank in turn may lend the funds (at $16\frac{1}{4}$ per cent) to a customer in need of dollar accommodation to pay for imports. The customer, as the final borrower, instructs (through his bank) the American correspondent to pay the funds to the account of an American exporter (held at bank C) to settle outstanding debts for goods shipped to Italy. Thus, the deposit has moved from a foreign account in bank A to a domestic account in bank C. The only document required is the dealer's confirmation slip (see Exhibit 1, page 325).

After the six months have elapsed the Italian importer must acquire dollars to repay the Italian bank, which in turn repays the UK bank – and so down the chain of intermediaries until the original owner is refunded.

d   Interest rates

Indications of the previous day's market for Euro-dollar rates printed daily in the *Financial Times* are for the call, 7 days' notice, 1 month's, 3 months', 6 months' and 1 year's bid and offered rates. An interbank transaction is rarely for less than $100,000, and would normally be of the order of $2 million. The size of the deal makes it possible for Euro-dollar operators to keep costs relatively low and so maintain both borrowing and lending rates that may be more attractive than in other markets. These large transactions are often referred to as 'wholesale' operations when compared with the smaller day to day more labour-intensive foreign business that is sometimes called 'retail' banking.

OPENING MARKET DEPOSIT RATES

Interbank market (% pa)	US dollars	Swiss francs	Deutsche-marks	Sterling	
				UK interbank	Euro-sterling
Market conditions	Very firm	Firmer	Firm	Firm	
Overnight	$8^1/_4 - 8$	—	—	$14^1/_2 - 14^1/_4$	
7 days fixed	$19^1/_2 - 19^1/_4$	$5^1/_4 - 4^3/_4$	$9^5/_8 - 9^3/_8$	$14^5/_8 - 14^3/_8$	
1 month fixed	$20^5/_8 - 20^3/_8$	$6^3/_8 - 6^1/_4$	$10 - 9^3/_4$	$14^9/_{16} - 14^7/_{16}$	$14^3/_4 - 14^1/_2$
2 months fixed	$19^7/_{16} - 19^3/_{16}$	$6^3/_8 - 6^1/_4$	$10 - 9^3/_4$	$14^{11}/_{16} - 14^9/_{16}$	$15^1/_8 - 14^7/_8$
3 months fixed	$19^3/_{16} - 18^{15}/_{16}$	$6^3/_8 - 6^1/_4$	$10 - 9^3/_4$	$14^{13}/_{16} - 14^{11}/_{16}$	$15^1/_8 - 14^7/_8$
6 months fixed	$17^{15}/_{16} - 17^{11}/_{16}$	$6^3/_8 - 6^1/_4$	$9^7/_8 - 9^5/_8$	$14^7/_{16} - 14^5/_{16}$	$14^7/_8 - 14^5/_8$
9 months fixed	$16^{13}/_{16} - 16^9/_{16}$	$6^1/_4 - 6^1/_8$	$9^5/_8 - 9^3/_8$	$14^1/_8 - 14$	—
12 months fixed	$16^1/_4 - 16$	$6^1/_4 - 6^1/_8$	$9^5/_8 - 9^3/_8$	$14 - 13^7/_8$	$14^5/_8 - 14^3/_8$

Following rates for information only

2 years fixed	$15^3/_8 - 14^3/_8$	$6 - 5^1/_2$	$9^3/_4 - 9^1/_4$	$14 - 13^1/_2$	
3 years fixed	$15^1/_8 - 14^3/_8$	$6 - 5^1/_2$	$9^3/_4 - 9^1/_4$	$14 - 13^1/_2$	
4 years fixed	$14^7/_8 - 13^7/_8$	$6^1/_8 - 5^5/_8$	$9^3/_4 - 9^1/_4$	$13^3/_4 - 13^1/_4$	
5 years fixed	$14^7/_8 - 13^7/_8$	$6^1/_4 - 5^3/_4$	$9^3/_4 - 9^1/_4$	$13^5/_8 - 13^1/_8$	

e   Origins of the market

The origin of the continental dollar market can probably be traced to the post-war period (around the early 1950s especially) when a number of Eastern European banks preferred to camouflage their ownership of dollar deposits by placing them with correspondents, principally in France and the UK. Subsequently the correspondent banks began to make use of these and other funds, offering them to those seeking dollar accommodation at lower rates of interest than those ruling in the US. Other holders of dollars took advantage of the developing market, which offered them a higher rate of return than they could obtain by placing their funds in the US (because of Regulation Q which limited the rate a US-based bank could pay a non-resident). Further factors influencing the development of demand for Euro-dollars have included the tightening of UK restrictions on overseas investment, and US curbs on both overseas investment and bank lending abroad. In 1968 the USA was a net borrower of Euro-dollars, and Japan also made substantial calls on the market. To meet those demands, funds continued to be made available at relatively attractive rates, and the total size of the market was estimated at some $35 billion. In 1971 massive flows of US dollars to Western Europe or Japan boosted the market to about $100 billion. As a result, controls were imposed in the USA which slowed the growth of the market considerably. The years 1976 and 1977 were years of stagnant loan demand in the USA, with the Comecon and the LDCs (lesser developed countries) absorbing a very sizeable amount of the total lending.

f   Supply

The raw material of the Euro-dollar is the pool of dollars owned by non-residents of the US. (It is certainly not limited, as the name may suggest, to holdings by Europeans.) But this pool is frequently enlarged as a result of transactions in which banks are able to accept deposits denominated in foreign currencies and 'swap' them into dollars that are then used for profitable investment in the continental dollar market. Also, temporary transfers to non-resident institutions of dollars owned by Americans help to swell the market.

In addition to Eastern European banks, suppliers of dollars now include commercial banks, a few central banks and, through their banks, non-banking institutions and individuals. Many banks are, of course, prepared to act as inter-mediaries, operating on both sides of the market and standing ready to quote interest rates for accepting and offering funds overnight, at call or for virtually any fixed period required by the potential depositor of dollars.

Some 60 per cent of dollar deposits in the Euro-currency market in 1975 originated from oil revenues, and were made principally by the governments of the OPEC (oil producing and exporting countries) and by oil companies.

g Demand

Most dollars obtained through this market are used in the private sector, and the financing of international trade appears to absorb a considerable amount. Commercial banks in many countries have taken advantage of the market to assist their customers in raising funds to finance international trade at a favourable rate of interest.

Other uses to which banks sometimes put these funds are:
- to provide capital for major production loans, such as for North Sea oil
- to engage in arbitrage operations
- to 'swap' into local currency in order to improve their liquidity position
- to employ the proceeds of 'swaps' for special purposes, such as the granting of short-term credits to local authorities or placing deposits with hire purchase finance houses without having to curtail credit extended to regular customers
- to finance a general domestic credit expansion – eg, Japan and, more recently, LDCs
- to finance outward direct investment for, say, UK companies
- to finance portfolio investment by private individuals, pension funds, management trusts and funds, and other professional investment bodies

h Types of Euro-currency loans

Fixed rate loans
Roll over loans (floating rate loans)
Stand-by credits
Syndicated credits

i Fixed rate loans

These can be described as medium-term fixtures for periods of up to five years, and very exceptionally up to ten years, with a bullet repayment at maturity. The benefit to the borrower is that he knows the cost to him over the period of the loan. They do lack the flexibility of variable interest loans described below, as the level of interest rates could drop during the loan period and most loan agreements preclude early redemption. Furthermore, market conditions strictly govern and limit the extent of the loan period that may be provided.

ii Roll over loans

Most funds currently (1981) raised on the interbank Euro-currency market tend to be short-term deposits on a fixed basis of up to one year. Such funds may be on-lent to commercial borrowers, subject to a renegotiation of rates at pre-arranged intervals of, say, three or six months. This is called a 'roll over'. The cost to the borrower for the 'new funding' on roll over will be a mark-up over the offered side of the rates quoted by the lending bank. If funds are to be raised on the London interbank market the interest rate to the borrower would probably be expressed as say, ¾ per cent over LIBOR (London interbank offered rate). An optional roll over period may be built into a loan agreement, allowing the borrower to choose to borrow at the next roll over for, say, six months or one year ahead at an agreed rate over that period. An additional flexibility is sometimes added to this type of loan in the form of a multi-currency option clause. This enables the borrower to switch into the potentially weakest currency which will cost less to obtain and to repay at maturity if it does in fact weaken against other currencies listed in the loan agreement. It is usually subject to the availability of the stated currencies at roll over dates. The cost of borrowing (interest rate) of a potentially weak currency is often considerable.

Roll over loans may carry an obligation to provide finance for up to, say, five years, but the interest is re-calculated on six-monthly roll over terms. This has the effect of matching maturities and helps the lending bank avoid the danger of borrowing short and lending long.

iii Stand-by credits

Similar in effect to overdraft facilities, stand-by Euro-currency credits are a commitment by banks to provide funds at an agreed rate or formula. A commitment fee is usually taken for undrawn funds, often 1 per cent or thereabouts.

iv Syndicated credits

These large loans are put together by a managing bank, or banks, which arrange by means of a placement memorandum for a syndicate of other banks to contribute. Documentation for these loans has become more complex since those arranged in the late 1960s, and they may to an extent have lost something of the speed and flexibility they once had. This is the result of costly experience by managers and syndicate participants when in the past insufficient precautions were taken and too great a reliance was placed upon the name of the borrower, the basic canons of lending being overlooked.

i Factors to consider before determining the best financing technique for a Euro-currency loan proposition

i Purpose of borrowing and the proposed use of the funds.

ii The amount required.

iii Length of time funds will be needed and the repayment terms.

iv The current ease and availability of funds of different forms (short-term v long-term, bond issues v equity).

v Security requirements for capital, including contingent liabilities such as guarantees.

vi Other borrowing conditions, such as negative pledges and covenants (eg, not to pay out dividends, not to subordinate debt, maintenance of a minimum current ratio, etc).

vii Precise details about the borrower and his control over his affairs.

viii Effect of capital raised on corporate liquidity and overall financial position.

ix   How funds are to be generated for servicing and amortising loans.

x   Requirements for subordination of debt.

xi   Cost of borrowing in 'real terms' as well as interest rate to be charged; charges, commissions, required balances, hedging and exchange risk costs.

xii   Possibility of roll over, multi-currency options, prepayment terms.

xiii   Local laws regulating debt-equity ratios, types of borrowing, inflow and outflow of capital.

xiv   Corporate relationship with local financial institutions and capital sources.

xv   Taxation, foreign and domestic, affecting the raising and use of funds and real interest rates.

xvi   Ability to protect funds against political and other difficulties such as nationalisation and exchange controls.

xvii   Evaluation of currency risks.

5.   CERTIFICATES OF DEPOSIT

a   Introduction

A certificate of deposit (CD) is a negotiable bearer instrument issued by a bank certifying that a stated sum of money has been deposited with the issuing bank. The rate of interest paid on the deposit and the date of repayment are also shown on the CD, which is the title document to the deposit.

The issuing banks are able to increase their deposits this way and thereby to provide for short- and medium-term advances for between 30 days and two years and two to five years respectively. A depositor of fixed-term money may wish to break the deposit and draw cash, in which case the bank would probably charge a penalty. A CD, on the other hand, may be sold to a London discount house without loss of liquidity, and the seller will receive all interest due to him up to the moment of negotiation. The interest rates may be slightly less than those applicable to the deposit rates for similar maturities quoted on the London money market.

b   London dollar negotiable CDs

These CDs are issued by a bank in London for a minimum value of US$25,000, for certificates with maturities less than one year, or US$10,000 when the maturity exceeds one year. In both cases they are usually issued for sums in multiples of US$1,000.

CDs may be bought from the bank which issued them, or from another bank, a discount house or London-based American stockbroker belonging to the International CD Market Association and operating in the secondary market for CDs. The primary market may be defined as existing between the original depositor and the issuing bank. CDs may be redeemed from the issuing bank at maturity or sold in the meantime to a secondary market institution. The majority of issues are in 'tap' form and made to individual depositors, although 'tranche' issues have been made which are managed issues along the line of a public offer of securities. A development in the CD market was the floating rate tranche issue introduced in 1977.

c   Sterling negotiable certificates of deposit

i   *Prime issues*

A document evidencing receipt of a deposit by a bank for a fixed period at a fixed rate of interest. Certificates are issued in minimum denominations of £50,000 and thereafter in multiples of £10,000 to a maximum of £500,000 per certificate. The period of issue is three months up to five years. Interest is paid gross on maturity for certificates up to one year and for others on the anniversary of the issue date and on final maturity. Certificates are in bearer form and fully negotiable, and may be sold before maturity through the secondary market.

ii *Secondary sterling negotiable certificate of deposit*
Certificates of deposit may be disposed of before maturity through the secondary market operated by banks and discount houses. A certificate is sold at a yield to maturity irrespective of the coupon rate at issue, the proceeds being calculated on the basis of the following formula:

$$\text{Proceeds} = \text{principal} \times \frac{36{,}500 \text{ plus (issued rate} \times \text{tenor in days)}}{36{,}500 \text{ plus (quoted yield} \times \text{days to run)}}$$

6. EUROBONDS

a Introduction
The need for capital expansion of the large multinational corporations has brought with it a need for long-term borrowing that is not subject to the national controls of any one country. This has been provided by Eurobond issues for periods of up to 20 years.

Eurobonds may be defined as bonds issued in a European capital market and denominated in a currency (or currencies) other than that of the country of issue. It is, however, possible for non-residents to raise certain domestic issues denominated in the currency of the country of issue, and in these cases subscription is sometimes confined to non-residents. In other words, these are issues outside normal local stock exchange channels. An example of this is a US dollar bond issue, listed on the London Stock Exchange, for, say, the Kingdom of Sweden (the borrower) and sold internationally. Issues are nearly always 'placed' (ie, the issuing consortium arranges for a group of selling banks to take up the offer) prior to funding. Sterling bonds may be issued by UK and by overseas borrowers, and subscriptions to these issues are not restricted in the UK. The UK investing public may subscribe to foreign Eurobonds, and UK companies may raise foreign currency loan stock without exchange control restrictions.

b The procedure of establishing a Eurobond issue
The borrower will appoint a bank to become lead manager to the issue. The bank chosen will probably be a merchant, investment or consortium bank. The lead manager usually invites one or more other banks or financial institutions to co-manage the issue, and the 'managing banks' so formed would normally expect fees of between 3/8 and 1/2 per cent of the total issue amount, plus expenses for their services. In due course, as the issue progresses, a subscription agreement is signed by the managers and the borrowers.

To ensure that the borrower receives the issue amount (less initial fees), the managers invite a group of financial institutions, mainly banks, to underwrite the issue, for a fee usually between 3/8 and 1/2 per cent of the amount underwritten. When the managers have received confirmation from the underwriting institutions that the issue will be covered, the managers (as agents of the borrower) and the underwriters enter into a underwriting agreement. At the same time as inviting the underwriters to cover the issue, the managers invite the financial institutions which they want to include in the selling group. The selling group, which invariably includes the underwriters as well as other financial institutions, is asked to subscribe to the proposed new issue for a commission usually amounting to 1½ per cent of amount allotted. The selling group members may decide to retain part of their allotment as an investment, but they will have clients, who may also wish to invest in this type of security, with whom paper may be placed. The selling bank's 'placing power' is vital to the successful launch of new issues.

The potential investor will naturally require to know about the borrower. What does he do? How successfully does he do it? These are two questions that will run through his mind. He will also want to know the terms and conditions of the issue, and who, if anyone, will represent his interest should he decide to invest. In order to meet these basic needs of the investor an 'offering circular', often called a 'prospectus', is prepared by the borrowers and the managers in conjunction with their solicitors. This 'prospectus' sets out:

i   The terms and conditions of the bonds or notes as the case may be.
ii   How the proceeds will be employed by the borrower – or in other words 'what does the borrower intend doing with the money raised?'
iii Historical background of the borrower.
iv   Nature of the borrower's business.
v   List of the borrower's directors.
vi   Financial statements covering five years and including the most recently available figures.
vii Auditors' report on the financial information given in the prospectus.
viii Details of stock exchange listing.
ix   Selling and underwriting information.
x   Any restrictions on the sale of the securities which must be observed.

The interests of the bond or note holders may be vested in a fiscal agent or in a trustee. It is usual for issues for UK borrowers to be constituted under a trust deed, whereas those for foreign borrowers are often subject to a fiscal agency agreement. This means that the bank selected to act as principal paying agent for the issue will also be responsible for representing the bond or note holders' interests in accordance with the terms and conditions of the issue.

c   Points for the borrower to consider

The corporate treasurer normally wants to secure his capital loan stock as cheaply as possible for as long as possible. The decision to acquire capital loan stock is sometimes taken in order to fund a major long-term commitment or investment, and sometimes to achieve capital adequacy for under-capitalised or fast-expanding borrowers and so to improve their gearing ratios and leverage. It is part of a treasurer's function to seek ways of achieving his prime objective by closely monitoring the market conditions, usually with the advice and assistance of his investment/merchant bankers. Market conditions reflect the preferences of investors and what terms they may be prepared to accept, but existing legislation (or changes in legislation) relating to tax, exchange control and other constraints often has an immediate and direct effect upon the investment demand. Other market forces include the volume of business of a similar nature which might be offered to the same investors at the same time. If investors are confident that the quality, taking into account borrower, currency and country of issue, of the security offered is good there is likely to be a demand for it at the right price.

The amount, the currency, the period, and the type of issue (straight, floating or convertible) will all have to be considered in the context of what the borrower needs and is prepared to pay for, and what the market conditions are likely to provide. Raising a capital issue can be an expensive procedure for the borrower. Up to 4 per cent of the capital raised may be syphoned off to pay the issue costs and fees in the form of 'front end' charges. The commissions payable to the paying agents for paying the coupons, and, later on, drawing and redeeming the bonds or notes, together with the trustee or the fiscal agent's fees (payable annually), all add up to swell the running costs of the issue.

A straight Eurobond issue will have a fixed rate of interest payable over the entire period of the loan. This means that while the borrower knows the exact cost of the interest, and therefore the full costs of raising the loan, he may find that he raised the loan at the wrong time, when interest rates had peaked. Most currencies most of the time have a positive yield curve, which is a lower interest rate structure for the short-date periods increasing in steps for successively longer periods, and this has the effect of costing the borrower more interest the longer the fixed period chosen for the loan. Some borrowers prefer to link the interest payable by them to short-term money market rates for this reason. The floating rate note interest structure is, in the case of US dollar issues, often a mark-up of say ¼ per cent over the rate of interest London banks will offer US dollars for six months (LIBOR). Every six months the rate is re-calculated by the reference banks chosen for this purpose, and the interest rate and coupon amount is published by the agent bank for the benefit of the note holders. In section 2 of this chapter it can be seen that one of the distinctions between a straight Eurobond and a floating capital notes issue is that for the latter no sinking fund is required. Since a sinking fund has the effect of shortening the life of the issue, it will reduce the period over which the cost can be amortised and is therefore more expensive from this point of view than a 'bullet' issue of similar final maturity, when the principal would be repayable in a lump sum at the end of the loan period.

Most floating rate note issues have a minimum interest rate which 'guarantees' a minimum return to the investor, but also 'guarantees' that the borrower is denied any benefit from subsequent interest rate reductions in the market that are below the stated minimum. The borrower should certainly be aware of the foreign exchange and/or tax exposure risks he might be running in raising foreign currency loan stock. Borrowers of medium-term and long-term Swiss francs and deutschemarks during 1973 will no doubt be reflecting upon the vastly increased cost of those currencies in terms of their own or other currencies into which the funds may have been transferred. In an attempt to provide the borrower with a long-term hedge against exchange risks some issues have been denominated in composite currency units. It is advisable that the assets being funded by long-term foreign currency issues be denominated in the same currency and preferably yield income in that currency. This is not by any means always possible because of the limited number of currencies in which Euro issues may be floated. The UK borrower should ensure that Treasury and Inland Revenue permissions are sufficient for the intended employment of funds without incurring risks of onerous taxation or other penalties in due course.

d   Points for the investor to consider

i   Security

Eurobonds and floating rate notes issued by high quality borrowers are negotiable bearer securities and as such offer the investor ready marketability and secrecy. The name and domicile of the borrower will affect the present and future market price of the security, and many issues where the borrower may not be too well known are guaranteed by the parent company or even a government. There may be restrictions on the sale of the securities to nationals of certain countries which could impede their marketability. A standard condition of an issue by a borrower of non-government status is the negative pledge clause in which the borrower undertakes not to give any prior charge during the life of the issue over the assets of the borrower that will (in the event of the borrower's liquidation) rank ahead of the rights of the investors.

Occasionally the rights of the investor will be subordinated to the rights of certain other creditors of the borrower. The capital issue of a commercial bank which ranks the rights of its depositors ahead of the bond or note holder's rights of repayment in the event of liquidation is typical. The bond or note holder's rights are therefore subordinated, and if more than one loan stock has been issued by the borrower the issues will probably rank *pari passu* without preference among themselves.

ii   Return on the investment

When falling interest rates are forecast, or are occurring, investors will tend to buy long-term fixed rate bonds; but when rising interest rates are forecast or occurring then CDs and floating rate notes tend to be in demand. The floating rate note will give a higher yield as a rule than a CD. The latter tends to be priced at about the London interbank bid rate whereas the floating rate note is usually ¼ per cent above the offered side of the rate. The investor is attracted to a high coupon price, a low issue or market price (discount) or under par, and date of redemption, but in the event these considerations must always be secondary to the question of security (*i* above). The relationship between these three factors gives rise to 'the yield'. It is a condition of the market place that the coupon on Euro-currency issues be paid gross, and the investor should examine his tax liability and any exchange control obligations which could render the intended investment unprofitable.

Convertible issues convey an option to exchange the loan stock for ordinary shares on terms defined in the conditions of the issue. If the borrower does well, and share value of the equity rises, holders of convertible loan stock may very well benefit by converting into the equity. While there are clearly some attractions to an investor in convertible stock, there are also drawbacks. The equity may be in a potentially weaker, or stronger, currency than the loan stock, the share price might never rise sufficiently to make converting worthwhile, and there are usually compensatory benefits to the borrower such as finer interest rates.

e   A comparison of the Euro and domestic capital markets

The Euro markets are not subject to any major national controls by the authorities in the host countries in which the transactions take place. A feature of the European capital markets is the queueing requirement, for all potential borrowers, by the regulatory authority of the currency of the issue to be floated. This is to ensure an orderly market. Domestic capital markets, which involve the home currency and are available to borrowers who are residents of the host country, are subject to national controls. These controls frequently limit access to the market by foreign borrowers, or can require that non-residents surrender part or all of the local currency raised for US dollars. During 1978–9 the German, Swiss, UK, Dutch, French and American capital markets were open, to a greater or lesser extent, to non-residents. Countries with strong economies may liberalise capital transactions from restrictive exchange control regulations, tighter controls being more commonly associated with countries with overall balance of payments deficits. Domestic issues are normally regulated in an orderly queue by the central bank or finance ministry of the host country. This is not the case with a Euro issue, the timing constraints of which are limited to market conditions.

Domestic issues are invariably listed on the local stock exchanges; the London stock exchange and the Luxemburg exchange are the principal listing centres for Euro issues.

The vast majority of Eurobond issues are US dollar bond issues floated in the London market, and to a lesser extent Canadian dollar and deutschemark issues. There have also been quite a number of issues expressed in composite currency units (mentioned in Chapter 8, section 17).

It is possible to draw an interesting comparison between the Euro-dollar bonds in London and the yankee bond (US domestic bond for a foreign borrower). The conditions required by the United States Securities and Exchange Commission (SEC) are more detailed than one would normally expect for a London issue, particularly in regard to financial disclosure. A London issue would probably be led-managed by a group of international investment banks and sold internationally through a larger syndicate of banks and brokers. A yankee bond, on the other hand, will be managed by a US investment house and sold within the United States. The yankee bond will probably be rated, which is less likely (but not unknown) for a Eurobond issue. Finally, it is usually possible, depending on market conditions, to raise larger US dollar amounts for longer periods and at lower coupon rates in the US domestic market than in London.

SPECIMEN DOCUMENTS

Illustrated on pages 325 to 329

Dealer's confirmation slip	*Exhibit 1*
London US$ certificate of deposit	*Exhibit 2*
Floating rate note	*Exhibit 3*
Fixed rate Eurobond	*Exhibit 4*
Tombstone	*Exhibit 5*

Exhibit 1   **Dealer's confirmation slip**

International Gourmet Bank Limited
100, Lombard Street, London E.C.2.

Our reference IGB 253/667   Date 18.4.19....

To: Wall Street Bank Limited, London

Dear Sir,

      We have pleasure in confirming the following transaction:

Your DEPOSIT with us for US $ 2,000,000.00
Which please pay to our New York Branch for the credit
of our account with them.
Value 20.4.19....
Period 6 months
Maturity 20.4.19....
Rate 5⅛% p.a.

Yours faithfully,

N. Gordon Graham
Manager
International Gourmet Bank Limited

Exhibit 2 **London US$ certificate of deposit**

NEGOTIABLE DOLLAR CERTIFICATE OF DEPOSIT

INTERNATIONAL WESTMINSTER BANK LIMITED

LONDON BRANCH

41, THREADNEEDLE STREET, EC2R 8AP.

Certificate No. 000000

U.S. ....

.... 19......

the sum of ....

.... U.S. Dollars

INTERNATIONAL WESTMINSTER BANK LIMITED CERTIFIES THAT

has been deposited on terms that it is payable to Bearer ....

on surrender of this Certificate, through the medium of a bank, at 41, Threadneedle Street, London, EC2R 8AP, on

the .... fixed,

together with interest at the rate of .... per cent. per annum,

calculated on actual days on a 360 day year basis from the date hereof to the date of maturity only, payable on or

after maturity if one year or less from the date hereof, and otherwise annually on the anniversary of the date hereof

and at maturity. Payment will be made by draft or telegraphic transfer on a bank in New York designated by us.

This Certificate shall be governed by English Law.

For and on behalf of INTERNATIONAL WESTMINSTER BANK LIMITED.

AUTHORISED SIGNATURE

AUTHORISED SIGNATURE

SPECIMEN

BRADBURY, WILKINSON & Cº Lᵈ NEW MALDEN, SURREY ENGLAND.

Exhibit 3   **Floating rate note**

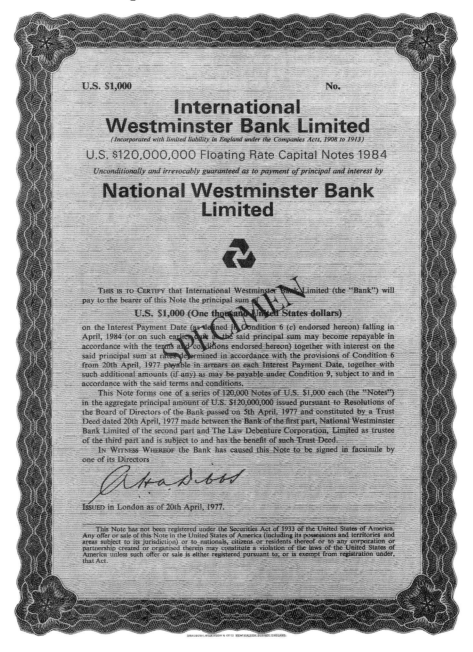

Exhibit 4 **Fixed rate Eurobond**

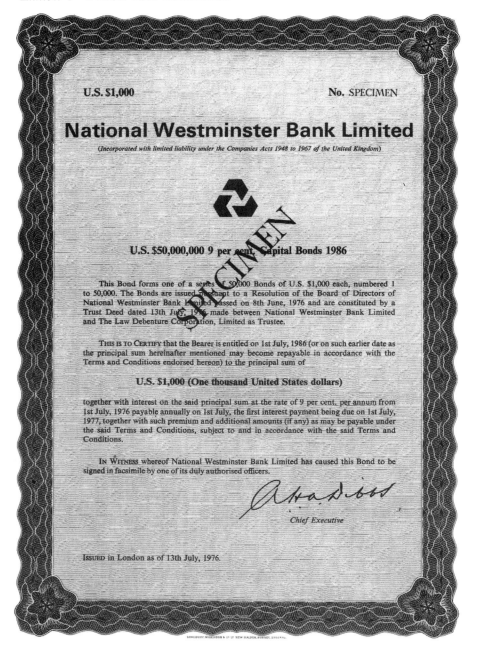

Exhibit 5   **Tombstone**

New Issue

These Notes having been sold, this announcement appears as a matter of record only.

April 1977

U.S. $120,000,000
International
Westminster Bank Limited

Floating Rate Capital Notes 1984

*Irrevocably and unconditionally guaranteed on a subordinated basis
as to payment of principal and interest by*

National Westminster Bank Limited

Orion Bank Limited   **County Bank Limited**   **Credit Suisse White Weld Limited**

Banque Nationale de Paris   **Banque de Paris et des Pays-Bas**

Banque Populaire Suisse   **Girozentrale und Bank der Österreichischen Sparkassen**
S.A. Luxembourg   Aktiengesellschaft
Société Générale de Banque S.A.   **Union Bank of Switzerland (Securities) Limited**

Westdeutsche Landesbank Girozentrale

Alahli Bank of Kuwait K.S.C.
Algemene Bank Nederland N.V.
Allied Irish Investment Bank
A. E. Ames & Co. Limited
Amex Bank Limited
Amsterdam-Rotterdam Bank N.V.
ASIAC—Asian International
 Acceptances & Capital Limited
Banca Commerciale Italiana
Banca del Gottardo
Banco Urquijo Hispano Americano
 Limited
Bank of America International
Bank Julius Baer International Limited
The Bank of Bermuda, Ltd.
Bank Gutzwiller, Kurz, Bungener
 (Overseas) Limited
Bank Leu International Ltd.
Bank Mees & Hope NV
The Bank of Tokyo (Holland) N.V.
Bankers Trust International Limited
Banque du Benelux S.A.
Banque Bruxelles Lambert S.A.
Banque Française du Commerce
 Extérieur
Banque Française de Dépôts et de Titres
Banque Générale du Luxembourg S.A.
Banque de l'Indochine et de Suez
Banque Internationale à Luxembourg
 S.A.
Banque Louis-Dreyfus
Banque de Neuflize, Schlumberger,
 Mallet
Banque Rothschild
Banque de l'Union Européenne
Banque Worms
Baring Brothers & Co., Limited
Bayerische Hypotheken- und
 Wechsel-Bank
Bayerische Vereinsbank
Berliner Handels- und Frankfurter
 Bank
Caisse des Dépôts et Consignations
Cazenove & Co.
Chase Manhattan Limited
Citicorp International Group
Clariden Bank
Commerzbank Aktiengesellschaft
Compagnie Monégasque de Banque
Continental Illinois Limited
Crédit Commercial de France
Crédit Industriel et Commercial

Crédit Lyonnais
Crédit du Nord
Credito Italiano (Underwriters) S.A.
Daiwa Europe N.V.
Delbrück & Co.
Den Danske Bank af 1871 Aktieselskab
Den norske Creditbank
Deutsche Girozentrale
 —Deutsche Kommunalbank—
DG Bank
 Deutsche Genossenschaftsbank
Dillon, Read Overseas Corporation
Dresdner Bank Aktiengesellschaft
Effectenbank-Warburg
 Aktiengesellschaft
Euromobiliare S.p.A.
 Compagnia Europea Intermobiliare
Eurotrading Limited
European Banking Company Limited
First Boston (Europe)
 Limited
First Chicago Limited
Robert Fleming & Co. Limited
Fuji Kleinwort Benson Limited
Antony Gibbs Holdings Ltd.
Goldman Sachs International Corp.
Groupement des Banquiers Privés
 Genevois
Hambros Bank Limited
Handelsbank N.W. (Overseas) Limited
Hessische Landesbank
 —Girozentrale—
Hill Samuel & Co. Limited
E. F. Hutton & Co. N.V.
IBJ International Limited
Interunion-Banque
Jardine Fleming & Company Limited
Kidder, Peabody International Limited
Kleinwort, Benson Limited
Kredietbank N.V.
Kredietbank S.A. Luxembourgeoise
Kuhn, Loeb & Co. International
Kuwait Foreign Trading Contracting &
 Investment Co. (S.A.K.)
Kuwait International Investment
 Co. (S.A.K.)
F. van Lanschot Bankiers
Lazard Brothers & Co., Limited
Lazard Frères et Cie
Lloyds Bank International Limited
London Multinational Bank
 (Underwriters) Limited

Manufacturers Hanover Limited
McLeod, Young, Weir & Company
 Limited
Merck, Finck & Co.
Merrill Lynch International & Co.
Mitsubishi Bank (Europe) S.A.
Samuel Montagu & Co. Limited
Morgan Grenfell & Co. Limited
Morgan Stanley International
National Bank of Abu Dhabi
The National Bank of Kuwait S.A.K.
National Westminster Bank Group
Nederlandsche Middenstandsbank N.V.
Nederlandse Credietbank N.V.
Nesbitt, Thomson Limited
The Nikko (Luxembourg) S.A.
Nomura Europe N.V.
Norddeutsche Landesbank Girozentrale
Österreichische Länderbank
Orion Pacific Limited
Peterbroeck, Van Campenhout,
 Kempen S.A.
Pierson, Heldring & Pierson N.V.
Postipankki
Rea Brothers Limited
N. M. Rothschild & Sons Limited
RoyWest Banking Corporation Limited
Salomon Brothers International
 Limited
Saudi Arabian Investment Company Inc.
J. Henry Schroder Wagg & Co. Limited
Skandinaviska Enskilda Banken
Slavenburg Oyens & Van Eeghen N.V.
Smith Barney, Harris Upham & Co.
 Incorporated
Société Bancaire Barclays (Suisse) S.A.
Société Générale
Strauss, Turnbull & Co.
Sumitomo Finance International
Svenska Handelsbanken
Swiss Bank Corporation (Overseas)
 Limited
Vereins-und Westbank
 Aktiengesellschaft
J. Vontobel & Co.
S. G. Warburg & Co. Ltd.
Wardley Ltd.
White Weld Inc.
Dean Witter International
Wood Gundy Limited
Yamaichi International (Nederland)
 N.V.

PAST EXAMINATION QUESTIONS

1   Write short notes on:
a   LIBOR, and
b   New York prime loan rate

(Foundation Course in Overseas Trade)

2   'The international capital market can be divided according to types of transactions:
    those involving the issue of foreign securities in the currency of the country of issue, and those involving the issue of Eurobonds.'
    Explain the difference between the types of transaction mentioned in the quotation.

(Institute of Bankers)

3   Explain what is meant by the term 'Euro-currency market', describe its main characteristics and outline how it works.

(Institute of Freight Forwarders)

Index

NOTES

NOTES

NOTES